The Polit

Berg French Studies

General Editor: John E. Flower

ISSN: 1354-3636

John E. Flower and Bernard C. Swift (eds), *François Mauriac: Visions and Reappraisals*

Michael Tilby (ed.), *Beyond the Nouveau Roman: Essays on the Contemporary French Novel*

Colin Nettlebeck, *Forever French: The French Exiles in the United States of America during the Second World War*

Bill Marshall, *Victor Serge: The Uses of Dissent*

Allan Morris, *Collaboration and Resistance Reviews: Writers and the Mode Rétro in Post-Gaullist France*

Malcolm Cook, *Fictional France: Social Reality in the French Novel 1775–1800*

W.D. Halls, *Politics, Society and Christianity in Vichy France*

David H. Walker, *Outrage and Insight: Modern French Writers and the 'Fait Divers'*

H.R. Kedward and Nancy Wood, *The Liberation of France: Image and Event*

David L. Looseley, *The Politics of Fun: Cultural Policy and Debate in Contemporary France*

Nicholas Hewitt, *Literature and the Right in Postwar France: The Story of the 'Hussards'*

Laïla Ibnlfassi and Nicki Hitchcott, *African Francophone Writing: A Critical Introduction*

Alex Hughes and Kate Ince, *French Erotic Fiction: Women's Desiring Writing, 1880–1990*

Jennifer E. Milligan, *The Forgotten Generation: French Women Writers of the Inter-war Period*

The Politics of Fun

Cultural Policy and Debate in Contemporary France

David L. Looseley

BERG PUBLISHERS

Oxford / New York

First published in 1995 by
Berg
Editorial offices:
150 Cowley Road, Oxford, OX4 1JJ, UK
70 Washington Square South, New York, NY 10012, USA

Paperback edition published in 1997.

Berg is the imprint of Oxford International Publishers Ltd.

Library of Congress Cataloging-in-Publication Data

A catalog record for this book is available from the Library of Congress.

British Library Cataloguing-in-Publication Data

A catalogue record for this book is available from the British Library.

ISBN   1 85973 013 2 (Cloth)
1 85973 153 8 (Paper)

Printed in the United Kingdom by WBC Bookbinders, Bridgend, Mid-Glamorgan.

For May and Len Looseley, and Avril and Rhiannon,
with love

Contents

Acknowledgements   ix

Abbreviations   xi

List of Illustrations   xv

Introduction   1

Part I: Culture and the State: The History of the Ministry

1   The Precursors: The Popular Front, Vichy and the Liberation   11

2   Heritage, Creation, Democratisation: The Malraux Years   33

3   From Malraux to Mitterrand: Creation and Creativity   49

Part II: A Socialist Ministry: Theory and Practice, 1981–86

4   Culture and the Economy: *les intellos au boulot*   71

5   Policies for High Culture: *la création dans la cité*   94

6   Beyond High Culture: Pluralism and *le tout-culturel*   113

7   A Certain Idea of the City: The Presidential *grands projets*   135

Part III: Policies and Debates, 1986–93

8   Lang and the Politics of Fun: Politicising the Cultural Debate, 1985–88   157

9   Popularising the Past: *Lang et Léotard, même combat?*   175

10   Culture and the Audiovisual   197

11   *A l'heure des bilans*: The Ministry in Question   212

Conclusion   233

Bibliography   246

Brief Chronology Since 1959   260

Index   265

Acknowledgements

I would like to express my thanks to a number of people for their assistance with the preparation of this book. For variously providing materials, discussion, advice or bibliographical assistance (in some cases several of these), I am indebted to the following Ministry personnel, past or present: Robert Abirached, Jean-Pierre Colin, Olivier Donnat, Jean Gattégno, Augustin Girard, Jack Lang, Alain Lennert, Pierre Moulinier, Marc Nicolas, Elisabeth Raynal and the Département de l'information et de la communication, and Jacques Renard. Special thanks are due to Jacqueline Boucherat and staff of the Département des études et de la prospective's Centre de documentation, particularly Anna-Michèle Schneider, for quite remarkable assistance and hospitality over the years. Thanks also go to a number of individuals not connected with the Ministry: Chantal Cransac (attachée de presse, RPR), Colette Flon (formerly of the Nancy festival), Véronique Falconnet (Bibliothèque de France), Michel Noir (Mayor of Lyon) and Yoland Simon (formerly of the Union des Maisons de la culture). I am also extremely grateful to librarians Grace Hudson (University of Bradford) and Sue Doran (Greenhead College, Huddersfield) for documentary assistance well beyond the call of duty; to Lecturer in French Dr Owen Heathcote and past students of Bradford University David Barefoot and Kate Sweetnam, for pointing out or passing on invaluable materials; and to my former French colleagues at Bradford for help with a heavy marking load at a particularly fraught moment. I also wish gratefully to acknowledge the Leverhulme Trust's funding of the project, which enabled me to take study leave on two separate occasions. Here too, I must thank my Bradford colleagues for withstanding my absences; and Professor John Green for facilitating them and being especially supportive. Lastly, I would like to thank a number of friends and relations whose help has been precious both materially and psychologically: Roselyne and Serge Allard, Maryvonne and Alain Besnard, Françoise and Gilles Cléroux, Jacqueline and Hubert Mazeaud, and Nellie and her late husband Jacques Termeau, for hospitality, documentation and indefatigable Lang-watching; Lynne and Gary Copley and Jennifer and Robert Tellez for taking an interest and giving moral support when it was in short supply; my parents and the Humble family for being ever supportive. And, above all, my wife Avril and my daughter Rhiannon for their unconditional good humour, kindness and love.

Abbreviations

ADLP	Association pour le développement de la lecture publique
ADMICAL	Association pour le développement du mécénat industriel et commercial
AEAR	Association des écrivains et artistes révolutionnaires
AFP	Agence France Presse
AGEC	Association pour la gestion des entreprises culturelles
AMC	Association des Maisons de la culture et des cercles culturels
APAM	Association populaire des amis du musée
ATOP	Association des théâtres de l'Opéra de Paris
BCP	Bibliothèque centrale de prêt
BD	Bandes dessinées
BdF	Bibliothèque de France
BN	Bibliothèque nationale
CAC	Centre d'action culturelle
CDN	Centre dramatique national
CFTC	Confédération française des travailleurs chrétiens
CGT	Confédération générale du travail
CNAC	Centre national d'art contemporain
CNAP	Centre national des arts plastiques
CNC	Centre national de la cinématographie
CNCL	Commission nationale de la communication et des libertés
CNL	Centre national des lettres
CNP	Centre national de la photographie
CNR	Conseil national de la Résistance
COIC	Comité d'organisation de l'industrie cinématographique
COREPHAE	Commission régionale du patrimoine historique, archéologique et ethnologique
CSA	Conseil supérieur de l'audiovisuel

DAGEC	Direction de l'administration générale et de l'environnement culturel
DAP	Délégation aux arts plastiques
DDC	Direction du développement culturel
DEP	Département des études et de la prospective
DGAL	Direction générale des arts et des lettres
DLL	Direction du livre et de la lecture
DRAC	Direction régionale des affaires culturelles
DTS	Direction du théâtre et des spectacles
EAC	Etablissement d'action culturelle
ENA	Ecole nationale de l'administration
EPBF	Etablissement public de la Bibliothèque de France
FIACRE	Fonds d'incitation à la création
FIC	Fonds d'intervention culturelle
FNAC (la)	Fédération nationale d'achat des cadres
FNAC, le	Fonds national d'art contemporain
FNESR	Fédération des élus socialistes et républicains
FNSP	Fondation nationale des sciences politiques
FRAC	Fonds régionaux d'art contemporain
FRAM	Fonds régionaux d'acquisition des musées
IFCIC	Institut pour le financement du cinéma et des industries culturelles
IHTP	Institut d'histoire du temps présent
IMA	Institut du monde arabe
IRCAM	Institut de recherche et de coordination acoustique-musique
MC	Maison de la culture
MF	million francs
MJC	Maison des jeunes et de la culture
MNAM	Musée national d'art moderne
PAF	Paysage audiovisuel français
PCF	Parti communiste français
PDG	Président-directeur général
PR	Parti républicain
PS	Parti socialiste
PTT	Postes télégraphes téléphones (the French Post Office)
RPR	Rassemblement pour la République (Gaullist party)
SFIO	Section française de l'Internationale ouvrière (forerunner of PS)
SOFICA	Sociétés de financement des industries cinématographiques et audiovisuelles

SYNDEAC	Syndicat national des directeurs d'entreprises artistiques et culturelles
TEP	Théâtre de l'est parisien
TNP	Théâtre national populaire
UDF	Union pour la démocratie française
UMC	Union des Maisons de la culture
UNEF	Union nationale des étudiants de France

List of Illustrations

I am most grateful to those listed below in parentheses for providing illustrative material and/or authorising its reproduction.

Figure 1   The Structure of the Lang Ministry, 1983 (Ministère de la culture et de la francophonie)

Figure 2   The Colonnes Buren (copyright Philippe Delacroix/ Ministère de la culture et de la francophonie)

Figure 3   La Villette

Figure 4   La Villette (David Shaw)

Figure 5   A Club Zénith electoral advertisement, Le Monde, 30 January 1986 (Jack Lang)

Figure 6   The Bibliothèque nationale de France, January 1995 (Jim Dolamore)

Figure 7   The Structure of the Toubon Ministry, April 1994 (Ministère de la culture et de la francophonie)

Figure 8   The Projected Ministry of Culture Budget for 1995 (Ministère de la culture et de la francophonie)

Introduction

'Les années Lang font partie de notre histoire culturelle'

attributed to Alain Carignon[1]

Shortly after the French general elections of March 1993, a *passations des pouvoirs* took place at the Ministry of Culture in the rue de Valois, the brief ceremony at which an outgoing minister hands over to his or her successor. Following the ruling Socialist Party's catastrophic defeat, a new centre-right government had just been formed by the Gaullist Edouard Balladur (RPR) and formally appointed by the Socialist President François Mitterrand, giving France its second period of *cohabitation* in seven years. At the rue de Valois ceremony, the new Minister, the RPR's Jacques Toubon, duly ushered out the Socialist incumbent Jack Lang, and in so doing rang down the curtain on what had undoubtedly been the most colourful and most controversial era in the Ministry's history since its creation by de Gaulle in 1959. Certainly, it had been the most enduring after the Gaullist decade, for Lang had been in office since Mitterrand's election in May 1981, apart from during the first cohabitation of 1986–8 when he had been ousted by the head of the Republican Party (PR) François Léotard, ousting him in turn after Mitterrand's re-election in May 1988.

This book is a study of the place of the Mitterrand-Lang era in the history of the Ministry. It lays no claim to being an exhaustive technical appraisal of government aid to culture during that time, though some consideration will be given to such matters when appropriate.[2] Evaluation of this kind is never easy, but it is much more of a problem when many of the measures adopted are still in progress and their long-term effects have yet to become clear. Nor has Lang been out of office long enough at the time I am writing (early 1994) for successors to have cast their own light on those measures by continuing or undoing them.

Why, in that case, examine the Mitterrand-Lang partnership now? Firstly, because it represents a fascinating episode in the contemporary cultural and political life of France. This episode is now quite clearly over given that, with Mitterrand leaving office in 1995, Lang's ambitions appear to have moved on (perhaps to include the presidency itself).[3] But it has left its mark both in France and further afield: for example in the British Labour Party's arts and media proposals for the 1992 general election; or in the Conservatives' involvement in Britain's first National Music Day in June 1992 modelled on Lang's Fête de la musique, to say nothing of their creation after that election of an innovative and broad-based 'Ministry of Fun', the Department of National Heritage, under a Secretary of State of cabinet rank. Secondly, although assessments of historical importance are just as perilous as evaluation at such an early stage and are clearly provisional, the Mitterrand years seem set to prove a significant stage in France's cultural history, independently of any technical judgments which may be made now or later of specific measures.

This is partly because the coming to power of the new Socialist Party (PS) which Mitterrand had carefully rebuilt from the ruins of the SFIO, and its remaining in power for much longer than earlier broad-Left governments, represent a critical moment, alongside the Front populaire or May 1968, in the long-standing relationship between culture and the Left in France. This moment forced both the French intelligentsia, which had largely identified with the Left since Dreyfus, and the PS, which had largely taken that identification for granted, to face up to some of the complexities of political power. But the Mitterrand years are also notable for the debate they provoked about culture, society and the state. As Jean-Pierre Rioux points out, France has always distinguished itself from other developed nations by 'l'effort séculaire que l'Etat et ses fonctionnaires ont consacré à la transmission, au partage et à l'enrichissement d'une "culture" largement entendue et dont ils ont estimé qu'elle relevait sans conteste du domaine de l'administration générale'.[4] A British or American observer accustomed to seeing governments kept safely at arm's length in cultural matters has mentally to change gear when first confronted with such direct intervention, with the degree of personal power wielded by a French Minister of Culture or the extent to which cultural life is enmeshed with the whole sense of nationhood. This singularity in itself makes French cultural policy generally a source of insight into the country's cultural and political make-up. But what makes the Mitterrand presidency specifically memorable is that Lang personalised this cultural power even further, intensifying the Ministry's voluntarism, popularising a specific doctrine, and projecting a charismatic image of himself. The President too contributed to this personalisation through his programme of *grands projets*, the grandiloquent cultural temples with which he recently transformed the face of Paris. The Socialist period therefore not only ruffled feathers but raised serious questions about the principle, nature and consequences of state intervention in the cultural sphere.

This has lately been demonstrated in a stream of publications which reflect critically on the period of Socialist governance, beginning in 1987 with the former *gauchiste* intellectual Alain Finkielkraut's controversial *La Défaite de la pensée*, a best seller which helped make cultural policy a subject of lively debate. Two biographies of Lang then appeared in 1990, by Richard Desneux and the American journalist Mark Hunter, the latter highly critical and attracting more attention than the former. More publicised still was another far from impartial book the following year by a professor and art historian at the Collège de France, Marc Fumaroli's *L'Etat culturel*, followed by a less noticed pamphlet by Henry Bonnier adopting much the same pugnacious standpoint, *Lettre recommandée aux fossoyeurs de la culture*. But most significant of all perhaps was a group of books by one-time cultural administrators: Jacques Rigaud's *Libre Culture* in 1990, followed in 1992 by Robert Abirached's *Le Théâtre et le prince* and Jean Gattégno's *La Bibliothèque de France à mi-parcours*. What criticisms these works contained were all the more persuasive for being formulated by experts and insiders, though on the whole all three undertook relatively serene dissections of recent policies. A fourth, however, *La Comédie de la culture* by Michel Schneider, a senior official in the Lang administration between 1988 and 1991, was much more aggressive and embittered. Published just before the 1993 general election, his assault was also more public, especially when Lang and Schneider appeared together on a stormy session of Bernard Pivot's TV programme 'Bouillon de culture' watched by 1.5 million people.[5]

What links most of these works, and many of the assessments in the press over the years, is that they have to a greater or lesser extent been influenced by Lang's undeniable taste for publicity and self-projection. Observers were often exasperated by what they took to be his vacuity, narcissism and shameless electoralism, some even accusing the government of using the Ministry as an organ of state propaganda to brainwash the young and impressionable. Inevitably, such judgments affected the way the measures themselves were perceived, with the result that cultural policy fell victim in the late 1980s to a process of discursive inflation for which the Minister and his most vocal opponents doubtless have to share blame. But the debates to which the Mitterrand era gave rise also posed more fundamental questions about the meaning and place of culture in the late twentieth century. The major issue here was exactly how the 'cultural' in cultural policy ought to be construed. In this context, there is, I believe, little to be gained by reviewing attempts by ethnologists, philosophers and others to define the term 'culture'.[6] Following the example of a Council of Europe evaluation of French cultural policy in 1988, I shall simply use the word as it has been used over the years by those conducting or debating policy, charting the shifts in meaning as they occur.[7] Nevertheless, a few preliminary remarks may be useful.

On a theoretical level, two basic meanings of the word are usually identified, though they are ultimately related. The first meaning embraces in its narrowest sense what is conveyed in English by the administrative term 'arts and heritage' (theatre, opera, the visual arts, music, literature, historic buildings, etc.). In a different register, such artefacts, together with the intellectual or spiritual enrichment they procure for an elite, are also known as 'high culture' – '*la haute culture*', '*la culture cultivée*' or '*classique*' in French. This is because the use of the term 'culture' has been extended in recent years, both by French cultural historians and by the discipline of cultural studies in English-speaking countries, to include 'low', 'minor' or 'popular' imaginative forms – from broadside ballads to pop, from vaudeville to soaps.[8] It is in this first sense, narrow or extended, that 'culture' or 'cultural' will most frequently appear in this study. The second meaning, however, is more extensive still: deriving from anthropology and ethnology, it subsumes the arts, heritage and popular cultures in the customs, models, rituals and general way of life by which a given community expresses and represents itself.

These two senses are fairly commonly accepted today but are none the less at the heart of the recent debates. Finkielkraut, for example, distinguishes between a humanist tradition he calls 'le détour par les œuvres pour comprendre la vie', and 'l'ensemble des pratiques d'une société, le mode d'être d'une communauté', his preference clearly going to the former conception. Lang similarly speaks of culture as on the one hand 'la production intellectuelle ou artistique' of human beings and on the other 'l'état d'une société, sa civilisation, ses mœurs, sa manière d'être, de vivre et de penser', but sees the work of his ministry as quite comfortably spanning the two.[9] As this already suggests, much of the sound and fury of the Mitterrand years was in fact about an alleged ministerial drift from the humanist to the anthropological sense, with all the perils that uncharted voyage was deemed to imply for the French classical tradition.

Be that as it may, in the more pragmatic discourse of administrative practice, the 'cultural' in cultural policy has generally meant four broad areas of state responsibility for the arts and heritage. The first is *conservation* , or maintaining and adding to the heritage (*le patrimoine*).

The second is '*création*', which entails state purchases and commissions of new works of art, aid to live performance, and measures to improve artists' living and working conditions. The third is '*diffusion*' and '*démocratisation*': these are sometimes used synonymously, though usually the former means measures to ensure that the arts and heritage find an audience at home and abroad, while the latter specifies a domestic audience which is sociologically and geographically diverse. The last is '*formation*': providing specialist training for professionals and amateurs outside the state education system (art schools, conservatoires, training for curators at the Ecole du patrimoine, and so on). Here what has caused controversy, both during Lang's stewardship and prior to it, is that over the years one or more of these activities has been prioritised over the remainder, although all four were written into the Culture Ministry's remit from the start.

In reviewing the significance of the post–1981 period, it is not particularly my intention to refute the various negative judgments of Socialist policy, which no doubt contain a certain truth. But I do consider many of them one-sided. My general purpose in writing this book is therefore to try to clear away the bravado and the brouhaha and provide a more balanced view. More specifically, my aims are threefold, as reflected in the book's three parts: to provide a short history of cultural policy so as to gauge the nature and distinctiveness of the Mitterrand years; to give as objective an account of those years as possible; and, particularly important, to analyse the debates they have stimulated, the better to assess the light they cast on the issues behind cultural policy – past, present and future. I shall pay particular attention to what has been the core of debate, namely the attempt to democratise access to culture. This essentially ideological ambition harks back at least to 1936 and constituted the founding mission of the Ministry in 1959, but it later came into conflict with more contemporary phenomena: post–1968 interpretations of cultural democracy, a stronger policy emphasis on encouraging new work, and most dramatically perhaps, the swift industrialisation and commercialisation of French leisure activities in the 1970s and 1980s in the wake of new communications technologies, which national policy-makers had some difficulty adapting to.

What I consider to be the central thread in the history of cultural policy over the last sixty years is in fact a persistent though sporadic and largely theoretical concern, emanating initially from the Left, to found state action on an all-embracing, or 'global', conception of culture more in tune with the times. This in turn meant attempting to design ministerial structures or funding mechanisms which might accommodate this wider conception and respond to a related conviction, again mostly among left-wing politicians and intellectuals, that the state's mission was to engage in what became known as '*action culturelle*'. This is a key term, almost as protean and polysemous as culture itself. In its original sense, the one in which it was first used in 1959, it is more or less synonymous with cultural policy itself. But as we shall see later, since the late 1960s the term most commonly refers to activities or institutions which attempt in whatever way to bring culture in whatever form nearer to people, communities and society. In this sense, it came reasonably close in the post–1968 era to yet another key notion, *l'action socioculturelle*, though strictly speaking the latter signifies activities and institutions which approach cultural practice not as an end in itself but as a way of socialising people, mostly the young and culturally deprived and usually by means of widely defined amateur activities. Jean Caune in fact sums up this distinction between cultural and sociocultural action quite simply: 'activités à caractères artistique et culturel pour le premier, activités orientées vers le loisir et la rencontre collective pour le second.'[10] To a large extent, the idea of basing state policy on a global conception of culture involved attempting to bring these two sets of activities into closer harmony, and it is with the first tentative steps in this direction, around 1936, that the contemporary history of cultural policy begins.

Notes

1. Carignon was quoted by Anne Sinclair on 'Sept sur sept', TF1, 7 February 1993.
2. A number of such works already exists, in particular R. Caron, *L'Etat et la culture*, Paris, 1989; A.-H. Mesnard, *Droit et politique de la culture*, Paris, 1990, and R. Wangermée and B. Gournay (Council of Europe report), *Programme européen d'évaluation: la politique culturelle de la France*, Paris, 1988. The Ministry of Culture's own research department, the Département des études et de la prospective (DEP), is also permanently engaged in evaluations of specific policies and of policy in general, which are published from time to time, usually by La Documentation Française. Full publication details of these and all other works cited in this study are provided in the Bibliography.
3. As the present study was being completed, Lang's political ambitions suffered a setback when in December 1993 he was formally deprived of his seat in the Assembly, hard won only months before at the March elections, for exceeding the stipulated limit on campaign spending. Nevertheless, in January 1995, as this

study was about to go to press, he put his name forward as one of three PS presidential candidates, though he withdrew it shortly afterwards.

4. J.-P. Rioux, 'L'Evolution des interventions de l'Etat dans le domaine des affaires culturelles', *Administration*, no.151, 15 April 1991, p.10.

5. A. Finkielkraut, *La Défaite de la pensée*, Paris, 1987; R. Desneux, *Jack Lang: la culture en mouvement*, Paris, 1990; M. Hunter, *Les Jours les plus Lang*, Paris, 1990; M. Fumaroli, *L'Etat culturel: essai sur une religion moderne*, Paris, 1991; H. Bonnier, *Lettre recommandée aux fossoyeurs de la culture*, Monaco, 1992; J. Rigaud, *Libre Culture*, Paris, 1990; R. Abirached, *Le Théâtre et le prince*, Paris, 1992; J. Gattégno, *La Bibliothèque de France à mi-parcours: de la TGB à la BN bis?*, Paris, 1992; M. Schneider, *La Comédie de la culture*, Paris, 1993. Pivot's TV programme was broadcast 19 February 1993.

6. On the meanings of the word culture, see in particular P. Bénéton, *Histoire de mots: culture et civilisation*, Paris, Presses de la FNSP, 1975; also B. Rigby, *Popular Culture in Modern France: a study of cultural discourse*, London and New York, 1991.

7. See Wangermée and Gournay, *La Politique culturelle*, pp.24–6.

8. On the notion of high culture, see Rigby, *Popular Culture*, pp.6–7.

9. Finkielkraut, 'The Late Show', BBC2, 12 October 1992 (see also *La Défaite*, p.11); Lang, 'The Late Show', 12 October 1992.

10. *La Culture en action. De Vilar à Lang: le sens perdu*, Grenoble, 1992, p.270. I am grateful to Pierre Moulinier of the Ministry of Culture for helping clarify these terms.

Part I

Culture and the State: The History of the Ministry

– 1 –

The Precursors: The Popular Front, Vichy and the Liberation

France's tradition of state involvement in the arts and heritage is a long one and is inseparable from the idea of a national culture.[1] In medieval times, the preservation of Europe's cultural heritage was largely the business of the Church. Gradually, however, with the disintegration of Charlemagne's empire, national cultures began to emerge and, in France, high culture was endowed with a political rather than religious purpose.[2] Successive monarchs patronised the arts by collecting works or distributing favours to artists, firstly in a purely private capacity but, from François I onwards, with a more public end in mind. Royal patronage, or *mécénat*, was intended to benefit the state by enhancing national prestige while also centralising and stabilising the intellectual life of the emerging nation-state by favouring a single national culture. It was, however, with the Sun King and his court, focal point of the artistic life of the age, that the idea of culture as an affirmation of nation really began. Classicism was able to become the harmonising force it did thanks to a number of institutional factors: royal patronage, the Surintendance des bâtiments du Roi under Colbert which supervised state involvement in the arts, and the various Academies under the Surintendance's sway, which laid down and taught the principles of their respective disciplines (literature, painting and sculpture, architecture, science). Louis XIV therefore benefited from the dissemination of a single culture which, in glorifying his own person, also glorified the nation.

The Revolution changed matters to a degree. With the expropriation of the monarchy, the nobility and the Church, their art treasures and monuments became the property of the nation and the responsibility of the state.[3] This transformed the notion of a national culture, which no longer meant a culture radiating from the centre of political power and monopolised by the few but one which was theoretically the legacy of all. In Revolutionary discourse, the nation was one and indivisible, having no place for elites, minorities or sectional interests, and the cultural heritage was the emblem of that unity. During the early years, a reasonably active state policy was conducted which included the opening of the Louvre as a museum and the creation of the Ecole nationale des beaux-arts and the Institut de France. Napoléon then laid the foundations of a state administration to oversee the heritage. What in fact characterises all the regimes before 1870 is their tendency variously to codify, censure or officialise cultural activity. Here, the role of the Institut de France was crucial, and more particularly its Académie des beaux-arts. Invested from 1797 with the right to choose the winners of the *prix de Rome*, the Academy, composed according to its critics of a self-recruiting and self-interested coterie, promoted what amounted to an official art. 'Académisme' as it became known was in theory classical but in practice merely conservative, disseminated through the new Ecole des beaux-arts' monopoly of education in music, painting, sculpture and architecture. It was summed up by Jeanne Laurent, a civil servant who began a career in arts administration at the end of the Third Republic, as 'l'application consciente et méthodique d'une doctrine'.[4] With the last years of the Third Republic, however, and with Laurent herself at the beginning of the Fourth, came an alternative state strategy.

The Third Republic set up a more developed administrative structure for what continued to be called *les beaux-arts* or fine arts – a term revealing the narrow conception of culture still in operation – which lasted until 1958. For Laurent, however, in her book *La République et les beaux-arts* (1955), this longevity led only to conservatism and limited ambition.[5] Certainly, the Republic was more concerned with democratising education through Jules Ferry's compulsory state system than with the *beaux-arts*, which did not have a ministry of their own – apart from briefly in 1881 – but were managed by a secretary or under-secretary of state within the Education ministry (L'Instruction publique). Beaux-Arts had only a small budget, was not seen as a prestigious appointment, and was generally attributed to lesser known figures with little political influence who usually did not stay long.[6] But the department's low profile also had to do with the Republican regime's liberalism. Cultural practices were deemed to be a private matter rather than the business of the state, whose duty was perceived as being largely restricted to conservation. Some efforts were made to bring about democratisation, by offering price reductions in state-run establishments for certain categories of citizen, or by setting up the Théâtre national populaire under Firmin Gémier in 1920, but they were limited.[7] As for creation, the state preferred to surrender its authority to a number of non-elected advisory councils on which the

Académie des beaux-arts was prominently represented. As a result, the training of future generations of painters, sculptors, architects and musicians, and what little state spending there was on new work, continued to be dominated by academicism. There was considerable resistance to acquiring the most significant contemporary art, much of which was sold abroad or privately. Hence the notorious refusal in 1895 of twenty-nine of the Impressionist canvasses bequeathed to the state by Gustave Caillebotte, whose collection included work by Cézanne, Monet and Manet. Municipal theatres throughout France, once flourishing centres of drama and opera, were similarly neglected and disappeared, leaving only tour companies to serve the regions with work from Paris. Popular entertainments and the rising mass-cultural forms – talkies, 78 records, radio – attracted very little government attention at all. Yet paradoxically, alongside this liberalism the state still perpetuated the Revolutionary myth of a single cultural heritage, supposedly national but in practice Parisian and middle-class, serviced by academicism and uniformly disseminated in elementary form by the centralised *école républicaine*. In this way, the Revolution's denunciation of anything which might threaten national homogeneity – regional languages, working-class, rural or avant-garde cultures – was upheld.[8]

But from the late nineteenth century, this *système des beaux-arts* slowly began to be challenged by a more voluntarist concern among intellectuals and militants with *éducation populaire*, that is, workers' or adult education. This was not a homogeneous notion, however. For some, it implied a Republican belief that educating those whom the school system had failed was a means of installing greater understanding and solidarity between classes. For others, it was a means not of unification but of revolution, of awakening the masses to their oppression. Bound up with this latter model was the revolutionary syndicalist belief in the specificity of working-class experience, a culture of the workplace and the trade-union rather than the bourgeois culture dispensed by the new compulsory primary education, which merely reproduced the existing social order. Evolving into a popular-culture movement, these two warring conceptions were to inform cultural-policy debate throughout the twentieth century.[9] At official level, however, it was primarily the former, more unitarian view which triumphed, becoming government policy at the time of the first real landmark in the history of contemporary cultural policy: the Popular Front.

The Popular Front, or 'Rassemblement populaire', was a short-lived alliance of the Left (Socialists, Communists and Radicals) formed in the mid–1930s in response to the growing threat of fascism and which came to power in May 1936 under Léon Blum. Its heyday was barely a year though it continued in some form until 1938, with some of its ministers remaining in office until the war. It grew out of a period of political uncertainty, cultural change, and intense activity by a broad-Left intelligentsia which played an important part in developing its ideas and in some cases putting them into practice. Not surprisingly, the formulation of a cultural policy became one of its main innovations.

What the Front meant by 'culture' and 'cultural', terms which began to enter official discourse at this time, was complex. Crucial to it was the evolution of those intellectuals close to the French Communist Party (PCF). In the 1920s and early 1930s, the newly formed PCF had repudiated the idea of a supposedly national high culture, considering it bourgeois and corruptive of authentic proletarian cultural practices. But with the menace of fascism in the mid–1930s, this doctrine was reversed. Suddenly discovering a patriotic pride in France's great artistic past, Communist spokesmen reclaimed it as the heritage of all and called for the setting up of a 'Ministry of Art'. At about this time, a large number of cultural associations and pressure groups sprang up, related in varying degrees to the Rassemblement and often linked with left-wing or trade-union organisations.[10] Perhaps the most important of these in size and influence grew out of the Association des écrivains et artistes révolutionnaires (AEAR) formed in March 1932 by PCF intellectuals to rally the non-party intelligentsia to its anti-fascist cause, which it succeeded in doing with the likes of Gide, the writer and autodidact Jean Guéhenno, and most significantly the future Minister for Cultural Affairs, André Malraux. Two years later, it called for the formation in Paris and the provinces of cultural groups bringing together workers, teachers and intellectuals. The result was the launch of a number of 'Maisons de la culture'. The AEAR itself became the Association des Maisons de la culture et des cercles culturels (AMC) in which Malraux was actively involved and which by 1937 claimed 70,000 members.[11]

What linked the AMC with the other Frontist cultural associations, some of which were affiliated to it, was the watchword 'popularisation', later to become 'democratisation'. 'Il n'y a pas deux cultures...', proclaimed the general secretary of the AMC, the Communist novelist René Blech, 'mais une seule, à laquelle ont droit les masses laborieuses aussi bien que les intellectuels'. This view was endorsed by the as yet unknown Jacques Soustelle, member of a group of museum curators and ethnographers formed in June 1936 called the Association populaire des amis du musée (APAM), who captured in a powerful image the quintessential Frontist ambition to take high culture to the people:

> Parallèle au grand mouvement politique et social du Front populaire, ou plutôt ne formant qu'un de ses aspects, se déroule dans notre pays un vaste mouvement culturel. Sa devise pourrait être celle-ci: ouvrons les portes de la culture. Brisons la muraille qui entourait, comme un beau parc interdit aux pauvres gens, une culture réservée à une 'élite' de privilégiés.[12]

Yet democratisation as the Front construed it did not involve high culture alone, but was based on a recognition that in a modern industrial society the worker has a right to recreation in all its forms. After the election, this doctrine was enshrined in the pioneering legislation setting up the forty-hour week and two weeks' paid leave, which allowed a new public to discover the seaside, youth hostelling and other healthy outdoor pursuits for the first time in the mythical summer of 1936. It was also encompassed in ministerial structures. Beaux-Arts remained within Education though without a secretary of state, both now placed under a young, dynamic minister, Jean Zay, also in charge of scientific research in the first Popular Front government. More importantly, the Front established France's first government department for those areas later circumscribed in the term 'sociocultural': youth, sport, popular education and leisure. A Sous-Secrétariat d'Etat à l'organisation des loisirs et des sports was set up under another young and energetic incumbent, the Socialist Léo Lagrange. Lagrange too was dedicated to widening access to the arts, but his chief ambition was to develop the whole person, mind and body, and his activities were suitably wide-ranging and powered by high idealism: 'Loisirs sportifs, loisirs touristiques, loisirs culturels, tels sont les trois aspects complémentaires d'un même besoin social: la conquête de la dignité, la recherche du bonheur.' Lagrange's department was later moved from Public Health into Zay's Education portfolio, further stressing the oneness of the high-cultural, the recreational and the educational, though to Zay's disappointment the radio service remained under the Ministère des postes.[13]

In practice, this broad conception of democratisation led to a variety of measures. As Education Minister, Zay attempted to make provision in schools for a creative-arts curriculum, though this did not come to fruition and has remained a failing of French education ever since. Instead, democratisation was pursued independently of formal education, in conjunction with the cultural associations, many of which similarly aimed to bring together educational, leisure and amateur or professional artistic activities and were often able to influence government policy considerably. The most productive relationships of this kind usually obtained between Lagrange's department and various sport and leisure organisations for workers. But arts and heritage associations also prompted some action. Collaboration between the government and the Association pour le développement de la lecture publique (ADLP), for example, led to the setting up of decentralised 'Centres de lecture publique' in Nantes and Bordeaux and a mobile library service known as the *bibliobus*, for which the Front is still remembered. Equally fruitful was the work of Soustelle's APAM which helped obtain more convenient night opening and reduced rates at the Louvre for trade-union members. A year after its launch, some 25,000 workers had taken part in its activities.[14]

One other, particularly significant instance for future state policy was the theatre. The Union des théâtres indépendants de France urged Zay to tackle the dearth of theatre in the provinces and suburbs, though in fact various itinerant troupes had already sprung up with this in mind. In 1924, the great Parisian actor-director Jacques Copeau had set up a small troupe in an obscure Burgundy village, touring the region with productions of classics or work adapted to local concerns. Either from its ramifications or independently, other troupes then began taking theatre to the regions, like Jean Dasté's Compagnie des quatre saisons, Léon Chancerel's scout-based Comédiens-routiers, or André Clavé's La Roulotte which later enlisted Jean Vilar.[15] None of these initiatives received financial assistance from the state, however; nor did Zay and Lagrange get far in altering the situation. Nevertheless, a vital blueprint was drawn up when a report on provincial theatre was commissioned by Zay from Charles Dullin, another actor-director close to Copeau, and plans were laid for a network of some 160 new or reopened theatres. The cultural historian Pascal Ory argues that in reality the government had neither the time nor the money for such a reform, though Zay did manage to bypass his budgetary restrictions to an extent by having 7.4 million francs redirected from the radio budget, which allowed some small help to be given to Dasté's Paris-based company and also, for the first time, to a provincial theatre group, Le Rideau gris de Marseille.[16]

In addition to democratisation, Ory identifies two other features of Frontist cultural policy, though he rightly points out that the three cannot be adequately separated. The first was the will to organise culture, exemplified in two attempts to regulate burgeoning mass-cultural forms by defining statutes for radio and cinema, which were considered to have an important educational function. Neither proposal, however, could be properly implemented before the outbreak of war.[17] A parallel instance was the bill on 'le droit d'auteur et le contrat d'édition' which tried to extend the Front's social legislation to 'travailleurs intellectuels'. Originally designed to protect authors specifically, the bill was broadened to include records, radio, film and so forth, redefining the notion of the work to embrace the new mass technologies. But with the Right and some big publishers ranged against the measure, negotiations led to delays and the bill was submitted too late.

These early audiovisual measures also illustrate Ory's second feature, which he calls *décloisonnement*, or decompartmentalisation: the acknowledgement of newer, popular forms of expression. The fact that the cinema of Gabin, Renoir and *Quai des brumes* is the form most often associated with the Front is significant in this respect. A quite different instance was the recognition of the existing folklore of France's still predominantly rural communities, illustrated in the creation of the Musée des arts et traditions populaires a matter of months after the elections. This dissolving of cultural boundaries also extended to those which isolated culture from society at large. Zay's multidisciplinary ministry was one manifestation of this, as was Lagrange's view of the complementarity of culture and leisure. A third was the Front's taste for bringing culture out into the open. Lagrange particularly set great store by the collective and the festive, seeing culture as a public activity which united people in a spirit of communal joy. 'Nous pensons', he proclaimed in December 1936, 'qu'il faut donner aux masses de grandes fêtes qui exaltent la conscience populaire aux dates significatives'.[18]

The best example of this was a massive revival in 1936 of Romain Rolland's play about the French Revolution, *Le Quatorze Juillet*, staged with government aid by the Paris Maison de la culture to coincide with 14 July. This was a vast, collective production with contributions by famous artists, composers and actors of the Comédie Française, while smaller parts were taken by members of the CGT. The play's first performance in 1902 had been unremarkable; in 1936 it succeeded because it captured the euphoria that prevailed that summer. As had already happened earlier in the day at a mass event at the Bastille, parallels between 1789 and 1936 were drawn and the audience, alternately chanting *La Marseillaise* and *L'Internationale*, was exhilarated. What this and similar spectacles demonstrated was the evolution of a Popular Front style characterised by an emphasis on joy, mass spectacle and a carnivalesque total theatre in which high and low cultures came together in celebration of a common heritage. The Exposition universelle of 1937, which the Front inherited and Zay helped organise, shared this mood, glorifying French achievement and the government's cultural eclecticism. Zay similarly turned the 150th anniversary of the Revolution into a festive, people's occasion with a mass rally outside the newly built Palais de Chaillot. Indeed, to a limited extent this style had echoes of the collective spirit fostered by European fascist regimes, as did some of the actual policies adopted, though the ideology was different and Lagrange was at pains to avoid the 'organisation of leisure' being interpreted in this fashion.

But what is most striking in such events, as in Frontist policies generally, is the incipient willingness to redefine the cultural in more sociocultural terms. High culture belongs among the people and the task of democratising it is integral to that of developing their intellectual and physical health and their personal happiness. This ecumenicalism, together with the pioneering social legislation, helped create the great sentimental myth of the Popular Front, which outlived it by many years. Nevertheless, its achievements in the cultural field need to be viewed somewhat more dispassionately. Firstly, although the Front was the first Republican government to abandon liberalism and place the arts and leisure on the political agenda, it actually failed to put the majority of its proposals into effect, albeit with extenuating historical circumstances. Secondly, a certain ambivalence surrounds its cultural policies because of what they in effect excluded. Elisabeth Ritaine and others argue that the Front's consensualism allowed no room for divergence or dissent since what was at stake was the rallying of the nation against fascism. Thus, those like André Breton or Jacques Prévert's revolutionary October group who did not associate themselves with it were soon marginalised.

In fact, despite gestures in the direction of the avant-garde and a general spirit of aesthetic openness, the Front was more preoccupied with democratising an accepted 'national' culture than with exploring new creative territories. Accordingly, the artistic output associated with it is fairly traditional. Clearly, this should not be taken too far. As Ory points out, Blum gave his backing to Le Corbusier's ground-breaking 'Pavillon des temps nouveaux' and Raymond Cogniat's experimental 'Théâtre d'essai' at the time of the Exhibition of 1937. Zay also involved the greatest contemporary practitioners of the performing arts in his reform of the Comédie Française and the Opéra de Paris. Nevertheless, Pierre Cabanne maintains that in the visual arts the Front fared little better than its predecessors at resisting the dominance of academicism. The national art collections at the time contained only one Picasso, classed under 'écoles étrangères'. In 1937, the Musées nationaux refused to acquire a second, while at the Exposition that year, Cabanne recounts, the Presidential cortege was discreetly steered away from the work by Surrealist or abstract artists.

Fumaroli also maintains (though with approval) that Zay himself was 'de tradition classique et rationaliste' and not susceptible to fashionable avant-gardism.[19]

None of which prevented the Front's global conception of the cultural becoming a reference point for future cultural administrators and commentators. Even Fumaroli, who is reproving of the whole notion of a state cultural policy, subscribes to the myth, though he does give it his own particular twist. What he most admires in fact is Zay's and Lagrange's insistence on seeing leisure and the arts as inseparable from learning rather than as substitutes for it. He therefore views the Front, *dirigiste* but in moderation, not as a fleeting exception to the Third Republic's abstentionism as Laurent does but as the very flower of the 'Athenian Republic' which was its model. For him, the Third Republic in its entirety was in fact a golden age of democracy and 'arm's length' modesty with regard to culture which did much to favour the artistic vitality of the period. This enables him to discredit the Mitterrand regime's and indeed the whole Fifth Republic's policies by arguing that their roots lie not in the Popular Front, of which both Malraux and Mitterrand have often been cast as heirs, but instead in Vichy, the very antithesis of the Front in Fumaroli's eyes. It is not within the scope of this book to explore this contention, but although research on the cultural policies and institutions of Vichy is still relatively scarce, what there is suggests that they continued Front policies more than they undid them, as indeed do Zay's own memoirs. This is not altogether surprising when one considers that Pétain's regime inevitably faced much the same social and cultural problems as the one it succeeded and that, although major agents of the Front's policies like Zay were removed from office, most of the second tier of decision-makers remained in post throughout the Occupation.[20]

Confronted with the energy totalitarian regimes appeared to derive from a collectivist ideology, many in defeated France felt the need to break with the abstraction and individualism they associated with Republicanism and rediscover a deeper-rooted spirit capable of reuniting the nation and curbing its moral decline. Drawing on extreme-Right thinkers like Barrès and Maurras, Vichy's 'national revolution' hinged on the belief that a new France could somehow be reborn by rejecting a rootless, cosmopolitan, elitist Parisianism and rediscovering a popular heritage enmeshed in the regional cultures of *la France profonde*. Hence a cultural and youth policy which favoured the revival of regional folklore in the form of traditional dances, music and costumes and gave limited encouragement to regional-language movements. Yet for the national revolution to be both national and revolutionary, a strong state was required and liberalism was condemned.[21] Central intervention in the field of culture was intensified accordingly. The Beaux-Arts administration under Louis Hautecœur, still within Education, was reorganised, with a tightening of its powers. The government also developed the youth and sport structures initiated by the Popular Front, creating a Secrétariat général à la jeunesse under Georges Lamirand, also within Education from September 1940, and a relatively autonomous Commissariat à l'éducation générale et au sport under Jean Borotra, whose sport policy owed much to Lagrange's.[22]

Ory tentatively suggests that this cultural interventionism in fact continued the Front's in three main ways: 'organisation', which included the ideological enlistment of various cultural movements such as the scouts and the creation of corporatist professional bodies such as the Comité d'organisation de l'industrie cinématographique (COIC); democratisation, which under Vichy found its most active form in decentralisation; and youth policies.[23] All three intersected in two bodies which were to mark future cultural policy. The first was the Ecole des cadres at Uriage, a state institution under the Secrétariat général à la jeunesse. Uriage began life as Pétainist in its mission to train the young leaders of the national revolution but soon evolved its own, more independent 'revolutionary humanism' which stood in covert opposition to the regime. It also developed an appropriate pedagogy in an endeavour to develop its tutees physically, intellectually and spiritually as Lagrange had sought to do, and foster a new team spirit.[24]

The other, more important body from the point of view of cultural policy was Jeune France, a semi-official association which had links with Uriage chiefly via the theorist of personalism and founder of the review *Esprit*, Emmanuel Mounier, who influenced both. Initially, Jeune France's aims were modest, but they rapidly evolved as its founder Pierre Schaeffer assembled around him a number of people from the various arts dedicated to bringing about a cultural renaissance, which could reinvigorate artistic creation and demonstrate that though vanquished militarily France's real sources of greatness, its cultural traditions, were still intact. Although Jeune France was legally a private association, Schaeffer had friends in government from scouting days, including Lamirand, and his organisation derived most of its funds from government departments. Like Uriage, it was initially in sympathy with the aims of the national revolution, as evidenced in the propagandist tone of some of its early pronouncements and its participation in national *fêtes* which celebrated and served the regime.[25]

In order to remoralise a new generation which might weld the nation together, it set out to renew cultural activity in the regions. Many of those active in reviving regional theatre before the war like Dasté, Clavé, Chancerel and Vilar continued their work either in or with Jeune France. Touring events involving libraries, music, poetry and exhibitions were also organised, while the Front idea of Maisons de la culture was adapted with the setting up of multidisciplinary cultural centres known as 'Maisons Jeune France'. But, again like the Front, its ambitions went beyond traditional high culture. It involved itself in existing local crafts and popular cultures such as folk dancing, choral singing and the kind of spectacular mass festivities and youth rallies favoured by the regime, often built on national or regional traditions and symbols. It became widely involved too in training by holding evening classes and creative workshops. The aim of such activities was to compensate for the sterile pedagogy of the state education system which, according to Mounier, had only succeeded in producing an 'abêtissement collectif' which had played its part in the downfall of 1940.[26]

As the Vichy regime hardened under Laval, it became aware that Jeune France's ambitions were not in keeping with its own, for many of the association's members came from the social-catholic or personalist Left (*Esprit*, the CFTC) and were far from being backward-looking traditionalists. The organisation was therefore dissolved in March 1942 after some seventeen months. Uriage too was closed down later that year by official edict and members of both, including Mounier, joined the Resistance. After the war, Jeune France was discreetly forgotten and until recently its place in the development of cultural policy remained largely unexplored. This is no doubt due to the discredit which befell it in view of its ideological ambivalence. Fumaroli makes much of its Vichy connections, seeing it as fostering an unthinking collectivism perfectly in tune with the regime.[27] Yet in the turmoil of the early Occupation, a refusal of Third-Republic liberalism and a discourse of national renewal were by no means exclusive to the pro-Vichy Right and can even be detected in the broadly left-wing Resistance. There is therefore a case for questioning Fumaroli's thesis and suggesting, as Ory does, a strong thread of continuity in cultural policy running from the Popular Front through Vichy and the Resistance into the post-Liberation period, with Jeune France as the missing link: condensing pre-war attempts at theatrical decentralisation, extending its activities to folk cultures and pedagogy, and involving the state in subsidising such non-Parisian initiatives. Fumaroli is right, however, to see Jeune France's critique of state education as the launch-pad for the subsequent creation of an autonomous Ministry of Culture, the way being prepared by the early policies of the Fourth Republic.

The unity and social levelling which war and clandestine struggle bring appeared to offer the French the chance of transcending pre-war divisions. The Resistance had spent the last years of the war laying plans for national reconstruction, enshrined in the CNR charter, and between 1944 and 1947, a broad-Left tripartite government, its composition modelled on the Resistance and therefore including Communists, set out to implement the charter's socialist-humanist principles. The need to rebuild France's economy and infrastructure also brought about economic planning which over the next thirty years of growth helped transform France into a modern consumer society. The early post-war years therefore saw a mentality of change which spawned a third brief age of cultural voluntarism, based on the Popular Front's recognition of new cultural needs alongside economic and social ones.

Like Jeune France and Uriage, many Resistance groups scattered across the territory had become involved in cultural dissemination and training. Consequently, a generation of cultural militants, some with experience dating back to the Popular Front, emerged from the Occupation convinced of the need to widen access to culture as a means of resisting the appeal of future totalitarianisms and building a more just society. For some, this implied revolutionary struggle. Yet it was not Marxism which became the dominant ideology of the movement but a combination of the socialist humanism and patriotism of the Resistance with the personalism and social catholicism of Mounier and *Esprit*, coupled with the ideals and aesthetics of early decentralisers like Copeau (also a Catholic) and Gémier.[28] Post-war democratisation was therefore not so much a political as an ethical and civic imperative aiming to transcend class struggle in favour of national consensus and individual self-fulfilment. Jean Vilar became one of its principal voices, proclaiming that theatre should be a public service because it meets a profound, almost physical need, as much in ordinary people as in the highly educated, and is capable of reconciling all social groups in a quasi-religious communion.[29] However, as in 1936, the objective of democratising high culture was part of a broader preoccupation with 'popular culture', a term which included workers' education, some recognition of the everyday cultural practices of ordinary people, and even in some cases a timid acknowledgement of a now rapidly evolving mass culture. The abiding ideology of the movement, however, was still edification, which usually meant a desire to liberate people from the alienating effects of the mass media by helping them accede to more fulfilling forms of cultural practice.[30]

This ideology was to find various outlets in the cultural landscape of the immediate post-war years, as private initiatives and cultural or sociocultural associations sprang up everywhere. Former activists of Jeune France or Uriage were behind the Editions du Seuil and the new daily newspaper, *Le Monde*. In 1944, André Philip, who had worked on *Esprit* and been an SFIO deputy, set up in Lyon the first of a nation-wide network of Maisons des jeunes et de la culture (MJC), youth clubs and cultural leisure centres making available a range of activities such as amateur theatre, crafts and choral singing. In much the same vein, the Clubs Léo Lagrange, a Popular Front initiative for young people, were developed into a federation in 1951 with the help of the SFIO's National Secretary for Youth, the future Prime Minister Pierre Mauroy. A network of *ciné-clubs* and later *télé-clubs* was set up, as were numerous other youth or cultural associations connected with political parties, religious movements or trade unions. The popular-education movement also grew rapidly, providing adult education or training in the arts, crafts and sport. Probably the best known of such groups was Peuple et Culture, formed from the Vercors maquis in 1944 by former members of Uriage and *Esprit* and with its roots in the Popular Front. Peuple et Culture too was concerned with moral improvement and much of its legacy lies in its training of the community arts workers who became known as *animateurs culturels*, whose job was to raise the cultural literacy, critical standards and civic sense of ordinary people.[31]

In state institutions, however, change was not as far-reaching, despite the inclusion in the new 1946 constitution of the right to equal access to culture and education. During the Fourth Republic, the attention of the major agents was largely taken up with reconstruction and later with colonial conflict, while the lesser figures usually placed in charge of the Beaux-Arts administration were not of the stature to command the budgets required for cultural reform. The new five-year plans introduced in the late 1940s were also silent on the matter. A further impediment was that many on the Left continued to see the Culture and Youth sectors as the natural preserve of the unwieldy Education Ministry, which is where both generally remained, as did Popular Education and Sport in various combinations. Given the broader conception of culture which had been developing since the 1930s, there was some logic in this. But the reality was that culture was placed second to the massive problems faced by an expanding but outdated state education system. Beaux-Arts itself was reorganised in August 1945 into a Direction générale des arts et des lettres (DGAL) under Jacques Jaujard, which remained the most stable structure for the arts throughout the Fourth Republic, subsumed sporadically into a Secrétariat d'Etat aux beaux-arts under André Cornu (1951–4), and 'aux arts et lettres' under Jacques Bordeneuve (1956–8), though even at these times it enjoyed no autonomy.[32] During the early 'heroic' period of the late 1940s, however, there were a few brief exceptions to the official inertia. Legislation was passed in 1945 introducing *comités d'entreprises*, leisure and cultural committees which became compulsory in all but the smallest firms. Harking back once again to Lagrange, a new 'Direction des mouvements de jeunesse et de l'éducation populaire' was set up within Education, placed for a short period under Guéhenno, which in 1948 became part of the Direction de la jeunesse et des sports, a dynamic body in the immediate post-war period. At the same time, other ministries were also beginning to take cognisance of the part played by the cultural in their domain, chiefly Foreign Affairs which set up its own Direction générale des relations culturelles, the first time the term 'cultural' was used in a ministerial connection. But the most significant step came in January 1947 when the Ramadier government created an autonomous ministry to coordinate youth affairs, sport and the arts, albeit one which lasted only until November that year. Under yet another young and dynamic minister, Pierre Bourdan, the Ministère de la jeunesse, des arts et des lettres embodied to a degree the Popular Front's comprehensive conception of culture, though it differed from the Zay ministry in that, for the first time since 1881, it separated Beaux-Arts from Education. It was, however, placed in charge of cinema once more and acquired most of the responsibilities of the Ministry of Information too, though still not the radio service.[33] Bourdan's ministry therefore broke new ground and, freed of the crushing weight of Education, was able to coordinate and assist many of the forces for cultural change which had emerged since the Occupation.

Some of these forces, however, had already found a champion in the DGAL before Bourdan: Jeanne Laurent, Sous-Directeur [*sic*] des spectacles et de la musique. The immediate post-war period saw a handful of state initiatives aimed at decentralising the arts, such as the new Direction des bibliothèques set up in August 1945 under Julien Cain, which took up the Popular Front's *bibliobus* idea and set up the first departmental collections called Bibliothèques centrales de prêt (BCPs) to supply the mobile libraries. But none was as successful as Laurent's initiatives to decentralise theatre.

Influenced according to Fumaroli by Uriage and Jeune France, Laurent believed the Third Republic had left the arts in the provinces in a parlous state. By the late 1940s, though, some signs of renewed activity were visible, particularly in the theatre. Although the municipal authorities had some degree of responsibility for their own cultural affairs, they depended on the state for any ambitious projects. Laurent implemented just such a project for theatre. The blueprint for it already existed in the report drawn up by Dullin, which had recommended that a number of permanent touring companies be set up in the provinces. Despite initial reluctance from central government, Laurent acted on its recommendations and by assiduous behind-the-scenes diplomacy at local level set up the first five Centres dramatiques nationaux (CDNs), theatre companies permanently based in a town and touring the surrounding region, jointly funded by the state and the appropriate municipality: Colmar (later Strasbourg), Grenoble (subsequently St Etienne) under Jean Dasté, Toulouse, Rennes and Aix-en-Provence.[34] Some of these companies already existed in some form, others were formed for the purpose. But what Laurent and the five directors succeeded in creating in the theatre world was a new mentality of 'implantation' rather than Parisianism, and a new cultural demand at local level. With her coordination, the Centres formed a broadly coherent movement in which the fundamental problems of decentralisation – how to become truly implanted in a community, how to reach audiences ill-attuned to appreciating high culture – could be tackled in common. This was mainly done by their developing a repertoire of reliably accessible classics and by experimenting with new approaches to production and new forms of relationship with the local public, known as *animation*.

Their success in these endeavours served to underscore the absence of similar work in the Paris suburbs. Accordingly, in 1951, Laurent appointed Vilar, founder of the Avignon Festival four years before, to revive Gémier's Théâtre national populaire (TNP). Influenced like the CDN directors by Copeau and Gémier, Vilar formed a company at the Palais de Chaillot in central Paris dedicated to performing a classical and modern repertoire and at the same time removing the social and scenic barriers which alienate ordinary people from such work. Further developing what were to become the classic techniques of *animation*, he made block-booking and subscription arrangements with workers' organisations and youth and educational establishments, speaking in factories to make his work better known and in the first years taking his troupe into the working-class suburbs and organising with trade unions the famous 'TNP weekends', which for a single price offered plays, food and entertainment.

Of course, decentralisation here was still very largely engineered and orchestrated by central government. Not only did the state bear the brunt of the cost but it also retained the right to appoint directors, often importing them from Paris or elsewhere. They in turn brought with them, in the early stages at least, a repertoire drawn from the national or international heritage – Molière, Marivaux, Giraudoux, some Shakespeare – rather than looking to regional or popular experience or daringly avant-garde work.[35] The state involved itself in this way because decentralisation was as much a national as a regional imperative. Firstly of course, the CDNs and the TNP were designed to remedy a dearth that was nation-wide. But a further political agenda was, as under the Popular Front, arguably to heal wounds by rebuilding a single national culture. Indeed, just as the Left at that time was not yet in favour of regional devolution generally, the ecumenicalism which provided the whole rationale of the democratisation movement militated against recognising pluralism or the extremes of experimentation. This at any rate was the feeling of those who in the 1950s and 1960s were radically to contest this 'boy-scout' approach as patronising and bourgeois, provoking a fundamental challenge to the whole ethic of democratisation.

Even at the time, enthusiasm for Laurent's offensive was far from universal, though for different reasons. In 1952, accumulated pressure against her from a variety of vested interests led to her being moved to another post, unrelated to theatre. This marked the end of state-driven decentralisation for the rest of the Fourth Republic and the beginning of a period of stagnating budgets for Beaux-Arts. It also brought to a halt the democratisation policy as a whole, as the onset of the Cold War and growing internal division nudged the Fourth Republic to the Right, away from social reform. But by this time, the terms of the democratisation question were shifting anyway, under the impact of a US-influenced mass culture disseminated by new media like records, cinema, radio and soon television, all of which operated according to a free-market philosophy rather than the humanist, improving principles which had inspired the democratisers and popular educators.[36]

The rise of mass culture in fact provides one last instance of state voluntarism immediately after the war: the cinema. The Liberation found the French film industry in poor health, its infrastructure decimated, its personnel scattered, and its production rate dramatically down. It also faced the prospect of potentially fatal competition from a huge pool of American films which had been building up during the Occupation and which the newly liberated French now yearned for more than ever.[37] It recovered largely as a result of state action. As indicated earlier, the Popular Front had been aware of the need to organise the industry, but a comprehensive bill drawn up by Zay had reached parliament too close to the war to be effective. Once again, Vichy followed in the Front's footsteps. Goebbels had ordered that the French industry be allowed to produce only 'des films légers, vides et, si possible, stupides'.[38] But one benefit of Vichy's corporatism had been to organise the industry and help it survive. In August 1940, the COIC was formed, along with a state cinema service which in 1942 became a *direction générale*. These two bodies together were able to salvage at least some of the Front's attempts at reform. After the Liberation, they were fused to form an original administrative structure which survives today: the Centre national de la cinématographie (CNC). Introduced by law in 1946, the CNC is a financially autonomous *établissement public* combining the functions of a professional body and a ministry directorate applying state policy. Its success rapidly led to a widespread acceptance of the principle of state involvement in cinema.

One of its early tasks was to protect against American market domination. Just before the war, a quota on the importing of dubbed films had been introduced and since 1942 US films had been banned. But as part of a package of measures negotiated between Léon Blum and the American Secretary of State James Byrnes in May 1946 to elicit American economic aid, the French government agreed to the unrestricted importing of American films, with the proviso that for an initial two-year period a quota would still operate, restricting the number of dubbed films imported and obliging cinemas to screen French films for sixteen weeks of the year, so that the industry could recover. Despite this condition, cinema professionals were generally hostile, especially when French film production fell from 119 in 1946 to 78 in 1947.[39] On 16 September 1948, the agreement was duly renegotiated, strengthening the regulations regarding the screening of French films and reintroducing the quota on dubbed imports. But the accord's impact went further than this for on the very same day parliament voted through the CNC's first major legislation, the 'Loi d'aide temporaire à l'industrie cinématographique', which instituted subsidies to film production and distribution, paid for by a tax on each new film based on length, and another on tickets sold. By this means, film-makers could be assisted with their next production and cinema-owners with the refurbishment of their auditoria. A new law in 1953 made the aid permanent. For Fumaroli, this marked the beginning of a 'frilosité protectrice' about the arts in general which led to the setting up of a ministry whose specific duty was to undertake equally damaging forms of interference.[40] However, the new law, which probably played a part in the emergence of the New Wave of the late 1950s, also contained an element of poetic justice since much of the money ploughed back into the French industry came from the screening of American films. It was also consistent with the ideology of democratisation in so far as it involved state intervention to preserve a precious national heritage, definitively recognising cinema as a cultural form rather than just an industrial product.

Voluntarism sometimes surfaced in other sectors too during the early Fourth Republic, such as the visual arts. In 1947, the Musée national d'art moderne (MNAM), closed since the outbreak of war, reopened under Jean Cassou who, with the help of Jaujard at the DGAL and Georges Salles, head of the newly renamed Direction des musées de France, had been pursuing a vigorous acquisitions policy, albeit still policed by the Académie des beaux-arts.[41] That same year, moves were already afoot to introduce the '1 per cent' rule, another unrealised Popular Front initiative which would require 1 per cent of the cost of building a new school or university to be devoted to commissioning a work of art to decorate the building, though the measure did not become law until 1951. But generally, after this short burst of activism in the late 1940s, Beaux-Arts settled back into relative quiescence for the rest of the Fourth Republic, mainly concerning itself with protecting the heritage, though this labour was not always devoid of innovation.

Laurent, however, was not prepared to let the era of voluntarism go by unsung. Three years after her removal, *La République et les beaux-arts* acerbically settled a number of scores and included the Fourth Republic in her indictment of the Third. A non-interventionist cultural policy influenced by academic conservatism has contributed to perverting public taste, she argued, which played its part in the moral decline leading to the defeat of 1940. Cultural voluntarism is therefore the moral duty of a secular state, 'non pour la gloire de Dieu ou du souverain comme sous l'ancien régime, mais pour procurer à la nation une des formes de vie spirituelle dont elle a besoin'.[42] Her model of a state policy hinged on the conviction that the state's role is not to give the public whatever it wants but to take the difficult paths of new, contemporary, living art, which will irresistibly win people over if only it is made available to them. Contemporary creation and democratisation are not in fact warring but indivisible. She therefore called for the revival of Popular-Front-style open-air *fêtes* for which new work should be commissioned; for two new opera venues on the Paris outskirts, recruiting a new public by keeping seat prices down and undertaking provincial tours yet still producing new work of the highest standard; and for state purchase of the work of living artists. The Ministry of Finance must vacate the Louvre and a second museum for contemporary art should be opened. Every provincial city must have its own contemporary art gallery and all municipalities should acquire their own collections. Art must be available in public places, and a well resourced creative-arts education provided in all schools.[43] And if all these innovations are to be achieved, what is needed is not a secretary of state within the Education Ministry but one daring, powerful personality at the head of an autonomous administration. In this and many other respects, her ideas proved influential, or at the very least prophetic. With the setting up in de Gaulle's new republic of a separate ministry under André Malraux, her book was to become a blueprint for the policies and perils of the next forty years.

Notes

1. A.-H. Mesnard, *L'Action culturelle des pouvoirs publics*, Paris, 1969. I am indebted to this work for the early historical material contained in this chapter; also to Gaudibert, Jackson, Laurent, Ory and Ritaine below. Throughout this study, I shall use an initial capital letter when I am making a short-hand reference to a specific government institution (e.g. Culture, Education), to distinguish the term from its general sense.
2. Mesnard, *L'Action culturelle*, p.30.
3. Ibid., p.81. The term *patrimoine culturel* was not yet applied to such artefacts. See pp.72–82 for a fuller analysis of culture under the Revolution.
4. J. Laurent, *Arts et pouvoirs en France de 1793 à 1981*, Saint-Etienne, 1982, p.37.
5. Laurent, *La République et les beaux-arts*, Paris, 1955, p.70. Laurent's version of the Third and Fourth Republics' approach to the *beaux-arts*, which has become almost a standard one, is based on both first-hand experience and, arguably, a degree of personal feeling since she had been unceremoniously transferred from her Beaux-Arts posting three years before the book's appearance. Mesnard, *L'Action culturelle*, however, does generally confirm her account, as does P. Cabanne, *Le Pouvoir culturel sous la Ve République*, Paris, 1981, though both writers, and a number of others like Bonnard, Rigaud and Fumaroli, are more willing than Laurent, with differing degrees of emphasis, to concede that one or other of the two Republics had virtues.
6. A notable exception was Dujardin-Beaumetz who remained Secrétaire d'Etat aux beaux-arts for seven years between 1905 and 1912.
7. Mesnard, *L'Action culturelle*, pp.111–12.
8. Ibid., pp.146–51.
9. E. Ritaine, *Les Stratèges de la culture*, Paris, 1983, pp.25–43. A more

recent and fuller analysis of the ideology of popular education and culture is J. Caune, *La Culture en action. De Vilar à Lang: le sens perdu*, Grenoble, 1992; also B. Rigby, *Popular Culture in Modern France: A Study of Cultural Discourse*, London and New York, 1991, pp.39–67, which usefully points up the ambiguities in the terms 'popular culture' and 'popular education'.

10. See P. Ory, 'Front populaire et création artistique', *Bulletin de la Société d'Histoire Moderne*, vol.8, 1974, pp.5–21, and 'La Politique culturelle du premier gouvernement Blum', *Nouvelle Revue Socialiste*, no.10–11, 1975, pp.75–93. In future, these articles will be referred to with the abbreviation BSHM for the first and NRS for the second.

11. J. Jackson, *The Popular Front in France: Defending Democracy, 1934–38*, Cambridge, 1988, p.121. See also P. Ory and J.-F. Sirinelli, *Les Intellectuels en France, de l'Affaire Dreyfus à nos jours*, Paris, 1986, p.97, Cabanne, *Le Pouvoir culturel*, p.16, and Ory, BSHM, p.7.

12. Blech quoted in Ory, BSHM, p.7; Soustelle (dated 26 June 1936) in, among others, L. Bodin and J. Touchard, *Front populaire 1936*, Paris, 1961, p.161.

13. Lagrange is quoted in Fédération Léo Lagrange, *1936, Léo Lagrange*, Paris, 1980, p.19. Zay too saw some of his cultural and educational measures as a single package, see M. Ruby, *La Vie et l'œuvre de Jean Zay*, Paris, no date, pp.213–14.

14. On the ADLP, J. Kergoat, *La France du Front populaire*, Paris, 1986, pp.366–7, and Jackson, *The Popular Front*, pp.125–6; on the APAM, Ory, BSHM, p.13.

15. D. Gontard, *La Décentralisation théâtrale en France 1895–1952*, Paris, 1973, pp.57–87.

16. Ory, NRS, p.85. See J. Zay, *Souvenirs et solitude*, Paris, 1945, pp.54–8 and 215–22; and Ruby, *Jean Zay*, pp.310–16.

17. Ory, NRS, p.88 and p.90. See also Zay, *Souvenirs*, pp.203–8.

18. Fédération Léo Lagrange, *1936*, p.23.

19. Cabanne, *Le Pouvoir culturel*, pp.18–21 (see also Laurent, *Arts et pouvoirs*, p.140); Fumaroli, *L'Etat culturel*, pp.87–8.

20. See Les Cahiers de l'IHTP, *Politiques et pratiques culturelles dans la France de Vichy*, no.8, June 1988, H. Rousso, pp.22–4, and Ory, pp.150–1.

21. See A. Shennan, *Rethinking France: Plans for Renewal 1940–1946*, Oxford, 1989.

22. Les Cahiers de l'IHTP, no.8, Rousso, pp.17–18 and p.22.

23. Les Cahiers de l'IHTP, no.8, pp.152–4. Ory's suggestions are tentative because he insists that not enough research has been done to confirm them.

24. B. Comte, *Les Cahiers de l'IHTP*, no.8, pp.117–30.
25. V. Chabrol, 'L'Ambition de "Jeune France"', *Les Cahiers de l'IHTP*, pp.105–15. Chabrol is also the author of a thesis entitled 'Jeune France: une expérience de recherche et de décentralisation culturelle', University of Paris III, on which Fumaroli's discussion of the association is based, *L'Etat culturel*, pp.94–113. See also Gontard, *La Décentralisation théâtrale*, pp.120–7; and C. Faure, *Le Projet culturel de Vichy*, Lyon, 1989, pp.57–65.
26. Quoted in Fumaroli, *L'Etat culturel*, p.103.
27. Ibid., pp.95–6, pp.111–12. On Fumaroli's view of Jeune France and Uriage, see the debate caused by his book in *Esprit*: J. Roman, 'L'Etat culturel', no.175, October 1991, pp.149–57, and M. Fumaroli, 'Les Anciens et les modernes', no.179, February 1992, pp.150–4. Further debate took place in a special issue of *Le Débat*, no.70, May–August 1992, pp.3–83.
28. J.-P. Rioux, *The Fourth Republic, 1944–1958*, Cambridge, 1987, pp.435–6; also M. Kelly, 'Humanism and national unity: the ideological reconstruction of France', in N. Hewitt (ed.), *The Culture of Reconstruction: European Literature, Thought and Film, 1945–50*, Basingstoke, 1989, pp.103–19.
29. For a fuller analysis of the ideology of cultural democratisation, see P. Gaudibert, *Action culturelle: intégration et/ou subversion*, 3e éd. revue et augmentée, Tournai, 1977, pp.13–46; and Ritaine, *Stratèges*, pp.62–5.
30. Rigby, *Popular Culture*, Chapter 2, especially pp.39–44.
31. On Peuple et Culture, see B. Cacérès, *Histoire de l'éducation populaire*, Paris, 1964, p.148; and G. and J.-P. Saez, 'Peuple et Culture et le renouveau de l'Education populaire à la Libération', paper read to the Colloque du CRHIPA on 'Education populaire et formation permanente en France et en Italie', Grenoble, 6–7 October 1989.
32. A.-H. Mesnard, *Droit et politique de la culture*, Paris, 1990, pp.79–83.
33. Ibid., pp.78–9.
34. On the setting up of the CDNs, see D.L. Looseley, 'Paris versus the provinces: cultural decentralization since 1945', in M. Cook (ed.), *French Culture since 1945*, London, 1993, pp.217–40; for a much more detailed account, see Gontard, *La Décentralisation théâtrale*.
35. Vilar did attempt to put on some new work at the TNP and there were increasingly exceptions to this rule in other cases too.
36. Rioux, *The Fourth Republic*, p.439.
37. J.-P. Jeancolas, 'The setting-up of a "method of production" in

the French cinema 1946–50', in B. Rigby and N. Hewitt, *France and the Mass Media*, Basingstoke, 1991, pp.59–60.

38. Goebbels is quoted in Ministry of Culture, *Cinéma*, Etat et Culture series, Paris, 1992, p.49; see also pp.49–51.
39. Statistics quoted in Fumaroli, *L'Etat culturel*, p.179. On Blum-Byrnes, see Jeancolas, 'The setting-up', pp.65–7; and Ministry of Culture, *Cinéma*, pp.54–8.
40. Ibid., pp.180–1.
41. Ministry of Culture, *Les Musées*, Etat et Culture series, Paris, 1991, pp.37–8.
42. Laurent, *La République*, p.82; see also p.147.
43. Ibid., Chapter 3, 'Pour une politique des beaux-arts', pp.163–226 *passim*.

– 2 –

Heritage, Creation, Democratisation: The Malraux Years

The formal creation of the Ministère d'Etat chargé des affaires culturelles by a decree of 24 July 1959, and the appointment of so prestigious a literary figure to head it, suggested that the day of a real 'policy' for culture, audacious and resolute as Laurent had advocated, had come at last. Malraux was after all de Gaulle's close ally, his 'ami génial, fervent des hautes destinées', and his ministry seemed set to enjoy a special relationship with the Elysée.[1] Indeed, he was to retain the post for a full decade under all four Gaullist governments, the only minister to do so. And yet in the setting up of his 'royaume farfelu' as he called it, there was little to imply a true sense of purpose.

De Gaulle returned to power determined to correct France's weaknesses and reinstate its international prestige. The Fifth Republic was to be a new order, constitutionally, economically, but also culturally. For if a more united, more assertive nation was to rise from Fourth-Republican immobilism and the near civil war caused by the Algerian conflict, it needed to believe in itself, in its 'grandeur' and in its heritage. To this extent, Malraux's appointment was a deliberate political symbol. For some, his links with the Popular Front, communism and the Spanish Civil War made him a wayward left-wing adventurer despite his conversion to Gaullism during the Resistance. But for others this was a persona which held the promise of a clean break with the drab officialdom and inertia of the Beaux-Arts administration. His primary task, therefore, was in Alain Peyrefitte's phrase to 'témoigner pour la grandeur'.[2] This, however, was a remit for the man, not the Ministry. Indeed, it had not even been obvious at first which job to give him. Malraux himself had expressed interest in the Youth portfolio but was initially appointed to Information, a post he had briefly occupied in 1945. After four months, the President informed his then *directeur de cabinet* Georges Pompidou that he intended to replace Malraux with Jacques Soustelle, more likely to handle the Algerian question with the necessary tact, and he instructed Pompidou to broach the subject with Malraux. After casting round for a diplomatic way of presenting the change, Pompidou told Malraux that it was the General's wish to create a great Culture ministry which only he was equipped to spearhead. Michel Debré, on the other hand, appointed de Gaulle's Prime Minister at the beginning of 1959, recounts in his memoirs that the President advised him to make a place for Malraux in his government as he would give it 'du relief'. Neither account suggests the new department was the result of a carefully laid plan.[3]

Nor was it exactly an administrative revolution. First, the name 'Cultural Affairs' did not herald a new definition of the cultural. From Education came the DGAL and the directorates responsible for architecture (including historic monuments) and archives, while the CNC was transferred from the Ministry of Industry and Commerce. This certainly brought the heritage and a number of the arts under one roof, but it was a long way from the updated, global conception of culture glimpsed during the Popular Front or even the Bourdan administration. The Education department's Haut Commissariat à la jeunesse et aux sports was originally to relinquish its Education populaire service but in the end refused and Malraux did not insist. He likewise declined to push for a say in books and libraries, leisure, cultural relations abroad, creative-arts education in schools, or the audiovisual media which were fast becoming a crucial vehicle of cultural influence. Second, there was the problem of staffing the new department. Jacques Jaujard, in whom some saw the incarnation of the old Beaux-Arts regime, was given a key if ill-defined position, where he remained until his retirement in 1967. The Education Ministry, while apparently not objecting to surrendering the arts themselves, did resist handing over its best civil servants, many of whom had in any case no wish to join an enterprise which nobody expected to last. Two-thirds of the senior staff given a choice in the matter did not wish to transfer. In the end, no more than 377 people made the move and the Ministry's staff in 1962 was estimated at only 4,745.[4] Lastly, the all-powerful Finance Ministry was equally sparing with its cash, so that Culture's share of the state's budget only ever averaged 0.39 per cent throughout the Malraux decade.

This is the paradox of the Malraux ministry: grand ideas, slim resources. More curious still is Malraux's own, widely recognised complicity in this state of affairs. In 1959, argues Jacques Rigaud, everything was possible: with his intellectual acumen and closeness to the centre of power, Malraux was better placed than any to redefine the state's mission and obtain a credible budget for the purpose. He did not trouble to do so. That the Ministry managed to survive to become as important as it is today was therefore the result not of ministerial drive or of a winning and timely formula being devised at the outset, but of an unpromising empty vessel being subsequently filled.[5]

An important factor here was the rise in the 1950s and 1960s of a 'civilisation of leisure' under the impact of reduced working hours, an improved standard of living during *les trente glorieuses*, and the development of automation in the workplace and the home. At the same time, Rigaud maintains that the rise of the mass media, and particularly the spread of television, helped bring the arts and their personalities into the public eye to an unprecedented degree, sensitising the population to the importance of the cultural as a means of social promotion and enhanced quality of life. A second major contributor was the handful of gifted senior civil servants who worked under Malraux. Decolonisation during the 1950s meant the repatriation of numbers of highly competent and adaptable state functionaries, many of whom found their way into mainland departments like Culture which were in need of extra personnel. These figures – such as Emile-Jean Biasini, who was to remain a leading agent of the cultural administration for the next thirty years – soon established a Ministry identity strong enough to attract younger, ENA-trained technocrats who from the mid–1960s began to show greater willingness to make careers there. The task of defining a philosophical purpose for the Ministry, however, fell to Malraux himself. And herein lies the key to his unwillingness to redefine the sphere he had in his care.

Malraux the Minister is an ambivalent figure. It is sometimes said that he was a visionary rather than an administrator, though André Holleaux, his *directeur de cabinet* between 1962 and 1965, depicts him as methodical, almost bureaucratic, hating disorder.[6] Admirers often bring to mind a Sampson at the mill with slaves: frustrated by bureaucratic structures and material constraints, stricken by personal tragedy and illness, and possessed of an inspirational vision which underpinned his portentous speeches and thunderous funeral orations on Moulin, Braque or Le Corbusier. He was also a tormented, increasingly reclusive man who saw less and less of his staff, often slipping notes under their doors at weekends. His acceptance of political office was entirely motivated by de Gaulle's national mission, not by the usual parliamentary or ministerial aspirations of the career politician, and it imposed upon him a role with which he never entirely coincided: 'Un ministre et André Malraux', he once told journalists, 'ça fait peut-être deux.'[7]

He also endowed his department with an almost cosmic significance. The starting point of his ministerial doctrine was democratisation: 'Il me semble indispensable [...]', he declared to the Constituent Assembly in 1945, 'que la culture française cesse d'être l'apanage de gens qui ont la chance d'habiter Paris ou d'être riches.'[8] The influence of de Gaulle, however, gave that ideology a somewhat more nationalist edge. What Malraux meant by culture was the highest and most lasting forms of artistic achievement of the past: 'un ensemble d'œuvres qui ont en commun ce caractère à la fois stupéfiant et simple, d'être les œuvres qui ont échappé à la mort.' In this sense, culture was a humanist alternative to religion and a source of immortality in an absurd universe: 'ce qui répond à l'homme quand il se demande ce qu'il fait sur la terre.' Furthermore, like religion, it was a means of national cohesion, creating a sense of belonging to a community of shared values which transcend divisions. But the cultural life of a nation is also the site of a Manichean struggle between the angels and demons of our imaginative experience. The great artistic heritage of the world constitutes 'un supplément d'âme', it is invested with a transcendental power which acts as a defence against both the absurdity of destiny and the harmful effects of cultural industrialisation. Malraux was not hostile to the media per se, only to their potential for spiritual damage when they are commercially exploited. Television and other mass-cultural forms in fact cynically manipulate the collective unconscious; they are 'dream-factories' pouring forth a 'deluge of imbecility' and playing for profit on the most primitive forces at work within the human psyche: sex, blood and death.[9]

The state's task, therefore, is to oversee the equitable distribution of those eternal products of the imagination which alone can compete with such elemental forces. As an internal report by his last *directeur de cabinet* Antoine Bernard put it: 'faire en sorte que le plus grand nombre et non plus seulement les privilégiés de la naissance ou de l'instruction, accède aux différentes formes d'art dans les conditions qui favorisent la communion avec les œuvres.' The word 'communion' here is essential. At the furthest remove from Fumaroli, Malraux was often at pains to demarcate his ministry's mission from that of Education of which it had long been no more than an accessory. Like Laurent, he held that great art has a mysterious ability to resonate within all; it does not need to be explained or taught but can be appreciated spontaneously if encountered directly; not mediation, but revelation. Bernard's report translated this rather primitive reception theory into more moderate technocratic terms: 'la communion avec l'œuvre d'art [exige] un minimum d'initiation ou de familiarité qui, sauf exception, ne s'acquiert pas du premier coup. Mais cette sensibilité au langage propre de l'art est indépendante de la connaissance et relève d'un autre ordre.'[10] Malraux was equally insistent on distinguishing culture from mere leisure. For him, how people amuse themselves in their free time was, one senses, a trivial matter, for the consumer society to address. It had nothing to do with the far greater task of helping them create significance. With the cultural thus epistemologically severed from the educational, sociocultural and recreational, small wonder that he was indifferent to gaining any jurisdiction over these sectors, even though this effectively denied him the chance of giving his quixotic crusade against the dream factories a truly operational form.

The practical implications of this philosophy were outlined in the Ministry's mission statement included in the July 1959 decree: 'Rendre accessibles les œuvres capitales de l'humanité, et d'abord de la France, au plus grand nombre possible de Français, assurer la plus vaste audience à notre patrimoine culturel, et favoriser la création des œuvres de l'art et de l'esprit qui l'enrichissent.' This same mission later informed the deliberations of the Fourth Plan (1962–5) which for the first time had a commission devoted exclusively to cultural provision.[11] Three broad areas of responsibility are implied here: promoting the national heritage at home and abroad; enriching it by encouraging contemporary creation; and, dominating and embracing these two, democratisation. In 1959, the three came together in the first, broad sense of the term *action culturelle*. The heritage mission was traditional; what was new was the voluntarism in the idea of creation and democratisation policies and it was these which proved most controversial.

One of Malraux's most popular measures for the heritage was the cleaning of Paris's historic buildings, begun in 1960. Then in 1962 came two seminal laws. The first was a five-year *loi-programme* (31 July) for the restoration of seven of France's most famous monuments including the Louvre and Versailles, extended in 1967 by a further act covering 1968–70 and involving 100 monuments.[12] The second was the famous 'Loi Malraux' of 4 August creating *secteurs sauvegardés*, which extended protected status to whole districts of historical or architectural significance. 1964 then saw the launch of the 'Inventaire général des monuments et des richesses artistiques de la France', one of the rare initiatives where the divorced Culture and Education Ministries collaborated successfully. The Inventory was the first complete survey, to be spread over some twenty-five years, of historic monuments and art objects of every description, 'de la cathédrale à la petite cuiller' as Malraux put it.[13] Together with the *secteurs sauvegardés* legislation, it widened the Revolution's definition of national heritage and encouraged the public's discovery of that heritage in the 1970s and 1980s. But for Malraux, such initiatives were also ways of asserting France's greatness. Although he was not narrowly nationalistic and dreamed of a planetary culture uniting the world, he felt that France, once 'le premier pays culturel du monde', had an historic role to play in achieving this.[14] Part of his work, therefore, in so far as his remit allowed, was as a cultural ambassador: visiting, speaking, even allowing France's most precious patrimonial assets to leave the country on temporary loan (the Mona Lisa to the United States in 1963, the Venus de Milo to Tokyo the following year). He also created a Service des expositions which organised numerous international exhibitions on French soil.

More original and more ambivalent was the second aspect of his remit: creation. As Caron points out, France's tradition of aiding artistic and intellectual innovation is over four centuries old.[15] But by 1959, after the Third and Fourth Republics' hands-off policy, any active support for new work appeared audacious. Laurent, however, maintains that, beneath the word 'cultural' in its title, the new Ministry actually retained much of the former Beaux-Arts spirit, allowing the retrograde influence of academicism on creation to continue despite Malraux's own opposition to it.[16] Others have portrayed him as too obsessed with the past to bother much with the present and it is perhaps significant that the July 1959 decree prioritised creation only in so far as it was a heritage in the making. Nevertheless, there was a modest revival of the neglected tradition of state commissions, which sometimes placed old and new work in a bold new partnership, stealing a march on academicism and eliciting howls of indignation, though in Laurent's opinion such exceptions were so much window-dressing. Chagall was commissioned to paint the ceiling of the Paris Opéra, for example, and André Masson that of the Odéon; modern artists like Arp, Masson and Miró undertook work for the Manufactures nationales (china and tapestry). Other artists – Le Corbusier, Cocteau, Braque – died before they could complete promising commissions, though in the case of Le Corbusier's unrealised plans for a museum of the twentieth century, Malraux was held to be responsible for delaying the project.

But what these deaths mainly serve to highlight is that commissions to younger, up-and-coming artists were rare in the early years. There was in fact loud disapproval of a speech Malraux delivered to the Assembly in January 1963, in which he made the 1 per cent scheme for visual art in new educational buildings seem like a form of charity the state could ill afford, sounding contemptuous of struggling unknowns and appearing to believe the money would be better spent on providing new work by established artists for universities and reproductions of masterpieces for schools.[17] A further problem was that the budget for acquiring contemporary work was still inadequate. To compensate, the inheritors of recently deceased artists were sometimes persuaded to donate, an undignified method which Cabanne dubs 'le thé chez les veuves'. Again, this brought in some admirable work by the established and the dead but was poor encouragement to the living.[18] There was nevertheless progress here during the decade. In addition to legislation in 1964 which extended social security benefits to artists, a law passed in December 1968 allowed works of art to be made over to the state in lieu of death duties. In 1962, a Service de la création artistique was formed within the Ministry under Bernard Anthonioz, shortly followed by a Commission of the same name to oversee state purchasing and commissioning. Thanks to these and other reforms, the 1 per cent was more efficiently used and tightly controlled from the mid–1960s. A Centre national d'art contemporain (CNAC) was set up in 1967 within Anthonioz's Service which, with Malraux's approval, pursued a much more audacious purchasing and display policy than the MNAM's penury had allowed it to, involving a wide range of new, often challenging work by younger or lesser known artists.[19]

In other areas of creation, Malraux's action was similarly uneven or incomplete. In 1959, the *avances sur recettes* mechanism was launched, a system of selective aid to new films to complement the automatic aid set up during the Fourth Republic and modified by Malraux at the same time. These changes were undoubtedly a step forward, but they needed to be completed by a much wider set of measures – better relations with television, modernisation of cinemas and reform of taxation – which did not materialise.[20] For theatre, a fund was established in 1964 to aid private theatres, another for subsidising experimental new work in 1967, and a number of new companies were given official recognition. Yet little was done to stop the decline of the TNP, from which Vilar resigned in 1963, or to help CDNs struggling with debts or municipal conflicts.[21] On artistic freedom too, the record is much the same. Often Malraux would side with the avant-garde or politically subversive against parliamentarians or local authorities, as happened when Genet's *Les Paravents*, staged in 1965 by Barrault at the Odéon-Théâtre de France, was taken as an affront to the French army. The revolt of May 1968 also revealed just how far he had filled key posts with artists or *animateurs* who were aesthetically challenging or hostile to the regime which had appointed them. At other times, though, he was inexplicably unsupportive and his relations with the arts world were not always good. His failure to intervene was resented when Jacques Rivette's controversial film *La Religieuse* was banned by the Information Ministry. His sudden sacking in early 1968 of Henri Langlois who had lovingly created the Cinémathèque caused considerable protest just prior to the events of May, while the events themselves led to the equally peremptory dismissal of the Renaud-Barrault company from the Odéon for having sided in the heat of the moment with those who had occupied it.[22]

Aid to creation was considered perfectly compatible with the Ministry's third objective, democratisation. For Malraux and his staff, a willingness to tackle cultural inequalities was the major way in which Cultural Affairs differed from Beaux-Arts and, because the received wisdom was that art could elicit a spontaneous emotion without apprenticeship or mediation, this was also felt to be a relatively straightforward business. Since this official dogma implied that 'cultural needs' existed in all, albeit latent in many, the Ministry could satisfy them or coax them out simply by the kind of adjustments to the geographical distribution of cultural facilities Laurent had already initiated for theatre: 'mettre un paysan de la Corrèze devant un tableau de Miró.'[23] Various structures were set up with this in mind. 'Permanent correspondents' of the Ministry at regional or departmental level were appointed; advisory committees, called 'Comités régionaux des affaires culturelles', were also formed which prefigured the first three Directions régionales des affaires culturelles (DRACs) set up at the end of the 1960s. A ten-year plan for musical development, one of the most effective initiatives conceived under Malraux, was launched just after his departure in 1969 by Marcel Landowski, who had been placed in charge of a separate Service de la musique created in 1966. As Malraux's biographer Jean Lacouture points out, the plan was a further example of what could be done when the Ministries of Culture and Education cooperated, for it included the creation of a musical *baccalauréat* as well as conservatoires, orchestras and new opera houses for each region.[24] For the theatre, Malraux designated another fifteen CDNs and gave smaller subsidies to a number of new companies classed as Troupes permanentes de décentralisation. The trouble with such measures, however, was that, as had been the case under Laurent, this remained centralised decentralisation, involving the unconsciously paternalistic importing of 'national' – that is, Parisian – values into the provinces, which Malraux himself was reluctant even to visit. But attitudes to regional devolution had been changing since the 1940s and the state's cultural paternalism was increasingly resented. It was above all the plan to set up a nation-wide network of Maisons de la culture (MCs) which brought this problem to a head, for the Maisons were the very incarnation of such benevolent condescension, Malraux even describing their purpose, in a speech inaugurating the MC of Amiens in March 1966, as being to ensure that 'avant dix ans ce mot hideux de Province aura cessé d'exister en France'.

The idea of 'Houses of Culture', with its starkly Soviet ring, was a reminder of Malraux's Popular Front past and he invested them with his own metaphysics and ideology, with the result that the actual role of the MCs was somewhat loosely defined. Funded equally by the state and the local authorities, with a third source of revenue from box-office receipts, they were intended to apply the lessons of Laurent's theatrical decentralisation to high culture as a whole, multidisciplinary arts centres housing facilities for theatre, music, cinema and television, science, exhibitions and lectures. Malraux likened their intended impact to the social transformation brought about by Ferry's education acts: 'il faut que, par ces maisons de la culture qui dans chaque département français, diffuseront ce que nous essayons de faire à Paris, n'importe quel enfant de seize ans, si pauvre soit-il, puisse avoir un véritable contact avec son patrimoine national et avec la gloire de l'esprit de l'humanité.' Again, this contact was to be unmediated. As Pierre Moinot, Malraux's head of Theatre and Cultural Action, told the Fourth Plan commission in 1961, a Maison, 'n'a pas le souci d'organiser l'enseignement, même des arts, et donne toujours le pas à l'œuvre. La confrontation qu'elle suscite est directe, évite l'écueil et l'appauvrissement de la vulgarisation simplificatrice'.[25] For Malraux himself, they were more places of worship than learning: if culture has replaced religion in a secular society, the Maisons would be its 'cathedrals'. They would be in the van of his struggle against the dream-factories and would also symbolise the greatness of the Gaullist nation, allowing France once more to be true to its unique past. More concretely, their mission was divided into three: to disseminate existing work of high artistic merit to town and region (*diffusion*), to mount new work of their own (*création*), and to encourage local people to feel at home in their MC and respond to the work available there (*animation*). This last aim did not, however, mean involvement in amateur, sociocultural activity. On the contrary, Malraux was adamant that they should only be centres of professional excellence and advanced creative 'research' rivalling the best Parisian work.

The actual implementation of the MC programme owed much to Emile-Jean Biasini who replaced Moinot in December 1961 and played a similar role to Laurent through his tireless labour at local and national levels. The first Maison was inaugurated in Le Havre in June 1961 and, by 1966, the Minister declared himself pleasantly surprised at their success. But in reality, they soon ran into fundamental problems which continued well beyond the Malraux years into the 1980s. To some extent, these were material. With their high running costs and sometimes splendid new premises (Grenoble, Amiens), they were inevitably a drain on local resources, while the state's Culture budget, stuck at less than half a per cent and unfairly weighted in favour of Paris, soon proved inadequate to implement the programme laid down in the Fourth Plan, which had initially proposed twenty. In the event, only eight were inaugurated before May 1968, though others were in the pipeline.[26] The shortage of staff qualified to run them was another problem. Individuals who combined an artistic gift with the breadth to pursue multidisciplinary community work and the managerial skills needed for such complex establishments were not two a penny. Usually, the difficulty was tackled by basing an MC on an existing theatre company, in several cases a CDN or Troupe permanente. But this presented problems of its own. Such directors were sometimes reluctant to pursue the aim of multidisciplinarity and criticised the state for forcing it on them, or were themselves criticised for the narrowness of their activities. A training school for *animateurs* was envisaged but soon abandoned for fear it would become in Malraux's words a 'school for professional agitators'.[27]

This fear was not entirely groundless. Brecht's politics and aesthetics had permeated the decentralised theatre by the 1960s and many became hostile to the conservative, bourgeois conception of culture they judged state policy to be promoting. Several MCs also ran into conflict with city councils, which resented the way their magnificent Trojan horse was undermining existing cultural facilities or were unimpressed by the avant-garde creations sometimes on offer, preferring more cost-effective, middle-of-the-road entertainment, or amateur events, to the music of Xenakis, the drama of Brecht or Beckett, or the sculpture of Calder. Ironically, the MC directors were usually supported in these skirmishes by the very state some were busy contesting and the early years of the MCs were fraught with three-way tensions. To make matters worse, by the late 1960s the contestatory spirit in the theatre was being intensified by a younger, countercultural movement which drew on Artaud, Grotowski and the happenings of American fringe groups like the Living Theater and Bread and Puppet, influences often brought to France by Jack Lang's Nancy World Theatre Festival launched in 1963, which became more radical as the 1960s wore on.[28] Left-wing agit-prop joined with a provocative, physical theatre to overthrow the traditional dramatist by means of improvisation and *créations collectives*, thereby challenging the whole patrimonial conception of 'the work' on which the state-driven policy of democratisation had been based since the Popular Front. The inevitable conflagration came in May 1968.

Although the events of May were ostensibly inspired by a Marxist-Leninist rhetoric of political insurrection, Mao's 'cultural revolution' of 1966–7 was also an influence, so that it was in practice the nation's cultural institutions which became the main target of the *gauchistes*. The Sorbonne and the Odéon were occupied and the MNAM closed 'pour cause d'inutilité', while that summer Vilar was savagely taken to task at Avignon for turning the festival into a 'cultural supermarket'. Provincial establishments too were occupied during May and a number of MCs sided with the protesters and made their premises available to them, though Malraux's flagships were themselves implicated in the critique of 'bourgeois' culture on which the movement was based. One of its preoccupations was the class nature of the high culture dispensed in France by schools, universities and cultural institutions. This seemed especially relevant to the MCs, which had failed to democratise not only quantitatively given that only a few existed, but sociologically. All the evidence suggested that the provincial inhabitants who benefited most from the new facilities were those who were already culturally literate: teachers, students, professionals.

Part of the trouble were the avant-garde and therefore unfamiliar types of *création* offered, for which local audiences were often ill prepared. But this was indissociable from a further cause, namely the democratisers' faith that, once confronted with great art, the masses could not fail to be transported by its ineffable truth. For the militants of 1968 as for the sociologist Pierre Bourdieu, the naivety of this position was flagrant. In his study of museum-going published in 1966, Bourdieu provided a model which could equally well be applied to the low level of working-class frequentation of the MCs. It showed that high culture is the key to social differentiation and that the working class is excluded from it because, not inheriting any 'cultural capital' from family or class, it has not learnt the codes needed to decipher it, a deficiency which schooling currently cannot remedy since it too is similarly encoded.[29] But in fact, the reactions of the provincial bourgeois, whose cultural capital in theory did open the door to the MCs but who were just as disconcerted by the avant-garde creations they found there, undermined the democratisers' idealism almost as effectively. To assume that *la culture cultivée*, whether traditional or avant-garde, is immediately accessible to all, that cultural deprivation can therefore be remedied by the statistical measurement of 'cultural needs' and a technocratic adjustment of provision, is to ignore the fact that these needs are socially and historically determined and only occur in those who already hold the codes required to satisfy them. But for the cultural revolutionaries of May, Malraucian democratisation was more than a naïve miscalculation: it was a vital weapon in the state's repressive attempt to impose on all the ideology of the dominant class, the very word culture, according to a blistering pamphlet by Jean Dubuffet, being 'associé à tout un appareil d'intimidation et de pression'.[30] True democracy clearly lay elsewhere.

Towards the end of May, the directors of MCs and CDNs, some of whom had worked in decentralised theatre since Laurent's time, met in Villeurbanne to review the impact of the events. The document they produced was a curious hybrid, demands for more state investment rubbing shoulders with a revolutionary discourse on cultural democracy. Its signatories acknowledged that May had brought about a dramatic *prise de conscience* and confessed to their objective complicity with an oppressive regime whose cultural policies had produced a vast 'non-public'. Spurning the state's comfortable concern with a fairer distribution of the cultural patrimony, they formulated a more radical conception of *action culturelle* founded on the notion of a culture in the making, its content constantly redetermined by the preoccupations of the non-public, which would thereby become aware of its situation, politicise and thus regain possession of itself.[31] In the event, this revolutionary enthusiasm was short-lived in most of the signatories. But Villeurbanne was one articulation of a more far-reaching desire to challenge the whole Fifth-Republic trilogy of heritage, creation and democratisation. In its place came a concern with genuine 'cultural democracy' in which, as Edgar Morin wrote the following year, 'chacun épanouirait son propre don, ses propres puissances de créativité'. The aim had this much in common with Malraux: it was not pedagogical. But in contrast to the Minister's insistence that the MCs be centres of professional high-cultural creation, post–1968 *animateurs* and cultural commentators like Morin proposed a sociocultural conception of cultural action in which, using new forms of *animation*, the Maisons would become 'des ateliers de créativité', placing their considerable resources at the disposal of the expressive needs of amateurs.[32] To the Gaullist dream of a unifying national culture, 1968 replied with 'le droit à la différence', calling for the validation of the authentic cultural identities of diverse micro-communities, that which particularises rather than that which unites.

Malraux described May 1968 as a crisis of civilisation; it also marked the collapse of his whole ambition as Minister. With the Maisons and decentralised theatre identified with subversion, a number of directors were sacked by exasperated local authorities. In November, Malraux addressed the National Assembly, announcing a package of reforms which responded to some of the more tangible demands of the Villeurbanne group, whose representatives he had met the previous summer. The creative units within the Maisons were to be given a separate status from the Maisons themselves, allowing the directors to concentrate on the artistic activity with which they were concerned. There would now be only one MC per region but there would also be smaller, more adaptable units in other areas: 'maisons dites "éclatées"' in which the diverse disciplines involved would each have their own premises; or 'relais culturels' which would place a greater emphasis on *diffusion*, a proposal which gave birth to the network of Centres d'action culturelle (CACs) set up in the early 1970s.[33] Clearly, these changes were a long way from the heroic vision which had founded the MCs. The following April, de Gaulle was defeated in a referendum on regional reform and stood down, replaced by Pompidou. Malraux left shortly afterwards.

In any assessment of the Malraux years, the achievements of the new Cultural Affairs department are obvious: restored and better protected public monuments, a big increase in regional cultural facilities, a ten-year plan for music which was to bring real change in music in the 1970s and 1980s, and the beginnings of an active creation policy. But the disparity between ambition and resources is equally conspicuous. However brilliant the ideas or metaphysical the vision, Malraux's failure to secure a viable budget, together with the narrowness of his conception of culture and his indifference to obtaining a say in contiguous areas vital to a modern cultural policy, set the limits of what his ministry could accomplish. So too, no doubt, did his own temperament. Many of those close to events at the time refer to the sporadic nature of much of his action: 'coups d'éclats sans lendemains, [...] percées audacieuses suivies de brusques retraites', writes Lacouture.[34] Some account for this by the contradictions within his own identity as writer and minister, which 1968 merely exacerbated. But more importantly, May revealed that the terms of reference of this supposedly innovative young ministry were already relics: national *rayonnement*, the eternity of the heritage, the struggle for the soul of the masses against the demons of mass culture, all had the austere ring of the epic 1930s more than the consumption-driven, self-indulgent, fun-loving 1960s which were seeing the rise of mass leisure, the mass media, new technologies and youth culture. May also exposed a dichotomy between the old, dominant discourse of democratisation – collective, civic, ethical – and an incipient, still muddled interest in personal creativity, be it esoteric avant-garde work in the MCs, experimental *créations collectives* which questioned the consecrated status of the artist, or simply people's desire to participate in fashioning their own culture, community and lives. By the end of the 1960s, the question of cultural democracy was therefore being posed in quite different terms from those which had characterised *action culturelle* since 1936.

Notes

1. Quoted from de Gaulle's *Mémoires d'espoir* in C.-L. Foulon, 'André Malraux, Ministre d'Etat et le Ministère des affaires culturelles (1959–1969)', in Institut Charles de Gaulle, *De Gaulle et Malraux*, Paris, 1987, p.221.
2. Alain Peyrefitte, 'Il y a un an mourait Malraux: le Ministre', *Revue des Deux Mondes*, November 1977, p.335.
3. For Pompidou, see ibid., pp.336–7. For Debré, see Rigaud, *Libre Culture*, Paris, 1990, p.62. The *cabinet* of a minister is his or her team of advisers headed by a *directeur de cabinet*, i.e. principal private secretary.
4. G. Poujol, 'The creation of a Ministry of Culture in France', *French Cultural Studies*, vol.2, no.6, 1991, p.254. Poujol provides more detail in an otherwise similar piece, also consulted here: 'La Création du Ministère des affaires culturelles', in R. Abirached (ed.), *La Décentralisation théâtrale*, 2 vols, vol.2, 'Les Années Malraux 1959–68', Paris, 1993, pp.25–37. (This volume appeared too late to make a substantial impact on the present study.)
5. Rigaud quoted in Poujol, 'The creation of a ministry', p.259. See also *Libre Culture*, p.62. I am indebted to both Rigaud and Poujol for the following analysis of the Ministry's beginnings.
6. Holleaux, 'Il y a deux ans mourait André Malraux: le Ministre des affaires culturelles', *Revue des Deux Mondes*, November 1978, pp.354–5, and 'André Malraux, ministre', in Ministry of Culture, 'Trentième Anniversaire du Ministère de la culture. Journées d'étude sur la création du Ministère de la culture', 30 November–1 December 1989 (dossier).
7. Quoted in 'Le Bilan Malraux', *Le Nouvel Adam*, no.9, April 1967, p.32.
8. Quoted in P. Gaudibert, *Action culturelle: intégration et/ou subversion*, 3ᵉ éd. revue et augmentée, Tournai, 1977, p.29, from a speech of 30 December 1945.
9. My analysis of Malraux's ideas is based on his speeches, particularly those given at the opening of the Maisons de la culture of Bourges (18 April 1964) and Amiens (19 March 1966), from which my two longest quotations come respectively. Most of his speeches are

unpublished but available in transcript at the Ministry. An extract of the Bourges speech appears in 'Malraux: paroles et écrits politiques 1947–1972 inédits', *Espoir*. *Revue de l'Institut Charles de Gaulle*, no.2, 1973, pp.58–9. The entire Amiens speech appears in Ministry of Culture, 'Trentième Anniversaire'. For further extracts and analysis, see J. Mossuz, *André Malraux et le gaullisme*, Paris, 1970, Part III.

10. *Le Ministère des affaires culturelles et la mission culturelle de la collectivité*, internal document dating from March 1968, published Paris, 1989, p.16, for inclusion in Ministry of Culture, 'Trentième Anniversaire'.

11. Commissariat général du Plan, *Rapport général de la Commission de l'équipement culturel et du patrimoine artistique*, Paris, 1961. Culture was previously covered by the 'Plan d'équipement universitaire et scolaire'.

12. The other monuments covered by the 1962 law were the châteaux of Vincennes and Chambord, Invalides, Fontainebleau and Rheims cathedral. A *loi-programme* is a law which sets up a framework for long-term government action.

13. Ministry of Culture, *Patrimoine*, Etat et Culture series, Paris, 1992, p.63.

14. Speech to the National Assembly, 27 October 1966, *Journal Officiel* of this day, 2ᵉ séance; partly reproduced in *ATAC Informations*, no.3, December 1966, p.3.

15. Caron, *L'Etat et la culture*, Paris, 1989, p.49.

16. Laurent, *Arts et pouvoirs en France de 1793 à 1981*, Saint-Etienne, 1982, pp.157–64. Poujol, 'The Creation of a Ministry', is cautious about Laurent's view, p.258.

17. P. Cabanne, *Le Pouvoir culturel sous la Vᵉ République*, Paris, 1981, pp.103–9.

18. Ibid., pp.93–100.

19. Ibid., pp.185–99; also Ministry of Culture, *Musées*, Etat et Culture series, Paris, 1991, p.41.

20. J. Lacouture, *Le Monde*, 9 July 1969, p.15.

21. Ibid., pp.1 and 15; also Lacouture, *André Malraux, une vie dans le siècle*, Paris, 1973, pp.376–7.

22. For all four episodes (Genet, Rivette, Langlois, Barrault), see Cabanne, *Le Pouvoir culturel*, pp.172–5, 211–17, 231–3.

23. J. Rouvet, quoted in P. Gaudibert, *Action culturelle*, p.24.

24. *Le Monde*, 9 July 1969, p.15.

25. Malraux is quoted in Mossuz, *André Malraux*, p.168; Moinot's statement appears in Commissariat général du Plan, *Rapport général*, p.71. For a more detailed introduction to the early MCs,

see J.-C. Bécane, *L'Expérience des Maisons de la culture, Notes et Etudes Documentaires*, no.4,052, Paris, 1974.

26. In order of opening: Le Havre, Caen, Bourges, the Théâtre de l'est parisien (TEP), Amiens, Thonon-les-Bains, Firminy, Grenoble.

27. Quoted in Lacouture, *Le Monde*, 8 July 1969, p.9.

28. On Nancy, see D.L. Looseley, 'Jack Lang and the politics of festival', *French Cultural Studies*, vol.1, no.1, February 1990, pp.5–19; and 'The World Theatre Festival, Nancy, 1963–88: a critique and a retrospective', *New Theatre Quarterly*, vol.6, no.22, May 1990, pp.141–53. The preceding analysis is partly based on my chapter 'Paris versus the provinces: cultural decentralisation since 1945', in M. Cook (ed.), *French Culture since 1945*, London, 1993, pp.224–7.

29. Bourdieu, *L'Amour de l'art*, 2ᵉ éd. revue et augmentée, Paris, 1969.

30. Quoted in Cabanne, *Le Pouvoir culturel*, p.141.

31. Reproduced in F. Jeanson, *L'Action culturelle dans la cité*, Paris, 1973, pp.119–24.

32. Both quotations are from Morin, 'De la culturalyse à la politique culturelle', *Communications*, special issue 'La Politique culturelle', no.14, 1969, p.32 and p.33 respectively. See also Caune, *La Culture en action*, Grenoble, 1992, pp.219–52.

33. *Journal Officiel*, 2ᵉ séance du 13 novembre 1968, pp.4,352–3; *Le Monde*, 15 November 1968, pp.6–7, also reproduces the part of the speech concerned with the MCs.

34. Lacouture, *André Malraux, une vie*, p.373.

− 3 −

From Malraux to Mitterrand: Creation and Creativity

Malraux's departure heralded a twelve-year period of uncertainty during which the Ministry went in search of itself. It had nine occupants before the Socialist victory of 1981, Ministers of Cultural Affairs, Secretaries of State for Culture and Ministers combining Culture with Environment or Communication. Only three stayed long enough to enact a policy: Jacques Duhamel (January 1971 to April 1973), Michel Guy (June 1974 to August 1976) and Jean-Philippe Lecat (April 1978 to March 1981), though even these enjoyed only a short term of office compared to Malraux's. Despite an overall rise in the department's budget in real terms, in percentage terms it remained low. In 1969, Malraux's budget had reached 0.42 per cent of state spending. Under Duhamel, it peaked at 0.61 per cent for 1974 but ended the decade at 0.47 per cent.[1] Even the 1974 figure is misleading, though, since it was the result of a one-off presidential intervention. Unlike his predecessor, Pompidou was an adept of contemporary art and filled the Elysée with it. It was consequently he who followed up the plan for a twentieth−century museum, transforming it into something closer to a Maison de la culture encompassing a number of art-forms. The Centre national d'art et de culture on the plateau Beaubourg was launched soon after his election and rechristened the Centre Pompidou following his death in 1974, an apt title in the circumstances since its conception was largely his own and he unashamedly used his powers to drive it through against unremitting opposition, making it the first of the major presidential construction works, the *grands projets*.[2]

In the course of the 1970s, the cultural, socio-economic and political conditions in which Malraux's policy had operated were transformed. The standard of living and level of educational attainment rose, patterns of employment and leisure-time shifted. As the CDNs and MCs helped the principle of *action culturelle* take root at local level, municipal authorities began to play a more active part in cultural provision, with institutions like libraries and museums sometimes becoming cultural centres in their own right, while new provincial initiatives cropped up everywhere. The expansion of broadcasting and communications technologies, the emergence of youth culture, and the post–1968 interest in the diverse cultural identities of micro-communities were also producing alternatives to *la culture cultivée*. Lastly, economic recession struck, followed by the election of the neo-liberal Valéry Giscard d'Estaing in 1974. All these factors meant that the principles of state cultural policy established under Malraux needed to be completely rethought.

For some years after the May events, relations between the state and the arts world were strained, soured further by occasional lapses of tact from ministers, as when Maurice Druon (April 1973 to March 1974) announced that those creators who came to him with a begging bowl in one hand and a Molotov cocktail in the other would have to make a choice. Nevertheless, some of the May movement's ideas about pluralism and difference began to infiltrate official thinking and, although ritual invocations of Malraux were still fairly common, an adaptation of his doctrine began shortly after his departure. *Action culturelle* was converted into *développement culturel*, an even vaguer notion from the discourse of economic planning and which viewed culture not as a transcendental artistic heritage but as something broader, more palpable and more vital to the quality of life and to social and economic progress. Around 1971–2, it was variously articulated by the Minister Duhamel, the Prime Minister Jacques Chaban-Delmas and the Sixth Plan's Commission des affaires culturelles chaired by the poet Pierre Emmanuel, which became an important think-tank on future directions. It was also explored at a colloquium held at Arc et Senans in May 1972 which brought together a number of experts, among them Edgar Morin, the cultural theorist Michel de Certeau and the head of the Ministry's research unit, Augustin Girard, to draw up a new strategy for presentation to the forthcoming conference of Culture ministers in Helsinki.[3]

For all the above, the issue for the 1970s was not access to high culture but how to foster creativity as a response to the human and social consequences of change in Western societies. Economic and industrial growth, urbanisation and mobility, continuing social divisions, the evolution of the nature of work, the rise of the mass media, all have caused societies to become fragmented and individuals alienated. Economic growth cannot be halted but it can be made to change gear from the quantitative to the qualitative, though this can only be achieved by 'un sursaut – de nature culturelle'. Clearly, 'cultural' here meant much more than it did for Malraux. According to the Arc et Senans declaration, when one speaks of culture today, the term designates a much wider field than the arts and humanities, embracing the education system, the mass media, and the so-called 'cultural industries': newspapers, books, records, video, film, advertising, habitat and fashion.[4] Here then was a further attempt to produce a global definition of contemporary culture as a basis for policy, though in the process a crisis was identified. On the one hand, the traditional culture prized by Malraux is largely irrelevant to the 'cultural reality' of the vast majority and certainly quite alien to the young and to some ethnic minorities. Marginalised in this way, it is becoming degenerate and nihilistic. Conversely, the unregulated cultural industries, especially the mass media, are dominated by the market and simply turn people into conformists and consumers. The cultural conditions of contemporary society are therefore depriving people of the possibility of expressing themselves. The remedy is for individuals and communities, particularly the underprivileged, to be empowered to make their own meanings through their choice of cultural practices and lifestyle. At Arc et Senans, Duhamel pointed out the dangers of thinking of *action culturelle* as mere distribution or *diffusion*, 'une culture de consommation arrosée d'en haut'. Instead, he called for a policy which facilitates individual creativity and recognises diversity. *Développement culturel*, then, was held to be about restoring what the Commission des affaires culturelles called 'le degré d'autonomie de la personne, sa capacité de se situer dans le monde, de communiquer avec les autres, et de mieux participer à la société tout en pouvant s'en libérer', though this humanist conception was accompanied by a more instrumental view of creativity as a factor of economic development.[5]

Not a great deal of the Plan or the Arc et Senans declaration actually found its way into policy, no doubt because, however strong the commitment, it was never strong enough to elicit an appropriate budget; nor was Duhamel in office long enough to see it through. The obvious corollary of a global conception of culture is close cooperation between Culture and a variety of other ministries, but as in 1959, the opportunity was largely missed other than in a few isolated instances. By far the most successful of these was the Fonds d'intervention culturelle (FIC) set up by Duhamel in 1971, a fund managed by Culture but also supplied by a number of other departments including Defence, Health, Aménagement du Territoire and Education. Its purpose was to provide short-term help with innovative or experimental initiatives conventional subsidy was unlikely to fund, often for new publics. During its first ten years, it financed some 1,300 projects, many of which, because of its strong local links, involved regional and ethnic cultures. In 1978, an interministerial committee was formed to supervise it, followed in 1979 by a Mission du développement culturel within the Ministry itself.[6]

Some 25 per cent of the FIC's activities during the 1970s involved educational establishments, another preoccupation of the Cultural Affairs Commission. This too was an implicit rejection of the Malraucian emphasis on the unmediated reception of art, for if cultural emancipation was to be taken seriously and each individual personally empowered to be creative, the state education system was the obvious place to start. But this was easier said than done. By tradition, the highly centralised school curriculum was concerned with developing the intellect not the sensibility and there was little room for creative self-expression. The two weekly hours devoted to music and drawing were usually of a formal, rule-bound nature (for example, *solfège* in music) and were often not taught by specialist teachers, or not taught at all due to shortage of staff. Cultural activities outside school-time or off the premises were rare. Worse still, parents and teachers frequently considered such lessons secondary and those who taught them second-rate. Once again, however, a push for change grew out of the late 1960s concern with creativity and cultural democracy. Landowski's ten-year plan included a reform of music teaching in schools which moved away from what he dismissed as the 'solfège de grand-papa'. The Sixth Plan then recommended, among other measures, that the hands-on creative work known as *activités d'éveil*, reserved at the time for only the youngest children, be extended to all age-levels. Some limited changes were implemented as a result, but the basic impediments to a full-scale arts training in schools remained.[7]

The Sixth Plan also recommended setting up an independent consultative body for culture. A Conseil de développement culturel was duly formed under Pierre Emmanuel, an 'organe de réflexion, de confrontation et de stimulation' linked to the Ministry but counterbalancing its concentration of power and superintending all interministerial activities.[8] It was short-lived. Little attention was paid to it and when Druon failed even to acknowledge its communications, the group resigned *en bloc*. The problem for all these initiatives in fact was that by 1973, with Druon introducing little by way of innovation during his brief term, the hour of the Sixth Plan was already past. This was even more self-evident when, after Pompidou's death the following year, the Gaullist regime was swept away with the arrival of Giscard d'Estaing, making 1974 the first real watershed in Fifth Republic cultural policy. Although *développement culturel* grew out of a questioning of Malraucian democratisation, it was still informed by the central Ministry dogma of state intervention to combat cultural inequalities. Giscardian liberalism came close to questioning that dogma.

Much has been made of the absence of a 'grand design' for culture during the Giscard era: its place reduced in the Seventh and Eighth Plans, the Ministry demoted to a State Secretariat between 1974 and 1977, and Giscard famously silent on the subject in his book *La Démocratie française* published in 1976. In addition, the President's background and style were more aristocratic than Pompidou's and his cultural tastes considerably more traditional. He disliked Beaubourg and fears about its fate might not have proved misplaced if the work had not been too advanced to undo, forcing him to inaugurate it, somewhat coolly, in January 1977. To compensate, he announced four *grands projets* of his own. Here, one of his chief concerns was to preserve 'une architecture à la française', just as for Les Halles he attempted unsuccessfully to introduce a 'jardin à la française'.[9]

The Giscard years also saw a drift from both pre– and post–1968 conceptions of *action culturelle*, towards a sharper distinction between professional creation and amateur creativity, art and *animation*. This was partly because many in CDNs and MCs became disillusioned after 1968 with what Robert Abirached calls 'l'utopie socio-culturelle' and even with the great civic vision of Vilar, Laurent and the early decentralisers, eschewing both in favour of a non-pedagogical, less socially conscious concern with themselves, as artists not activists. It was also a result of a shift in policy under Giscard's first Secretary of State for Culture, Michel Guy, who, having launched the Festival d'automne in 1972, had numerous contacts in the contemporary arts and a real interest in creation, particular theatrical.[10] To an extent, the ground here had been prepared by Duhamel. In an interview in 1972, he drew a firm line between *animation*, designed to encourage creativity in all, and the Maisons' 'rôle de référence' as centres of professional work of a high standard. The MCs, he said, were not yet suited to developing creativity, which was the job of sociocultural establishments like MJCs.[11] The same year, he also introduced triennial contracts for the CDNs, to free them of annual worry about renewal of their subsidy. The effect of this was to focus the CDNs on a more clearly defined, fixed-term creative plan, or 'project'. Duhamel had also begun bringing relatively young artistic directors into the national theatres, one of whom was Jack Lang, brought from Nancy in 1972 to undertake what proved to be an ambitious, costly and contested redesigning of the home of the TNP, the Théâtre de Chaillot. In the same reshuffle, Duhamel decentralised the TNP itself to the CDN at Villeurbanne (Lyon) run by Roger Planchon, who was now joined there by Patrice Chéreau. Two years later, Guy controversially sacked Lang but continued to appoint young creative talents, often with Parisian backgrounds. Where decentralised institutions were concerned, this implied a demotion of the founding 1940s and 1950s notions of *animation* and *implantation*, long-term work rooted in the local community, in favour of a more detached, Parisian standard of creative excellence. This intensifying of Parisianism, coupled with the abandonment by many of militant civic action, brought about a fundamental shift in the decentralisation movement as Laurent had originally conceived it.[12]

This shift has to be set against the background of two further factors which were beginning to transform attitudes to *action culturelle* by the mid- to late 1970s. The first was the rise of economic liberalism as a response to recession; the second the blossoming of the cultural industries. Both brought about an attempted redirection of cultural policy under Giscard. Where culture was concerned, liberalism meant a new reliance on market forces rather than state intervention and was particularly in evidence in book policy. In 1975–6, responsibility for books, municipal libraries and BCPs was transferred from Education to Culture with the setting up of a Direction du livre working closely with the Centre national des lettres (CNL), an *établissement public* akin to the cinema's CNC created in 1973. In July 1979, however, it was the Minister of the Economy, René Monory, who took the radical step of freeing book prices, regulated for the previous 120 years by the recommended-price system (*prix conseillé*). This, together with a decision to end the state's small subsidy to the CNL and the government's acquiescence to a proposed merger of the publishing firm Hachette with the industrial giant Matra, signified for many the rejection of a long-standing acceptance that books had to be treated differently from other commercial products.[13]

Liberalism also meant alternatives to direct state subsidy. Towards the end of the decade, Lecat began to look at corporate sponsorship, bringing fears that culture would be further commercialised. In practice, though, much more interest was shown in recognising the local authorities as funders of the arts. Through the 1970s, a network of outposts of the Culture Ministry, the DRACs initiated under Malraux, was slowly set up in the regions, with the aim of deconcentrating funds and to an extent decision-making. With their help, Guy rationalised central and local spending on culture through what were called '*chartes culturelles*', contracts between the state and a tier of local government (municipality, department or region) involving one-off initiatives proposed by the local agency but which it could not handle so effectively alone. The charters marked a significant departure from the Gaullist view of the state as prime mover in decentralisation by acknowledging local authorities as partners rather than mere recipients. Some twenty-seven were signed between 1975 and 1979, after which the policy was abandoned, although by then it had already aided a large number of initiatives, often linked with regional cultures, such as folk museums called *écomusées* and a multitude of restorations of various rural buildings. The charters were not without their critics. Some on the Left saw them as central interference in local affairs, others as a prelude to state withdrawal from the arts. In fact, it was under Lecat rather than Guy that a degree of disengagement came about, with his notorious claim in 1979 that decentralisation (in the Laurent-Malraux sense) was 'une idée dépassée'. This prefigured a cut in government subsidies to decentralised establishments and a reduction in the Culture Ministry's share of the state budget. The MCs' and CACs' grant went down in real terms, leading to a rise in seat prices (kept artificially low to widen access), further retreat from *animation*, and the erosion of ever more costly *création*. There was, it has to be said, a genuine problem with the MCs, for their escalating operating costs were an increasing drain on public resources and they were often troubled by industrial disputes. But savaging the institutions most closely associated with Malraux was all the same an Oedipal act. Hand in hand with it came a partial return under Lecat to giving conservation a higher priority than creation and democratisation, with the setting up in 1978 of a fully fledged Direction du patrimoine, the designation of 1980 as 'l'Année du patrimoine', and most important of all, adjustments to the budget. In the 1978 exercise, while the performing arts were slashed, over 208 million francs were given to museums and around 315 million to historic monuments as opposed to 131 million and 231 million respectively in 1977.[14] There was simultaneously a reconcentration of resources on select prestige institutions, particularly Parisian. In 1977, the budget for all the MCs, CACs and similar institutions outside Paris was half that of the Opéra de Paris alone.

The cultural industries furnished yet another justification for reining back state intervention. In 1978, the head of the Ministry's research department, Augustin Girard, was one of the first to point out the need for modern policy-making to take stock of the new technologies which were rapidly expanding these industries and producing a paradox for cultural policy in the process: 'le progrès de la démocratisation et de la décentralisation est en train de se réaliser avec beaucoup plus d'ampleur par les produits industriels accessibles sur le marché que par les "produits" subventionnés par la puissance publique.' His aim was not to pass judgment on this state of affairs, but simply to urge decision-makers at national and local levels to act accordingly, whether by relying more on the cultural industries or by controlling their negative effects. It was the first option the Giscard regime favoured, though it has to be stressed that there was never any question of abandoning state involvement altogether. But on the Left, a considerably more Manichean view of the cultural industries prevailed and PCF and PS alike attacked Girard as the mouthpiece of a fundamentally right-wing, capitalist ideology.[15]

The new Socialist Party which had evolved from the moribund SFIO and other groups between 1969 and 1971 had in fact fallen behind in developing a cultural policy of its own, as its First Secretary François Mitterrand freely admitted. But his defeat as joint PS-PCF candidate in the 1974 presidentials had brought home the need for a more clearly defined position on the issue and from then until 1981 a number of different influences at work within the party more or less converged to make a PS cultural doctrine of sorts. One of these was the party's Secrétariat national à l'action culturelle (SNAC) created the previous year under Dominique Taddei. Soon after the 1974 defeat, the SNAC went on the offensive by organising a series of debates at the Avignon Festival, rounded off by a press conference on 28 July 1974 by Mitterrand. The debates centred on a draft document entitled 'Orientations générales d'une politique d'action culturelle', drawn up by the SNAC. This also formed the basis of 'Rencontres nationales de la culture' held the following January, after which the document was redrafted and officially adopted.[16]

Both the SNAC document and Mitterrand's 28 July speech were part of a strategy to win over a constituency of left-wing artists and intellectuals who had traditionally identified with the PCF. Consequently, as Jean Caune points out, the SNAC text particularly combines the conventional economic analysis of Marxism with an idealist belief in workers' self-management (*autogestion*) learnt from the *gauchistes* of May. No cultural revolution is possible without an end to capitalist domination and exploitation, but economic liberation alone will not guarantee cultural liberation and there is a need in a planified economy to ensure that 'l'initiative créatrice' remains free. Both documents also share the Sixth Plan's global definition of culture, though the SNAC observes that, for all the talk of globality, the current Secretary of State Michel Guy is still mainly concerned with the professional *beaux-arts*, quite divorced from the sociocultural. For the SNAC, a truly global conception of culture must mean that it is no longer simply the business of professional artists but is defined in much broader anthropological terms: 'Nous proposons donc d'appeler culture un ensemble de représentations collectives qui est explicité par le savoir, justifié et modelé par l'idéologie et vécu dans les comportements quotidiens. Ainsi conçue, la culture totalise les idées, les règles, les usages, conscients ou inconscients, qui définissent un type de société.'[17] As such, culture is in one sense a collective phenomenon which each individual passively and involuntarily reproduces. But each can also contribute creatively to it and change it, thereby making it an active, dynamic culture.

Marked by May 1968, however, the SNAC refuses any instrumental view of culture of the kind the Sixth Plan had in mind. For an active culture implies a *prise de conscience* which brings about change. Part of this new awareness comes from the physical and intellectual pleasure which the discovery of art, the acquisition of new knowledge or of a new means of self-expression bring. This pleasure has its own 'cultural value' irrespective of the practical consequences or usefulness of the experiences in question. Indeed, precisely because such experiences and such pleasure are gratuitous, they can open the mind to radical change: 'changer la vie', as the party slogan ran. This is one reason why capitalist society cannot tolerate active cultures, be they working-class, regional or 'extra-territorial' (i.e. immigrant or ethnic), for capitalism depends on stable mass–consumption to maximise profit. Transferred to a planetary scale, this commercial imperative similarly requires the suppression of national cultural identities. So it is that French culture 's'efface elle-même progressivement devant le cosmopolitisme à l'américaine. La pop-music, le western, le feuilleton télévisé, la bande dessinée nous permettent d'imaginer ce que pourrait être demain une culture de masse à l'échelle planétaire'.[18] Monopolising the main means of expression, capitalism also brings passivity and alienation by turning all cultural goods into merchandise and all who are not professionals into mere consumers.

Influenced by Gramsci, the document therefore defines a strategic position for *action culturelle* in the wider political struggle, the objective of *autogestion* being inseparable from that of popular creativity, which implies not just 'une culture pour tous', but 'par tous'.[19] Capitalism leads to a policy of conserving a bourgeois heritage rather than favouring creation. Socialism, the SNAC claims, reverses this order, though in practice the document pays only lip-service to creation in the sense of new work by professional artists. What is clearly of much greater importance is fostering amateur group creation, for this collectivises and mobilises people whereas the work of art only isolates them and turns them into passive spectators. Creation, then, as process, not product. In this post-Malraux, *gauchiste* sense, *action culturelle* is complementary to formal education but naturally implies a complete reform of the education system, including the development of creative-arts training in schools. What is needed therefore is a powerful, properly funded central-government department to coordinate all types of cultural action. Mitterrand had told *Le Monde* that 1 per cent of the state budget was 'un minimum indispensable' but that this alone would be purely symbolic without a policy integrating the cultural spending of the diverse ministries. Thus, one purpose of the proposed new ministry would be to bring about flexible interministerial structures capable of obviating the traditional compartmentalisation of the arts, science, town-planning, the army, and of course education and broadcasting.[20]

The SNAC document was a first working out of a Socialist theory of cultural policy, woolly, earnest and verbose. But the SNAC was not the only determinant of that policy within the party. Between 1975 and 1981, as the full implications of *le giscardisme culturel* became clearer, its position was overlaid and to an extent overtaken by other emphases. One feature which did not change was the hostility to the mass media and cultural industries, voiced even more vigorously in the general policy statement drawn up for the 1981 presidentials, *Le Projet socialiste des années 80*: 'Exaltant la rentabilité financière, l'industrie culturelle oriente les désirs vers la consommation passive de marchandises, source de profits pour quelques-uns, remède illusoire au mal de vivre du plus grand nombre.'[21] But where the PS's attitude did evolve was on the issue of creation and creativity, shifting in the late 1970s in favour of the former, though not always decisively. This change may be explained more by pragmatics than ideology. Firstly, as Giscard's stress on preserving the heritage grew, promoting creation became an ideal niche for the PS to occupy. Secondly, in 1978 the PCF chose to return to a more *dirigiste* approach to creation, prompting a haemorrhage of creators to Mitterrand's party.[22] Lastly, there was the vital impact on national policy of PS-controlled local councils. At the same time as the state was looking for ways of off-loading some of its responsibilities onto local authorities, some authorities were themselves realising that the presence of lively creative talent in their region was an asset and were upping their cultural spending accordingly. In Socialist councils particularly, cultural policy became a priority, even more so after the 1977 local elections when the party took a number of new municipalities. By 1981, some Socialist councils in the bigger cities had earned reputations for cultural dynamism, like Pierre Mauroy's Lille or Grenoble under Hubert Dubedout. Belfort was devoting 14 per cent of its budget to culture, Montbéliard 16 per cent and Avignon 22 per cent. This produced a shift towards more spectacular, costly creation activities, often provided with prestigious new facilities whose running costs committed the councils to high expenditure at the expense of *animation*.[23]

The extent of the shift at local level can be gauged from another PS encounter, held in Rennes in October 1980 by the Fédération nationale des élus socialistes et républicains (FNESR) and entitled 'La création artistique dans la cité', which brought together local politicians and creators and was followed up by a further session at Avignon in July 1981.[24] As in the SNAC document, the essential problem was defined as the massification of culture by the cultural industries and sub-standard American imports. But the part the SNAC had previously allotted to sociocultural *animation* in combatting this was now said to have underestimated the equally valuable contribution made by artistic creation. Indeed, some *animateurs* had apparently become rather a nuisance, seeing themselves as omnipotent mediators between artist and public and failing to distinguish creation from popular creativity. A resolution of this problem, the colloquium concluded, would be for creative artists to become better integrated in local communities and take on the *animation* work themselves.

Even so, the less spectacular objective of popular creativity was not completely abandoned by the PS, at least not at local level where there was a rich network of sociocultural associations. Shortly after the 1981 presidentials, Claude Petit-Castelli published a survey of the cultural action pursued by Socialist town halls over the previous four years which, though devoting considerable space to creation and the Rennes conference, also showed that cultural democracy was still a live concern, though the objectives of the activists concerned were no longer those of the SNAC. In the 1960s, *animateurs* had often been politically militant volunteers or part-timers, whereas increasingly through the 1970s they were replaced by a corps of trained professionals, with the result that popular creativity became an end in itself more than a political weapon. 'Pas de militantisme exacerbé [...],' one local PS official told Petit-Castelli, 'simplement, laisser prendre la parole.' In *Le Projet socialiste des années 80* too, creativity was no longer cast as a way of contesting the establishment and opening the mind but as much closer to what the Sixth Plan had in view: 'la culture, moyen de la responsabilité.'[25]

Creation and creativity were also very much the concerns of the man who would soon be implementing Socialist cultural ideology at national level, Jack Lang. The Lang who had launched the Nancy Festival in 1963 could see no real antagonism between the most avant-garde forms of creative art and *animation* work in the community. In his early days, this was a reasonably easy stance to adopt because the festival was an amateur, exclusively student event until 1968 when professional troupes were allowed to participate. Its aim had in fact been to explore new dramatic languages and at the same time encourage the participation of students and the wider community, as actors, spectators or volunteer helpers, frequently all three. Such participation was believed to be a learning process, a way of provoking in local people an informed, critical response by sustained exposure to challenging international work. In this way, the spectator would cease to be 'l'homme que l'on alimente en culture standard, en culture de confection, comme on alimente les bœufs en foin'.[26] Participation also took a startlingly different form with the arrival of Bread and Puppet in 1968, which launched a phase of street theatre in which the traditional barriers between stage and spectator were abolished. To some extent, this early work makes Lang the classic 1960s *animateur*, working to radicalise and stimulate the creativity of local amateurs. But his position was actually more complex than this, for he never went as far as to demote professional creation in the way the SNAC did. Indeed, when in the wake of May 1968 the conventions which make the work of dramatic art recognisable as such had been so thoroughly contested that Nancy had become, as one commentator put it, a festival not of drama but of psychodrama – and a countercultural carnival increasingly at odds with the local authority – Lang dramatically backed off, using the 1971 event to dissociate himself from the excesses of its recent past.[27] His daring appointment as director of the new national theatre at Chaillot the following year, with Antoine Vitez as his artistic director, then completed this move into professional theatre, their controversial, esoteric work there becoming one further manifestation of the shift from *animation* to creation in the theatre of the 1970s.

Lang's sacking only two years later by Guy was a watershed in his career, nudging him out of theatre into politics where he could implement the view he had expressed in his doctoral law thesis that cultural democracy was a political rather than cultural matter.[28] In the 1974 presidentials, he supported Mitterrand. In 1977, he was elected to the Paris city council as a left-wing independent but promptly joined the PS. Vocal in council debates on Jacques Chirac's plans for the site of the demolished Les Halles, Lang was appointed head of the Délégation nationale à l'action culturelle which replaced the SNAC in August 1979. From this position, he spoke up for creation. At the SNAC sessions of January 1975, even before joining the party, he had objected to its demotion of creation. He had also deplored criticisms of the massive subsidies to prestige Parisian institutions, asserting that even under socialism 'les grandes institutions de création' would need to be increased.[29]

But again, his position was actually less straightforward than this. Another of his hobby-horses was the way an atomised society enslaved to consumption was destroying the old sense of community. Once more, television was identified as the chief culprit, locking people in their solitude and turning them into passive onlookers. His remedy lay in what he claimed to have learnt from Nancy and Chaillot, which was the possibility of a renaissance of 'un art communautaire':

> A côté d'une part irremplaçable de créations individuelles et solitaires, la voie est largement ouverte à tous ceux qui seront des initiateurs et des rassembleurs. Je crois à l'avenir d'actions culturelles de groupes, capables, plus que des créations érigées en spectacles traditionnels, de tirer les Français des forteresses où ils s'enferment (leur logement – leur voiture) ou d'ôter les glaces qui les séparent.

The *animateur* here is necessary because creativity does not well up spontaneously in everyone but has to be nurtured and taught, to be part of an individual's environment from an early age. But it is an error to train a separate corps of *animateurs* to perform this task. Creative artists must carry it out, becoming part of the community, particularly in schools.[30] Thus, by enlisting art in the wider task of transforming society, Lang was resolving the creation-creativity duality in much the same terms as the FNESR's 'la création dans la cité'. Arguably, however, this apparent resolution simply concealed a refusal to choose between the two, an approach which was to become a hallmark of Socialist policy from 1981. During the election campaign of 1981, it was reiterated in very similar terms in the *Projet socialiste* and formed the cornerstone of an overall cultural strategy which candidate Mitterrand unveiled to the nation in its finished form.

Among the four front runners in 1981 – Chirac, Giscard d'Estaing, Marchais and Mitterrand – there was a measure of consensus on such policy issues as arts education in schools and devoting 1 per cent of state expenditure to culture.[31] There was also fairly widespread agreement among observers that the new president, whoever it turned out to be, must at last translate the global conception of culture into policy, a policy which should be conducted, according to the pro-Gaullist Marcel Landowski, by a great Ministry of Arts and Culture which should encompass education, youth and sport, radio and television, because only a ministry of such stature could respond to an imperious necessity today: 'donner une âme à nos sociétés industrielles.'[32] The party which seemed most likely to achieve this was the PS. Mitterrand argued that current policy was spiked by having no 'dessein d'ensemble', whereas socialism was a complete 'cultural project' in itself, 'moins un choix de société qu'un choix de civilisation'.[33] He also highlighted Giscard's sacrificing of contemporary creation to *patrimoine*, contrasting this with his own view that 'memory is revolutionary' since creative exploration needs to grapple with the heritage in order to contest and transcend it.

The high point of Mitterrand's cultural campaign was a symposium on science and culture organised by the PS in March at the Palais de l'UNESCO in Paris, its theme 'Créer aujourd'hui' and its participants an impressive array of political and cultural personalities from the international Left. Clearly, the event was meant as a symbolic spectacle and Mitterrand, who gave the closing address, used it to launch his 'new deal' for culture, which centred on three 'commandments'. The first was 'réensemencer': irrigating 'les terres de l'esprit' which had become parched and impoverished under preceding administrations. This would require an entirely new *loi-programme* for technical and artistic education throughout the education system, a new policy for the development of libraries, and a reorientation of television towards cultural and educational programming. All three measures would combat the 'déculturation' of millions of French citizens 'par des médias trop souvent pauvres en imagination'. In a campaign questionnaire, he also testily called for television to expiate its deleterious effects on literature and other art forms.[34] The second commandment was 'décentraliser', which implied building on the successful experiences of Socialist municipalities like Lille and Grenoble; developing regional television so that, as in West Germany, the major part of national programming would consist of regionally produced work; and installing a wider network of centres for creative 'research' throughout the country. The last commandment was, inevitably, 'créer'. A true creation policy meant saying no to the ethic of financial viability and audience ratings and yes to multiplying the funds and opportunities available 'aux chercheurs et aux défricheurs' of all kinds. But creation would also be served by the initiation of a number of 'réalisations de référence', such as an international music complex and a vast national exhibition to mark the bicentenary of the Revolution.[35]

In addition to these specific proposals, Mitterrand, like Lang and the FNESR, presented culture as deeply embedded in society. However, even more than at Avignon in 1974, his position diverged from a standard Marxist one in that he presented culture as embracing those very economic and political conditions which Marxism sees it as determined by. True, culture cannot isolate itself from them, but the relationship works both ways: 'Rien ne change qui ne change d'abord dans les consciences, les cœurs ou les intelligences.' Everything has a cultural dimension and culture can play a determining role in the development of society. And this, he said, is precisely the meaning of the idea that Socialism is a cultural project.[36] Culture is in fact 'un vaste dessein mobilisateur des énergies et des talents'. Mitterrand also complained of the too rigid compartmentalising of creative disciplines, particularly science and art. One aim of the symposium was to bring scientists and artists together and stress the complementarity of their contributions to the rebirth of France. In his book *Ici et maintenant* (1980), he also spoke of his cultural project as 'un plan de changement capable d'englober l'éducation, l'information, la science, l'art, en un mot ce que les marxistes appellent les superstructures. Les séparer serait vain'.[37]

More pragmatically, the UNESCO event was intended to demonstrate the kinship between the party and an international community of intellectuals from all fields and thereby to help disseminate an image of the PS as a hive of cultural activity. Mitterrand assured scientists and culturalists that they would not be the icing on the cake of socialism but its architects, as demonstrated, he claimed, by the numerous colloquia on cultural and scientific matters organised by the party over the past year. Several of these occasions, like the symposium itself, had been the work of Lang, whose theatrical talents, media flair and contacts in the international arts world were used to good effect in the run-up to the 1981 elections. As the campaign got under way, Lang also launched a 'manifeste pour la République' with which numerous personalities were associated. On 31 January, a double-page close-up of Mitterrand appeared in *L'Express* and *Le Point* accompanied by a short laudatory text by Françoise Sagan. This was the first stage in what amounted to a parallel campaign, planned well in advance by Mitterrand's publicity manager Jacques Séguéla working closely with party officials like Lang. Playing on the fact that Mitterrand had some small reputation as a writer, the campaign team set out to construct an identikit picture of him as statesman and *homme de culture*, combining political wisdom and intellectual vision. The culmination of it, again the work of Lang, was a special issue of *Le Matin* entitled *François Mitterrand vu par...* in which twenty-three writers, not all of them Socialists or even supporters, gave their views of the presidential candidate, the intellectuals' intellectual.

François Mitterrand vu par... carried a subliminal message. In much the same way as de Gaulle was supposed mysteriously to have incarnated the French nation, so too was Mitterrand constructed as personifying the union of culture and politics. In him is the global conception of culture made flesh, proof that the Socialist project is not an arid set of technical proposals but a living totality. Naturally, the culture of Giscardism was represented as the antithesis of this via a lexis of sterility, conformism, atomisation. Giscardian technocracy, so the argument went, is in fact an object lesson in what happens when the cultural is excised from the political. Party intellectual Catherine Clément therefore saw the prospect of a second septennium in apocalyptic terms: 'si Giscard, par malheur pour nous, était élu, c'en est fait de la pensée de gauche, c'en est fait de la poésie, c'en est fait de la vie même de ce vieux pays.' But if only this empire of evil could be vanquished, France could experience a new cultural revolution which would tear down the Bastille of Giscardian individualism. 'Avec la victoire du socialisme,' a portentous Mitterrand proclaimed at the symposium, 'il faut s'attendre à un déferlement de la joie populaire, à une explosion d'enthousiasme, au bouillonnement et à l'effervescence des imaginations. A l'aurore d'un nouveau devenir, je dis simplement: bonjour la vie!'[38]

And for a few days in May, he seemed to have been proved right. 'Dans un grand élan populaire et national, le peuple français vient d'élire François Mitterrand à la présidence de la République,' rejoiced the new party leader Lionel Jospin on 10 May.[39] A huge street party took place that night at La Bastille, with a little prompting from Lang, where participants spoke of a happening which recalled the great moments of left-wing mythology: 1968, 1936, 1789. A comparable mood prevailed on the 21st, the day of the investiture. Its centre-piece, also staged by the indefatigable Lang, was Mitterrand's visit to the Panthéon in the late afternoon, a monument usually ignored for official ceremonies but situated in the heart of the Latin Quarter and therefore recalling both Mitterrand's inter-war intellectual roots and the May events. Walking relaxedly along the Boulevard St Michel, he was escorted by a retinue of Nobel Prize winners and other personalities from the arts and sciences. Parisians had been invited to assemble to greet him as he passed and did so in great numbers. *La Marseillaise* and Beethoven's *Ode to Joy* played by the Orchestre de Paris under Daniel Barenboim lent a touch of majesty to the carnival mood. At the Panthéon, Mitterrand then entered the crypt, alone but for the TV cameras, to lay a rose on the tombs of Jaurès, Moulin and the anti-slavery campaigner Victor Schoelcher, again signifying the continuity between his victory and the great heritage of the Left. In such a supercharged atmosphere, expectations were high. The writer Elie Wiesel, one of the new President's guests that day, felt that France might now be transformed by a new politics and a new humanism. In a quite different vein, the singer-songwriter and novelist Yves Simon wondered, a trifle optimistically, whether Bob Dylan, soon to begin a European tour, was aware that the generation which had grown up with his songs now walked the corridors of the Elysée, that millions of French people had made the lyrics of *The Times They Are A-Changin'* their own and voted Mitterrand accordingly.[40] Strange days indeed.

Notes

1. See Chronology for the various other holders of the Culture portfolio. See *Développement Culturel*, no.67, October 1986, special issue on the budget 1960–85, for full budget details, especially p.2.
2. For Pompidou's major statement on cultural policy, see his interview in *Le Monde*, 17 October 1972, pp.1, 12 and 13.
3. See also P. Emmanuel, *Pour une politique de la culture*, Paris, 1971, and J. Chaban-Delmas, 'Jalons vers une nouvelle société', *Revue des Deux Mondes*, January 1971, pp.6–16.
4. Extracts from the declaration are reproduced in *Développement Culturel*, no.13, May–June 1972, pp.2–3. Girard defines the 'cultural industries' as the transmission or reproduction of a 'work' (undefined) by industrial and therefore commercial means.
5. Duhamel is quoted in *Développement Culturel*, no.13, p.3; the Sixth Plan quotation is from Commissariat général du Plan, *Rapport de la Commission des affaires culturelles*, Paris, 1971, p.14.
6. On the implementation of the Sixth Plan, see A.-H. Mesnard, *Droit et politique de la culture*, Paris, 1990, pp.104–9.
7. Ministère de l'éducation nationale et de la culture, *L'Art à l'école: enseignements et pratiques artistiques*, Paris, no date [1993], pp.20–2. Landowski's remark is on p.18. *Solfège* is music theory.
8. J. Rigaud (Duhamel's *directeur de cabinet*), 'La Politique culturelle: bilan de deux années d'action', internal Ministry document taken from the review *Défense nationale*, February 1973, p.1 (pagination of the internal document).
9. F. Chaslin, *Les Paris de François Mitterrand: histoire des grands projets architecturaux*, Paris, 1985, pp.15–18. A coolly technocratic critique of Giscardian cultural policy appears in Commission du Bilan (F. Bloch-Lainé), *La France en mai 1981*, vol.3, pp.295–317.
10. Abirached's phrase comes from *Le Théâtre et le prince 1981–1991*, Paris, 1992, p.14. See also Caune, *La Culture en action. De Vilar à Lang: le sens perdu*, Grenoble, 1992, pp.256–61. It is difficult to establish to what degree the state prompted or merely reflected this change. Abirached believes it did both, p.115.

11. 'L'Avenir des Maisons de la culture', interview with J. Duhamel, *Le Monde*, 4 May 1972, p.17.
12. See A. Busson, *Le Théâtre en France: contexte socio-économique et choix esthétiques*, *Notes et Etudes Documentaires*, no.4,805, Paris, 1986, p.103.
13. 'Sept Ans de culture', *Les Nouvelles Littéraires*, 23 April 1981, p.34. The CNL replaced the Caisse nationale des lettres created in 1930; it is chaired by the Directeur du livre. Fuller discussion of the book prices issue can be found in Chapter 5.
14. The figures regarding the *patrimoine* budget are quoted in E. Loyer, 'La politique culturelle sous Valéry Giscard d'Estaing (1974–1981)', *Cahiers Français*, 'Culture et société', no.260, March–April 1993, pp.36–8.
15. Girard, 'Industries culturelles', *Futuribles*, no.17, September–October 1978, pp.597–605; also personal interview, 30 July 1993.
16. My sources here are four documents. The first is Mitterrand's 28 July speech at Avignon, reprinted as 'Action culturelle débat majeur de notre temps', *Nouvelle Revue Socialiste*, no.4, 1974, pp.5–11. The other three are all variants of the draft document: 'Orientations générales d'une politique d'action culturelle', ibid., pp.12–31, dated June 1974; a typed document with the same title but somewhat different wording, probably written by B. Pingaud and dated July 1974; and what appears to be the final draft (also typed) produced from the Rencontres nationales and dated January 1975, entitled 'L'Action culturelle dans le combat politique', dated January 1975. I have also consulted Caune's analysis (pp.210–17) of a seemingly identical document from January 1975 though with different pagination and the original title, 'Orientations générales...'.
17. 'L'Action culturelle dans le combat politique', p.2.
18. Ibid., p.9.
19. Ibid., p.18.
20. 'Un Entretien avec M. F. Mitterrand', *Le Monde*, 2 May 1974, p.2.
21. *Projet socialiste pour la France des années 80*, Paris, no date [1980], p.283.
22. G. Sandier, 'Avignon: les débats sur la politique culturelle', *Le Matin*, 4 August 1981, p.22.
23. D. Wachtel, *Cultural Policy and Socialist France*, New York, 1987, pp.27–30.
24. Typed report (dated January 1981) of the 24–5 October 1980 meeting; a report on this and the 21–3 July 1981 meeting appears in *Communes de France*, no.16.

25. Petit-Castelli, *La Culture à la une, ou l'action culturelle dans les mairies socialistes*, Paris, 1981, p.50; *Le Projet socialiste*, p.279.
26. Quoted in D.L. Looseley, 'Jack Lang and the politics of festival', *French Cultural Studies*, vol.1, no.1, p.10, from a 1966 article by Lang in *Théâtre et Université*.
27. André Bercoff, quoted from *L'Express* in ibid., p.13. For a fuller discussion of the 1971 change, see D.L. Looseley, 'The World Theatre Festival, Nancy, 1963–88: a critique and a retrospective', *New Theatre Quarterly*, vol.6, no.22, May 1990, pp.144–5.
28. Lang, *L'Etat et le théâtre*, Paris, 1968, pp.255–6.
29. Handwritten anonymous summary of the SNAC draft document and the ensuing discussions in the various working parties at the Rencontres nationales, pp.12–13. Lang's intervention further highlights the debate in the party between creation and popular creativity as it was prompted by a remark by Taddei that creators must be defended but that 'ce n'est pas l'essentiel'.
30. Lang's views are taken from his conversations with Jean-Denis Bredin about Nancy and Chaillot, published as *Eclats*, Paris, 1978, especially p.215; and from two interviews with Lang and Bredin, at the time of *Eclats*'s publication, in *Le Monde*, 28 February 1978, pp.1–2 (the quotation is from p.1) and 1 March 1978, p.2.
31. Giscard accepted the need for a budget increase but did not specify a figure.
32. *Le Monde*, 26–7 April 1981, p.12.
33. Speech to symposium on science and culture, 19 March 1981, reprinted in 'François Mitterrand vu par...', *Le Matin*, numéro hors série, no date [April 1981], p.25.
34. Ibid., p.25. Campaign questionnaire, *Le Matin*, 21 April 1981, p.30.
35. 'François Mitterrand vu par...', p.25.
36. 'François Mitterrand', interview in *Les Nouvelles Littéraires*, 7–14 May 1981, p.27.
37. First quotation, 'François Mitterrand vu par...', p.25; second, *Ici et maintenant*, Paris, 1980, p.156.
38. Clément, 'François Mitterrand vu par...', p.39; Mitterrand, ibid., p.25.
39. Quoted in *Le Monde*, 12 May 1981, p.11.
40. Wiesel is quoted in *Le Monde*, 23 May 1981, p.14; Simon, 'Les Temps changent', *Le Monde*, 18 June 1981, p.17.

Part II

A Socialist Ministry: Theory and Practice, 1981–86

− 4 −

Culture and the Economy: *les intellos au boulot*

The 10 May triumph was followed by an equally overwhelming victory for the Left in the June general election, giving Mitterrand an opportunity for sweeping change. Where culture was concerned, however, one thing was very soon clear: there was to be no super-ministry of the kind called for by Landowski. Instead, the importance of culture was asserted through the inclusion in Pierre Mauroy's government of the first fully-fledged and self-standing ministry since 1974, under Jack Lang. Still divorced from Education, the Ministry of Culture was also separate from Communication, with which it had been twinned under Lang's predecessor but which now had a full minister of its own (Georges Fillioud), and from a newly created Ministry of Free Time under the trade-unionist André Henry. The latter department, which Mauroy had personally pushed for with the Lagrange model in mind, was also allocated a 'delegate minister' (*ministre délégué*) for Youth and Sport (Edwige Avice) and a secretary of state for Tourism (François Abadie).

Lang depicted his ministry as a revolution and an act of faith: 'Nous nous sommes engagés à changer la vie, c'est-à-dire pas seulement à faire mieux que nos prédécesseurs, mais aussi à faire autrement. Je ne prends donc pas la succession de M. Lecat ou de M. d'Ornano. Mon but, ma démarche, m'en écartent radicalement.'[1] At the same time, he projected a much more unassuming image of himself, confessing to a sense of awe at the task now before him and creating the impression that he had been invested with a power he was anxious to devolve at the first opportunity. The cultural state's ultimate purpose, he said in Marxist vein, was to disappear, though he was careful to stress that the state must retain a role where endangered sectors like cinema were concerned. He was also at pains to distance himself from his own reputation. Lang had always polarised opinion and his appointment was given a mixed reception. Many from the theatre welcomed him as an *homme de métier* and authentic regional voice. Yet his cultural background was not unanimously held to his credit, some still insisting on thinking of him as the madman of Chaillot. His appointment was also rumoured to be unpopular with some local-party workers for whom he was the urbane Parisian arriviste who lacked the *gravitas* which only grass-roots militancy and a firm political base could confer. He thus found himself faced with the difficult task of reassuring one side without disappointing the other. 'L'individu doit changer de peau quand il devient responsable', he ambivalently informed a journalist.[2]

During the first weeks, everybody was sure a new cultural doctrine was in power though nobody quite knew what it was. 'Si mon opinion d'homme privé est faite, celle du responsable national reste à faire', Lang remarked. Indeed, he saw it as his duty to stay silent and 'sillonner la France' for suggestions and criticisms and he was reluctant to commit himself to any specific measures, resorting instead to a handy pirouette which remained serviceable for some time: nothing would be a priority because everything was.[3] If pushed, he would fall back on Mitterrand's three commandments or a few left-wing aphorisms about building bridges between art and the worker, redistributing power, and encouraging minority or community cultures. To help him flesh out such principles, he commissioned a number of reports during the summer. Some concerned established sectors of the Ministry's activities: the heritage, the MCs and CACs, now known collectively as 'Etablissements d'action culturelle' (EACs), the plastic arts, books and libraries. But others had a more innovative focus. The sociologist Pierre Belleville chaired a working party studying *action culturelle* in the workplace. Regional and minority cultures were investigated by an Occitan militant and literature specialist at the CNRS, Henri Giordan. Lyric writer Pascal Sevran was given the job of examining the state of the *chanson*. Where the audiovisual sector was concerned, the situation was complicated by the existence of the separate Ministry for Communication, which led to the setting up of two linked but distinct commissions. One, on broadcasting, was headed by Malraux's collaborator Pierre Moinot who reported direct to the Prime Minister, while his vice-president Jean-Denis Bredin was also appointed to chair a second group to investigate cinema, which reported to Lang. Though Bredin was instructed to work closely with Moinot, this arrangement did not augur well for a harmonised audiovisual policy.

In the meantime, the Minister set about putting his own house in order. Lang was said to have wanted to keep Communication and he publicly committed himself to pressing for more coordinated policies for culture, television and education. Yet he had inherited a department which, still aglow with the reflected glory of its Gaullist period, by 1981 was in reality as under-resourced and undervalued as Malraux's had been, and he would often claim to have found its drawers and cash-box empty.

It was soon clear, however, that he had no intention of letting this state of affairs continue: 'Je veux que ce ministère s'épanouisse, qu'il abuse de son prestige – car, paradoxalement, il est prestigieux autant que misérable, – qu'il contamine l'Etat, l'ensemble du pays.'[4] Some small progress was made here straightaway. The Ministry at least retained the title 'Culture', suggestive of more than the administrative technicalities implied in 'Affaires culturelles'. In early June, a decree transferred back a number of responsibilities for protecting the heritage lost to Environment in 1978. More importantly for future controversy, it also moved the Bibliothèque nationale (BN) from the Ministry for Universities.[5] That same month, Lang announced one thousand new posts for culture and was soon able to set up two new directorates, for Développement culturel and Arts plastiques, though subsequently his opponents were to see such manoeuvres as the first steps towards a vast and disturbing new bureaucracy (see Figure 1).

In terms of personnel, many of the secondary administrators in post under Giscard (and in some cases Malraux) remained. But Lang installed his own unconventional, highly creative team at the top, 'toute une génération issue de l'extrême-gauche "algérienne"' as Ory put it.[6] Jacques Sallois, *énarque* and former PSU member, was appointed director of Lang's cabinet. Another of its members was Claude Mollard, one-time general secretary of the Pompidou Centre, who was made responsible for budget matters and was to play a key role in securing the now legendary increase in the department's budget that year, before being moved to the Délégation à la création, aux métiers d'art et aux manufactures, successor to Anthonioz's Service de la création artistique. Dominique Wallon, radical president of the student union UNEF in the early 1960s and head of the Grenoble MC, was appointed to the cabinet to set up the new directorate for Développement culturel, while Bernard Gilman, director of the same MC and former worker-activist in Peuple et Culture, was to develop relations with the local and regional authorities. Two of Lang's friends from festival days were also appointed as advisers, Jean-Pierre Colin and Christian Dupavillon. The autumn then saw a wave of appointments to the various directorates. Professor of theatrical aesthetics, critic and writer Robert Abirached, also a friend since Nancy, took charge of Theatre. Jean Gattégno, a university teacher of English and education trade-unionist, was appointed Directeur du

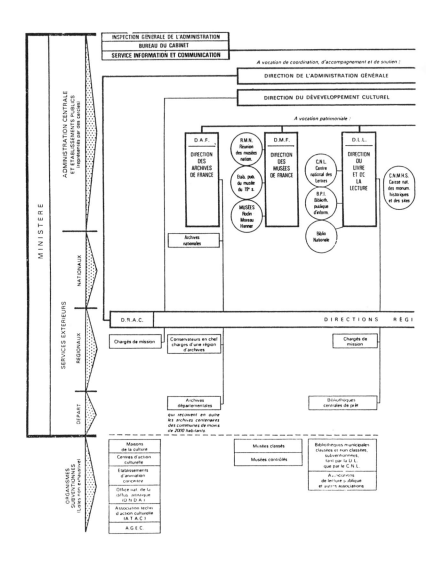

Figure 1. The Structure of the Lang Ministry, 1983. Source: Ministère de la culture et de la francophonie.

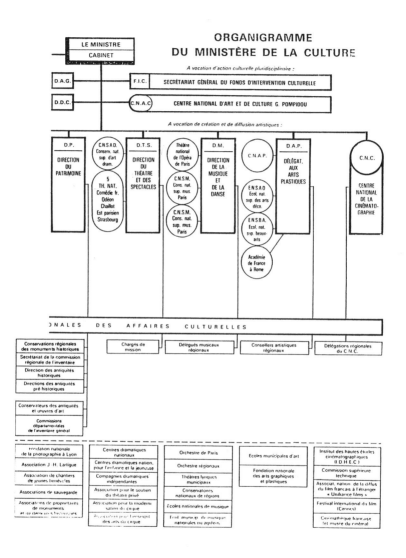

ORGANIGRAMME
DU MINISTÈRE DE LA CULTURE

livre et de la lecture. And Maurice Fleuret, *Le Nouvel Observateur*'s music critic and director of the music festival in Mauroy's Lille, became Director of music and dance. A scattering of immediate measures acted as further markers of change. One of Mitterrand's first acts was to facilitate the long-awaited naturalisation of two well-known writers exiled in France for their opposition to totalitarian regimes: the Argentinian Julio Cortazar and the Czech Milan Kundera. Lang was also quick to act in the sector he knew best, the theatre, appointing or confirming the appointment of several rising creators as CDN directors in early July. The 'Loi Lang', undoing Monory's freeing of book prices, was drawn up immediately after the presidentials and rushed through Parliament by early August. In October, it was announced that museums would be free to all on Wednesdays and to school parties throughout the week. Mitterrand also intervened personally to ensure that works of art were exonerated from the government's new wealth tax.

But apart from these isolated measures, during the early months in power while policies were being formulated and the budget drawn up, the PS government's cultural revolution was largely a matter of words and gestures, as it tried out a variety of identities. One was that of heir to the old Left, already prefigured in the election campaign and the Panthéon ceremony. Pierre Mauroy, with his roots in the SFIO's popular culture and youth movement, proudly drew parallels with 1936, pointing out the cultural nature of the current government's early social legislation – the thirty-nine-hour week, the lowering of the retirement age to sixty, the improvement of working conditions – and its continuity with the Popular Front's. Much the same lineage was invoked that July when Mitterrand visited the Avignon Festival on the tenth anniversary of Vilar's death. Accompanied by a cluster of ministers, among them Lang in a soon-to-be celebrated pink jacket, Mitterrand was the first Fifth-Republic president to grace the event and his mere presence was enough to establish a symbolic link between the Socialist project and Vilar's civic humanism. Lang too took to evoking the authority of Vilar and Laurent around this time, though much of his inspiration and rhetoric was actually drawn from a more recent era, the 1960s. This became clear in September 1981 when, after the summer lull, the government's cultural project caused real controversy for the first time with an issue which harked back to the Blum-Byrnes agreements but which Lang managed to give a contemporary, *tiers-mondiste* inflection: the threat of Americanisation to national culture.

In his first press conference in September, Mitterrand gave an outline of cultural policy and announced a big increase in the Culture and Research budgets for 1982, though not the famous 1 per cent, now promised for 1983; culture was also to be reintroduced into the Plan. Lang himself gave major interviews to *Playboy* and *Le Monde* which revealed that audiovisual matters particularly were on his mind. He would often stress the urgency of a complete overhaul of 'la fabrication de l'image' embracing cinema, television, radio, video and the new technologies. He wanted TV to be decentralised, to become one big video library for France's theatrical and musical heritage, and most of all to develop as a creative medium in its own right, becoming quite simply 'la meilleure télévision du monde'. Among other things, this would have to mean an end to 'l'importation à bas prix des sous-séries américaines'.[7] It was this last ambition in particular which prompted him to refuse to attend the American film festival held annually in Deauville. It would, he said, be 'an anomaly' for him to do so: 'Un ministre doit choisir entre les exploitants et les exploités. Le rôle d'un ministre n'est pas de participer à des réceptions mondaines financées au demeurant par des compagnies américaines, mais d'être où est la vie.'[8]

The gesture attracted considerable attention. While some accused him of a simplistic cultural nationalism or even xenophobia, the Comité pour l'identité nationale which had been lobbying since May for the dissemination of France's culture and language, published a manifesto supporting his crusade against 'cultural imperialism' and calling for the existing quota of French films on television to be increased from fifty to sixty per cent.[9] In reality, however, the debate revealed somewhat more about French sensitivities on issues of national identity than about Lang himself. His boycott and subsequent self-justification were no doubt inept but scarcely warranted the accusations of a *France seule* mentality worthy of Maurras or Vichy, for his position on national culture went well beyond jingoism. Much of the indignation it caused was in fact based on a parody which had him dismissing all American art from Dos Passos to 'Dallas', or resistant to foreign influences of any kind, and he was to spend the next ten years trying to live the reputation down.

Yet Deauville was no blunder. Firstly, he was taking a stand against American 'majors' like Warner Brothers and MGM which, he believed, were trying through the Motion Picture Export Association to thwart European cinema policies.[10] But his stance was also bound up with the new government's foreign policy, one of whose aims was to encourage dialogue between the prosperous 'North' and the under-privileged 'South', to which a summit conference was to be devoted in Cancun, Mexico, that October.[11] In June, Lang had already spoken of the need to develop cultural ties with other nations, particularly those which had emerged 'du même creuset que nous', which covered countries from Mediterranean Europe to Asia and South America. Citing Léopold Sédar Senghor, he had boldly declared that 'chacun doit être un métis culturel' and called for a cultural third force, independent of the two superpowers. In the *Playboy* interview, he even described this policy as one of the main planks of his programme.[12] Then, shortly after Deauville, he attended the first conference of Francophone culture ministers and delegations held in Cotonou, capital of the Marxist republic of Benin, where his speech on the French language as a shield against the penetration of multinationals and American mass-cultural products anticipated a much more notorious one the following July at the world conference of some 150 culture ministers organised by UNESCO in Mexico City.[13]

In the Mexico speech, made just after a controversial visit to Cuba where he had enjoyed the hospitality of Castro, he aggressively adopted the theme of cultural 'decolonisation', arguing that too many countries today are passively accepting 'une certaine invasion, une certaine submersion d'images fabriquées à l'extérieur et de musiques standardisées'. Statistics, he maintained, show that across the world television schedules are saturated with such productions, which erode cultural differences. Unable to reciprocate, the nations of the world have therefore become 'les vassaux de l'immense empire du profit' and need to mount 'une véritable résistance culturelle' against 'cet impérialisme financier et intellectuel', which today no longer seizes land but minds, ways of thinking and living. The airwaves must be 'decolonised' by greater diversity in TV programming and greater collaboration in cultural production between 'pays de culture voisine' and 'alliés immédiatement naturels'.[14]

Not surprisingly, the speech caused further uproar, starting with the American delegates at the conference. Some in France like the writers Hervé Bazin and Tahar Ben Jelloun took his side, while Alain Finkielkraut, acknowledging the problem he raised, felt he was using America as a scapegoat for the mediocrity of France's own mass culture. Another intellectual, Bernard-Henri Lévy, linked Lang's position with the Right or even fascism, while the extreme-right publication *Royaliste* came out in Lang's favour.[15] Again, the Minister himself spent the following weeks protesting his innocence. His position, he insisted, had simply been part of the government's drive to make French industries more competitive, win back domestic markets and put an end to the balance of trade deficit.[16] But this reading was disingenuous to say the least given the vocabulary of ideological warfare he had used at Cotonou and Mexico, where it had clearly been politically expedient to do so. But there was also a weakness in his whole argument. Deauville, Cotonou and Mexico were all based on his objection to inauthentic 'multinational cultures', which were rootless and alienating because they were not the natural expression of organic communities but manufactured from a lowest common denominator and then imposed on all. This, he seemed to feel, was a phoney internationalism, quite distinct from genuine exchanges between 'natural cultural allies'. But what exactly is 'natural' about such allies in the age of the global village? If one may just go along with the argument that, for Francophone nations at least, the French language serves as a common cultural heritage, it is difficult to see why France should automatically have a greater cultural affinity with, say, a developing South American nation on the strength of an obscure idea of *latinité* than it does with the United States, an advanced industrial state like itself whose cultural productions have been a lingua franca in Europe since the war. Replying to Lang, the writer Guy Konopnicki said he would personally prefer the crassest Broadway revue any day to the 'l'affligeant spectacle des danses folkloriques en sabots', maintaining that if Walt Disney and the Western have become more successful in France than its own indigenous popular cultures, it is not simply because of the supremacy of US export machinery but because American mass culture is more relevant to the new, urbanised lifestyle of the majority of the French, and because the cosmopolitanism of that culture has made it eminently exportable. Far from being a commercially manufactured internationalism, the American presence in Europe was in fact a feature of the natural evolution of advanced capitalist societies towards a universal culture which has now outgrown the confines of national identities.[17] From this standpoint, the mistake in Lang's position on America lay not in cultural poujadism but in his tendency to clothe opposition to US market domination in a left-over *tiers-mondisme* inappropriate to the France of today. As has been regularly pointed out ever since, not least by the Americans themselves during the 1993 GATT negotiations, the only effective means of challenging the USA is not to put up trade barriers but to beat it at its own game, by encouraging creative excellence in all fields and by chipping away at its own brand of cultural protectionism, a reasoning which by 1982 Lang, behind a smokescreen of left-wing rhetoric, was already moving towards.

His distaste for the standardisation and passivity associated with American mass culture was tied in with his own past and indeed his whole conception of his mission as Minister. The Culture department was a posting to which temperamentally at least he seemed ideally suited, for it was arguably he more than Mitterrand who combined the *homme de culture* with the politician. And this combination made him an *animateur* on a national scale, as Antoine Vitez had already glimpsed at Chaillot. Lang, wrote Vitez in 1978, is in his way an artist, but his creative medium is reality itself: 'faire bouger des personnes et des personnages sur la scène du monde [...], leur faire jouer un rôle dans un spectacle fomenté par lui.' This, Vitez went on, is perhaps what also makes him a politician: 'Inventer des événements plutôt que des œuvres.' That same year, Lang himself claimed that his role in theatre had been to 'Faire parler, faire aimer', dragging people from their domesticated solitude. It was precisely this talent as a kind of countercultural redcoat which he brought to ministerial office: 'chef d'orchestre doublé d'un animateur pour entretenir l'enthousiasme, et si possible d'un sourcier capable de découvrir "ces gisements inexplorés de notre intelligence et de notre sensibilité".'[18] This conception of his duties was also fundamental to the philosophy which was soon to take him a long way from his and the PS's original Leftist rhetoric: the relationship between culture and the economy.

In the PS's view, the predominance of American pap on French TV and the liberation of book prices under Giscard merely provided further evidence of the negative effects of market forces. But the party's ideological position midway between historical materialism and idealism implied that the relationship between culture and the economy was dialectical and therefore potentially positive. This assumption had been hinted at in Mitterrand's address at the UNESCO symposium but was spelt out in the speech Lang gave to the National Assembly on 17 November 1981 to introduce his first full budget. Over the following eighteen months, it was to be sharpened under a variety of influences and pressures, reaching its finished form in 1983.

Like the Panthéon ceremony, the Culture budget debate was made into a mythic Socialist occasion. Mauroy and other ministers turned out for it, arts celebrities were invited to hear it, and the Chamber was fuller than for any of the earlier budget debates that year. What those present witnessed was certainly unprecented in the Fifth Republic: the doubling of the Ministry's budget, from 2.96 billion francs or 0.47 per cent of the total state budget, to just over 5.99 billion francs or 0.75 per cent. As Lang had promised to make all areas a priority, there were increases across the board, though some areas benefited more than others to make up for past neglect. The ascendency Giscard had given conservation and Paris over creation, the provinces and *action culturelle* was reversed quite spectacularly. With public reading now the top priority, the Book directorate's income was tripled and central spending on municipal libraries multiplied by twelve. Funds for the acquisition of new works of art were increased by 185 per cent and expenditure on cinema and the audiovisual went from 35.2 to 120 million francs. Rises in the traditionally favoured areas were somewhat more modest: *patrimoine monumental*, for example, went from 1.2 billion francs to 1.73 and museums from 642.5 million francs to 1.07 billion.[19]

The speech itself was the first theoretical treatment of cultural issues since Mitterrand's the previous March and was an appropriately flatulent affair which began with an evocation of the French nation on 10 May stepping joyfully from darkness into the light. Lang also ceremonially laid the ghost of Druon in the name of the 1968 generation: 'Désormais, il n'y aura plus d'un côté l'imagination des uns tendant leur sébile et le désespoir des autres fabriquant des cocktails molotov. Désormais, le Pouvoir s'emploiera, lui aussi, à retrouver, sous les pavés, la plage.' Like Mitterrand at UNESCO, his message was still an integrated culture remotivating society, but he now placed noticeably more stress on its economic dimension. This had a curious ring coming from a socialist regime, but during the summer, indeed as early as 21 May, the new government had had to wake up to the economic situation it faced. At a Cabinet meeting on 23 July, the President had stressed the need for unemployment and job creation to be the number-one priority and Laurent Fabius, in charge of the budget, had likewise asked ministers to consider whether their expenditure plans actively aided employment.[20] Lang, however, had fought hard to extract his increase from the Finance department and with Mitterrand's support had pushed it through, though the Finance Minister Jacques Delors had insisted on the 1 per cent being spread over several years. Consequently, the pressure on Lang to justify his increase in economic terms was intense.

'Doubler le budget de la Culture en temps de crise, est-ce bien raisonnable?', he duly began (p.1). With Malraux doubtless in mind, his answer hinged on the belief that the time when culture was deemed to hover, beautiful yet remote, above the material realities of the everyday, is gone. Culture is certainly 'la vie de l'esprit', but it is life in all its other forms too. As he had told *Playboy*, it should not have connotations of pedantry, obligation or excessive respect but should be an earthy, physical experience enjoyed by all, 'la culture comme plaisir, jouissance, nourriture, soif'.[21] In saying this, he was not demeaning culture but, rather than see it as Malraux's *supplément d'âme*, was setting it to work as the source of the creative energy and sense of purpose which drives a living society. For encouraging creativity, enterprise and the presence of beauty will dynamise not just France's art but its economy too: 'Pas d'espoir de redressement économique', he told the Assembly, 'en un pays qui laisserait les intelligences et les talents en friche, et les hommes sans idéal' (p.4). 'Une société qui ne crée pas meurt', he went on (p.18), enlarging on the point at Mexico City: 'Une société qui retrouve le sens de l'invention et de la création pourra redonner à chacun de nos pays l'idéal mobilisateur dont nous avons besoin pour vaincre la crise.' Far from cutting public spending on culture at a time of recession, therefore, the duty of the state is to invest in intelligence and imagination as a means of resisting 'la fatalité des prétendues lois internationales'.[22]

In proposing a functional culture, Lang like Mitterrand also proposed an enlarged definition of it. Culture was not simply his business but the whole government's, which included not one but forty-four ministers of culture, whose various new measures were all cultural in the fullest sense in that they were statements of what he had already called 'a new morality', a proposed value system and lifestyle for the national community.[23] Casting his own ministry in the role of overall orchestrator, he placed great stress on the need for interministerial cooperation, particularly with Communication to ensure that broadcasting companies did not work against state cultural policy, and with Education to enable the law on *éducation artistique* to be drawn up. But just as culture is not the preserve of one ministry, neither should its highest institutions – theatre, museums, libraries – be the privilege of one class as they were at present, or of one city, Paris. Nor should it be restricted to such high-cultural temples. There must be no hierarchy between major and minor arts and the private sector should not be despised for its commercial nature, any more than private sponsorship as long as it is not a substitute for state funding. His two watchwords, then, were creation and decentralisation. He concluded by stressing that the government was now treating creators as allies and that the cultural world was giving the new regime unprecedented support.

The importance of the budget speech, whose principles were confirmed in a 'Plan intérimaire' for 1982–3 hastily produced the same month, lay in its bringing together in a single though not particularly homogeneous form the various strands of thought which had influenced the PS's attempts to shape a cultural policy since 1974: the democratisation advocated by the Popular Front and Malraux; the post–1968 preoccupation with pluralism, creativity and difference; and the Sixth Plan's idea of an integrated global culture, with more stress now on the power of such a culture to reinvigorate the economy. The same three strands were later apparent in a decree dated 10 May 1982 which enlarged the Ministry mission statement drawn up by Malraux in July 1959. The result of a compromise, according to Jacques Sallois, between the internationalists and regionalists within the PS and those who favoured creation or popular creativity, the new mission was to

permettre à tous les Français de cultiver leur capacité d'inventer et de créer, d'exprimer librement leurs talents et de recevoir la formation artistique de leur choix; de préserver le patrimoine culturel national, régional ou des divers groupes sociaux pour le profit commun de la collectivité tout entière; de favoriser la création des œuvres de l'art et de l'esprit et de leur donner la plus vaste audience; de contribuer au rayonnement de la culture et de l'art français dans le libre dialogue des cultures du monde.[24]

Like the budget speech, this statement suggested a number of overlaid and not automatically compatible aims, though all came together in the implied hostility to the American-influenced mass media and the corresponding foregrounding of French creation and creativity. The speech was generally well received. For many in the arts world, any doubts it raised were outweighed by the sheer novelty of a Western government in the early 1980s declining to sacrifice culture to austerity. At the same time, it was easy to be sceptical about talk of darkness and light and forty-four ministers of culture, which, twelve years on, Lang had still not lived down. Nor was it difficult to identify the confusion in his voracious definition of culture and its relationship with the economy. Although this relationship could be understood on a perfectly pragmatic level, Lang at first insisted on presenting it in much grander humanist terms, using a half-learnt Malraucian lyricism which came to sound fatuous and absurd as time went by and for which he was soon notorious. The idea thus became confused with the rhetoric and the budget speech marked the beginning of a period of suspicion of both Minister and Ministry. 'Les éclats d'éloquence de Jack Lang devant l'Assemblée, le 17 novembre 1981', Fumaroli ironised in 1982, 'sont un seuil dans l'histoire des Affaires culturelles. Le voile est déchiré.'[25] For the Right particularly, out of power for the first time in twenty-three years, the speech certainly did seem to produce an abrupt awakening after six months of aphasia. The conservative press immediately set about portraying Lang as a dangerous sectarian who was diabolically using his theatrical skills to mask a more sinister intent. Throughout 1982 and early 1983, his adversaries contrived to discover in his propensity to turn everything into culture and his alleged wish to be 'Minister for Desire' an Ubuesque appetite for ideological domination. The Right, however, was not alone in having such misgivings. 'Oui, si l'on veut,' said Bernard Frank in the pro-government *Le Matin*, 'tout est culturel et tout est politique, mais par un de ces tours de passe-passe globalisant [*sic*] où l'humble, l'affolante réalité des choses de la vie n'a que peu de choses à voir.' A generally sympathetic *Le Monde* piece covering the speech noted that Lang's notion of culture turned happiness and the art of living into a ministerial portfolio and advised caution.[26] But there was also a more specific objection to Langian discourse. In the speech, there was unmistakable triumphalism in the way Lang announced an end to hostilities between the arts and the state. But the question the writer and journalist Guy Hocquenghem raised in *Libération* was whether this sudden benevolent interest in the welfare of the cultural community might not amount to a fatal embrace. Hocquenghem detected in Lang's lyricism what he called 'un barrésisme progressiste' which, while seeking to appeal to modernity and youth, also turned on traditional, often right-wing themes: 'L'éloge du travail, du "réel", du "vital"', and 'le ventre fécond de la terre'. Hocquenghem did not doubt Lang's sincerity. On the contrary, what worried him was the genuine passion for reconciling art and the state such eloquence betrayed, which he saw as unconsciously totalitarian. His fear was that the idea of everything being cultural would mean the end of almost a century of intellectual dissent.[27]

That such doomsday scenarios were formulated more in response to words than deeds was indicated by the fact that the government had actually refrained from setting up a ministry broad enough to carry out such a hegemonic enterprise. On the contrary, there were those who, for all the talk of forty-four ministers of culture, were already forecasting that, with neither television nor creative-arts education in the Ministry's purview, its cultural revolution would be a damp squib. Even Lang was fond of quoting the saying attributed to Malraux that 'deux fois trois sous ne font que six sous'. Even so, the threat of the dead hand of socialism on art and thought if not the entire nation was to become a recurrent theme of the Ministry's adversaries in the ensuing years. Hocquenghem's doubts in fact reflected a more general reticence felt by a number of intellectuals towards the government as a whole. Around autumn 1981, a mysterious 'silence' of left-wing intellectuals particularly was diagnosed, probably triggered by Deauville. It peaked in 1983 with two significant events: an international colloquium organised by the Ministry in February which asked intellectuals and people from the arts to consider how culture could remedy world recession, and an on-going debate in *Le Monde* that summer launched by the novelist, historian and government spokesman, Max Gallo. Gallo's piece was a good instance of the bewildered disappointment felt by the Socialists at the fact that, with the Left at last in power, the intellectuals of all people – the very 'motor driving its world views' in Diana Pinto's phrase – appeared to have abandoned it, leaving the Right free to attack at will.[28] There were of course exceptions to this abstention, like Catherine Clément who lyricised about the regime's cultural policy in her book *Rêver chacun pour l'autre*, or Régis Debray who was an adviser at the Elysée.[29] But the most obdurate or critical intellectuals were also the most prominent in the media – Lévy, André Glucksmann, Michel Foucault, Philippe Sollers – and their silence could be deafening. The reasons for it could not all be laid at the government's door. Disillusionment after May 1968, the onset of economic recession, and the market-oriented, mediatised nature of society all meant that intellectuals were no longer as publicly influential as before and some had preferred to withdraw into literary or university careers. If those who remained in the public eye were anti-Giscard, it was not usually in the name of a party but of the universal values at stake in issues like the death penalty. Few, at any rate, had ever seen Mitterrand as the incarnation of their political beliefs. Thus, the 10 May victory was greeted in some quarters with indifference, while in others it brought a more obscure sense of dispossession. In a perceptive diagnosis of this latter position, Jean-Denis Bredin attributed the silence to the fact that the Left's victory had completely disrupted their instinctively oppositional mind-set by removing the object of their dissent.[30]

Some intellectuals, however, felt they had more palpable reasons. In the 1970s, a number had turned dramatically against the Marxist dogma of the PCF and no longer recognised themselves in the kind of ideological language the PS, now in partnership with the Communists, was using in 1981. While the crowds had celebrated on the evening of 10 May at the Bastille, Alain Finkielkraut had looked on with a sense of uneasy distance: 'J'étais sur la place avec un groupe d'amis. J'ai eu l'impression de participer à une sorte d'hystérie collective et je me suis surpris à chanter *l'Internationale* avec la foule. Cela m'a rendu triste: ma joie ne pouvait plus passer par ce chant-là.' Finkielkraut's remark hints at an historical irony in the PS's position which was analysed further by Jean Baudrillard in his contribution to the *Le Monde* debate. The Left arrived in power, Baudrillard argues, not as the logical culmination of an historical process as the PS liked to think, but at the end of history itself, bursting expectantly on-stage just as everyone else had gone home. May 1968 had been the last explosion of 'toutes les énergies de dépassement, les énergies sociales de rupture, les énergies culturelles alternatives' and had signified merely 'la perte du sens', the installation of a new 'immorality' ungovernable in terms of the old strategies for maintaining balance and control. The PS, however, had understood none of this: 'renouant avec leurs vieux principes, ils ont pris gentiment la suite des réformes de 36 ou de la fin de la dernière guerre, enchaînés à une histoire (la leur et celle de leurs réformes) qui n'a pas eu lieu.'[31] From Baudrillard's perspective, it is easy to see that by enthusiastically reviving the old ideological discourse the new government was flogging a very dead horse. Evocations of Jaurès and Blum, talk of nationalisations, banning private schools and solidarity with national liberation movements, and above all the appointment of Communist ministers, all evoked an ideology the intellectuals had turned their backs on and from the first they were on their guard.

This watchfulness seemed vindicated in December 1981 after the military coup in Poland, when the French Minister for External Relations Claude Cheysson declared that the government would 'of course' be doing nothing. The statement provoked a swift response from a number of artists and intellectuals, including Foucault, Glucksmann and Patrice Chéreau, who signed a communiqué which drew a bitter comparison with other French Socialist 'démissions' at the time of Spain in 1936 and Hungary in 1956. Lang reacted strongly, accusing the signatories of wanting to 'disloquer la majorité politique française' more than help Poland. This sensitivity to intellectual opinion, already visible in his responses to the Deauville incident, reappeared over his Mexico speech when he intemperately rebuked the 'jacasseurs professionnels de la société parisienne, plus attachés à s'enivrer de leurs propres logomachies qu'à regarder le monde en face'.[32] Lang, however, was himself a further cause of the intellectuals' suspicion, not only because of his supposedly 'Pétainist' lyricism but also because of his *tiers-mondiste* hostility to the USA at a time when many former leftists were looking to America as a haven of individual liberties and resistance to state centralism.[33]

Thus, by the time of the *Le Monde* series in 1983, French socialism was for a number of intellectuals quite simply an irrelevance, 'incapable', in Jean-Edern Hallier's words, 'de tenir le discours de la modernité'.[34] By this time, however, the PS itself was frantically throwing its ideological baggage overboard and embracing the very 'modernity' it was accused of ignoring. This was chiefly the result of its confrontation with economics, though given the importance of intellectuals to the party's identity, their silence undoubtedly played its part. But by the start of 1983, months of grappling with inflation, devaluation and creeping unemployment had led to a new realism, 'une vision détrompée des choses', as Jospin put it in August 1983.[35] Where cultural policy was concerned, this change was made quite easily, under cover of the culture-economy linkage. In the early days, the party's Leftism prevented it from fully grasping or openly stating the more 'modern' (i.e. pragmatic) implications of the idea. But the economic difficulties, together with the period of reflection launched by the Ministry in 1981 through the various reports it had commissioned, brought about a refocusing of the argument. A revealing stage in this process was the report entitled *L'Impératif culturel* which formed the basis for the chapter on cultural policy included in the Ninth Plan in March 1983.[36]

The report was written by Marc Guillaume and drew on *La Culture au pluriel* and other writings by Michel de Certeau. Its mandate was to plan a long-term strategy for cultural development as a factor of economic and social development. Unlike the depression of 1929, Guillaume argued, the economic crisis which began in the early 1970s is bound up with a deeper cultural crisis dating from the late 1960s, cultural in that it calls into question the whole value-system which industrial capitalism and economic growth were founded on. The inertia which is its outcome is not therefore susceptible of purely economic or technological remedies. Instead, the solution must involve a remobilisation which, like the crisis itself, must also be cultural. But, as Guillaume went on to say, we must be clear what the cultural implies here. He restated the need for a global definition of the field of culture, which should embrace not only those forms by which human beings represent the world, death, human relations and so on, but also the humbler, more limited, often ephemeral representations and practices connected with everyday living: 'la culture de l'ordinaire' or 'la culture au pluriel'. Such representations and practices are inseparable from their economic, technological and social contexts – the workplace, the home, the new technologies – which themselves become part of this enlarged field. To exclude them is to reject modernity and turn culture into a decorative extra. What the report proposed, then, was that the state cease to concentrate exclusively on encouraging and democratising high culture and recognise also the autonomy and equality of all practices, including those hitherto seen as minor and insignificant.

Guillaume evidently saw this approach as having both human and material benefits. On the one hand, it would allow people to 'appropriate' their own cultures, their work and their lives, releasing new creative energies and making them whole. On the other, the increased activity and consumption this would stimulate would have a direct economic pay-off in terms of job creation, productivity and consumer spending, though Guillaume insisted that the 'cultural mobilisation' he had in mind must lead to the subordination of the economic to the human and the cultural. On paper, the government also took this view. But as its financial difficulties worsened, it became particularly eager to highlight the material side, as evidenced in February 1983 at the international colloquium on the theme 'Création et développement', held at the Sorbonne.

By asking its participants to reflect on the contribution creation and creativity might make to curing the world's economic and social ills, the colloquium was meant as the ultimate demonstration of the new reconciliation between the cultural milieu and the state. It was the kind of glittering occasion only Lang could stage. Participants came from a range of fields: economists, scientists, and a long list of creators, thinkers and stars, from Jacques Derrida to Sophia Loren. In the programme for the colloquium, the 1981 notion of culture as a remedy for 'la crise' was restated in the usual lyrical terms. Mitterrand's closing address was similarly couched in the high-sounding discourse of his UNESCO speech, drawing a parallel between today's technological revolution and the Renaissance. But this time, the humanism was accompanied by a hard-headed statement of culture's economic usefulness in partnership with modern technology and industry: 'la création devient facteur de développement et les activités culturelles s'affirment parmi les secteurs en expansion', he declared, continuing a little later: 'Les industries de la culture sont les industries de l'avenir. Industries de la communication ou industries du savoir, industries de programmes ou industries de loisir, nous pensons, j'y insiste, qu'investir dans la culture, c'est investir dans l'économie, que c'est du même coup dégager l'avenir et contribuer de la sorte à rendre à la vie tout son sens.'[37]

As *Libération*'s Laurent Joffrin commented, there was something quite new here: not in the assertion that the cultural and communication industries were the way forward, which was unquestionably true, but in the transformation the Socialists' cultural ideology had undergone since the 1970s and even since 1981. For evidently, the Left had signed an extraordinary peace treaty with the market-place.[38] Between 1981 and 1983 the entire balance of the culture and economy argument had in fact subtly shifted. As Lang had made clearer after the budget speech, its initial premise was that the economic crisis is cultural in so far as it is the result of a deeper spiritual loss of direction in post-Christian societies. The crisis can consequently be beaten if culture, or more precisely the chance to be personally creative and have access to works of art in our daily lives, is offered as an alternative form of transcendence in contemporary civilisation. This is the idealist and most Malraucian dimension of the argument, and the most questionable since there is surely a good chance that providing people with a new source of spirituality will, if anything, turn them away from the material. *L'Impératif culturel* then presented a more temperate version by arguing that the recession was linked with a loss of faith not in God but in the economic values of industrial capitalism and that a creativity-releasing fulfilment could be achieved by allowing people to appropriate their own cultures.

But a third, considerably more utilitarian interpretation is that culture today, as a branch of the ever-growing leisure industry, is an important economic resource which can make a significant impact on employment, investment and the balance of trade. And as Lang began to argue, where trade in particular is concerned the exporting of a country's 'biens informationnels et culturels' can have an impact on the overseas sales of its other products. In fact, the American example amply shows in his view that a country's intellectual and cultural independence is closely bound up with its ability to remain economically competitive in world markets, since an industrially dominant nation will end up exporting its entire lifestyle.[39] All three of these meanings cohabited in the culture-economy argument. It therefore provided a conveniently passe-partout formula which allowed the government to activate its different meanings as appropriate while appearing to be self-consistent, the humanist dimension providing an ideologically acceptable front for making the leisure and communication industries a priority of cultural policy, as was to be the case in the Ninth Plan.

Mitterrand's speech at the colloquium included an invitation: 'J'invite les hommes, les femmes de culture à venir partager leur savoir, à s'associer plus que jamais à la vie de la communauté.'[40] Behind it was the implication that despite the earlier friction, here was a concrete task for intellectuals to perform with a government now less obsessed with the ideological gestures of the past and more in tune with modernity. Some of the participants were favourable to this idea, others less convinced. Derrida was not against the notion of state intervention in so far as it means state regulation and is operated with discernment. Nor did he believe that creators can claim to stand outside or even in opposition to state institutions since such opposition itself inevitably draws its legitimacy from a counter-institution of some kind. But he was quite clearly challenging the more pragmatic implications of the culture-economy link when he insisted that the relationship of cultural communities with the state must be one of absolute independence: 'un mot d'ordre tel que "la culture pour sortir de la crise" ne serait pas seulement impuissant, il serait choquant s'il était interprété comme la mission d'un nouvel auxiliariat au service de finalités techno-économiques commandées par la valeur de "production" ou de "croissance".' Umberto Eco went further still. The 'homme de culture' and the 'homme de pouvoir' had quite different conceptions of the notion of crises. The politician's aim is to cure them as a form of illness within the body social, whereas the job of 'hommes de culture' like himself is to establish a new way of seeing the world: 'je ne résous pas les crises', he exclaimed, 'je les instaure.'[41]

Both interventions illustrated the perils of asking intellectuals to address the problems faced by governments, for in truth neither side was speaking the other's language. Discussing the colloquium, Jacques Renard, one of Lang's pre–1986 *directeurs de cabinet*, stresses the need to 'intégrer la création artistique dans le processus même de production', one economic role of the artist being to help sell French products by ensuring that they are aesthetically pleasing. He does acknowledge Eco's point and considers whether it is not a misunderstanding of the function of art to harness the artist to the cause of social progress in this way; but he soon reassures himself that creators will be free to choose whether to 'répondre à l'attente qui se manifeste à leur égard'. Nevertheless, as Derrida and Eco had recognised, this potentially instrumental conception was the central problem behind the whole culture and economy dialectic. 'Les Intellos au boulot!', read a *Libération* headline in response to Gallo's piece in *Le Monde*.[42]

Shortly after the colloquium, changes of a different kind came about. In the municipal elections of 6 and 13 March 1983, the Socialists lost a number of their flagship councils, whose cultural policies were in a number of cases swiftly dismantled. Furthermore, after a first wave of austerity measures the previous June, Jacques Delors announced on 24 March an even more draconian package including further devaluation, so that the 1 per cent for Culture was again postponed. But March had worse in store for Lang personally, for the municipals were followed by a Cabinet reshuffle in which he was demoted to *ministre délégué*, which removed his automatic right to sit on the Council of Ministers, though it was not clear whether this was as a result of mistakes made (*Libération* blamed the 'pantalonnade de la Sorbonne'[43]) or of the need for a leaner cabinet. The Ministry for Free Time too was demoted and merged with Jeunesse et Sports under Edwige Avice, also a *ministre déléguée*. Communication became a *secrétariat d'Etat* answerable to the Prime Minister, though still under Fillioud. Lang's ministry did at least remain autonomous, however, and culture also remained a priority in the 1984 budget despite the austerity measures, though Lang was obliged to look for more aid from local authorities and private sponsorship.

In the last chapter and this one, I have looked at PS theories regarding cultural policy: at what influenced them and at how they evolved, first between 1974 and 1981 and then between the May 1981 victory and the turning point of 1983. In the following three chapters, I shall examine how this set of somewhat heterogeneous and potentially conflicting principles affected the policies themselves, where change had in fact already begun the year before. The policies are divided – somewhat artificially but for convenience – into those for high culture, those concerned with wider forms of cultural practice, and the President's *grands projets*.

Notes

1. Interview with Agence France Presse, 18 June 1981.
2. Interview with *Le Quotidien de Paris*, 1 June 1981, p.16.
3. Interview with *Les Nouvelles Littéraires*, 4–11 June 1981, p.16.
4. Interview with *Le Monde*, 5 September 1981, p.8.
5. Décret 81–646, *Journal Officiel*, 6 June 1981.
6. P. Ory, 'La Politique du ministère Jack Lang: un premier bilan', *French Review*, vol.58, no.1, October 1984, p.80.
7. All 3 brief quotations are from an interview with Lang, *Le Matin*, 18 June 1981, p.7. See also *Playboy* (édition française), September 1981, pp.21–103 *passim*.
8. Quoted in *L'Est Républicain*, 8 September 1981.
9. *Le Monde*, 17 September 1981, p.23.
10. *Journal du Dimanche*, 6 September 1981.
11. On the government's international cultural policy, see J. Forbes, 'Cultural policy: the soul of man under Socialism', in S. Mazey and M. Newman (eds), *Mitterrand's France*, London, 1987, pp.141–5.
12. Lang's June remarks are from Agence France Presse, 18 June 1981; *Playboy*, p.22.
13. Typed Ministry transcript of the Cotonou speech dated 18 September 1981.
14. Speech published as 'Intervention de M. Jack Lang, ministre de la Culture', in *Après-Demain*, no.250, January 1983, pp.4–7 (quotations pp.5–6).
15. Bazin, Jelloun and Finkielkraut are quoted in *Le Nouvel Observateur, En France aujourd'hui: idées, arts, spectacle*, Paris, 1987, pp.14–15. Lévy's comments were quoted by J. Garcin in a TV interview with Lang, 'Ouvert le dimanche', FR3, 12 September 1982, from an article in *Le Matin* [3 August 1982]. In *Le Quotidien de Paris*, 8 March 1983, p.35, Lévy again singled out Lang as the

exponent of a 'social-nationalist' line drawing its inspiration from 'la tradition intellectuelle du pétainisme'. *Royaliste*'s discussion of the Mexico speech is in 'Faut-il brûler Jack Lang?', 16–29 September 1982, pp.6–7.

16. See for example his interview '"Je ne suis pas un ayatollah!"', *L'Express*, 10 September 1982, pp.8–11.
17. Konopnicki, *Le Monde*, 7 August 1982, p.2.
18. Vitez's comments appear in Lang and Bredin, *Eclats*, Paris, 1978, pp.208–9. Lang's 1978 comment appears in *Le Monde*, 28 February 1978, p.1. The last quotation is from Agence France Presse, 18 June 1981 (the inner quotation is from Mitterrand).
19. Budget details are from various sources, in particular Ministère de l'économie et des finances, 'Projet de loi de finances: budget de la culture', *Les Notes Bleues*, no.43; *Le Monde*, 17 November 1981, p.27; and *Libération*, 18 November 1981. The increase included some 200MF for the newly transferred BN, without which Culture's share of the state budget stood at 0.73 per cent. I use 'billion' in the sense of 1,000 million throughout.
20. P. Favier and M. Martin-Roland, *La Décennie Mitterrand*, Paris, 1990, vol.1, pp.49–61. The July Cabinet meeting is reported in 'Un Effort pour la recherche et la culture', *Le Figaro*, 24 July 1981. I have used a typed Ministry transcript of Lang's speech headed 'Discours prononcé par M. Jack Lang, Ministre de la Culture, à l'Assemblée Nationale le mardi 17 novembre 1981, lors de la Session Budgétaire' (my quotation here is from p.3), since the version reproduced in the *Journal Officiel* (2ᵉ séance du 17 novembre 1981, pp.3,870–3) is apparently abridged: it does not, for example, contain the notorious claim that 'les Français ont franchi la frontière qui sépare la nuit de la lumière' (p.1 of transcript). Future references to the transcript in this chapter will appear in the text.
21. *Playboy*, September 1981, p.103.
22. 'Intervention de M. J. Lang', *Après-Demain*, January 1983, p.7.
23. Interview with *Le Monde*, 5 September 1981, p.8.
24. Décret no.82–394, 10 May 1982, *Journal Officiel*, 1 May 1982, p.1,346. Sallois is quoted in Foulon, 'André Malraux, Ministre d'Etat et le Ministère des affaires culturelles (1959–1969)', in Institut Charles de Gaulle, *De Gaulle et Malraux*, Paris, 1986, p.239. Lang later told Foulon that the decree had been drafted some 40 times and that he would not personally have worded it in this exact form. See also P. Ory, 'La Politique du ministère Jack Lang', on the early ideology of PS cultural policy and its influences, especially pp.77–80.

25. 'De Malraux à Lang: l'excroissance des Affaires culturelles', *Commentaire*, no.18, summer 1982, p.256.
26. *Le Matin*, 8 January 1982; *Le Monde*, 19 November 1981, p.1.
27. 'La Culture par la joie', *Libération*, 18 November 1981.
28. Pinto, 'The Left, the intellectuals and culture', in Ross, Hoffmann and Malzacher, *The Mitterrand Experiment: Continuity and Change in Modern France*, Oxford, 1987, p.217; Gallo, 'Les Intellectuels, la politique et la modernité', *Le Monde*, 26 July 1983, p.7. Gallo's article was followed by two more under the heading 'Le Silence des intellectuels de gauche', both by P. Boggio, surveying intellectuals' attitudes to the government, 27 and 28 July 1983, pp.1 and 6, and p.6 respectively. A series of responses from intellectuals was then published over the following months.
29. Clément, *Rêver chacun pour l'autre*, Paris, 1982.
30. Bredin, 'Les Intellectuels et le pouvoir socialiste', *Le Monde*, 22 December 1981, pp.1 and 22. K. Reader identifies further factors to explain the intellectuals' distance, including the '"decentralising" tendencies of May' and 'the perceived shortcomings of Theory', *Intellectuals and the Left in France since 1968*, Basingstoke, 1987, p.139.
31. Finkielkraut is quoted by Boggio, *Le Monde*, 27 July 1983, p.6; Baudrillard, *Le Monde*, 21 September 1983, pp.1 and 10.
32. Lang is quoted respectively in *Le Monde*, 22 December 1981, p.5, and *Les Nouvelles Littéraires*, 28 October 1982, p.12.
33. Pinto, 'The Left', p.223.
34. *Le Monde*, 10 August 1983, p.6.
35. Jospin quoted in *Le Monde*, 27 August 1983, p.7.
36. Commissariat général du Plan (Marc Guillaume), *L'Impératif culturel*, Paris, 1982.
37. The contributions to the colloquium were collected in *Le Complexe de Léonard ou la société de création*, Paris [1984]. The quotations from Mitterrand are from pp.365 and 367.
38. *Libération*, 14 February 1983.
39. See interview with Lang, *Les Nouvelles Littéraires*, 28 October 1982, p.12.
40. *Le Complexe de Léonard*, p.369.
41. Ibid.: Derrida, pp.77–92 (quotation p.92); Eco, pp.57–60 (quotation p.57).
42. Renard, *L'Elan culturel: la France en mouvement*, Paris, 1987, pp.20–9 (quotations pp.21 and 29). 'Les Intellos au boulot!', *Libération*, [26] July 1983, quoted in *Le Monde*, 27 July 1983, p.6.
43. G. Dupuy, 'Sous le corset, la peau', *Libération*, 24 March 1983.

– 5 –

Policies for High Culture: *la création dans la cité*

In July 1981, Guy Hocquenghem, noting that Socialist cultural policy had so far produced only symbolic gestures, attempted to extrapolate from them a philosophy. He concluded that a traditional interpretation of culture had come to power which would exert a 'dictatorship' over the new, audiovisual forms of today. Personified respectively in Mitterrand and Lang, books and theatre were the only real cultural paradigms of the Left, he contended: 'les seuls auxquels le poids des ans, la poussière des bibliothèques, la tradition de l'Antiquité aient donné leur poids d'humanisme. Arts "naturels", où nulle technologie (suspecte de froid cynisme) ne s'interpose, qui s'éloignent de l'immédiateté consommatrice propre au cinéma ou à la télévision.' He then summarised the links between this humanism and the whole public-service tradition of Vilar, Laurent and Malraux.[1] Although time was to prove him wrong in some important ways, Hocquenghem's piece today is a useful reminder of the old-Left, old-fashioned, high-cultural image PS policies had in 1981 and of the parentage they shared with Gaullism.

On one level at least, the government too cast itself in this tradition, as the President's appearance at Avignon indicates. Despite all the talk of radical change, therefore, Malraux's heritage-democratisation-creation trilogy was not fundamentally questioned and, like the Gaullian decade, Lang's first ten years were to see considerable advances in high-cultural facilities. The network of departmental BCPs begun in 1945 was completed to improve access to books; new establishments called Centres de développement culturel were added to the existing EACs, while the network of CDNs and comparable establishments increased from twenty-three to forty-two between 1981 and 1990. The ten-year Landowski plan for music bore fruit and was extended, bringing significant increases in the number of national schools of music and Conservatoires nationaux de région, while new orchestras were set up in several regions. A new Agence pour le développement régional du cinéma in 1983 helped more than 600 local cinemas open or be renovated, and so on. And of course, with the doubled budget, the funds available to these and other decentralised establishments were greatly increased.[2]

Nor was *le patrimoine* neglected to the extent the opposition was increasingly to make out. 78 museums were opened or renovated with over 200 more in gestation. A vast number of new monuments was listed and the listing procedure deconcentrated to the regions, with consultative commissions called 'COREPHAE' set up to give local people a say in the process. Additionally, Lang continued to widen the definition of the heritage as Malraux had already begun to do. Ethnological artefacts (industrial, rural, maritime) were included within it as recommended by the Querrien report of 1982, and so were a number of examples of twentieth-century architecture.[3] He also attempted to widen access to it by various forms of popularisation and *mise en valeur*: improved opening hours, the use of audiovisual aids and better explanatory documentation, free entry to monuments for schoolchildren, and so on. The launch of the yearly Journée portes ouvertes dans les monuments historiques in 1984, which threw open the Elysée palace and a number of other historic buildings for a day, was also an instant success and by 1990 was drawing some two million visitors.

All the same, *le patrimoine* was undoubtedly not the priority it had been for Malraux, as evidenced in the fact that the doubling of the budget in 1982 did not bring about a corresponding doubling for historic monuments until almost ten years later. The justification for this was that, as an official review of France in 1981 by François Bloch-Lainé pointed out, the Giscard years had already given quite enough emphasis to the heritage at the expense of new work.[4] What distinguished Socialist high-cultural policies in fact was that the approach to both of Malraux's priorities, the heritage and democratisation, was slanted towards the objective he had probably pursued least: creation.

The question of high-cultural creation was still a complex one for the PS in 1981 because of its earlier insistence on placing community work and popular creativity above what it had still insisted on calling the *beaux-arts*. For although it had now reversed this hierarchy, it was not yet ready to discard the community ethic completely. The result was a compromise, summed up in the Rennes and Avignon colloquia formulation, 'la création artistique dans la cité'. Creation was now accepted as 'une valeur irremplaçable' but artists were still tacitly expected to be in some obscure sense useful, or at least integrated, in touch with their community and aware of their civic function. Accordingly, Lang emphasised in his budget speech that creation and decentralisation were to be twin priorities. 'Un ministre de la culture n'est pas un ministre des "artistes"', he even proclaimed in 1981, 'mais un militant au service de tous.'[5] In practice, however, 'la création dans la cité' was more problematic than it looked, quite simply because of the inescapable clash between established tastes and artistic innovation. As *L'Impératif culturel* pointed out, 'le créateur ne se pose qu'en s'opposant à des formes, une sensibilité, des valeurs qui paraissent acquises'. Of course, by interrogating accepted cultural norms in this way, Guillaume went on to stress, living artists can still make a valuable contribution to social change and preserve a community from immobilism, as long as they are in a position to grapple with those norms as embodied in an average audience.[6] But however reciprocal the need may be in theory between the creator and the community, if contemporary creation does go against the dominant culture, it is unlikely to be understood or welcomed and may not therefore find the audience it requires to retain a *raison d'être*. This was no doubt the greatest of a number of paradoxes the idea encountered when it was implemented.

Putting creation back into the community took a variety of forms but can best be illustrated in three sectors: books and theatre as Hocquenghem correctly observed, and the visual or plastic arts. After 1981, the mechanisms for aiding creation established since 1959 were generally maintained or extended: grants to novelists, poets and composers to enable them to take sabbatical leave; financial assistance with mounting exhibitions or to remedy the shortage of studio space; state prizes or the purchase and commissioning of new work. The Socialists' chief originality here lay simply in increasing the budget for such operations. Lang also updated less direct forms of aid, reviving the Popular Front's endeavours to demarginalise artists by improving their rights and benefits, as with an important act passed on 3 July 1985 concerning *les droits des artistes-interprètes*, which both modernised and considerably extended the range of the 1957 legislation on copyright, long since overtaken by advances in communications and reproduction technology.[7] A third form of aid to creation involved tackling *diffusion*, as book policy amply demonstrates.

Books and public reading were one of main planks of the PS's electoral programme for culture. This was partly because the book industry was in trouble during the 1970s, as audiovisual leisure took over from the paperback revolution of the 1950s and 1960s and as Giscard's economic liberalism began to bite. Public reading was in fact one of the neglected areas of cultural policy identified in the Bloch-

Lainé report. But books and libraries were also integral to the Left's whole tradition of democratisation and popular education. 'Nous menons ce combat', declared the Socialist deputy Rodolphe Pesce at a colloquium in Valence on the subject in January 1981, 'parce que le livre reste un élément fondamental de notre culture. Il est associé à la lutte pour les libertés, pour l'éducation, pour la démocratie et pour l'indépendance et l'identité culturelle nationale.'[8] Under Jean Gattégno, the Book directorate, now called the Direction du livre et de la lecture (DLL), increased aid to new writing and publishing via the CNL and tackled the nation's lamentable library provision by helping increase the number of municipal libraries by over 50 per cent in six years, while the new BCPs raised the numbers served by the network by ten million.[9] But the library shortage also made it essential to preserve France's dense network of bookshops. This was the purpose of Lang's very first bill, which abolished the 'arrêté Monory' of 1979 freeing book prices and replaced it with a mandatory single price system, the *prix unique du livre.*

One of the few general priorities Lang had been prepared to disclose in his very early interviews as Minister was the need to 'corriger les lois du marché', which rule 'la production de la pensée' and treat cultural forms as commercial products.[10] Book-pricing was an ideal example. It was also an illustration of how far new writing was dependent on *diffusion*: 'Au centre de ce débat', Lang told the Senate when presenting his bill, 'c'est l'avenir de la création littéraire en France qui est en cause.'[11] Monory's measure was proving disastrous for the small or medium-sized bookseller. Under the previous *prix conseillé* system, the publisher had made known a recommended cover price, on which a bookseller might offer a discount of around 10 per cent to selected customers. But in the mid–1970s, the market began to change as the traditional specialist booksellers came into competition with more modern outlets: book-clubs, the self-service leisure chain FNAC, even hypermarkets and department stores. Because of their turnover, these retailers were able to buy in bulk, receive a generous discount and, in the large conurbations where demand was high, pass it on to customers by offering 20 per cent, sometimes 40 per cent rebates, undercutting the smaller specialists who could not buy in such quantity. Under pressure from some sectors of the industry, Monory responded by applying free-market principles, allowing all distributors to set prices themselves. This only made matters worse. Best sellers tended to go down in price whereas books classed as slow sellers went up. For the first time in ten years, prices rose in 1980 by some 16 per cent as against a 13.2 per cent rise in the general cost of living.[12] Furthermore, the new uncertainty about how much to pay meant customers were no longer impulse-buying, or were simply not buying at all. Hence a fall in the turnover of bookshops and publishers in 1980 and in the number of books printed. The virtue of the smaller specialist retailers is the width of their stock. Supermarkets and department stores tend to concentrate on best sellers to be sure of a rapid turnover. But the smaller suppliers stock both best sellers and a selection of other books in print, the cost of providing this service being offset by their sales of best sellers. If their customers buy these elsewhere, this delicate economy breaks down and shops close. According to the abstract laws of market forces, this is simply a case of the weakest going to the wall, but to the PS it showed up the limits of applying a narrowly commercial reasoning to a cultural artefact. For Monory meant concentration not only of distribution but of production too, affecting literary output itself. Because of their wide stock, the smaller independents offer a lifeline to the more experimental or specialised publishing houses which are prepared to take a risk with young unknowns or slow sellers such as scholarly works or poetry. They also provide a service to readers based on the expertise of the staff, who are able to advise on quality and in some cases guide them to the less publicised new editions. It was this diversity in terms of both *diffusion* and *création* that the new government was bent on protecting. Its stand was neither original nor heroic, since the alternatives to Monory were few and its opponents many, including the major presidential candidates save Giscard.[13]

The government had hoped to introduce the measure by decree but this posed a number of legal difficulties, so a bill was hastily tabled. This did away with both Monory and the *prix conseillé*. The publisher determines the retail price of a book and outlets across the country are allowed a 5 per cent margin of flexibility. Although the 'Loi Lang' received almost unanimous support in Parliament with few amendments, its true significance for the Socialists was ideological. It placed the cultural value of the book above its value as a commodity; it said that small was beautiful; and it rejected the industrialisation of literature which turned writers into 'des robots produisant à la chaîne des quantités calibrées de textes commandés pour répondre à un besoin de consommation connu d'avance'.[14] It was an unashamedly interventionist step designed to democratise books, preserve France's literary heritage and protect contemporary creation all in one go.

The law, however, which came into effect from 1 January 1982, was not without its opponents or its paradoxes. Many in publishing and retail welcomed it, while naturally the three biggest booksellers, the FNAC and the supermarket chains Leclerc and Carrefour, were utterly opposed to it. The FNAC's managing director André Essel argued that, as 60 to 70 per cent of the public buy at discount through clubs, mass outlets, or bookshops offering reductions and would now have to pay more, there would inevitably be a decline in sales and therefore in the publishing industry.[15] Some also feared that, with pricing power transferred to the publishers, prices would rise even further. These misgivings proved largely unfounded; but they accentuated the paradox of a law which sought to democratise access by increasing prices and penalising those distributors like the FNAC who had unquestionably demystified books and introduced them to a wider public. The Centres Leclerc began enthusiastically flouting it, claiming it went against European legislation. However, further campaigns of non-application and legal manoeuvrings eventually brought about a ruling by the European Court of Justice in 1985 which confirmed France's right to legislate and the act's general conformity, after minor adjustments, with the Treaty of Rome. In 1986, the new Chirac government did not undo the act and by its tenth anniversary it was widely accepted, though small bookshops were still disappearing. In 1992, Jean Gattégno took the view that a true assessment of the *prix unique* was difficult because indicators were not objective, but that those bookshops which were in a position to modernise had been saved by it, whereas those which never were commercially viable did not become so. Meanwhile, some distributors continued to find ways round the legislation and by 1993 the Ministry was gloomily anticipating that the need to harmonise legislation as a result of the single European market would start up another offensive.[16]

Another, more controversial effort to bring new creative work into communities involved the plastic arts. According to Bloch-Lainé, this was another sector where creation had been neglected, the budget for state commissions being particularly inadequate.[17] Lang's purpose in creating a new directorate to replace the Délégation à la création in October 1982, the Délégation aux arts plastiques (DAP), was to repair this neglect and under Claude Mollard's stewardship the DAP became an emblem of a whole new philosophy. To assist it, a new *établissement public* was also set up, the Centre national des arts plastiques (CNAP), which became the main vehicle for creation and decentralisation policies. The CNAP proved particularly innovative in throwing open the Ministry's doors to previously ignored forms of visual art,[18] but it was equally enterprising in assisting the more traditional high-cultural disciplines like painting and sculpture. The mechanisms for aid to creation and *diffusion* in the regions were considerably diversified in the early years: a partly deconcentrated Fonds d'incitation à la création (FIACRE) created in 1982 to provide direct aid to projects of an experimental nature; newly created Centres d'art (thirty or so by 1992) which undertook exhibitions, colloquia and other activities; some forty '*artothèques*' which aimed to loan contemporary works to organisations and in some cases the general public; and, to help operate these new regional initiatives, a team of twenty-two regional artistic advisors (*conseillers artistiques régionaux*) appointed to the DRACs. But the CNAP's most remarkable initiatives concerned state purchases and commissions.

Under Lang, the Ministry's acquisitions budget rose from an initial 5.55 million francs to 33.56 million in 1985.[19] One beneficiary was an existing structure taken over by the CNAP, the Fonds national d'art contemporain (*le FNAC*), which acquires recent work for the state to be circulated among various national institutions including embassies, ministries and, more recently, provincial museums. But in order to decentralise acquisitions procedures, the Ministry created two further funds in 1982: the Fonds régionaux d'acquisition des musées (FRAMs) and the Fonds régionaux d'art contemporain (FRACs). Both are co-financed by state and region and according to Mesnard have transformed the regional landscape, particularly the FRACs, which assist contemporary art by exclusively purchasing work by living artists – in some cases local, in others national or international – and familiarising the local public with it by travelling exhibitions, *animation*, loans of work to local institutions, and so on. The FRACs have also contributed to creating a nation-wide rather than simply Parisian art market. By 1992, some 8,500 paintings, photographs and other artefacts by around 2,000 artists had been acquired and made available outside the established network of museums.[20]

The FRACs were not always seen positively, however. Some felt they were diverting resources and decision-making away from the existing museums and galleries which were better equipped to make purchasing decisions. Others argued that they sustained the art market artificially.[21] But there was also friction caused by aesthetic differences. Mesnard considers that, as mostly 1901 associations, the FRACs are more deconcentrated than fully decentralised, for the DRACs play an active part in their management. The state-appointed regional artistic advisor generally proposes work for consideration by a committee of experts, which then advises the fund's governing board (*conseil d'administration*) composed of a majority of local councillors, the latter body usually ratifying the experts' recommendations. But sometimes, particularly in the early stages, this led to conflict between artistically conservative local representatives on the governing board, often interested in buying only rather conventional work by regional artists, and those on the committee of experts who were enthusiasts of aesthetic experimentation or fashions in the international art world, with some local officials complaining of being pressured by the Ministry into going along with the experts' choices. In one case, the FRAC Franche-Comté, it took two years for local- and central-government officials even to agree on the composition of the committee of experts, while the FRAC Ile-de-France had its state subsidy withdrawn by Mollard because of the failure of the experts, the *conseil d'administration* and the DAP to agree on its artistic policy.[22] Many other FRACs, however, were set up reasonably successfully, albeit with somewhat uneven results in terms of the artistic merit of the collections assembled.

The Lang ministry also prided itself on reviving the tradition of state commissions (*commandes*), which had all but died out since the early days of the Third Republic, other than in the shape of the '1 per cent for art' mechanism set up in 1951. Acting on a forgotten recommendation of the Sixth Plan, Lang began by extending this mechanism to virtually all public-building work subsidised by the state and, after the decentralisation law of 22 July 1983, by local authorities as well. Then, in 1983, a new commissioning procedure was devised, the Fonds d'aide à la commande publique, initially for Paris but later used to help local authorities undertake their own commissions. The purpose of the fund, which had increased sixfold by 1989, was to take contemporary art out of the gallery and into the community. This was mostly done by commissioning sculptures, usually of well known public figures in the first years, for a variety of outdoor settings: parks, squares, stations, deprived urban areas. The style of such works was seldom conventional and often encountered public disapproval. But the fund was at its most controversial when the setting in question was a cherished historic monument, as was frequently the case.

In reality, state commissions are provocative by their very nature. Firstly, as Claude Mollard has pointed out, they bring contemporary art into people's daily field of vision while at the same time freeing the artist to be more daring than museum display allows.[23] Secondly, any policy of state aid to living artists raises difficult issues about which artists to choose and what criteria to adopt when choosing. Who is to judge what is today's great art? How can the state avoid developing an 'official art' by imposing its own taste? And lastly, as the CNRS specialist Raymonde Moulin asks, 'faut-il donner aux contribuables ce qu'ils ont envie de voir ou quelque chose pour lequel ils ne sont pas prêts?' Where the purchase of existing work is concerned, the FIACRE or *le FNAC* are guided by expert committees as the FRACs are (though Moulin also wonders how expertise can really be defined here). But Mesnard maintains that commissioning a work which does not yet exist is a different matter entirely, for it is, as the presidential *grands projets* amply testify, much more a deliberate affirmation of a state style.[24] Under the Socialists, this was all the more apparent because of increased presidential and ministerial intervention in culture generally and because the works commissioned often appeared defiantly avant-garde, as if intended to convey a politico-aesthetic message about the dawning of a new age. But when, to boot, such work was selected to grace a loved and supposedly timeless monument, there was more often than not a hue and cry.

One of the most notorious instances of this were the 'Colonnes Buren', erected in the *cour d'honneur* of the Palais Royal.[25] The courtyard, adjacent to an historic formal garden and framed by the elegant colonnades and archways of the Conseil d'Etat, the Comédie Française and the Ministry of Culture itself, was state property and, since it was being used only as a car-park, seemed an ideal site for an exemplary commission. But the plan for a series of sculptures by contemporary artists in both courtyard and garden soon encountered resistance. First, the design submitted for the courtyard specifically was rejected by the Commission supérieure des monuments historiques. The Ministry then approached Daniel Buren, whose subsequent proposal was chosen by Mitterrand personally. Buren's sculpture was to fill the 3,000m² courtyard with a base composed of asphalt squares each containing at its centre a truncated column, all of which would exactly reproduce the diameter and spacing of the existing colonnades. Taller columns would also protrude from three sloping trenches dug below ground level along which water would flow. Like Buren's previous work, all the columns would be adorned with vertical stripes, in this case black and white, and the entire construction was to have a formal geometry in keeping with the linear, repetitive composition of the site (see Figure 2).

The historic monuments commission rejected this design too. The Minister, however, was not obliged to heed its recommendations and this time chose not to. His decision occasioned a flurry of opposition in December 1985 when the model of the project was exhibited at the CNAP. Those living near the site, led by a representative of the Société pour la protection des paysages et de l'esthétique de la France, submitted the case to the administrative tribunal. The RPR leader Jacques Chirac also became involved as Mayor, which automatically politicised the affair only two months before the forthcoming general election. The real issue, however, was not political, nor even aesthetic in the strict sense, but patrimonial.

What most of Buren's opponents objected to was the incongruity of locating a challenging new sculpture in an historically significant

Figure 2. The Colonnes Buren (architect: D. Buren). © Philippe Delacroix. Source: Ministère de la culture et de la francophonie.

setting. Some, for example, suggested that it might be perfectly appropriate in a modern location like La Défense or one of the new towns. But as Buren himself recognised, this argument merely placed creation in a ghetto hermetically distinct from the evidently more respectable and respected heritage, when the real question was how that heritage ought in fact to be 'respected'. For many, this simply meant not tampering with it. But Buren and others pointed out that not even the Palais Royal had been respected in this sense and that to do so would be to mummify the heritage, whereas to call on contemporary artists to work in an historic site was to have a true sense of history, 'vivre et faire vivre le passé'. 'Il me paraît évident', wrote Mollard, 'qu'au Palais Royal, l'œuvre des artistes, si elle s'inscrit dans un espace, se trouve aussi confrontée au passé du lieu, et à son avenir.' What was ultimately in question, then, was a conviction that for contemporary creation truly to have a place in the community, it must be allowed to interpellate the community's past, to reinterpret and revivify an inherited urban environment which has become, as Mollard put it, 'le champ ordinaire de la vie sociale, banalisé, aseptisé'.[26] Today, as passers-by weave through the completed columns or leapfrog over them, sit on them to contemplate the classical architecture which frames them or watch children fishing coins from the sunken trenches, it is difficult not to conclude that this conviction was well founded.

Behind such debates lay a more complex problem, outlined by Robert Wangermée in the Council of Europe's 1988 report on French cultural policy. Unlike the early 1900s, when the burgeoning modernist movement was championed by great private buyers like Daniel-Henri Kahnweiler, the late twentieth century is characterised by the absence of a coherent avant-garde. This places an especial burden on the limited circle of today's buyers responsible for purchasing work for the proliferating number of public institutions such as museums or FRACs, who, rather than being champions of an existing movement like Kahnweiler, find themselves arbiters of artistic value. For official acquisitions are now the chief means of recognition for contemporary work, and public institutions and private galleries tend to form a closed circuit of mutual influence which in turn influences individual collectors.[27] This burden has been made all the greater by what might be described as the Caillebotte neurosis: the dread of letting significant new work slip through the state's net. One consequence of it is that too much credit is given to whatever is spectacularly new, to the exclusion of more classical or less recognisably innovative styles, which means that the art market is inevitably skewed. This has led some to identify a new 'academicism of the avant-garde' and a recentralisation of artistic legitimation, neither of which chimes with the original notion of putting creation back into communities. Nevertheless, where state intervention has succeeded according to Wangermée is that by maintaining a domestic 'assisted market' in a sector where a free market was virtually non-existent, it has stimulated a regional demand, as well as a market abroad among private collectors and museums, though he acknowledges the risk that such aid might merely become a form of welfare provision for struggling artists.[28]

A comparable problem arose in another area in which the government endeavoured to restore the community function of creation: the theatre and the EACs. Much of the system of aid to creation here dates back to Malraux or Laurent. It includes grants to playwrights, commissions to companies and grants to encourage them to mount innovative new productions. In addition to the public sector (national theatres, CDNs and numerous 'independent companies'), the state also offers assistance to commercial theatres to encourage them to depart from safe Boulevard material which is often little more than a star vehicle, by means of Malraux's Fonds d'aide au théâtre privé. In some cases, as with the CDNs, state aid may include a requirement to put on newly written work. This is an attempt to remedy the dearth of new playwrights which has come about since the 1960s, hand in hand (whether as cause or effect) with the tendency mentioned earlier for directors to become creators in their own right and lose sight of their role in the community.

By 1981 a number of CDNs had indeed drifted away from the Laurentian model of a light, mobile company regularly mounting new productions and *animation* activities in its home town and surrounding area. Instead, a new production often did not involve a permanent company at all (costly and restrictive of a director's freedom) but actors on a short-term engagement, including an expensive Parisian star for a key role. Ever more complex sets also imposed constraints on touring. These developments irritated Jeanne Laurent who soon after 10 May wrote an open letter to Lang which argued that such practices laid CDN directors open to the charge of being more concerned with their own power and Parisian standing than with genuine decentralisation.[29] A not dissimilar evolution took place in the MCs too, most of which were still based on theatre. Both types of establishment were also experiencing rising operating costs with increasing professionalisation, while the government cutbacks in the late 1970s had only worsened their financial plight. Thus, in the subsidised sector generally, while democratisation and *animation* were being sacrificed, creations too were becoming rarer and dearer.

Although Laurent was accused of taking a nostalgic view of decentralisation, her position seemed to match the government's own and her letter was dutifully circulated to CDNs and the smaller independent companies also receiving subsidy. Lang expressed his intention to reassert 'l'idée simple et saine de Jeanne Laurent' and remoralise decentralised theatre by restoring its 'civic', 'educative' purpose. He also spoke passionately of the two lessons he drew from her work and from that of Dasté: a refusal of Parisian domination of taste and the absolute right of creators to 'vivre et travailler au pays'.[30] Appropriate policies were elaborated with his advisor on theatre and *action culturelle*, Robert Abirached, who in September 1981 became head of the Direction du théâtre et des spectacles (DTS). Against Abirached's own wishes, however, and those of the SYNDEAC which represents the directors of EACs and CDNs, he did not regain the EACs, which had been taken out of the DTS by Lecat and were soon to come under Dominique Wallon's new directorate for *développement culturel*. Abirached sees this as an error resulting from the divorce between creation and community action and one which merely exacerbated it.[31]

Nevertheless, when the first measures were announced, the will to return theatrical creation to the community still seemed very much in evidence. An increase of some 80 per cent in the overall theatre budget for 1982 was obtained, with creation and decentralisation again the priorities. In the summer, Lang's new appointments to decentralised establishments followed Guy's example of promoting promising young creative directors, though some of the appointments had been in the offing under Giscard.[32] New decentralisation measures unveiled in October included an average 40 to 50 per cent increase for the CDNs, to restore their 'moyens de création' and help them set up permanent troupes, the only condition being that their aesthetic experimentation be compatible with their public-service mission. For some, like Jérôme Savary, such strings after years of penury were 'aussi douces que de la crème de chantilly sur un "pet de nonne"'.[33] But this rediscovery of the lost values of Laurent was soon to assume some unexpected forms, as Vilar's public-service ideal became identified with better quality control and a more market-oriented conception of their operation.

The triennial contracts system in use in the CDNs since 1972 was extended to the established independent companies, while the others were subject to more stringent regulations to prevent their receiving grants irrespective of quality. As for the CDNs themselves, a new *contrat-type de décentralisation dramatique* was introduced in December 1984 which revised the 1972 contracts but reiterated the injunction to mount a certain number of new productions, plays and performances in the regions. It also required a CDN to earn at least 20 per cent of its overall budget from the box-office (the proportion had fallen as low as 10 per cent in some cases) and to restrict administrative and technical costs to a maximum of half that budget. A comparable approach was applied to other performing arts. Measures were devised to help orchestras or opera houses cut production costs, improve their managerial efficiency and marketing, and attract private-sector finance. A special body was set up in 1982 to further these objectives in the public sector generally, the Association pour la gestion des entreprises culturelles (AGEC). This developed regional structures to help cultural establishments find new sources of funding from private sponsorship, while from 1988 the Ministry also encouraged them to seek expert advice on management and promotional skills from outside agencies by defraying part of the cost.

In the fifteen MCs and thirty-eight CACs, essentially similar reforms proved more controversial. By 1981, the cultural landscape in the regions was unrecognisable in comparison with the 1960s. Competing with younger or more flexible forms of *action culturelle* and the rising audiovisual media, wrestling with the government cuts and their inflated administrative costs, some EACs had become little more than receiving-houses. Cumbersome and grandiose, the MCs in particular were increasingly viewed as budget-hungry dinosaurs. In an interview in July 1983, Lang's irritation at the way they were monopolising cultural debate with their 'vieille querelle post soixante-huitarde' was patent. His policy, modelled on his success with the theatre sector generally, was, he said, to transform them from the inside by placing each one in the care of 'une personnalité forte', which in practice meant a new, nationally known creator capable of giving an MC a clear artistic identity.[34] The Puaux report on the EACs, published in Paris the previous year, had similarly recommended placing creation above *animation*, which would also entail redefining their statutes and managerial standards. This was eventually done by focusing on a new, finite 'cultural and artistic project' for each establishment, a detailed creative and financial plan drawn up by a candidate for the directorship of an EAC and submitted for consideration as a possible basis for a contractual agreement to a jury of state and local representatives.

One implication of the notion of the project was that it made the director personally responsible for his or her 'product'. But this came up against a structural difficulty since it was an EAC's local management association, not its director, which was responsible for the institution's budget. The attempt to revise the EACs' statutes accordingly was to cause some friction between the Ministry and the SYNDEAC on the one hand, and the body representing the associations, the Union des Maisons de la culture (UMC), on the other. The SYNDEAC had been pressing for some time for the EACs to be put firmly in the hands of their directors, who had often begun their careers in the turbulent 1960s and now feared that the PS government's decentralisation laws of 1982 and 1983 would place them even more at the mercy of local authorities with a different conception of the EACs' mission. The directors therefore expected prompt central-government reform, much as they had in 1968, to protect them from provincialism. Their fears appeared to prove justified after the Right regained a number of municipalities in March 1983. While some new councils like Avignon and Grenoble merely carried on as before, in others contracts were rescinded, budgets slashed, and there were even closures. The reasons often related to the local history of the establishments concerned but in general inadequate management was cited, as were unjustified costs, Marxist bias, and – most significantly – the elitism or avant-garde impenetrability of the creative work being produced. Local protests and a national movement initiated by Antoine Vitez had little effect. Although this was the last of the major ideological clashes concerning the EACs, it brought out even more clearly the kind of conflicts which creation in the community could produce, and which the new contractual agreements were designed to address.

Two such agreements were drawn up, a long-term one defining the EACs' public-service obligations, and one for a limited period of three to four years which laid down each establishment's priorities. Apart from Lang's idea of appointing 'une personnalité artistique forte', the chief impact of the reform was to reduce the managerial powers of the local associations. Like Puaux, it stopped short of removing association status altogether as the SYNDEAC had urged, allowing instead for some flexibility in the type of legal status adopted. But it did nudge the EACs towards a more commercial conception of their role, turning directors into something closer to company managers by placing executive and budgetary authority squarely in their hands. Not surprisingly, it was generally welcomed by the directors themselves and, by spring 1986, 75 per cent of the EACs had accepted the new contracts.[35]

What in fact all these reforms in the performing arts were premised on was the idea of converting the conventionally subsidised institution into an *entreprise culturelle*, more akin to a private business. Since public funding was no longer given permanently to an institution but on the basis of a specific, finite undertaking, it became selective rather than automatic. In this way, the subsidised sector was to be kept on its toes by making creators rediscover a degree of competition, accountability and responsiveness to public demand, instead of languidly relying on a guaranteed income. In Renard's view, this was not simply to ensure the efficient deployment of taxpayers' money but a means of both stimulating creation and at the same time encouraging the sector to seek out a bigger public by such techniques as marketing, variable seat-pricing and sales to the audiovisual sector. Nor in his judgment was this variant of Lang's culture-economy argument incompatible with the Socialist ambition of cultural emancipation but rather indissociable from it.[36] Even so, it sat rather uncomfortably with the traditional discourse of democratisation.

The impact of the reforms was also somewhat equivocal. Clearly, better management and budgetary standards and a revival of a sense of purpose after the aimless 1970s were all necessary. But the longer-term effects have not always been consistent with the government's other objectives. One contradiction is identified in the Council of Europe report which considers that the 20 per cent rule imposed on CDNs has in practice acted as a deterrent to staging new work and has merely reinforced the recent tendency to reinterpret classics.[37] Conversely, some believe that fixed-term projects, the appointment of nationally known creators, and other devices like short-term residencies by dance or theatre companies in CDNs or MCs, have simply furthered the undermining of the notion of 'implantation', since a handful of 'consecrated' figures, usually with Parisian backgrounds or reputations, have regularly rotated among subsidised institutions as a matter of policy. Thus, it is argued, the Parisianism Lang spoke so passionately against in 1981 has remained as strong as ever – stronger in fact due to developments in transport like the TGV network which has had a marked recentralising effect.

There are also those who feel that the new emphasis on selectivity in funding, rather than encouraging an entrepreneurial responsiveness to demand, has failed to alter an existing inflationary spiral in both costs and aesthetics. According to the American economist William Baumol, the performing arts fall victim to an inflexible economic law which causes their production costs to rise faster than their income from the box-office, thereby creating a situation of structural deficit. As Alain Busson has shown, the natural result of this is for the theatre to rely ever more closely on public subsidy. This in his analysis leads to an ever greater aesthetic sophistication which generates either more spectacular and expensive productions intended to 'faire événement', or more self-consciously 'different', avant-garde ones. Both of these strategies are adopted solely in order to gain recognition, which is achieved not by winning over the public but by simply impressing one's peers in the profession and the powerful critics of the Parisian press. Both strategies therefore tend only to reinforce the trend towards an aestheticism turned in on itself, introducing an imbalance in the complex three-way relationship between creator, public and financial sponsors which traditionally regulates the economy of theatre, and giving the state as principal benefactor a subjective and arbitrary artistic power it should not possess.[38] Measures like the 20 per cent rule were of course designed to correct this imbalance and restore the public as interlocutor in this relationship. But although Busson agrees that this entrepreneurial discourse is being assimilated by the theatre world, he does not detect a fundamental break with past practices. Indeed, some even believe that the sudden increase in the theatre budget in 1982 may have exacerbated the inflationary trend.[39]

Clearly, then, the Socialists' 'création dans la cité' policy, moderately successful in the case of books and bookshops, inevitably ran into greater difficulty in the plastic arts and theatre, which involved the much more thorny matter of acclimatising the general public to contemporary high culture and vice versa. But in the meantime, the Ministry was also striving after a quite different conception of cultural democracy.

Notes

1. 'Les Culturocrates', *Libération*, 21 July 1981, pp.20–1 (quotation p.20).
2. All details are taken from the following Ministry of Culture documents: 'La Politique culturelle 1981–1985: bilan de la législature' (12 booklets); 'Les Orientations de la politique culturelle de Jack Lang', 1990; and 'La Politique culturelle 1981–1991', 1991 (12 booklets).
3. M. Querrien, *Pour une nouvelle politique du patrimoine*, Paris, 1982.
4. Commission du Bilan (F. Bloch-Lainé), *La France en mai 1981*, vol.3, p.299 and p.307.
5. Interview with Agence France Presse, 18 June 1981.
6. Commissariat général du Plan (M. Guillaume), *L'Impératif culturel*, Paris, 1982, pp.78–9 (quotation p.78).
7. For further details of legislation regarding creators and their rights, see the various booklets in Ministry, 'La Politique culturelle 1981–1985' (see 'Cinéma', pp.9–10 for the July 1985 law); also A.-H. Mesnard, *Droit et politique de la culture*, Paris, 1990, pp.394–400, and

R. Caron, *L'Etat et la culture*, Paris, 1989, pp.49–66.

8. Quoted in P. Parmantier, 'Feu le livre?', *Communes de France*, March 1981, p.23.

9. Ministry, 'La Politique culturelle 1981–1985': 'Le Livre et la lecture', pp.13–14; Lang's press conference, 24 May 1989, Ministry press dossier no.DP388, p.17.

10. Agence France Presse, 18 June 1981.

11. *Journal Officiel* (Sénat), séance du 29 juillet 1981, p.1,205.

12. Ibid., p.1,206, and Parmantier, 'Feu le livre?', p.22.

13. Even Giscard's replies on the matter in the run-up to the election suggested he was wavering. Mitterrand, however, prompted by Les Editions de Minuit's Jérôme Lindon, had been constant in his commitment to the *prix unique* since 1977, well before Monory's measure.

14. 'Dix Ans après une loi qui fait fureur!', supplement to a special Salon du Livre edition of the DLL's newsletter *Lettres* marking the 10th anniversary of the law, March 1991, unnumbered page.

15. Note to the Senate of 22 July cited in *Le Monde*, 24 July 1981, p.15.

16. Ministry of Culture, *Le Livre*, Etat et Culture series, Paris, 1993, pp.92–6. Gattégno is cited from a personal interview 7 April 1992.

17. Commission du Bilan, vol.3, pp.307–8. Gournay disputes this view of the pre–1981 period, R. Wangermée and B. Gournay, *Programme européen d'évaluation: la politique culturelle de la France*, Paris, 1988, pp.329–32.

18. See Chapter 6.

19. Ministry, 'La Politique culturelle 1981–1985': 'Arts plastiques', p.12.

20. A.-H. Mesnard, *Droit*, pp.298–9 and pp.310–12; 1992 figures quoted in 'L'Art et l'état, 1: les FRAC en question', *Beaux-Arts*, no.104, September 1992, p.66.

21. D. Wachtel, *Cultural Policy and Socialist France*, New York, 1987, pp.50–1.

22. Mesnard, *Droit*, p.125, p.256 and pp.311–12; *Beaux-Arts*, no.104, September 1992, p.66; and J. Warnod, 'Les FRAC: une bonne idée trop souvent détournée', *Le Figaro*, 12 March 1986, p.34.

23. C. Mollard, *La Passion de l'art*, Paris, 1986, pp.141–2.

24. Mesnard, *Droit*, pp.381–2; see also R. Caron, *L'Etat et la culture*, Paris, 1989, pp.54–5. Moulin is quoted in 'L'Art et l'état, 3: les politiques de l'art', *Beaux-Arts*, no.106, November 1992, pp.98 and 99. See also the previous issue, 'L'Art et l'état, 2: la commande publique', no.105, October 1992, pp.65–72.

25. Other examples were the wrapping up of the Pont Neuf by the artist Christo and of course the Pyramide du Louvre (see Chapter 7).

26. Buren is quoted in 'La Modernité souffle où elle veut', *Le Figaro*, 21 January 1986; Mollard, *La Passion*, p.145 and p.143 respectively.

27. Wangermée and Gournay, *La Politique culturelle*, pp.157–8.

28. Ibid., p.157 and p.243.

29. 'Lettre ouverte au Ministre de la culture', dated 13 August 1981, reproduced in *Acteurs*, no.1, January 1982, pp.68–72.

30. The first quotation is from Lang's interview with *Le Monde*, 5 September 1981, p.8; the second from his speech inaugurating the Théâtre J. Dasté, 'Discours de Jack Lang', unpublished, 5 vols, vol.1, July 1981–September 1982, p.161.

31. *Le Théâtre et le prince 1981–1991*, Paris, 1992, p.14.

32. The appointees were J. Savary, A. Delbée, J.-L. Martin-Barbaz and D. Llorca. Lang also appointed G. Lavaudant to the Grenoble MC and, a little later, Chéreau, together with the administrator Catherine Tasca, to devise a new institution out of the beleaguered MC and CDN at Nanterre. The following year Lang took the daring step of moving J.-P. Vincent from Strasbourg to take charge of the Comédie Française, the first director from decentralisation to do so.

33. Savary, intervention at Lang's and Abirached's press conference, 3 December 1981, 'Discours de Jack Lang', vol.1, July 1981–September 1982, p.149.

34. *Le Monde*, 19 July 1983, pp.1 and 15.

35. G. Saez, 'Politique culturelle: suivez le guide!', *Pour*, no.101, May–June 1985, pp.44–5. For further details of the reform, see Ministry, 'La Politique culturelle 1981–1985': 'La Décentralisation', pp.4–6; and Renard, *L'Elan culturel: la France en mouvement*, Paris, 1987, pp.64–73.

36. *L'Elan culturel*, pp.200–2 and p.225.

37. Wangermée and Gournay, *La Politique culturelle*, p.155.

38. Busson, *Le Théâtre en France: contexte socio-économique et choix esthétiques*, Notes et Etudes Documentaires, no.4,805, Paris, 1986, pp.59–64 (Baumol), pp.81–5 and pp.110–28. See also Abirached, *Le Théâtre*, pp.40–3 and p.130.

39. See for example Wangermée and Gournay, *La Politique culturelle*, p.155. Abirached also notes this phenomenon, not only in the French subsidised theatre but in other countries too, *Le Théâtre*, p.95.

– 6 –

Beyond High Culture: Pluralism and *le tout-culturel*

The Socialist government was well aware, after the socio-economic and cultural changes of the 1960s and 1970s, of the need not to confine itself to a Malraux-style *beaux-arts* policy. As I noted earlier, the period after 1968 had seen a more sophisticated reading of the problem of cultural democracy emerge, which set greater store by creativity, pluralism and difference. Already built into the Sixth Plan's notion of *développement culturel*, this reading was taken up again in *L'Impératif culturel* and given pride of place in the May 1982 decree, which presented the Ministry's first mission as being to 'permettre à tous les Français de cultiver leur capacité d'inventer et de créer, d'exprimer librement leurs talents et de recevoir la formation artistique de leur choix'. This task fell to the new Direction du développement culturel (DDC) under Dominique Wallon, which in May 1982 took over from the inadequately funded Mission of the same name set up by Lecat in 1979.

The DDC's sphere of activity was complex and perhaps incoherent, cutting across the disciplinary boundaries of the other directorates and to an extent of other ministries. One of its concerns was the traditional form of cultural action undertaken in the EACs, which often led to demarcation disputes with Abirached's DTS. But it also became the instrument of the most distinctive and innovative policies of the new government: decentralisation, the recognition of new practices and publics, and the cultural industries. Accordingly, it enlisted a number of dynamic, unconventional civil servants, often politically committed *hommes de terrain* in tune with cultural action at local level.[1] For all these reasons, it was to become the most controversial, heterodox and ideologically contested department in the Ministry.

Creativity, Democracy and Difference

Under the influence of post–1968 *gauchisme*, the new PS had acquired a faith in local democracy and cultural specificity which had led it to abandon the Left's traditional jacobinism and proclaim, as Mitterrand did in a speech in March 1981, 'le droit à la différence'. The political and administrative 'colonisation' of the regions by Paris consequently became an important feature of its election campaign. Cultural facilities were a particular focus here because libraries, museums and art and music schools were owned by municipal authorities but kept under the paternal scrutiny of the state in return for specific subsidies. Accordingly, Lang's first statements demonstrated a will to satisfy each province's aspiration to autonomy, even presenting centralism as a form of mental illness. Yet when the Minister of the Interior Gaston Defferre unveiled his draft decentralisation legislation at a Cabinet meeting in July 1981, Lang was far from enthusiastic.[2]

As well as generally reducing legal and financial controls over local-authority decision-making and establishing the regional councils as executive bodies in their own right, the decentralisation laws of 1982 and 1983 devolved certain state powers and introduced a system of block grants which aggregated the individual subsidies given by ministries to local authorities for specific purposes. A *dotation générale de décentralisation* to finance these transfers was created and a further, exceptional grant of 500 million francs for culture, the *dotation culturelle spéciale*, was also released to help towns (350 million francs) and regions (150 million francs) make up for past deficiencies. Naturally, the rationale of the block-grants system was that local government would be empowered to spend them as it saw fit. But for Lang, this would mean handing over funds he had only just obtained after a summer's hard lobbying. So, in common with several other ministers, he argued forcefully that the wholesale delegation of funds and powers was premature in his particular sphere, where a coherent national policy had only recently been put into effect. With presidential support, he had his way. The only actual transfer of powers, and of corresponding resources via the *dotation générale*, was the making over of the BCPs and departmental archives to the departments. Funds for municipal libraries were also absorbed into the *dotation générale* but Lang ensured that they could not be spent on any purpose other than libraries. In all remaining sectors, the previous practice of negotiated specific subsidies, which of course meant continued ministerial supervision, was retained.[3]

Rather than full devolution, the Ministry preferred various forms of deconcentration or partnership such as the FRACs, the FRAMs and the regional heritage commissions (COREPHAEs). It also completed the network of DRACs and increased their human and financial resources. More importantly, the DRACs and the DDC were closely involved in reviving and enlarging Michel Guy's contracts policy. The regions' share of the special block grant was earmarked to help them draw up cultural policies of their own, but their freedom to spend the money, spelt out in the 1982 law, was once again curtailed in practice by means of two-year contracts signed with the DDC, called *conventions de développement culturel*. In 1984, these were replaced by broader, five-year commitments introduced into the *contrats de Plan*. Conventions were also drawn up with the communes and departments on an annual basis, seventy-eight in the first year (1982). But although the policy enabled the provinces to benefit from the national budget increase, it was sometimes seen as a cloak for continued state paternalism in the early years. In October 1985, an opposition conference on cultural decentralisation was held in Lyon chaired by Raymond Barre, Michel Guy and the RPR's Jacques Baumel, which deplored the incompleteness of Lang's decentralisation generally, while the opposition parties' joint electoral programme signed in 1985 asserted that 'une authentique décentralisation suppose la suppression des mécanismes pseudo-contractuels par lesquels elles [les collectivités locales] paient de leur liberté, en matière culturelle, les moyens financiers qui leur sont octroyés'.[4]

It was (and remains) true that the DRACs received annual instructions from the rue de Valois about the priorities they should encourage local authorities to adopt, some of which bore little resemblance to a municipality's own, while in other cases it was only too easy for local officials unversed in this sort of bargaining to be coaxed towards, or spot for themselves, the projects likely to win favour, which the Ministry could then present as the product of genuine dialogue.[5] In the *contrats de Plan*, for example, the state was keen to push *culture scientifique et technique* and its social policy for the deprived urban districts (*quartiers*). In one case, Saez recounts, the DDC even refused to accept a region's proposals. In the end, Defferre, already irritated with the contracts for 'sabotaging' his reform, insisted that the *contrats de Plan* be negotiated without DDC involvement, effectively marginalising it in the state-regions relationship.[6]

Even so, by the time of the Right's return to power in 1986, the contracts policy had generally proved popular at local level, with both the Left and the Right. Although Wallon's claim that he could find no mayor who shared the sentiments expressed at the Lyon gathering doubtless owed a little to wishful thinking, the policy had quite clearly avoided the trap of only favouring councils sympathetic to the government.[7] All the regions had signed up in 1982 and almost all had negotiated *contrats de Plan* in 1984. Better still, the contracts were acting as a spur to further local-authority investment. Lang had made it clear that his doubled budget should not be regarded as a pretext for councils to scale down their own efforts. On the contrary, state funds would be proportional to local investment, so that towns would be cajoled into stepping up their own expenditure by the promise of ever greater state aid. Today, with more than 1,200 conventions signed between 1982 and 1991 involving a total of one billion francs of joint expenditure, French local and regional authorities are well on the way to providing two-thirds of public spending on culture;[8] and although this development had begun long before 1981, the contracts policy certainly boosted it, contributing in the process to *l'aménagement culturel du territoire*. As a result, these authorities are now in a better position to negotiate with the Ministry as equal partners. Nevertheless, the Ministry's reluctance to entrust funds fully to local government is revealing of the continuing paradox of a centrally planned, national policy for decentralisation. True, Lang had a much less unitarian view of national culture than Malraux and genuinely wished to free the regions to develop their own identities as partners of the state. But at the same time, he and others in the party and the arts feared local-authority philistinism after years of conflict over decentralised institutions. The Ministry could not therefore resist the reflex to harmonise those identities in a single chorus and, to this extent at least, continued the Gaullist concern with culture as an affirmation of nationhood.[9]

The most distinctive area of the DDC's work was concerned with new cultural practices and publics. It was carried out in conjunction with a member of Lang's cabinet team, Jean-Pierre Colin, who in his book *La Beauté du manchot* presents it as embodying a conception of humanity and society. With the post–1968 reform of the PS, he argues, there emerged a new humanism on the Left, more concerned with human rights than class warfare or revolutionary change. Yet human rights were not conceived as an abstract function of national unity, but rather as integral to the party's new commitment to multiplicity and difference. In the wake of May, there came a chorus of demands for rights, from regionalists, women's and gay movements, the disabled, *les exclus* of all kinds. Colin believes that by responding to them, despite disapproval from some jacobin elements within the party, the Socialists found a new legitimacy and distinctiveness. None the less, just as Lang thought of central-government policy as harmonising diverse regional identities, so too does Colin view multiculturalism as an opportunity for the national culture to be redefined and survive; again, unity in diversity.[10]

In practice, this philosophy meant a programme of work with various minorities or underprivileged communities, partly to remedy inequality of access to high culture but also as a way of demonstrating that such groups already had a cultural life of their own which was equally rich and significant. One instance was the policy directed at the world of work. The Belleville report published in 1982 emphasised that a culture of the workplace existed alongside that of leisure, embracing both the traditional kinds of activities organised by unions and *comités d'entreprise* and a broader sense of identity and community based on individual workers' relationships with the instruments of their labour and on the solidarity with others this brings. *L'Impératif culturel* also argued that by recognising such activities and allowing workers to 'appropriate' their working lives, industry could be made more dynamic and productive.[11] These principles led the Ministry to extend its contracts policy to the *comités d'entreprise*, with which seventy conventions were signed, again some involving traditional initiatives such as *bibliobus* and libraries, others more community-specific activity to do with the industrial heritage or '*la mémoire ouvrière*'.

Other communities were also identified in the programme. One aim was to help maintain the identity of rural areas by preserving their heritage or setting up structures enabling those living in such areas to express themselves, such as the Agence nationale pour la création en milieu rural or the Association pour la promotion des radios rurales. Much of this work, however, given the serious problem of 'cultural desertification' brought about by the rural exodus, concerned *diffusion*, for example the opening or renovation of cinemas in more remote areas. Disadvantaged suburban districts, a priority area in the Ninth Plan, were similarly catered for, with particular attention paid to the problems of illiteracy. In other cases, the communities concerned were regional, as proposed in the Giordan report entitled *Démocratie culturelle et droit à la différence* (Paris, 1982). The contracts between the state and those regions with strong cultural identities like Brittany and Languedoc-Roussillon aimed to assist local associations which promoted regional languages, traditional musical forms, or patrimonial facilities. In 1985, the Conseil national des langues et cultures régionales was set up to act as a consultative body and intermediary between government and the diverse organisations representing specific communities. To extend the right to difference beyond the mainland, a Fonds de promotion des cultures d'outre-mer was also created.

There were, of course, limits to how far a regionalist policy could go. One was the constitution itself with its stress on the indivisibility of the Republic. The absence of a real consensus within the PS – in particular the survival of a tradition of jacobinism – also acted as a restraint, as did the links with extremism and the Right which some regional movements retained. Finally, as Colin points out, the fact that the most active and visible regional-language movements, the Breton and the Occitan, were concerned with cultures identified with the past made the regionalist issue look archaic at a time when the internationalisation of English and the advancement of European integration were the major concerns, though the living languages of border regions like Alsatian, Catalan and Flemish could, he felt, play a vital role in creating the new Europe.[12]

There was also something of a problem over the relationship between regional and 'community' or ethnic cultures. Colin regrets that the Giordan report did not choose to consider the latter, for both he and the DDC saw them as a priority. The Ministry placed particular stress on assisting the integration of ethnic minorities through the notion of *l'interculturel*, a non-hierarchical, two-way exchange or even *métissage*. It therefore worked closely with a variety of associations, for example giving financial support to the Beur movement and the SOS Racisme organisation which grew from it. This culminated in SOS Racisme's first 'Touche pas à mon pote' open-air concert at the Place de la Concorde on 15 June 1985 which, according to Colin, was carefully orchestrated by Lang himself. In fact, this concern, more forward-looking and electorally attractive than giving backing to regional cultures, dominated DDC policy as the years went by.[13] It did, however, meet with opposition from some in government who detected in the Langian model of a national multiculture a threat to the traditional concept of national unity. This was clear when the Conseil national des langues et cultures régionales was first mooted. It was initially agreed that the Council would be called 'des langues et cultures de France' and would therefore represent both regional and community cultures. But this definition, Colin relates, was not to the liking of certain ministries, in particular Education under Jean-Pierre Chevènement. Not only was it considered to undermine the status of French, but it also placed on an equal footing an historically rooted territorial language like Breton, and Arabic which was perceived as alien. The President finally settled the matter by opting for 'langues et cultures régionales', effectively excluding community cultures.[14]

The DDC also turned its attention to other kinds of minorities: the disabled, the military, and those confined in institutions like prisons and hospitals. In such cases, contracts were often negotiated with other ministries since Lang was only too aware how little he could achieve alone, though the FIC proved especially useful here as it provided a pre-existing structure for interministerial cooperation. Again, integration or reintegration was the aim but through the encouragement of specificity and difference. Colin himself was involved with measures for the handicapped, particularly the deaf, and he makes a revealing historical comparison between the state's refusal to countenance regional languages and its hostility to the use of sign language in state schools. Still frowned upon today in some educational circles, sign language was actively opposed by the Third Republic; and its infant practitioners, like those caught speaking Breton, were punished. Instead, the deaf were forced to learn to lip-read, simply because it required knowledge of French and was therefore consistent with the idea of a national monoculture, while sign language was seen as dangerously separatist.[15]

One final means of achieving cultural democracy, which also involved the DDC to an extent, was creative-arts training in state education. This was a boat the PS could ill afford to miss, not only because of Mitterrand's campaign pledge but because, as Bourdieu argues, only familiarity with the codes of artistic expression from an early age is likely to stimulate cultural practices in the form of either personal creativity or simply a demand for ready-made cultural forms. The *enseignements artistiques* issue also offered an ideal opportunity to demonstrate Lang's commitment to a coordinated interministerial strategy. However, if this was the policy on which most depended, it was one of those in which least was achieved.

In 1981, the creative subjects taught in schools still comprised only music and art and were still available to only 10 per cent of the school population. The problem was that change could only come from within the vast and ponderous Education administration and would necessarily be massive, complex and costly. Hence Mitterrand's promise to table a bill on the matter. During his first months in office, Lang unwisely undertook to have a joint draft ready for the Assembly by the autumn of 1982. But liaison between Culture and Education officials proved frustrating and at one stage Mitterrand had to remind Lang and the Education minister Savary of the need to push ahead. Admittedly, a number of promising collaborative ventures did materialise. In 1982, week-long field-trips to historic monuments called '*classes du patrimoine*' were introduced, followed two years later by similar sessions called '*classes arc-en-ciel*' (later '*classes culturelles*') involving children in creative work with artists. In 1983, an agreement between the two ministries was signed; 1984 saw the introduction of creative workshops in audiovisual media and drama and, in fourteen pilot *lycées*, of film and theatre studies options in the A3 baccalaureate. At the same time, the DDC was also coordinating initiatives involving the two ministries and local authorities through its 'Mission Education-Culture' under Jean Ader. But with Education taken up with more weighty matters like the vexed private education issue, the bill itself never saw the light of day. By 1986 more than 600,000 pupils were still without even music or art lessons.[16]

Despite their innovativeness and diversity, all the Socialists' accomplishments in respect of new publics and practices in fact need to be put into perspective. Firstly, the DDC was not popular. At the Lyon conference, it was clearly the *bête noire* of local opposition parties – 'un péché contre l'esprit, un crime contre le pluralisme culturel', said the Mayor of Orléans Jacques Douffiagues – because of its alleged bureaucracy and interference in local affairs.[17] But at central-government level too, both the DDC and the FIC went against ingrained civil-service habits by working directly at local level. Moreover, by virtue of its 'horizontal' vocation (i.e. straddling all the areas covered by the 'vertical', or discipline-based, directorates), the DDC was sometimes resented for encroaching on other people's territory. Also, and again like the FIC, it was considered spendthrift. In the 1985 budget, the FIC itself was wound up, reputedly made obsolete by the DDC and the now fully developed DRACs, though in Colin's estimate this was 'une ténébreuse affaire' whose real motives he cannot discern.[18] At any event, the FIC's fate prefigured the DDC's own after the change of government in March 1986. Secondly, and more importantly perhaps, the status of the DDC's work within the Ministry should not be exaggerated. Colin concedes that the administrative measures for regional and community cultures were modest, as was the budget allocated to them, while the Council of Europe report points out the limited resources for *action culturelle* generally, compared to those available for disseminating high culture or funding prestigious new facilities. It concludes that the pursuit of true cultural democracy was a policy more symbolic than voluntarist, which needed to be conducted and funded more systematically.[19]

In the absence of such voluntarism, and with little real ascendency over the creative arts in schools or television, the Ministry's options for carrying out a successful *développement culturel* programme were limited. To compensate, it increasingly fell back on a festive conception of culture, which owed much to Lang's own background. For some in the party, the idea of organising popular, politico-cultural festivities harked back to the Revolutionary *fêtes* or the Popular Front's great outdoor assemblies celebrating a revived national spirit. Lang on the other hand gave this old-Left notion a more modern reading, influenced by his experience of street theatre at Nancy and of staging more directly political happenings like the Panthéon, whose significance for him had gone beyond its immediate usefulness as a propaganda stunt: 'Au fond, était-ce de l'art, était-ce de la politique, lorsque nous avons, pour célébrer la journée d'installation du nouveau président de la République, convié le peuple de Paris au Panthéon? Un peuple immense était rassemblé. J'ai vu des milliers de jeunes chanter spontanément "L'Hymne à la joie". J'ai été personnellement bouleversé, comme le furent beaucoup d'autres.' 'Spontanément', lyricised Mauroy, 'dans toute la France, le 10 mai, et aussi le 21 mai, des fêtes se sont organisées partout, du moindre village à la place de la Bastille. J'y vois le signe de cette vitalité qui me réjouit: lorsque la fête est là, c'est un signe qui ne trompe pas.'[20] Indeed, what the Popular Front, Nancy and the Panthéon all seemed to demonstrate to the party was that a joyful, public, cultural event could release an energy and imagination capable of breaking down the very barriers which Mitterrand's socialism was dedicated to demolishing: between the individual and the collective, professional creation and amateur creativity, culture and the economy.

It was with this in mind that the Ministry launched the first Fête de la musique held on 21 June 1982, brainchild of Maurice Fleuret with help from Christian Dupavillon and Jacques Sallois. By 1981, the big increase in specialist music-education facilities after the Landowski plan had meant a surge in amateur musical activity. Soon after arriving at the Ministry, Fleuret had unearthed figures which indicated that France now had five million people who played a musical instrument, half of them under twenty years old.[21] The aim of the Fête was to recognise and encourage this practice. But what distinguished it particularly was the stress it placed on spontaneity and improvisation. Part of this derived from the fact that the idea was only dreamt up some three weeks before the launch date, but it was largely because the organisers wanted both professionals and amateurs of every description, even those who might have to improvise an instrument, to come out into the street and play or sing for thirty minutes, in a kind of pagan ritual marking the summer solstice. Thus, despite the flood of notified events which blocked the Ministry's switchboard, the real spirit of the occasion was provided by the element of unpredictability and fun, recalling the SNAC document's insistence on the gratuitousness of pleasure as a force for change. The Fête, wrote *Le Monde*, was 'une idée assez folle [...] Une idée de mai 68, l'art dans la rue, la musique pour tous – et par tous'. Hunter relates that Lang in fact saw the idea as so mad as to be positively dangerous, but was daring enough to let it go ahead.[22]

Despite press efforts to belittle it, the first Fête was a modest success. There was a wide variety of events spread across France, though also a tendency – ever more pronounced in the following years – for the organised to overshadow the spontaneous. Some dismissed the initiative as demagogic, others as devaluing professionalism and the slow apprenticeship musicianship demands. But Fleuret later recounted that Mitterrand had called it the most important thing the Ministry had ever done.[23] For here was a government which had succeeded in bringing happy crowds together in the street to celebrate the arts in carnival mood. Finally shedding the last obstinate vestiges of the fusty Beaux-Arts, France's Minister of Culture could now step forward transfigured: Lord of the Dance, leader of a giant Dionysian conga weaving unsteadily across the national territory.

'Au carrefour de la création et du loisir', Ory had written in 1974, 'la Fête est sans doute une nécessité politique, si on l'approche comme "simulacre" d'une révolution qui n'eut pas lieu – qu'on ne veut pas faire.'[24] Certainly, the idea of a state-initiated spontaneity was a curious one, and potentially awkward for Lang personally since through him the subversive, countercultural energy of Nancy now found itself harnessed to national or political interests. Nevertheless, the Minister was quick to read the signs. Over the next decade, one grimly frolicsome, playfully titled occasion – La Ruée vers l'art, La Fureur de lire, Les Arts au soleil – spawned another, eye-catching substitutes for more costly or laborious cultural action in schools and communities. Indeed, the image-conscious, media-wise fun culture which now became Lang's trademark was almost a travesty of the post–1968 principles of grass-roots creativity, pluralism and difference the DDC had been created to implement. But this was just one irony of the much bigger shift which came about in Socialist policies between 1982 and 1983. For in parallel with the DDC's legitimation of neglected amateur practices, the Ministry also began incorporating in its global definition of culture those forms of professional creation which had similarly been ignored as minor. And this new orientation soon came to overshadow the work of the DDC.

Mass Culture and the Cultural Industries: *le tout-culturel*

In December 1982, commenting on a recently published Ministry survey of cultural practices in France, Augustin Girard drew attention to the fact that, as the survey indicated, subsidy to the various cultural forms was inversely proportional to public consumption of them.[25]

The justification for this state of affairs is obvious enough, since it is precisely limited public demand which makes state aid necessary, if France's cultural kaleidoscope is not to be deprived of experimental and costly new work by renowned artists which often has only an infinitesimal following. But this argument works both ways. If the preservation of diversity is to be the touchstone for propping up art forms few demand, how can the state justify ignoring other forms which are very much in demand but also in need? This reasoning became central to Socialist policy during the first quinquennium and the term '*décloisonnement*', or decompartmentalisation, was used to describe it. Like 'democratisation' which it replaced or at least subsumed, *décloisonnement* was polysemous, signifying the breaking down of barriers between art and the people, artistic disciplines, the amateur and the professional, and so on; and in all these senses, the Fête de la musique was the perfect illustration of it. But it chiefly came to mean doing away with the hierarchy between 'high' and 'low' cultures. Rather than batter heroically at the non-public's door as the Ministry had habitually done, Lang very soon began to look for another way in, tackling the problem of cultural inequalities not in terms of audiences but of creative forms.

Ministerial recognition was accordingly bestowed on a number of hitherto neglected 'popular' arts: puppet theatre, operetta, circus, cookery, in some cases involving prestigious new institutions like the Ecole nationale des arts culinaires near Lyon or the Centre national supérieur de formation aux arts du cirque in Châlons-sur-Marne. But to decompartmentalise any further in the high-tech 1980s, the Ministry was obliged to grasp the nettle of mass-cultural, industrially produced forms which operate in a market economy and which have no public-service mission. In his National Assembly speech of November 1981, Lang publicly acknowledged the legitimacy and respectability of the cultural industries. What counted above all, he proclaimed, was to dynamise French society by encouraging creation wherever it was found; therefore 'pas de modèle unique. A chacun son choix: l'art savant ou l'art populaire, l'art nouveau ou l'art traditionnel. [...] De la création audiovisuelle à la création industrielle, de la commande publique à la création plastique'. It was time, he said, for the state to acknowledge the private sector 'without complexes' and to have dealings with it that were 'adult' and 'serene' and he spoke of reconciling 'création et production marchande', implying that the cultural industries were not just means of *diffusion* but could be creative forms in their own right.[26]

One of the Ministry's first interests here was youth culture, which chiefly meant popular music. In ministerial usage around 1981, this was a broad category which included folk, *chanson* old and new, and variety and jazz. But it was dominated by pop and rock, and as early as June Lang signalled his intentions by being seen at a Stevie Wonder concert in Paris. In 1981, the French pop music and record industry was certainly in need of assistance. Its market share was dwindling after the boom of the 1960s and 1970s, due to the domination of English or American products. The maximum luxury-goods VAT rate of 33 per cent was imposed on records, which particularly penalised young French unknowns. French record companies were being swallowed up by multinationals like EMI. And the conditions of comfort, visibility and safety at concert venues were often deplorable even in Paris. Nevertheless, the idea of the state becoming involved with pop, still seen as a frivolous branch of the entertainment industry, was a novel one in 1981, despite the process Ory calls the 'respectabilisation' of minor forms during the 1970s. Rock music, of course, was something else again, the term usually denoting music with a harder, more aggressive edge than pop and a sub-culture of little known groups, often suburban or provincial, struggling to make their way with limited resources and in poor conditions. Rock was also seen as a crude, disaffected form with associations of drugs, vandalism and delinquency. Yet all of this only served to make it an ideal vehicle for the government to make a daring statement about *décloisonnement*.

In February 1982, Lang, prompted initially by Fleuret, unveiled a new music policy which included a number of measures for pop.[27] Among them was aid to young musicians in search of rehearsal facilities. The difficulty for amateur rock bands of finding a space which could accommodate their equipment and avoid the problem of noise was addressed with the help of the FIC and the DDC. A guide to rehearsal facilities, also containing advice and information for the estimated 25,000 rock groups in France, was produced entitled *Maxi-Rock, Mini-Bruit*. Aid to local bodies to help them provide and equip rehearsal facilities themselves was also forthcoming, including the provision of technical expertise. More spectacular, however, was the action taken for professional rock venues, where the most eye-catching measure concerned the capital. Rock music did not have its own major concert venue in Paris, which meant that impresarios were obliged to book halls used for other purposes, where acoustics and visibility were often poor. At the President's request, Lang set out to remedy the problem. A concert hall holding ten thousand people originally planned for the Porte de Bagnolet was shelved due to cost, replaced by a more flexible structure at La Villette capable of seating between three and six thousand. Put up in a matter of months, Le Zénith opened in January 1984 and was intended to spawn smaller structures in the regions, though these were slow in coming. Some dismissed such initiatives as mere vote-catching, but the Paris Zénith clearly responded to a need. By 1991, it had been used by in excess of two hundred performers and five million spectators.

Aid to pop also came in other forms, including the July 1985 law on copyright which entitled both record producers and performers to earnings when their records were played on the air and imposed a tax on blank cassettes to compensate for private copying. But like the DDC's activities, all these measures need to be seen in context. The 19 million francs spent on jazz, *chanson* and variety in 1985 were 10 million below the subsidy to Boulez's experimental music centre (L'IRCAM) alone, and represented under 5 per cent of total Ministry spending on opera.[28] While it may be argued that popular music, being a commercial form, does not need to rely as heavily on state subsidy as these high-cultural forms do, the Council of Europe report points out that aid to pop also lagged behind the more comparable cinema industry. The promised reduction of VAT on records, for example, a campaign issue in 1981, was not in the end achieved by the Socialists, even though this would have been an effective way of supporting creation since the high cost of a record meant the buyer was often dissuaded from trying out unknown artists.[29] There was also a certain unease in some quarters that through state aid the elements of revolt and provocation in rock were being officialised and tamed, though again the danger needs to be set against the widespread acceptance of pop as a mainstream commercial medium by 1981 and the limited nature of the measures and the spending. Lang's support for popular music was more symbolic than hegemonic.

Much the same could be said of the Ministry's aid to *bandes dessinées* (BD), or comic strips, also identified with the young. At a press conference held in January 1983, Lang spoke of the disdain which had previously caused BD to be seen as a 'sous-produit littéraire' harmful to youth. Asserting its legitimate place among other visual or literary forms of expression, he stressed its social function in fostering a kind of aesthetic literacy in those whom traditional artistic forms had failed to touch.[30] In reality, however, with Ory's process of 'respectabilisation' in the 1970s, BD had already become extremely popular and was being increasingly taken over by big publishing houses. Between 1975 and 1981, its share of publishing's total turnover had gone from 1.7 to 3.4 per cent.[31] At the same time, it was rapidly catching up with film and photography as a branch of the arts worthy of academic study. As with rock music, then, the chief innovation in the Ministry's recognition lay in its receptiveness to an existing trend. And here too, the measures taken appear relatively limited compared with the publicity given them. In April 1982, the Minister launched a period of consultation with BD professionals. This led to a 'plan BD' the following January, many of whose measures simply extended existing aid to authors or visual artists. More spectacular was the plan for a Centre national de la BD et de l'image in Angoulême bringing together an *atelier-école*, a documentation and research centre and a museum, eventually inaugurated in January 1991.

Because the comic strip usually comprises both written text and drawing, these measures did not only involve the Book directorate and the CNL but also the DAP, which was particularly active in broadening the range of ministerial intervention. One example was photography, for which a Centre national de la photographie was created under Robert Delpire, akin to the CNC and CNAP, and a School of Photography in Arles in 1982. More distinctive, however, was the interest taken in advertising and fashion. As with pop and BD, the first gestures were made quite early on, though for advertising, after the transformation in October 1982 of the Musée de l'affiche into an advertising museum, tokenism was more prominent than action and it is not one of the areas the Ministry's own balance-sheets in 1985 and 1991 highlight. More was done for fashion. On 25 March 1982, Lang accompanied Danièle Mitterrand to the opening of the Journées du prêt-à-porter organised by the head of Yves Saint-Laurent, Pierre Bergé, at which the autumn and winter collections were on show. This was symbolic beyond their mere presence for Lang had also authorised the event to take place in the Louvre's Cour carrée. On the same day, he also announced that a fashion museum would be created within the Louvre's Musée des arts décoratifs, a project which in fact predated the Mitterrand victory. Fashion was promoted via various grants and subsidies distributed to designers by the FIACRE, while Lang himself took a more personal interest by making a point of sporting stunning designer clothes.

The DAP's activities also extended to other forms of industrial design (*création industrielle*). In early June 1982, Lang launched an international competition to design office furniture for a new Finance Ministry at Bercy and other ministries. The five winning designs would be put into production by five selected French firms and would have a guaranteed market worth over forty million francs. This was intended both to encourage creation and help dynamise the French furniture industry, just as aid to fashion was meant to stimulate the textile trade. Contemporary designers were brought in to equip and redecorate the offices of the Ministry's various directorates, while a commission was given to Philippe Starck to refurnish the Elysée apartments. An Ecole nationale supérieure de la création industrielle opened in November 1982 and the following year saw the creation of a special Mission for industrial design within the DAP, as well as an interministerial agency.

It was the Ministry's willingness to involve itself in such an extensive range of industrialised forms of creation which gave rise to the largely pejorative media label *le tout-culturel*, a term which by the end of the 1980s had become commonplace and which underscored the distance the Ministry had travelled since 1959. Its theoretical foundations are hazy but can be summed up in Lang's statement in June 1982 that 'il peut y avoir autant acte de culture dans le dessin d'une robe, le design d'un objet ou l'élaboration d'un film annonce-publicitaire que dans l'écriture musicale, l'art graphique ou l'architecture'.[32] In Lang's lexicon, 'an act of culture' is one in which three elements are present. The first is 'le beau', a convenient camouflage which allows the eternal essence of an ineffable aesthetic pleasure to be equated with the merely decorative. The second is creation, here simply the production of an artefact which did not exist before. The third is representation. In the same speech, Lang quoted Henri Michaux's 'l'habillement est une conception de soi que l'on porte sur soi' and went on to suggest just as unexceptionably that in addition to being a statement about oneself, fashion is a statement about the society from which it springs. Renard in fact maintains that it is impossible to create a fashion style, a dish or an advertisement without in some sense reflecting the state of a society, its currents of opinion and its form of social organisation.[33]

With the word 'culture' or 'cultural' thus applied easily and non-judgmentally to many more artefacts than those originally anticipated by Malraux, great art was increasingly placed on an equal footing – at least where its right to ministerial aid was concerned though not necessarily its aesthetic worth, Ministry officials insisted – with various lesser forms of creative 'talent'. In December 1984, Juliette Peyret, formerly in advertising but now working in Lang's cabinet as an advisor on 'communication', spoke of making his department 'le ministère de la créativité, de la stimulation du talent, de l'imagination peut-être', an ambition which, she insisted, Lang and everyone at the Ministry shared.[34] The term 'creativity', a buzzword by the mid–1980s suggestive here of the noun *créatif* or *créative* used to denote someone working in design, was unintentionally revealing for it served to underscore just how far the idea of 'talent' – a range of applied skills of direct use to the world of commerce – had taken over in ministerial discourse from the revolutionary popular creativity favoured by the SNAC a decade earlier. In October 1985, the Ministry became involved in the Galeries Lafayette's promotional event 'La France a du talent' where many of the objects in which it has traditionally been involved – ceramics, glass, museum pieces – were available for sale. It also staged its own event the same year, 'Coup de talent dans l'Hexagone', organised as part of International Youth Year.

From this sketchy theoretical position, it was only a short step to the most pragmatic dimension of the culture and economy linkage referred to in Chapter 4. Here, the tendency to see 1983 as a dramatic turning-point is slightly misleading since the promotion of the cultural industries and 'l'art utile' was, as we have seen, already written into Lang's November 1981 script and was activated from early 1982, though it is true that the cultural industries were promoted much more energetically from early 1983. But what particularly changed at this time was the ideological emphasis. Although rock, fashion and so on were all private-sector activities functioning in the marketplace and were already classed as industries, the initial preoccupation was more with their right in a cultural democracy to be recognised as popular expressive forms. This preoccupation was never overtly abandoned but became indistinguishable around 1983 from the idea that the Ministry must now also address the commercial, technological and industrial structures associated with such forms. Furthermore, as the 1983 colloquium exemplified, the government began vigorously promoting the notion that culture is a major asset in France's overall industrial strategy, capable of affecting foreign trade, the balance of payments and unemployment. While not strikingly socialist, this new emphasis was not entirely surprising either. By 1984, cultural activity in France was indeed accounting for 4 per cent (almost 150 billion francs) of the gross domestic product, more than the automobile industry, and employing around 500,000 people.[35] Furthermore, with a boom in new audiovisual technologies (video, CD, walkmans, IT) and in cultural and leisure spending over the previous decade, the cultural industries were one of the few growth areas in the economy and could be relied on to remain so.

But even before the February colloquium, Lang expressed the belief that France had fallen behind in this field, for despite being full of creative talent, it had failed to invest sufficiently in its industrial exploitation. He would regularly point out that for twenty years the copies of foreign films distributed in France had been made not in French laboratories but abroad, or that the French BD artist Mœbius had worked on the American computer-based Disney cartoon *Tron* because the technology required for such ground-breaking work was not available at home. Still importing too many musical instruments, movie cameras and too much audio, video and computer equipment, France needed to invest more in research and the industrial production of cultural and related goods.[36] Part of the problem was that many of the cultural industries in France, especially those described as 'industries of content' (books, records, film production, the audiovisual media and new technologies like video and software), involved small or medium-sized firms which carried little weight in political and financial circles. As Renard points out, a record company might well have no staff other than its founder. Even France's most important record-pressing concern, MPO, which had taken the risk of launching into the internationally competitive compact-disc market, employed only 300 people in 1986.[37] Such industries were often disadvantaged because, as producers of 'immaterial' goods whose commercial success could never be guaranteed, they found that banks and finance houses were reluctant to become involved, which prevented them from enjoying the normal credit facilities available to most other industrial sectors. Accordingly, government aid to the cultural industries, rather than taking the form of direct subsidy, was mostly aimed at boosting investment from other sources.

Apart from the funds made available by the various directorates, such aid was again the responsibility of the DDC, to which the budget for 1982 had already allocated 10 million francs for the cultural industries. This was doubled the following year and complemented by a further 50 million for 'new technologies'. These sums were meant to assist firms which were in financial difficulties, launching risky new products, or developing a new commercial strategy, though in practice the aid often fell foul of the Finance Ministry's administrative apparatus which could veto such moves. After the 1983 election, support from the Culture Ministry became more strenuous still. The DDC was equipped with a new Mission économie culturelle et communication which took over the cultural industries budget and coordinated the various activities it financed. In May, a Ministry-initiated 1901 association, the OCTET agency, began operating (also funded by several other ministries, as well as private banks), designed to advance new cultural technologies in France such as video and animation and to encourage creators and financiers to be more aware of each other.

On 3 October 1983, Lang announced that the cultural industries were to be prioritised as part of a new 21 billion-franc package for the communication industries over the next five years, one of twelve priority programmes in the Ninth Plan. 750 million francs were to be earmarked for the Culture Ministry and new structures set up. These included a limited company entitled the Institut pour le financement du cinéma et des industries culturelles (IFCIC), designed to make it easier for companies engaged in creative content, technical production (musical instruments, printing, stage equipment), and distribution (video outlets, cinemas, theatres) to obtain credit. Another initiative, announced in October 1984, was the Plan Son. Lang was aware that the huge music boom in France had scarcely benefited the French music and recording industries. The Plan Son, developed in conjunction with the Ministry for Industrial Redeployment, was therefore intended to win back the domestic market and boost exports by modernising those industries through research, development, and the improved production, distribution and marketing of French-made products such as CDs or musical software. For visual technology, a parallel initiative, the Plan Recherche Image, had already been launched in 1983 involving computer-aided image processing of particular use in making cartoon films. Measures were also taken to develop a French industry in computer and video games, while the OCTET agency assisted the production of French pop videos and the creative use of new technologies.[38]

A different means of encouraging investment in culture was corporate sponsorship (*mécénat d'entreprise*), already widespread in the USA but limited in France, where the established tradition of private patronage had largely died out by the Occupation. In the 1970s, however, the economic crisis began to stimulate a new interest in alternative means of arts funding. 1979 saw the creation of the Association pour le développement du mécénat industriel et commercial (ADMICAL) under Jacques Rigaud and a government enquiry into business sponsorship. But again it was ironically the Socialists who took the first steps, with the budget laws of 1982 and 1985 setting up new tax incentives. More lucrative still for businesses was the arrangement, also dating from 1985, which authorised sponsorship to be entirely deductible from taxable profits as publicity expenses. The benefit for companies of course, at least in theory, was a certain brand image as a 'caring' firm. Not everyone was convinced of the benefits for culture however. For a start, the income remained modest, averaging some 350 million francs annually.[39] More importantly, corporate sponsors tend to be big companies, which often favour established reputations rather than innovation. Finally, private sponsorship is notoriously unreliable and often short-term, making the financial situation of the artists involved precarious. For all these reasons, the Ministry argued that the US model should not be adopted as an absolute and that *mécénat* should never imply state withdrawal but rather a mixed economy. Nevertheless, Lang and others pointed out in its favour that it loosened the hold of officialdom and gave the artist a third interlocutor in addition to the state and the local authorities.[40]

Lang was aware of the need to give maximum publicity to the cultural industries if investing in them was to gain acceptance. In 1985, a series of media events brought the idea to public attention: gold, silver and bronze *'puce'* awards for cultural innovation in the new technologies, a three-month Fête de l'industrie et de la technologie at La Villette, and most of all an 'Art et industrie' exhibition, mounted in October 1985 in conjunction with the Industry Ministry. The exhibition was the apotheosis of the whole new ideology of commercialism and talent. On display were cartoon films, advertising clips, computer software, fashion garments, designer furniture and other objects: style-conscious modernity combined with commercial functionalism in a 1980s 'look' intended to attract young people to careers in creative design. Lang accordingly presented the event as 'un manifeste, un credo, une fenêtre ouverte sur l'avenir'. Here was apparent proof that a cultural democratisation of sorts had come about almost overnight, for many of these products, no longer impersonal but associated with the names of now famous designers like Philippe Starck, were already on sale at reasonable prices in mass retail outlets.[41]

But Lang also insisted that in promoting such commodities, his purpose was not purely economic. On the contrary, he claimed to be supporting the cultural industries because of their impact on the very nature and boundaries of artistic creation. He stressed that, because they involved high-risk economies, they were fragile and needed a special type of help which combined free-market principles with regulation against unfair competition. This idea of a synergy between the economic and the cultural, already visible in the *prix unique du livre*, became one of his hallmarks, though once again it was made more problematic by the fact that some of those industries lay beyond his superintendence. Where this was so, all he could do was stress the legitimacy of his interest and attempt to make agreements with the appropriate ministries: PTT, Industry and, most of all, Communication.[42]

The *tout-culturel* and the support for cultural industries were Lang's most distinctive and controversial initiatives. Yet he was not alone in making either policy or headlines. Equally distinctive, possibly more controversial, was the programme of major building works known as the *'grands projets culturels'* or *'grands travaux'*, initiated not by the Culture department but by the President himself.

Notes

1. G. Saez, 'Politique culturelle: suivez le guide!', *Pour*, no.101, May–June 1985, p.38. On the DDC, see also Saez, 'La Politique de développement culturel de 1981 à 1986', unpublished paper read to the Séminaire du Centre de Recherches Administratives, FNSP, 31 January 1987; and A.-H. Mesnard, *Droit et politique de la culture*, Paris, 1990, pp.120–1.
2. P. Favier and M. Martin-Roland, *La Décennie Mitterrand*, Paris, vol.1, 'La Rupture', 1990, pp.145–6.
3. I am grateful to the Ministry's Pierre Moulinier for clarifying a number of technical aspects of the decentralisation measures.
4. For the Lyon event, see *Un Projet culturel pour demain dans le cadre d'une véritable décentralisation*, actes du colloque de Lyon, 21 October 1985. The opposition's electoral programme for culture and communication is reproduced in the Ministry's *Lettre d'Information*, no.191, 28 April 1986, pp.3–4.
5. Mesnard, *Droit*, pp.314–15.
6. Saez, 'La Politique de développement culturel', p.5 and pp.14–15.
7. Ibid., p.13.
8. *Développement Culturel*, no.98, February 1993, p.1. The Ministry's DEP also produces an annual analysis of the previous year's contracts: see F. Moulin and P. Moulinier, *Les Conventions de développement culturel*, DEP, May 1993.
9. See Saez, 'De l'autonomie des politiques culturelles territoriales', n *Les Papiers du GRESE*, no.6, autumn 1989, Presses Universitaires du Mirail, pp.7–8; and R. Wangermée and B. Gournay, *Programme européen d'évaluation: la politique culturelle de la France*, Paris, 1988, p.109.
10. *La Beauté du manchot: culture et différence*, Paris: Publisud, 1986, pp.11–26 and pp.55–6.
11. P. Belleville, *Pour la culture dans l'entreprise: rapport au Ministre de la culture*, Paris, 1982; and Commissariat général du Plan, *L'Impératif culturel: rapport du groupe de travail long terme culture*, Paris, 1982.
12. Colin, *La Beauté*, pp.57–8 and p.101. See also Mesnard, *Droit*, pp.322–3. Regional languages were mainly the responsibility of Education nationale.
13. Colin, *La Beauté*, p.105. On the policies for regional and community cultures, see Saez, 'La Politique de développement culturel', p.11, and his much fuller analysis, 'Emergence et institutionnalisation des cultures régionales et minoritaires comme

objets de politique publique', unpublished paper read to colloquium on 'L'Etat devant les cultures régionales et communautaires', 23–5 January 1986.

14. For an account of this debate, see Colin, pp.114–18. Colin does point out that community cultures were to be represented on the Council but inadequately and unevenly, pp.118–19.

15. Ibid., pp.73–5.

16. See two documents by the Ministère de l'éducation nationale et de la culture (Délégation au développement et aux formations), *L'Art à l'école: enseignements et pratiques artistiques*, Paris, no date (1993), p.26–7; and 'Les Enseignements artistiques de 1981 à 1986. Ce qui a été fait, ce qui reste à faire', no date.

17. Douffiagues, *Un Projet culturel pour demain*, p.45.

18. Colin, *La Beauté*, pp.96–7; see also his contribution to *Commentaire*, no.50, summer 1990, p.346. In a letter to me dated September 1993, Pierre Moulinier also contends that the FIC disappeared to avoid duplication with the DDC and the DRACs.

19. Colin, *La Beauté*, p.112; and Wangermée and Gournay, *La Politique culturelle*, pp.218–19 and p.248.

20. Lang interviewed in 'Les Deux Urgences du Ministre de la culture', *France-Soir*, 12 June 1981; Mauroy in 'Ce qu'ils nous veulent', *Les Nouvelles Littéraires*, 4–11 June 1981, pp.14–15.

21. M. Hunter, *Les Jours les plus Lang*, Paris, 1990, pp.143–51.

22. *Le Monde*, 4 June 1982, p.25; Hunter, *Les Jours*, p.146.

23. Fleuret quoted in a personal interview in 1983 with D. Wachtel, *Cultural Policy and Socialist France*, New York, 1987, p.45. See also Hunter, *Les Jours*, pp.150–1, on the political importance of the Fête de la musique.

24. 'Front populaire et création artistique', *Bulletin de la Société d'Histoire Moderne*, vol.8, 1974, p.17.

25. 'Pratiques et politiques', *Le Monde*, 8 December 1982, p.13.

26. 'Discours prononcé par M. Jack Lang, Ministre de la culture, à l'Assemblée Nationale le mardi 17 novembre 1981, lors de la Session Budgétaire', typed Ministry transcript (the quotation is from p.18, the shorter references from pp.11–12).

27. Shortly before his death, Fleuret told Hunter, *Les Jours*, p.144, that Lang himself had not thought of an all-embracing policy for music until Fleuret insisted on it in October 1981; though Lang's presence at the Wonder concert the previous June perhaps suggests otherwise.

28. Ministry of Culture, 'La Politique culturelle 1981–1985': 'La Musique et la danse', pp.13, 17 and 23.

29. Wangermée and Gournay, *La Politique culturelle*, p.174.

30. 26 January 1983 (Paris), speech reproduced in 'Discours de Jack Lang', unpublished, 5 vols, vol.3, October 1982–March 1985, pp.7–8.
31. H. Starkey, 'Bande dessinée: the state of the ninth art in 1986', in J.Howorth and G.Ross, *Contemporary France: A Review of Interdisciplinary Studies*, 3 vols, vol.1, London, 1987, p.181.
32. Press conference speech announcing the setting up of the Musée de la mode, 26 June 1982, reproduced in 'Discours de Jack Lang', vol.1, July 1981–September 1982, p.95.
33. Quotation from Michaux, ibid., p.95; Renard, *L'Elan culturel: la France en mouvement*, Paris, 1987, p.53.
34. 'Le Ministère de la culture deviendrait-il le ministère de la pub?', interview with J. Peyret, *Stratégies*, 2 December 1984, p.56.
35. Ministry, 'La Politique culturelle 1981–1985': 'Economie et culture', p.2.
36. My analysis of Lang's views here draws particularly on his press conference on the communication industries, 7 December 1982, in 'Discours de Jack Lang', vol.2, October 1982–March 1985, pp.7–12; and on his speech inaugurating the Salon des techniques de l'image et du son, 14 April 1983, ibid., pp.13–19.
37. Renard, *L'Elan culturel*, p.96 and p.101.
38. On all these matters, see: Lang's press conference of 3 October 1983, 'Les Orientations nouvelles de la politique des industries de la culture', Ministry, dossier d'information no.118; Ministry of Culture, 'La Politique culturelle 1981–1985': 'Economie et culture', pp.4–10; and Lang's speech presenting the Plan Son, 23 October 1984, unpublished transcript. See also Renard, *L'Elan culturel*, pp.95–103.
39. Wangermée and Gournay, *La Politique culturelle*, pp.87–8; see also pp.85–8.
40. For Lang's views on *mécénat*, see his speech to a colloquium at the Ecole des hautes études commerciales, 29 November 1984, unpublished Ministry transcript, pp.8–11.
41. Quotation from Lang, 'La Création industrielle sera le pétrole de l'an 2000', interview with *Le Matin*, 11 October 1985. On this form of democratisation and the theme of art and industry, see also the feature by F. de Gravelaine *et al*, 'Art et industrie', *L'Unité*, no.622, pp.22–8, especially 'Look, soif d'aujourd'hui?', pp.24–7.
42. See Chapter 10 for the audiovisual issue.

– 7 –

A Certain Idea of the City: The
Presidential *grands projets*

Despite their distinctiveness and number, Mitterrand's *grands projets* represent a strong element of continuity with the past, particularly the Pompidou and Giscard years. De Gaulle was relatively indifferent to art and architecture which he happily left to Malraux. He is not therefore remembered for any major building projects, other than the Maisons de la culture or perhaps the controversial urban development project for Maine-Montparnasse. Indeed, what Pompidou's single-minded success with Beaubourg shows, in marked contrast to the uneven distribution of the MCs or the years of toing and froing over Les Halles, is that a direct presidential resolve, with the combination of centralised power and political longevity which only the Elysée confers, is essential if a state plan to build a costly monument to culture is ever to come to fruition.[1] But Beaubourg was exemplary in other ways too. First, an open international competition to find a design was organised which attracted 681 submissions. The international jury was then left to make up its own mind, with the result that a design was chosen which Pompidou reportedly did not like.[2] Second, he set a precedent Mitterrand was to follow, which was to create a modern institution dedicated to demystifying the museum and opening it to as wide a public as possible, in the heart of the city.

Giscard attempted to better Pompidou's achievement by launching four more projects: the Musée d'Orsay; the much-needed science and industry museum and park at the redundant abattoirs of La Villette; the 'Tête-Défense' which was to complete the business centre to the west of the city with a monumental building; and the Institut du monde arabe (IMA). Yet he crucially departed from the Pompidou model by making the final choice of architects for three of the four projects himself with no guidance from a properly constituted jury, which led to his being taxed with monarchism – the notorious *fait du prince*. The lessons of the 1970s were therefore contradictory. On the one hand, *le fait du prince* was deplored, not least by the Socialist opposition. On the other, the messy compromises over Les Halles were evidence of the chaos which can ensue in the absence of a coherent political will. Beyond doubt, Mitterrand's own *grands projets* owed considerably more to the second of these lessons.

At the end of his first press conference on 24 September 1981, Mitterrand outlined what the 'réalisations de référence' he had touched on at UNESCO the previous March would comprise. Further proposals were added subsequently to form a major building programme, supervised and coordinated by a team of four senior officials including Lang. Having first obtained the blanket approval of the RPR Mayor of Paris Jacques Chirac, whose support was vital if the projects were not to be obstructed, Mitterrand then issued a communiqué dated 8 March 1982 which unveiled the full programme of 'grandes opérations d'architecture et d'urbanisme'. Three of Giscard's projects were to be completed, though with alterations. For La Villette, Giscard's chosen architect, Adrien Fainsilber, was retained but his plans for the park were abandoned and a new competition held. The Giscardian head of the *établissement public* responsible for Orsay was replaced by Jacques Rigaud, with the left-wing historian Madeleine Rebérioux as his vice-president, their job being to redefine the museum's programme. The IMA was, as La Ville de Paris wished, to be moved from the proposed Boulevard de Grenelle site, though less to placate the city council than to dislodge the architect, for it was not the council's alternative site which was adopted but another, adjacent to the university facilities at Jussieu. Jean Willerval's project for La Défense, which Mitterrand did not like, was simply scrapped.[3]

Of the new initiatives, the most radical was the decision to move the Ministry of Finance out of the Richelieu wing of the Louvre where since 1872 it had prevented the entire building being made over to the museum. The idea of a 'Grand Louvre' had long been cherished by curators and arts officials, including Laurent, in whose blueprint it figured, and Malraux. Even Mitterrand's adversaries had therefore to admit that it was an audacious step and it caused considerable excitement in the Louvre administration itself, where staff had for years coped with the lamentable conditions in which the museum functioned: overcrowding, inadequate display, information and reception space, poor facilities for storage and restoration, shortage of staff, and frequent industrial unrest. Small wonder that it received fewer than three million visitors annually, 70 per cent of them non-French and therefore unlikely to return. A new Ministry of Finance was to be built to the east of the city, in the Bercy district.

Mitterrand's other plans included a Cité internationale de la musique, already pencilled in under Giscard as part of Fainsilber's plans for La Villette, consisting of new premises for the Conservatoire national de musique which had long since outgrown its supposedly temporary home in the rue de Madrid, a 3,000-seater auditorium, research and creation facilities, and a music museum. To celebrate the bicentenary of the Revolution, the government would be bidding to hold a Universal Exhibition in Paris, to be known as Expo 89. As for the Tête-Défense, this was now to be the site of a Centre (later 'Carrefour') international de la communication, which would bring to a district entirely given over to commerce 'la dimension culturelle et l'animation nécessaires à son parachèvement' and demonstrate France's determination to take its place in 'le monde de l'audiovisuel, de la communication et du cinéma'. Also to be transferred to the Centre were the Ministries of Urbanism and the Environment. The aim, it was said, was a grand monument that would mark the 1789 bicentenary as the Eiffel Tower had done the centenary. In addition, the communiqué alluded to a new popular-music concert hall at la Porte de Bagnolet; the rebuilding of Guy Rétoré's Théâtre de l'est parisien (TEP); and a package of research and technology facilities for the Montagne Sainte Geneviève. But perhaps most spectacular of all was the proposal for a second opera-house, 'moderne et populaire', to be built at the Place de la Bastille which, together with the Cité musicale at La Villette, would remedy the inadequacy of concert facilities in the capital. Lastly, to counterbalance this programme for Paris, the Minister of Culture was asked to draw up a list of projects of national or international stature in the regions in conjunction with the appropriate authorities. Amongst these were the BD museum in Angoulême and the Photography school in Arles, training schools for dance in Marseille and music in Lyon, and in a later list Les Archives du monde du travail in Roubaix and a number of smaller Zéniths.[4]

After the March announcement, the job of selecting architects began. Under Giscard and long before him, it had been customary to nominate French public-service architects armed with a *grand prix de Rome* for construction projects of this kind, which left no opening for the brilliant outsider. Like Pompidou, Mitterrand broke the mould, allowing Parisian architecture to come under fresh influences from abroad, the young, and in some cases the unknown. International competitions were held for three of the most important projects, La Défense, the opera-house and the park at La Villette, none won by French architects. Furthermore, the President was often prepared to heed the expert advice of juries and even be talked into choosing designs he did not appreciate, though he did not follow Pompidou so far as to relinquish the final decision completely except in the case of the La Villette park, won by the Swiss-born Bernard Tschumi with a design distinguished by the bright red *folies* placed at regular intervals throughout the site (see Figure 3). For La Défense, Mitterrand accepted the jury's selection of the little-known Danish academic Johann-Otto von Spreckelsen's open cube in white marble, which became one of his two favourites. For the Opéra-Bastille, in what was considered a lacklustre set of submissions, he somewhat begrudgingly went along with the choice of Carlos Ott, a young Paraguayan equally unknown in France, though with the proviso that the plan be further worked on. In the national competition organised for the Ministry of Finance at Bercy, the choice went to Paul Chemetov and Borja Huidobro whose low, rectangular building swung a giant leg across the Quai de la Rapée into the Seine like a Dali painting and was widely disliked. Once more, Mitterrand himself did not seem unduly enthusiastic, describing it as 'un peu mastoc', but accepted the jury's recommendation though again insisting on alterations.[5]

Some of the competitions did, however, prove controversial, particularly when a foreign architect was nominated, but chiefly because of the way the choices were made. The preference for the rising star Jean Nouvel for the IMA from only a small number of invited French candidates in a hastily conducted competition provoked *Le Quotidien de Paris* to mount a long-running campaign against what it took to be a politically inspired decision. When during the Cité musicale competition the President took the extraordinary step of eliminating one of the two favourites of the jury for the second round, some jury members resigned.[6] But most controversial of all was the choice of the Chinese-American Ieoh Ming Pei to work on the extension of the Louvre. This was not simply because Pei was not French, nor because he proposed to build a huge glass pyramid at the heart of the museum precinct, the Cour Napoléon. It was because this was the only occasion on which Mitterrand decided entirely alone, launching no competition and taking no advice from a jury, *fait du prince* par excellence.[7]

The presidential nature of the projects was reinforced in other ways too. Most of them were given the semi-autonomous legal status of *établissements publics*, a procedural device which bypassed the controls and interference of the central administration, linking the *grands projets* directly to the minister concerned and, for the major appointments and budgetary decisions, to the President himself. In the process, Lang's own responsibility for the projects, not all of which came under his jurisdiction anyway, was also reduced.[8] But even when his ministry was directly in charge of a project, as with the Opéra-Bastille, the

Louvre and Orsay, Mitterrand's involvement was closer still and it was he, not the Culture Minister, who chose Jacques Rigaud and E.-J. Biasini to head the respective *établissements publics* for Orsay and the Louvre extension. Like Giscard, Mitterrand would also have the architect's model left in his office for weeks on end and would often take time making the final decision. He took an interest in the Saint-Gobain glass being used in the Louvre pyramid and the marble proposed for la Grande Arche; for the Opéra-Bastille, he even chose the fabric for the seats.[9] Furthermore, keen to avoid the problems caused to Les Halles by delay or dissent, Mitterrand used every means at his disposal to take his projects to a point where cancellation after the 1986 elections would be more expensive than completion. There was a tendency to bypass correct administrative and legal procedures, to announce a project before it had been costed or to start building before costing was complete, to ignore the views of consultative bodies and to impose tight schedules on juries, such as the seven days granted the La Villette park jury to assess 470 projects.

What were the motives behind this grim resolve? These are complex, but broadly speaking one may recognise in the *grands projets* programme the ambition that was driving Socialist cultural policy generally: to reassert but redefine a national culture. One official justification commonly put forward was the commitment to creation. Mitterrand believed that neither Paris nor France had made enough room for contemporary architecture and he was keen to contribute to its development. After all, he told *Le Nouvel Observateur* in 1984, 'il serait fâcheux que l'architecture de mon septennat fût celle des péages pour autoroutes'.[10] For both aesthetic and political reasons, he rejected Giscard's classicism and opted for a familiar modernism of form and materials: pyramid, sphere, and cube; steel, marble and glass. Yet at the same time, this was to be understood not as a callow repudiation of the past but rather a continuation of it: 'Il n'existe pas d'architecture innocente', wrote E.-J. Biasini in 1990, by then Secrétaire d'Etat chargé des grands travaux: 'les Grands Travaux participent de ces gestes qui défient le temps et signifient solennellement la continuité de notre culture et de notre histoire.' Indeed, art historian Pierre Vaisse, a sceptical observer of the projects for some time, claims that Mitterrandian architecture is actually based on a rather conventional monumentalism, 'modern' only by virtue of its quotations from the founding fathers of modernism some sixty years ago.[11]

Secondly, the *grands projets* were intended as a further application of the culture-economy principle, enhancing France's international prestige and Paris's tarnished image as cultural capital of the world.

They were also, Mitterrand believed, a wise investment in times of austerity because they would create 10,000 jobs a year, keep alive a host of crafts and skills which otherwise would be lost, and act as a showcase of the French construction and design industries. And most of all, they would energise French society itself, restoring France's self-confidence: 'Ils sont une façon de dire aux Français qu'ils doivent, qu'ils peuvent croire en eux-mêmes.' As Lang too put it, a certain number of 'grandes réalisations de portée nationale ou internationale' was actually essential because of their ability to mobilise, to incite French people up and down the country to 'coaliser les efforts, les énergies et les imaginations'. This mobilisation theory was particularly in evidence in the idea of Expo 89 which, said Mitterrand, must like those before it 'solliciter l'imagination architecturale, favoriser la création des artistes, des artisans, des ingénieurs, et offrir ainsi à notre génération l'ambition de s'inscrire à son tour dans l'histoire'.[12]

The notion of a generation inscribing itself in history points to another common reading of the motives behind the *grands projets*. Rulers are generally remembered less for their economic or foreign policies than for the monuments they leave behind and a number of observers felt that Mitterrand's compulsive attention to the projects suggested he saw them as emanations of himself rather than as objectively necessary institutions. Favier and Martin-Roland evoke a President anxious to engrave his passing in stone, while his close friend Paul Guimard referred to his wish to 'griffer le temps'. Critics were not slow to read Pharaonic aspirations into his choice of a pyramid for the Louvre, *Le Canard Enchaîné* coining the term 'Tonton-Khamon'.[13] In Mitterrand's own explanations, however, the personal cannot be so easily disentangled from the public or political. 'Il est vrai qu'une force me pousse à tenter de soutenir la création d'une architecture. J'ai toujours eu ce goût', he confided to Catherine Clément in 1982, describing how he liked to spend time studying buildings, looking for the harmonies in the shapes of doors and windows, following the lines of the rooftops from the presidential helicopter.[14] Yet central to the appeal architecture has for him is also the way it combines this individual, creative dimension with both social usefulness and power: 'C'est l'architecture, par son utilité et par sa qualité, qui peut tout entraîner', he told *Le Nouvel Observateur* in 1984. While to Clément he explained thus the coherence of the *grands projets*: 'bâtir, c'est répondre à une utilité, proposer un contenant pour qu'il y ait un contenu. C'est créer, c'est composer un nouveau paysage pour la ville, un corps familier pour les millions d'hommes qui vivent là.' He also clearly believes in a correlation between architectural ambition and the greatness of a nation, as if a country's willingness to invest in magnificent buildings which will inspire its citizens were in itself a harbinger of national rebirth. Demonstrating just such an ambition, Mitterrand thus represents himself both as an individual concerned to make his mark on history by shaping people's aesthetic lives, and as the vehicle of the nation's greatness: 'Modeler le regard', he said to Le Nouvel Observateur, 'la mémoire, l'imagination des générations et des générations... Ce n'est pas une ambition pour moi, mais pour la France.'[15] Mitterrand was also of the view that the grands projets 'rally behind a certain idea of the city'. In his estimate, the divorcing of architectural values from town-planning has given rise to two equally undesirable alternatives: the development of tower blocks or grands ensembles, and, in reaction to this, what he calls 'dispersion'.[16] At the time of the 1981 election, he argued that the trend towards individual housing outside towns was not a natural evolution in demand but a result of Giscard's urban policy which, like Giscardism itself, had encouraged a nervous individualism which made people anxious to avoid the communication, conviviality and exchange that previously existed in urban communities: 'Nous n'aurons rien fait', Mitterrand said of the grands projets, 'si nous n'avons pas créé dans les dix années à venir les bases de la civilisation urbaine', which he also proclaimed to be the very essence of socialism.[17] Precisely how such costly, prestige projects for the capital were supposed to achieve this was not apparent to everyone. The architect and former soixante-huitard Roland Castro, for example, contended that it was in 'l'architecture ordinaire' that a Socialist government ought to be making its mark, a comment which prompted the government to back a scheme called Banlieues 89, under Castro himself, intended to beautify the disadvantaged suburbs and help rebuild the 'urban civilisation' the President had spoken of.[18] But the grands projets were still thought to have their own part to play in this task, for their very scale and prestige would allow them to act as beacons of urban and civic renewal, and their 'vertu de mobilisation' would encourage local authorities to emulate them.

The projects were similarly meant as beacons of Socialist cultural policy as a whole. They were monuments to the boost given to creation. They illustrated the Ministry's belief in reinterpreting the heritage by commissioning new work like the Pyramid or by converting historic buildings to new purposes as with the Orsay station. And in particular, they enshrined the traditional conception of democratisation. 'To provide easy access for all to the works and wisdom of the past and present', wrote Mitterrand, 'such is the prime ambition of France's major building projects.'[19] This ambition was most in evidence in the idea of a 'popular' opera-house, proposed by

Laurent in 1955 and even pursued for a time at Malraux's request by Vilar though in the event to no avail. In a report submitted in January 1977, François Bloch-Lainé wrote of the Opéra de Paris that it combined minimum democratisation with maximum expense. In 1981, opera-goers did indeed represent only 2 per cent of the nation,[20] and little about its home, the Palais Garnier, was likely to remedy this. Firstly, seats were in too short supply to cope with a growing demand in the wake of the music boom of the 1970s. Secondly, it was extremely expensive to run, accounting for over a third of the Ministry's music budget, each spectator's enjoyment being subsidised to the tune of 800 francs. This was partly because of the high costs of all opera productions, leaving them particularly exposed to the Baumol law, and partly because Garnier had followed the evolution of the performing arts generally in that the practice of maintaining a permanent troupe had given way to seasonal engagements, 'starisation' and ever higher-quality productions. This accounted for the tendency no longer to alternate different productions, which in turn led to a drop in the annual number of performances and therefore spectators. The appallingly high price of tickets which ensued inevitably compounded the problem. A further difficulty, as with the Louvre, was a shortage of adequate support facilities, particularly rehearsal space and workshops for making sets. As Garnier's director Massimo Bogianckino confessed in 1984, the Opéra was thus limited to three shows a week so that the rest of the time the stage could be used for rehearsals: 'Nous payons les gens pour attendre.'[21]

The Opéra-Bastille was conceived as the antithesis of all this, attracting people who had never been to an opera before. Bloch-Lainé had called for a modern facility offering 3,000 seats. In the summer of 1981, Lang took up the challenge, commissioning a report from Jean-Pierre Angrémy, at the time Director of Theatre at the Ministry.[22] Angrémy recommended the creation of a new facility within the La Villette music complex; La Défense was also considered a possibility for a time. In the end, the Bastille site prevailed because of its convenient ideological symbolism, which tacitly equated the throwing open of an elitist art-form with the celebrations of 10 May, the Popular Front rallies which used to begin there, and the epic of 1789.

Democratisation was equally central to the Grand Louvre project. Firstly, Pei's pyramid sought to democratise architecturally. Biasini identified the need to 'dédramatiser le monument', an objective which in fact applies to most of the *grands projets*, while Lang spoke of their 'philosophy of transparency'.[23] As a metaphor, transparency suggests modernity rather than fusty monumentalism, and openness instead of the feeling of closure and intimidation created by the cultural architecture of the past. It was already at work in the Pompidou Centre, whose architects tried to deconstruct it as an institution by displaying its inner workings on the outside.[24] But transparency also becomes literal in the use of glass. Pei's glass pyramid, as well as dematerialising the structure itself and allowing the Louvre to be visible beyond, lets the visitor hesitating on the threshold see what is inside before entering. This principle was later applied more ambivalently to the last of the *grands projets* (along with a new conference centre on the Quai Branly), the Bibliothèque de France. Indeed, contemporary critics like Pierre Vaisse doubt whether glass can ever achieve the 'utopia' of transparency, to say nothing of whether it is suited to the various buildings' purpose.[25] But in addition to the use of glass, democratisation in the Grand Louvre became indistinguishable from the brasher, trans-Atlantic concern with making the heritage more approachable and entertaining. Pei described the Pyramid as 'rejuvenating' the historic building. It was to offer a 'Louvre "à la carte"' by providing, in one vast open-access forum underground, a range of facilities designed to attract a non-specialist public and ease its contact with the museum proper: from temporary exhibitions, a bookshop, educational activities and information and rest areas, to cafés, a post-office and gift-shops. In this way, the fortunate post-modern visitor 'pourra, comme c'est le cas dans les musées américains, organiser librement sa journée au Louvre',[26] combining eating, shopping and art appreciation.

Other *grands projets* were meant as beacons not of high culture but of the newer doctrine of the *tout-culturel*. In the early days, some of them exhibited a residually *gauchiste* quality which reflected the ideology of the DDC, like the Archives du Monde du Travail or the original plans for the Carrefour de la communication at La Défense which stressed regionalism and pluralism. Others, however, focused on commercial forms: the Zénith, the BD museum at Angoulême, and so on. But perhaps the richest, most fascinating instance was La Villette, which seemed to synthesise all the various approaches (see Figures 3 and 4). From the start, the Socialists had declared an interest in what they called *la culture scientifique et technique*, which meant demystifying science and technology. Its roots lay in the creation of the Palais de la Découverte under the Front populaire and subsequently in the Fourth Plan, though the policy had only been implemented in a small number of MCs like Grenoble in the late 1960s. Lang shed light on the Socialists' conception of it at a study session on La Villette in February 1982, maintaining that the new facility must avoid the mistake of other science museums, which

Figure 3. La Villette. A section of the park seen from a *folie* (architect: B. Tschumi), Le Zénith (background left; architects: P. Chaix and J.-P. Morel), and two further *folies*.

Figure 4. La Villette: part of the Cité des sciences et de l'industrie, with the spherical mirror-clad cinema, la Géode, in the background (architect: A. Fainsilber). Photo: David Shaw.

display technology simply for its own sake, detached from its historical and social contexts. Rather than demonstrate a triumphalist vision of scientific gadgetry in this disembodied way, he argued, 'réintroduisons l'homme, réintroduisons l'histoire, réintroduisons aussi le futur'. The museum was to be, in its director Professor Maurice Lévy's words, an 'instrument de connaissance et d'appropriation'. Indeed, the term *musée* was abandoned because it implied a passive gaze directed at scientific objects; a 'Cité des sciences' on the other hand was suggestive of a human community, an ethos of participation and plurality.[27]

This humanist and humanised notion of science and technology implied *décloisonnement* and interdisciplinarity, which were also the theme of the site as a whole. This was embodied in the simple cohabitation of the science museum, the Cité musicale, and later the Zénith. But it was also enshrined in the park itself, described by Chaslin (p.217) as perhaps the only *grand projet* founded on an authentic left-wing philosophy. To merit *grand projet* status, Lang made clear, the park was to be of an entirely new kind. Neither 'espace vert' nor theme park, it was to consummate the wedding of science and art, the natural and human worlds. As François Barré put it in the report he drew up on the project: 'entre nature et ville, le jardin est un entre-monde qui parle de Dieu et des hommes, du pouvoir et de la société.'[28] Such an intermediate universe was the ideal arena for cultural and sociological *métissage* and for realising Mitterrand's urban culture. It was to be a park rooted in the city and in its district and it would provide as many forms of sociability, creative and recreative activity as the imagination could invent: spaces where children can do gardening and families can gather, spaces for libraries, eating, jogging. Science and art, nature and culture, learning, leisure and pleasure would all combine in a '"civilisation de la rencontre"', an outdoor urban idyll for which Lang's historical referent was the Renaissance of Rabelais's Thélème.[29] The park was thus a metaphor of the global conception of culture, not as a collection of compartmentalised, rarefied and narrowly defined art-forms experienced in solitude or in a closed Malraucian temple, but a culture at large, that can be physically entered and shared with others in an affirmation of community.

This emblematic importance of the *grands projets* helps explain the hostility they increasingly attracted. Lang cheerily welcomed this for it placed debate about architectural issues in the public domain. But much of it was party-political and represented a potential threat to some of the projects in the event of a change of government in March 1986. Indeed, for one of them, Expo 89, the threat materialised well before then, with the municipal elections of March 1983. Crucial to the Expo issue was the position of the Mayor of Paris. Common interests and a shared desire to avoid further conflicts like Les Halles had meant that reasonably cooperative relations had been established between the state and the Hôtel de Ville regarding the *grands projets*. After a meeting with the President in February 1982, Chirac gave the entire programme the go-ahead, though he did emphasise from the start that he foresaw a problem over cost. A year later, with the municipals approaching and several of the projects under fire in the press, he was already being more guarded, declaring himself 'satisfied' with the programme as Mayor but as a tax-payer 'paniqué, terrorisé, stupéfait'.[30] As for the Expo specifically, although his signature had appeared on France's application to the Bureau international des expositions in April 1982, he now warned that he would have to be 'vigilant' about its financing. The PS's poor showing at the March municipals then prompted the opposition to bolder advances. In May, the bill on the Expo went through Parliament but the RPR and UDF voted against. Talk circulated of insuperable traffic and accommodation problems caused by the anticipated sixty million visitors. Then, on 2 July, Chirac and Michel Giraud, RPR President of the Ile-de-France region, announced that it could not be held in Paris after all. In its present form, France could not afford it and it would cause Parisians untold disruption and expense. Jacques Toubon, RPR mayor of the thirteenth arrondissement, did pull punches a little, declaring that they were not yet saying either yes or no; but the message was quite clear. Mitterrand cancelled the operation three days later.

In the ensuing furore, there were two readings of the cancellation. One was that the technical difficulties the Expo posed had already been overcome in a report by Gilbert Trigano and the projected costs brought down, but that Chirac's spoiling tactic had forced Mitterrand's hand. By immediately cancelling the event, then, the President had gained a moral victory, showing himself to be capable of dignity and restraint, while Chirac appeared 'une girouette' as Lang put it. The alternative reading, however, was that Chirac had merely been used as a scapegoat for a cancellation which, in the aftermath of devaluation and economic austerity, was already inevitable. Chirac's announcement therefore offered Mitterrand a way out without losing face. Even Lang, at the time the most disappointed as his intemperate attacks on Chirac showed, recognises with hindsight that in a time of economic crisis the event as planned was 'peut-être un peu somptuaire' and that, if Mitterrand had not backed down so quickly, a compromise might have been reached.[31] But what the Expo episode demonstrated most clearly was the political escalation of the culture issue in the wake of the March municipals. In this supercharged climate, intensified by the simultaneous polemics over the treatment being meted out to EACs by some of the new right-wing councils, the opposition's focus now swung over to other *grands projets* even though, as Mayor, Chirac himself generally maintained his readiness to assist procedurally.

The battle of the Grand Louvre began when the project was submitted to the Commission supérieure des monuments historiques in January 1984. The meeting was stormy, partly because the Commission was manoeuvred into deciding in a single vote on both the Pyramid specifically and the entire extension of the Louvre; and partly because of the shock caused by the design. Again, the polemic was highly politicised, with the right-wing press generally against and the left-wing for. 'La meute glapit', thundered Pierre Cabanne, for in France today any cultural act is political. Roland Castro too saw the controversy as more political than aesthetic, symbolic of the eternal struggle in France between progressivism and conservatism. Vaisse, however, disputes any automatic equation between aesthetic and political affiliation. Indeed, although as Chaslin points out the Association pour le renouveau du Louvre formed by Michel Guy and others to oppose the Pyramid drew a number of its members from Barrists and Giscardians, Chirac (RPR) declared himself in favour, albeit with tactical caution. The debate was nevertheless, as Chaslin also shows, a 'querelle des anciens et modernes'.[32] The anti-Pyramid faction included the Société pour la protection des paysages et de l'esthétique de la France, which was also active against Buren and, much earlier, Le Corbusier's 'cité radieuse' in Marseille; while most well-known representatives of the contemporary arts were in favour. There was also conflict between those who recognised the need for a new entrance and new facilities for mass tourism, and those *habitués* who wished to preserve the Louvre's ancient dignity. Michel Guy argued that, although the extension was a bold and necessary step, the museum needed to be protected from desecration for, with *animation* and commercial activities laid on for a mass public, 'tout cela aura un aspect mi-RER, mi-Forum des Halles'.[33]

Other criticisms of the *grands projets*, in particular the Opéra-Bastille, were more concerned with timing and cost. After the Expo's cancellation, Mitterrand tersely reminded the projects' coordinator Yves Dauge that they must be completed within the time but also the budget allotted, though these demands were not easy to reconcile. The estimated cost of the Opéra-Bastille, the project Mitterrand had been least sure of and which was in jeopardy with every Finance bill, rose from 1,766 million francs in 1983 to 2,170 million in 1985. Between 1981 and 1983, the cost of the Cité des sciences had gone up 22 per cent. Mitterrand insisted that it return to the 1981 estimate, which meant that not all of the museum was ready in time for the opening. In addition, only about half of the proposed park could be authorised in the budget for 1985, while the Cité musicale was similarly divided into two phases, as was the Louvre project.[34] Bagnolet was abandoned altogether. This deceleration made some of the projects look even more vulnerable as March 1986 approached. By 1985, the opposition had declared that it would cancel the Opéra-Bastille unless it had gone past the point of no return. Furthermore, the Ministry of Finance would not move out of the Louvre and the Bercy building would be sold off as office-space.

These threats only increased the urgency. At La Villette, La Grande Halle was hastily opened in 1985, then the Géode only two days before the election. To avoid the Bercy ministry having to wait for buildings in its path to be demolished, it was simply extended in a different direction. As this sense of improvisation grew, opposition hostility focused all the more on the programme's profligacy, while Lang and others in the team tried constantly to put the spending into perspective. The practice of costing the *grands projets* as a single budgetary item, for example, gave a false impression, the Minister argued, since it concentrated attention on one astronomic figure while the costs of far more expensive projects like nuclear power stations were not aggregated in this way. Furthermore, this figure included sums taken from the ordinary budgets already allocated to the various contributing ministries, thereby counting them twice. It also took no account of income to the state from the *grands projets* (to say nothing of their less quantifiable cultural benefits) or of other investments, including those of the private sector as with the Grande Arche (1.7 billion francs).[35]

Another familiar complaint was that the projects were benefiting the capital alone. True, there was the parallel programme for the provinces. But this represented a fraction of the cost to the state, involved the local authorities in forking out for a substantial part of a presidentially imposed project they were not always delighted to have, and enjoyed little of the status of the Paris projects. Furthermore, with the provincial *grands projets* as with the *conventions de développement culturel*, Ministry aid under the scheme was only forthcoming when it considered the project 'exemplary' and consistent with its own options.

Worse still, the Paris projects became a budgetary priority from 1984, absorbing a growing portion of spending and undoing earlier progress made towards a better balance between Paris and the provinces. When the Ministry's budget for 1985 was examined in the Assembly in October 1984, despite an overall increase of 6.4 per cent, concern was expressed on both sides at the preponderance of the *grands projets* and their future operating costs. Largely as a result of the projects, *autorisations de programme* (funds earmarked in the annual budget for long-term capital expenditure) were up 36.7 per cent, while the money made available to the provinces for *action culturelle* and facilities like monuments, archives and municipal libraries fell. The following year, the budget for cultural decentralisation plummeted by a further 50 per cent, with the DDC taking nearly a 25 per cent cut.[36] Despite increases in spending on the various regions of between 60 and 120 per cent, the Ministry's overall outlay on Paris in 1986 represented 58.6 per cent of its budget and on the provinces (excluding the Ile-de-France) only 31.6 per cent, which contrasted markedly with 44.3 per cent and 40.2 per cent respectively in 1981.[37] Even more worrying was the future commitment the programme represented, as the operating costs of such monster institutions, added to existing ones like the Pompidou Centre and the Opéra-Garnier, were certain to absorb a huge portion of Ministry funds. Arguing its way out of the irony of this recentralisation became a political albatross for the government as the elections approached.

Less publicly perhaps, other disparities between theory and practice were also apparent. Mitterrand's idyll of a living community of the city and his talk in the 1981 campaign of a 'contre-pouvoir associatif'[38] that would guarantee the participation of citizens in the creation of their built environment contrasted strangely with the centralised, personalised and statuesque *grands projets*. Vaisse maintains that rather than having a living relationship with their urban environment or driving the process of renewal in a district, the projects are often isolated monuments, the Bastille opera-house particularly being squeezed for the sake of symbolism into a site with which it fails to mesh.[39] It is in fact ironic that, to build the opera-house, it was necessary to break up an existing community which by all accounts displayed precisely the organic sociability Mitterrand had once wished to restore. As one of the members of the Association des expulsés du 12ᵉ arrondissement put it: 'C'est un tissu urbain très riche, très vivant, qui est condamné par le projet.' Indeed, one effect some projects are having is the gentrification of formerly working-class or run-down districts.[40]

All of the objections encountered by the *grands projets* ultimately point back to their being highly personalised presidential initiatives and confirm the contradiction this chapter began with, between resentment of the *fait du prince* and a fairly widespread agreement that in France only a supreme political authority is capable of bringing off so ambitious a building programme, one which has undoubtedly enhanced France's cultural standing and Paris's attractiveness to tourists. And, although one should be wary of taking official self-justifications at face value, it is equally unwise to dismiss the projects simply as the product of extravagant self-interest or even megalomania as some have, for their overall significance is more complex than such reactions allow. As has often been pointed out, part of that significance lies in the progressive emergence of culture as a presidential *domaine réservé* since Pompidou and a key issue on any political agenda. But as I have tried to show, the projects are also bound up with the Left's entire cultural policy in power, which they illuminate and are illuminated by. Their full significance, and more particularly their full impact on the Socialist project, has therefore to be viewed in relation to that policy's evolution, and also to the debates it increasingly inspired. For although the period after the March 1986 elections saw political conflict with regard to cultural policy lessen somewhat, a vigorous intellectual debate began around that time about its very principles.

Notes

1. F. Chaslin, *Les Paris de François Mitterrand: histoire des grands projets architecturaux*, Paris, 1985, p.13, to which I am indebted for some of my pre–1985 material. S. Collard defines other Gaullian projects as *grands travaux* (e.g. Concorde or the ocean liner France), though she also makes a distinction between *grands travaux* and the specifically cultural nature of *grands projets*, 'Mission impossible: les chantiers du Président', *French Cultural Studies*, vol.3, no. 8, June 1992, pp.130–2.
2. On the competition system, see Collard, 'Mission impossible', p.107, note 55.
3. For details of the fate of specific projects, see the appropriate chapters from Chaslin, *Les Paris*; also P. Favier and M. Martin-Roland, *La Décennie Mitterrand*, Paris, 2 vols, vol.1, 1990, pp.562–71.
4. See Chaslin, *Les Paris*, p.27, footnote, for the full lists. My quotations in this paragraph are all from the 8 March communiqué.
5. On the circumstances behind the choice of Ott, see Chaslin, *Les Paris*, pp.199–202. Mitterrand is quoted in Favier and Roland, *La Décennie Mitterrand*, vol.1, p.567.

6. See Chaslin, *Les Paris*, pp.231–3, for full details.

7. According to Chaslin's sources, it was in fact difficult to persuade Mitterrand of the need for a competition for other projects too, ibid., p.35.

8. On the *établissement public* formula, see A.-H. Mesnard, *Droit et politique de la culture*, Paris, 1990, pp.240–1; and Collard, 'Mission impossible', pp.116–17, which also lists which ministries were responsible for individual projects.

9. Favier and Roland, *La Décennie Mitterrand*, vol.1, p.568.

10. 'François Mitterrand: "Parce que je suis amoureux de Paris..."', *Le Nouvel Observateur*, 14 December 1984, p.66.

11. Biasini, 'Les Grands Travaux: l'héritage de demain', *Après-Demain*, no.322, March 1990, p.8; Vaisse, 'Dix Ans de grands travaux', *Contemporary French Civilization*, vol.15, no.2, summer/fall 1991, pp.324–5.

12. The last three quotations are respectively from Mitterrand, '"Parce que je suis amoureux"', p.70; Lang, debate on the *grands projets* with the PS, in 'Discours de Jack Lang', unpublished, 5 vols, vol.1, October 1982–March 1985, 3 December 1984, pp.129–30; and Mitterrand's *lettre de mission* to Robert Bordaz dated 20 November 1981, Ministry of Culture press release, 3 December 1981.

13. Favier and Roland, *La Décennie Mitterrand*, vol.1, p.562, p.565 and p.570. Guimard's remark is quoted in '"Parce que je suis amoureux"', p.69.

14. C. Clément, *Rêver chacun pour l'autre: sur la politique culturelle*, Paris, 1982, p.289.

15. The quotations from *Le Nouvel Observateur* are from '"Parce que je suis amoureux"', p.68 and p.69 respectively; Mitterrand's remark to Clément is from Clément, *Rêver*, p.287.

16. The English quotation is from *Connaissance des Arts*, special issue *Grands Travaux* (English edition), 1989, p.5; Mitterrand's views on 'dispersion' appear in '"Parce que je suis amoureux"', pp.68–9.

17. For Mitterrand's views on architecture, Giscardism and socialism, see his article, 'La Démocratisation voie de la vraie réforme architecturale', *Architecture*, no.22, April 1981, p.43, and Chaslin, *Les Paris*, p.21. The quotation is from a presidential statement made 29 January 1982 and reproduced in the Ministry of Culture's *Lettre d'Information*, 4 July 1988.

18. Chaslin, *Les Paris*, p.172; and '"Parce que je suis amoureux"', p.68.

19. *Connaissance des Arts*, *Grands Travaux*, p.5.

20. Bloch-Lainé is quoted in Chaslin, *Les Paris*, p.187; the statistic is taken from R. Wangermée and B. Gournay, *Programme européen d'évaluation: la politique culturelle de la France*, Paris, 1988, p.192. On Vilar's planned 'TNP lyrique', see P. Cabanne, *Le Pouvoir culturel sous la V*ᵉ *République*, Paris, 1981, p.200.

21. Quoted in 'Le Grand Air de Carlos', *Le Nouvel Observateur*, 14 December 1984, p.86. On opera and its problems, see Wangermée and Gournay, *La Politique culturelle*, p.192. Fuller discussion of the new opera-house project appears in Chapter 9.

22. Both Bloch-Lainé and Angrémy were later to become the chief planners of the Bastille project, alongside Michèle Audon.

23. Biasini is quoted in S.H. Riggins and K. Pham, 'Democratizing the arts: France in an era of austerity', *Queen's Quarterly*, vol.93, no.1, spring 1986, p.151; and Lang in an interview with *Paris Match*, 3 February 1984, p.26.

24. On the architectural conception of Beaubourg, see Renzo Piano paraphrased in Riggins and Pham, 'Democratizing the arts', p.151.

25. Vaisse, 'Dix Ans de grands travaux', pp.326–7.

26. *Beaux-Arts* (text by J. Girard and G. Boyer), special issue *La Pyramide du Louvre*, no date, unnumbered pages. Pei's 'rejuvenation' comment is quoted in Riggins and Pham, 'Democratizing the arts', p.151.

27. Lang, speech of 9 February 1982, 'Discours de Jack Lang', vol.2, July 1981–September 1982, p.78; Lévy and others are quoted in 'Le Temple du Dieu futur', *Le Nouvel Observateur*, 14 December 1984, p.75.

28. Barré is quoted by Lang in his 9 February 1982 speech, 'Discours de Jack Lang', vol.2, July 1981–September 1982, p.76.

29. Ibid., p.77; and his speech launching the competition for the park, 17 May 1982, 'Discours de Jack Lang', vol.2, July 1981–September 1982, p.89; the inner quotation is from Mitterrand.

30. 'Tous les grands chantiers de Paris ne pourront être financés déclare M. Chirac', *Le Monde*, 23 February 1983, p.44.

31. Favier and Roland, *La Décennie Mitterrand*, vol.1, p.569.

32. Cabanne and Castro are cited in Chaslin, *Les Paris*, p.124. Vaisse, 'Dix Ans', pp.313–14. On the aesthetic and political nature of the whole debate, see Chaslin, *Les Paris*, pp.123–33. A polemical pamphlet linked with the Association pour le renouveau du Louvre also appeared, picking up a number of the main issues and summarising the warring positions: B. Foucart, S. Loste and A. Schnapper, *Paris mystifié: la grande illusion du Grand Louvre*, Paris, 1985, see particularly pp.52–7.

33. Guy's remark appears in *Le Figaro Magazine*, 20 September 1984.
34. The statistics and other details are from Chaslin, *Les Paris*, p.210, pp.73–4 and p.224 respectively.
35. See ibid., pp.239–42, for fuller details of these arguments.
36. For the 1985 figures, see *Journal Officiel*, séance du 25 octobre 1984, pp.5,215–22 *passim*, statistic on *autorisations de programme*, p.5,219; for 1986, see D. Wachtel, *Cultural Policy and Socialist France*, New York, 1987, p.75.
37. Wangermée and Gournay, *La Politique culturelle*, p.132.
38. Mitterrand, 'La Démocratisation voie de la vraie réforme architecturale', p.43.
39. Vaisse, 'Dix Ans', pp.314–16.
40. *Le Nouvel Observateur*, 14 December 1984, p.85; and D. Wachtel, *Cultural Policy*, p.75.

Part III

Policies and Debates, 1986–93

Lang and the Politics of Fun: Politicising the Cultural Debate, 1985–88

What the preceding analysis of Socialist policy between 1981 and 1986 has generally shown up is a certain disparity between word and deed. Despite the PS's apparently comprehensive interpretation of the field of culture, the progress made in the direction of a truly global policy, and of true cultural democracy as defined in the late 1960s and early 1970s, was still fairly limited, less a revolution than an adjustment of focus. Firstly, Malraux's democratisation-heritage-creation trilogy for high culture was not fundamentally questioned; and though creation was foregrounded as promised, the efforts to bring it closer to local communities did not always yield the desired result. Secondly, the most radical proposals for change – an *enseignements artistiques* bill and the recognition of new rank-and-file publics and practices – either did not materialise or were not given enough weight compared to the more traditional arts and heritage. Instead, the post-1968 concern with cultural democracy was translated into a highly publicised binary policy: a festive approach to amateur practices and participation, and a *tout-culturel* approach directed at professional creation and the cultural industries. Lastly, the *grands projets* programme, which magnificently summarised the non-selective conception of culture the PS had originally preached, turned out to be too imperious and grandiloquent – too concerned with national symbolism, too Gaullian in style and Giscardian in practice – to make much of an impact on everyday cultural democracy.

Part II also revealed that, although the new cultural-industries discourse around 1983 seemed to go against the PS's previous suspicion of mass culture, it had already been written into the budget speech of November 1981 and was beginning to be implemented by early 1982. The watershed of 1983, then, had somewhat less to do with policy than with presentation, for that year the Ministry in a sense came out, adjusting its image to match its measures. This was a result both of the economic U-turn which caused the government to espouse modernity and entrepreneurialism, and of the more or less simultaneous collapse of the original left-wing cultural project under a remarkable hail of blows. The silence of the intellectuals issue came to a head with the February colloquium and the *Le Monde* debate; the disaster of the municipals led to the undoing of the Left's cultural action in its flagship communes and an assault on the *grands projets*; Lang was demoted and the 1 per cent again postponed; and, most symbolic of all, Expo 89, laden with Popular-Front symbolism and entangled with the PS's whole sense of itself as a party of the Left, was cancelled. In July 1984, Prime Minister Pierre Mauroy, himself saddled with an old-Left image, was replaced by the considerably younger Laurent Fabius representing a new generation of well-groomed, middle-class, often ENA-trained Socialists. The party role-model ceased to be the hirsute, *baba-cool* intellectual or local militant and became the smart-suited, socially minded entrepreneur à la Bernard Tapie. In the cultural sector, this brought about the reconstruction of Jack Lang.

As Lang became better known to the press during his first two years in office, there was widespread recognition of his talents, in particular his extraordinary energy and capacity for work. Less than a year after coming to office, he was having fifty meetings a day and receiving more than 300 hundred requests for interviews from the foreign press alone. The switchboard at the rue de Valois had had to be doubled, the amount of post had trebled, and the Minister seemed to be everywhere at once. 'Ce n'est plus un ministre', commented his bodyguard, 'c'est Fantomas.'[1] But as glimpsed earlier, he had also attracted less favourable comment. In 1982, when it was still too early for opponents to carry out a critique of policy, the new ministry's weakest point was Lang himself: the ideological character of some of his pronouncements, gaffes like the trip to Cuba, his growing reputation for sycophancy towards the President. Some also disliked his style: the Byronically tousled perm, the year-round tan, the open-necked shirts and designer suits. 'Pour la première fois', exclaimed the indignant editor of *Le Figaro Magazine*, Patrice de Plunkett, 'voilà un ministre de la République dont tout acte soulève un commentaire dans le ton de la haute couture.'[2] Then there was his taste for political theatre and celebrity occasions, already at work in the party events he had organised before 1981 and still visible in the lavish Sorbonne colloquium, giving rise to media labels like *Disneylang* and *la gauche-caviar*. All of these criticisms were condensed in a virulent pamphlet by de Plunkett, *La Culture en veston rose* published in autumn 1982, which presented him as both a dangerous ideologist and a semiliterate fop, his totalitarian designs made all the more obvious by his preciousness and taste for mixed metaphors. Zhdanov, Maurras and Barnum rolled into one, Lang became the man the Right loved to hate.

Of course, this image did no harm at all to his political credibility and those on both sides who had initially thought of him as a liability were proved wrong. Despite the lapses and the lyricism, he had soon demonstrated that a high public profile, however controversial, pays dividends. For all that the 1983 colloquium had been shouted down as meretricious, its success lay in its having drawn attention to the fact that famous creators and intellectuals from across the world were willing to come to Paris to discuss the government's cultural project; and whether this was for love or a free flight on Concorde as cynics suggested mattered little. Another case in point was the Fête de la musique, which some worked hard to ridicule but which by its second year was a public-relations triumph. As Vitez had already spotted in 1978, Jack Lang was a more complex phenomenon than he seemed and provoked equally complex reactions. 'Depuis deux ans', wrote Jean-Paul Enthoven after spending ten days with him in 1983, 'le style Lang – boy-scoutisme charmeur, saturé de convictions; look d'éternel Chevalier à la rose... – irrite autant qu'il séduit.'[3]

Naturally, it was the seductiveness which was mobilised as the prospect of defeat in the 1986 elections loomed. A change in his public image actually began with the cultural industries policy, which required a more business-like persona. And like the government as a whole, he also struggled even more vigorously to divest himself of his anti-American tag: Deauville and Mexico were forgotten, references to solidarity with national liberation movements dropped. Although he did not ever retract his strong words, he now campaigned against American domination at European level and in more conciliatory terms. With France occupying the presidency of the EC in 1984, he chaired the European Council of Culture Ministers in Luxembourg in June. Just before, he had blamed the Europeans themselves for allowing US imports to dominate European markets and declared he was going to Luxembourg with one message: 'let's imitate America's spirit of enterprise, its spirit of adventure and the conquest of new intellectual frontiers'.[4] Then, in September 1985, as if to complete the metamorphosis, he attended the Deauville Festival, throwing a dinner-party at the Hôtel Royal for some thirty guests.

But the most important way in which Lang strove to adjust his image concerned youth. It took the PS government a short while to realise that the young of the mid–1980s were quite indifferent to the brand of ideological rhetoric Lang had used in his first months in power. Raised on American mass culture, accepting it as their own, they were mobilised much more by planetary issues like human rights and ecology, or pop-humanitarianism like Live Aid, than by grim crusades against cultural imperialism. At the 1983 colloquium, Lang explicitly recognised this. The days of barricades and insurrection are over, he said, and today's 'Internationale de la Jeunesse' is very different from that of the 1960s: 'Regardez-la, elle se moque des frontières, des idéologies fatiguées, elle se ressemble partout, et elle se rassemble, malgré les espaces, musique à l'oreille, tee-shirt sur les épaules, elle a son langage commun avec son uniforme (pacifique) commun, ses artistes en commun, et elle est en train de bâtir une société parallèle à la nôtre, mais porteuse, elle, de l'avenir.'[5] Whether or not this world-wide cultural revolution would prove any more lasting than 1968's, and how far the 'common language' of tee-shirts and walkmans was distinguishable from the 'false internationalism' and standardisation brought about by Americanisation, were questions he left unanswered. But his speech certainly heralded a closer, perhaps more in-touch concern with youth culture and a willingness from the mid–1980s to recognise whatever seemed to be the fashion of the moment. One instance was world music. To an extent, this term recalled Lang's 1981 concern with preserving authentic cultural identities. But in the main, it suggested not so much an exchange of such identities as a melting-pot where they were dissolved since, although world music implied an interest in African or Asian musical styles, it usually involved mixing them with Western rhythms and instrumentation and in France was bound up with SOS Racisme and the Beur movement. *Métissage* accordingly became a major theme in Langian discourse in the mid–1980s.

Predictably, the interest in youth meant a good deal of standard-bearing pageantry. In November 1983, Lang joined a march against racism. He was later one of those responsible for bringing together Desmond Tutu, Mother Theresa, the founder of Amnesty International Sean MacBride and naturally Mitterrand at the Rencontres internationales sur les libertés et les droits de l'homme of May 1985. And most visibly of all, he associated himself directly with the 'Touche pas à mon pote' rock concert a fortnight later, also attended by Fabius. Not surprisingly, his popularity among the young and elsewhere soared. In an early poll in January 1982, only 30 per cent of respondents had viewed him favourably. By February 1985, a Harris poll had given him a score of 52 per cent and showed that his *tout-culturel* approach had found particular favour: 70 per cent considered it normal for the Ministry to aid BD, 74 per cent French TV production, and 77 per cent popular music. The Fête de la musique was approved of by 77 per cent, and by 89 per cent of 15–17 year-olds. In June that year, a SOFRES survey placed him top of the ministerial popularity chart, while a survey of opposition voters in late 1985 revealed that he was one of the very few they would like to see remain in post in the event of a PS defeat.[6] This was a fine irony. As the Socialists' star waned, here was the party maverick some had thought of as the madman of Chaillot, too 'artistic' and arriviste by half, now the government's one *valeur sûre* in a volatile climate and, more ironically still, a consensual figure bestriding the gulf between Left and Right.

The Fabius government soon latched on to his usefulness, restoring his ministerial status in December 1984. Not long afterwards, the press began to notice that in the process he had been moved up into the front line, appearing more frequently on television and acting as unofficial presidential spokesman. In a TF1 interview in April 1985, Mitterrand paid homage to his achievements. On 3 June, Lang's second appearance on Antenne 2's 'L'Heure de vérité' revealed him to be shedding his 'artistic' persona and demonstrating the all-round grasp of world events of the accomplished politician. 'Tout se passe', *Le Point* commented after the programme, 'comme si Laurent Fabius avait fait de lui le porte-parole du nouveau langage, le préposé au sourire et à la jeunesse, le délégué général au new-look officiel.'[7] Cultural policy was becoming entangled in a politics of fun.

Part of the reason for this was that the Centre and Right had begun to strike back. Having under Giscard lost sight of the strategic importance of culture, the opposition was swiftly reminded of it by Lang's *modus operandi*, some even being converted to Gramsci's contention that political hegemony depends on cultural power. Chirac's Ville de Paris had already made culture a priority and Conservative mayors of other big cities followed suit. Cultural provision became an electoral issue in the 1983 municipals and it was the Right's new assertiveness in the wake of its success which provoked the subsequent feuds over the EACs and *grands projets*. In September that year, the first 'Rencontres de Fontevraud' brought together at the historic abbey three oppositional organisations, the Association des élus pour la liberté de la culture created that year, Art et Lumière, and the Alliance pour une nouvelle culture, also launched in 1983. According to *Le Monde*, the three were closely related, and membership of the last two was said to be drawn from a wide spectrum of right-wing opinion including the extreme-right. Culture, *Le Monde* commented just before the cultural budget debate in November, was in the political arena as never before.[8]

With this escalation on both sides, it was inevitable that culture would also play a key role in the run-up to the general election. In October 1985, the Culture budget for the following year, by virtue of a 15.8 per cent increase, came within a whisker of the promised 1 per cent (0.95 per cent).[9] No opportunity was missed to help Lang hit the headlines. On 17 April 1985, he arrived to address the Assembly wearing a black jacket with a Chairman Mao collar concocted by the vogue designer Thierry Mugler. For some, the jacket, coupled with his long dark curls and seemingly worn without the obligatory tie, was too provocative to bear. 'Habillez-vous comme tous les Français!', insisted one opposition deputy. 'C'est une tenue de Chinois!', expostulated another. 'Kadhafi! Kadhafi!', chanted UDF and RPR members alike. The matter of the tie will probably never be cleared up to the satisfaction of the scrupulous investigator; 'En a-t-il ou n'en a-t-il pas', *Libération* disingenuously enquired the following day. But with the incident widely reported, even eliciting a reaction from Tripoli, Lang clearly emerged the winner, having cast the Right as petty and bigoted.[10] But such provocations were only one weapon in Lang's arsenal. Another were the new Ministry-initiated jamborees which sprang up that same year: the historic monuments open day, a Fête du cinema, a Ruée vers l'art and an Oscars de la mode ceremony. Lang also criss-crossed the country with press conferences, inaugurating or visiting cultural institutions by the score or pursuing his own campaign to represent Loir-et-Cher, where he had finally been parachuted after trying a number of constituencies. In November 1985, he had an audience with the Pope. The following January, he was filmed in his kitchen cooking a homely pot-au-feu and obligingly passing on the recipe to viewers.

Naturally, the Right did its best to deflect the Lang roadshow. His old enemy Michel Guy, for example, articulated the standard opposition view that the Left had merely improvised its cultural policies. It had spread the budget too thinly (*saupoudrage*), subsidised ill-defined creation projects of dubious worth, prioritised the trendy, the spectacular and the Parisian at the expense of the heritage and decentralisation, and failed to address major issues like reading and libraries (particularly the BN), the audiovisual and arts education, all of them priorities of the 1981 cultural project. Articles in *Le Figaro* and its magazine also raged against what Lang was doing with the Ministry. 'Mais non, son bilan n'est pas bon!','Mais non, cet homme n'est pas "sympa"!', read the exasperated subtitles in one piece by de Plunkett. RPR deputy Jacques Baumel saw the *tout-culturel* in particular as bringing about 'la ruine d'un certain classicisme à la française' with one aim in mind: 'dissoudre les formes de la société et promouvoir une contre-société culturelle.'[11] Much heat was also generated by the

Buren Columns and a dispute over Pierre Mauroy's wish to have the 'plans-reliefs' of 102 fortified towns transferred from Les Invalides to his mayoral domain of Lille, which the opposition hotly contested.

What Lang's colourful personalisation of state intervention had in fact brought about was a tendency to look back nostalgically to a more restrained, Beaux-Arts conception of cultural administration, in the name of the up-and-coming 'neo-liberal' values the Right was espousing at the time, suspicious of statism and all its works. The question 'faut-il un ministère de la Culture' therefore became a theme in the run-up to the election. A feature in Le Figaro with this title argued that the Ministry must cease to 's'ériger lui-même en créateur, de prêcher des idéologies, d'édicter des normes' and must return to being 'un ministère des affaires culturelles voire, plus simplement, du patrimoine'. Christian Langlois, architect and member of the Institut de France, took a comparable view in a short pamphlet, Pour une véritable culture, which wanted the replacement of the Ministry by one entitled 'du développement artistique et du patrimoine'. The Académie des beaux-arts likewise called for the word 'culture' or 'cultural' to be expunged from the Ministry's title and for patrimoine to become its chief focus. It demanded the dismantling of the CNAP, the CNAC, le FNAC and the FRACs, all 'sectaires, tentaculaires et paralysants', and insisted that creation policies, which currently allow too much favour to go to the fashionable and the experimental, be restrained by 'collegial authorities' such as the Academy itself.[12]

In the meantime, a growing number of artists and intellectuals was rallying round Lang. In January 1986, a group of young 'creators' working in the fashionable areas he had become identified with formed le Club Zénith to defend him. They held a rock concert in early February, complete with badges and tee-shirts bearing the Club's motto 'Pourvu que ça dure' and intended for all those who identified with 'le formidable élan culturel que connaît la France depuis quatre ans'.[13] They also took a full-page spread in the press (see Figure 5), bearing the same slogan and the sketched faces and names of four attractive young artists: an actor, a black musician, an Oriental stylist with a modish bobbed haircut and an illustrator. Squeezed between them (though larger than they) was a fifth face in the same flattering style, hair tousled, shirt open, studded leather jacket and collar turned up, with the caption: 'Jack Lang ministre 46 ans.' The text expressed faith in the marriage of culture and enterprise, in creation, métissage, and 'le sens de la fête'.[14] In February, the monthly magazine Globe published a manifesto which, while not actually supporting the Socialists, listed ten of their measures it would not accept to see undone if the Right returned, including aid to creation and the grands

Figure 5. A Club Zénith electoral advertisement, *Le Monde*, 30 January 1986. Permission to reproduce: Jack Lang.

projets. It was signed by some significant names given the earlier reticence of intellectuals: Bernard-Henri Lévy, Guy Konopnicki, Philippe Sollers and two of the signatories of the Poland petition, Costa-Gavras and Chéreau. Guy Hocquenghem, however, remained an obdurate unbeliever and published an acerbic attack on former leftist intellectuals whom he accused of selling out.[15] Even more useful to the government was an appeal which appeared in *Le Matin.* 'Amis français', it read, 'Depuis cinq ans, sous l'impulsion du président de la République et de Jack Lang, la France connaît un formidable élan culturel et a reconquis un grand prestige international. Faites en sorte que ce mouvement se poursuive!' It was launched by an international group of artists and intellectuals, some recognisable from the 1983 colloquium or the May 1981 celebrations, like Elie Wiesel, Umberto Eco, William Styron; others more singular: Alberto Moravia, Ingmar Bergman and, most extraordinary of all, Samuel Beckett. Beneath their names was a long list of further signatories, again some known supporters, others not. New names were added as the weeks went by, including the editor of the scarcely pro-government *Le Quotidien de Paris*, Dominique Jamet.[16] The opposition press did its best to discredit the list but it was a hard knock for the Right. Christian Langlois launched a petition of his own, announcing 500 signatures, but his list was unimpressive in comparison. It was perhaps frustration at losing the cultural campaign which made some lash out intemperately at an RPR meeting on 27 February. Jacques Toubon, at the time general secretary of the RPR, was reported to have described Lang as a megalomaniac, speaking of his 'politique de strass, une politique de paillettes' and of the 'millions and millions' being spent on the Théâtre de l'Europe entrusted to 'an Italian Communist director', Giorgio Strehler, who was in fact a Socialist.[17] This only alienated further a number of theatre professionals unsettled by talk of municipalising the EACs and denationalising the CDNs. At a press conference held at the Odéon on 8 March by Patrice Chéreau, Ariane Mnouchkine, Peter Brook and others, there was fulsome praise for Lang. Strehler commented 'Les ignorants me font peur', while Chéreau, whose grant for Le Théâtre des Amandiers at Nanterre had just been slashed by its RPR-dominated departmental council, exclaimed: 'au secours! La droite revient.'[18]

Although the PS remained the biggest party in the Assembly after the election on 16 March, the UDF-RPR partnership, promising tough measures on immigration control, law and order and terrorism, had the majority. The Front National, only five years after being unable to field a presidential candidate, won thirty-five seats as a result of Mitterrand's introduction of proportional representation, raising fears that the government formed by Chirac would now be cajoled into taking an even harder line. In this new climate of uneasy cohabitation, the choice of a Culture Minister to replace the emblematic Lang was clearly a significant one. As Lang was quick to point out, the appointment on 20 March of François Léotard, the general secretary of the PR tipped as a future president, was testimony to the transformation Culture's standing had undergone since 1981. Combined with Communication as under Lecat, Léotard's ministry acquired yet more clout and was ranked fourth in the government hierarchy. Léotard made much of this position, which he believed to be unprecedented. This was a ministry with a future, he said, though it was rumoured that he would have preferred Defence and had only accepted Culture on condition that it be combined with Communication and allocated a budget which matched Lang's.[19] A Secretary of State was also appointed to assist him, Philippe de Villiers, aged thirty-six and like Léotard an *énarque*, though he had chosen to retain his local roots in the Vendée rather than make a career in Paris.

In many ways, Léotard was a judicious choice to follow Lang. He too was young for the office and publicity-conscious, with a strong media identity of his own: more the jogging executive than the artistic dandy and, having once been a novice Benedictine monk, more austere than fun-loving. Some on the Left attempted to diabolise him, and the video artist Kiki Picasso even produced an electronic portrait designed to equate him with the Front National, entitled 'Léopen'. But most frequently, he was depicted as an ambitious moderate, a pro-American advocate of 'libertarian liberalism'. Expectations of hard-line conservatism were more common at first with regard to de Villiers, formerly a leading member of the Alliance pour une nouvelle culture and described by *Libération* as 'une personnalité ambiguë, enraciné en pays chouan', whose strong anti-government stand and other political views in the early 1980s were often dredged up by the press straight after his appointment. Yet here too, commentators generally agreed that today he mixed left- and right-wing approaches to culture and had mellowed with age, while in his own statements he made it plain that he shared Léotard's liberalism.[20]

Of course, this liberalism itself caused some in the cultural world, panicked by Lang's prophecies of doom, to expect a return to cultural giscardism which would leave them high and dry. The RPR-UDF platform had after all focused on the need to diminish the role of the state in culture. Léotard too made it quite clear that he conceived his job in considerably more modest, business-like terms than his predecessor who, he remarked with terse disapproval, 'a été perçu comme ayant réussi par des gens qui n'ont pas la notion de l'argent'.[21]

Liberalism was also the justification put forward for the planned privatising of one if not two public-service TV channels. To make matters worse, although there was to be no formal division of labour between Léotard and de Villiers, privatisation seemed set to take up most of the Minister's time in the near future, with Culture playing second fiddle. It was indeed some while before Léotard made a major statement on his cultural programme.

Given the pre-election polemics, the *plans-reliefs*, the Buren Columns and the *grands projets* looked especially vulnerable. After 16 March, the Conseil de Paris voted in favour of the removal of Buren's work, which gave Léotard the ideal pretext if he wished to stop it. Before the elections, two of Chirac's henchmen, Toubon and Alain Juppé, had promised that some of the *grands projets* would be halted. A number of these fears were swiftly confirmed after 16 March. Juppé and Edouard Balladur, now the Budget and Finance Ministers backed by powerful *inspecteurs des finances*, objected to the costly opera-house, while Balladur pointedly moved his ministry back into the Richelieu wing of the Louvre, which his predecessor Pierre Bérégovoy had only vacated in January. On 2 April, a communiqué announced that the transfer of the *plans-reliefs* would not go ahead. On the 16th, despite assurances which Léotard had obtained from Chirac and Balladur, the government's 'Projet de loi de finances rectificative' for 1986 (also known as the *collectif budgétaire*), which aimed to reduce its predecessor's planned public spending by 10 billion, slashed the Ministry's budget by 4 per cent (421 million francs) while other departments took only a 1 per cent cut.[22] This included a saving of 200 million on the Opéra-Bastille and the Cité musicale at La Villette. The Carrefour de la communication project for the Arche de la Défense (not financed out of the Culture budget) was stopped altogether. Furthermore, all of the Ministry's directorates suffered except Patrimoine and Musées, which Léotard said had been neglected under Lang. Hardest hit was the DDC, with a loss of 75 million francs.

The Minister tried to minimise the cuts but had to acknowledge that they would make him unpopular. This was certainly the case. 'Voici revenue la vieille idée selon laquelle la culture, c'est du superflu', thundered Lang.[23] Dominique Wallon resigned noisily from the DDC, the first of the old guard to do so though he was shortly followed by Maurice Fleuret, equally acrimoniously and also over funds. In his resignation letter, Wallon made it clear that he saw the cut as a choice of economic rather than social concerns and of traditional policies over innovative action for the deprived.[24] The following June, Léotard announced that the DDC in its present form would be dismantled and its tasks divided between a new coordinating structure, the Direction de l'administration générale et de l'environnement culturel (DAGEC) and Abirached's DTS, which took charge of the EACs. As Léotard himself acknowledged, this replacement of 'development' by the more modest notion of 'environment' also suggested a shift away from the idea of the state actively intervening for change. The DDC's contracts policy, however, also under threat before March, was finally retained though Léotard stressed the need for greater selectivity to avoid the infamous *saupoudrage*.[25] Together with the decision, amid general surprise and dismay, to privatise the flagship of public broadcasting, TF1, these were Léotard's most ideological measures.

On 25 June 1986, with bills reforming the press and broadcasting now passing through parliament, Léotard and de Villiers at last held a press conference on their cultural policies. Only three months into 1986, the Minister said, 40 per cent of the Ministry's funds for operating the major institutions had already been committed, leaving him no room for manoeuvre in absorbing the recent budget cut. He drew attention to an estimated 4,000 associations subsidised by the DDC and often only loosely connected with culture, five times as many as in 1982. The Lang administration had shown 'un manque de sérieux', typified in the 2.4 billion francs estimated costs of the Opéra Bastille which had been the subject of no preliminary evaluation. As for his own policies, he announced three priorities: the heritage, the international dimension of French culture, and creative-arts education in schools, none of them new but all of them areas where Lang's record had been questioned. With them came Ministry changes, including a new, much-reduced unit to replace the DDC within the DAGEC, the Délégation aux enseignements et aux formations under Michel Tourlière, Claude Mollard's predecessor at the DAP, whose chief mission was to coordinate relations with Education with a view to placing a law on arts education on the statute book. At the DAP, Mollard himself was replaced, as was Lang's recently appointed Director for Patrimoine, Thierry Leroy. Lastly, Léotard promised to restore the coordination between the various ministries responsible for cultural action abroad (Foreign Affairs, Francophonie, Co-operation) which, he pointedly remarked, had operated until 1981.[26]

Quite clearly, this was a package meant to suggest a liberal new broom; but actually Léotard had very little leeway. The universal popularity of his predecessor's policies meant that reversing them would be suicide and he was doubtless aware of the rumour that in being appointed to Culture he had been handed a time-bomb in the hope he would damage his presidential chances. He was therefore careful to stress that he had no intention of being a 'destructeur'. The difficulty of his position had already become clear over Buren. Chirac was keen for him to stop the project, as was the conservative press. But whatever his personal feelings, Léotard knew the peril of starting his term by destroying a work of art and he refused, to the fury of Buren's opponents. He also made it plain that the *grands projets* programme would remain more or less intact, Juppé, Toubon and Balladur notwithstanding.[27] It was equally striking that two of his three priorities, *enseignements artistiques* and *action internationale*, had numbered among the Socialists' original priorities. On the third, *patrimoine*, de Villiers cautiously emphasised the need to avoid the opposite extremes of 'le "patrimoine naphtaline"' and 'le "patrimoine-cobaye"'. But he did urge in somewhat Langian terms that in future *patrimoine* be considered as 'plural', 'creative' and 'living'. The Secretary of State even trod reasonably softly where the *tout-culturel* was concerned. 'Nous garderons une acception large de la Culture', he said, 'mais nous pensons que si tout est culturel, tout n'est pas ministériel.' Nor was there any sign that Léotard had heeded the calls for a 'liberal' Ministry reduced to a more modest heritage role. On the contrary, its remit had been widened by the addition of Communication.[28]

For all these reasons, the break between the Lang and Léotard years was much less dramatic than many had feared. Yet this did not stop Lang doggedly politicising cultural issues, a task made easier by the fact that Léotard's cobbled-together broadcasting bill caused widespread discontent. More generally, Lang's strategy was to play the Minister-of-Culture-in-exile and upstage Léotard at every opportunity, turning up like a bad penny alongside him at events Lang had previously been identified with. The ex-Minister also made a point of stressing that he had never been busier or more solicited, particularly by the young who, he claimed, would often plead with him not to abandon them. His showing in the polls was still massive and there was even talk of his being presidential material. To capitalise on this popularity, in April he launched his own, short-lived movement based on the Club Zénith called 'Allons z'idées', with the help of Bernard Tapie, the PDG of Yves St-Laurent Pierre Bergé and Jacques Séguéla. Its declared programme was simply the Ministry's record over the previous five years: multiculturalism, the abolition of cultural hierarchies, the indissolubility of culture and the economy, and the need for everyone endowed with creativity and enterprise, on Left or Right, to pool ideas and, as usual, 'liberate initiatives', 'create events' and 'invent encounters'. A more pragmatic purpose was simply to keep Lang in the limelight and attract to Mitterrandism a more fashion-conscious, fun-loving electorate, those young people he had spoken of at the Sorbonne who had rejected traditional political ideologies in the name of 'les nouvelles solidarités, les droits de l'homme, leur défense sous des formes originales'.[29]

In December 1986, the organisation helped fan the discontent of the arts world when in Léotard's 1987 budget regular subsidy to twenty-eight independent theatre companies was withdrawn. The Minister was also accused by the SYNDEAC of massively cutting funds to the EACs, de-prioritising creation, and reducing the Culture budget generally by a further 8 per cent in the Finance bill for 1987. Léotard coolly pointed out that the overall Theatre budget had actually gone up a little, that the measure concerning the companies, on which in any case he quickly gave ground, simply continued the reforms set in train by Abirached and Lang, and that the 8 per cent cut only involved the *grands projets* budget. But he was unable to ward off an embarrassing rally on 18 December outside the Ministry in protest at his whole cultural and audiovisual package, while he himself was appearing on 'Questions à domicile'.[30]

By the end of 1986, however, Lang had found more effective ammunition elsewhere to use against the government. Firstly, unemployment remained intractable and by December had topped 10 per cent, an increase of 5.5 per cent in a year. Secondly, since March Chirac had been pushing through reforms at a remarkable pace – privatisations, the abolition of the wealth tax, hard-line law and order and immigration measures – some of which were not popular. Most damaging of all, however, was the uproar caused by the proposed reform of higher education. Coming as it did against this background of rapid and defensive legislation, the 'Loi Devaquet' assumed a greater importance than it probably deserved, becoming a symbol of the repressiveness of the Right's whole programme. Massive demonstrations were held late November and early December and confrontations with the security forces culminated in the death of a young student. This forced Devaquet to resign and a humiliated Chirac to withdraw the bill and halt his reforms. Some on the Right overreacted, fearing another May '68 and failing to recognise that the December movement actually rejected ideology and party politics in favour of the more universal preoccupations Lang had astutely harnessed in Allons z'idées. Now back in a university post as professor of law at Nanterre, Lang in fact marched with the students and spoke in their name, prompting Louis Pauwels in *Le Figaro Magazine* unwisely to lambast them as 'des produits de la culture Jack Lang [...] atteinte de SIDA mental'.[31] A few months later, Lang was given yet another unhoped-for opportunity to play the debonair free-thinker when in April 1987 the Minister of the Interior Charles Pasqua condemned a number of publications, including material in *Gai-Pied*, as pornographic. In response, Lang presented him with the complete works of Rabelais and two erotic lithographs by Picasso, suggesting that Pasqua might follow Mussolini's example of covering Roman statues with fig-leaves.

Facile though they were, tactics of this kind were part of a more complex strategy. Thrust against his will into cohabitation, Mitterrand had opted to keep his distance from the new government by casting himself as the Gaullian guarantor of national unity above the party-political melee, emphasising during the 1988 presidential campaign the need for 'ouverture' and a united France. Lang followed suit, diabolising the Right further by presenting the Chirac government as sectarian and Mitterrand as the only hope of a more moderate spirit of *rassemblement*, embodied in the Allons z'idées slogan 'la grande famille de la France qui bouge'. The 1986 movement was right to be suspicious of parties, he declared, 'car l'époque est finie où un parti pouvait tout chapeauter, tout organiser'.[32] Again like Mitterrand, the Lang of 1987 thus seemed to be distancing himself not only from his own past but from his own party. Of course, by so doing he was still tacitly undermining Léotard, who as leader of the PR could not avoid having a party-political identity. But he was above all consolidating his own political base by building on his cross-party appeal, and improving his chances of a place in a future government of *ouverture* by placing that appeal once again at the service of a president who was himself trying to climb above party-political dog-fighting. By 1987, however, it was no longer certain that he wanted that place to be Culture: 'Je n'aime pas cheminer deux fois sur les mêmes routes', he was reported to have replied to a question about his future.[33] But like it or not, after Mitterrand's eleventh-hour bid for a second term at the Elysée proved successful, it was indeed to Culture that Lang returned in the first Rocard government, on 12 May 1988.

The itineraries of both Left and Right between 1985 and 1988, and of Lang and Léotard specifically, testify to a shift in cultural policy and debate. Just as Lang and the PS were busy shuffling off an outdated leftism, the Right too was shedding its technocratic indifference to culture, while the Minister Léotard, by circumstance or conviction, was in a number of ways picking up where his predecessor had left off. Thus, despite Lang's initial attempts to turn culture into a battlefield, the reality was that the opposing sides were drawing closer to the middle ground, a process which the appointment of a markedly more ecumenical Lang, crusader for Mitterrand's 'France unie', only reinforced.

The Politics of Fun

Notes

1. 'Culture: suivez Jack Lang!', *Le Point*, 5 April 1982, p.121.
2. *La Culture en veston rose*, Paris, 1982, p.19.
3. 'Jack Lang comme si vous y étiez', *Le Nouvel Observateur*, 25 November 1983.
4. 'France launches American-style drive to save European cinema', Reuter's bulletin, 21 June 1984.
5. Lang, *Le Complexe de Léonard*, Paris, [1984], p.124.
6. For the 4 polls, see, respectively, *Le Matin Magazine*, 9 January 1982; Louis Harris-France, 'Les Français et la culture', 1985, p.16, p.5 and pp.10–11; AFP dispatch, 21 June 1985, reporting a survey taken 7–11 June 1985; *Le Journal Rhône-Alpes*, 15 November 1985.
7. 'Jack Lang: la grande parade', *Le Point*, 10 June 1985, p.127.
8. 'La Culture dans l'arène politique. Serpents et sorcières', *Le Monde*, 5 November 1983, pp.1 and 20. On the Fontevraud encounter, see 'Les Nouveaux Chouans', *Le Monde*, 3 November 1983, p.8.
9. 15.8 per cent increase in *crédits de paiement* (i.e. funds to cover capital expenditure in the coming year), 14 per cent in *autorisations de programme*, *Journal Officiel*, 2ᵉ séance du 28 octobre 1985, p.3,575–6.
10. *Journal Officiel*, séance du 17 avril 1985, p.235 and p.239; The *Libération* quotation is from 'Assemblée nationale: en avoir ou pas', 18 April 1985.
11. M. Guy, 'Michel Guy au *Quotidien*', *Le Quotidien de Paris*, 25 July 1985, pp.12–13; de Plunkett, 'Le Système Lang', *Le Figaro Magazine*, 25 January 1986, pp.15–23; Baumel, 'Quelle action culturelle demain?', *Le Figaro*, 1–2 March 1986.
12. *Le Figaro*, 21 May 1984, p.2; Langlois, *Pour une véritable culture*, 1985 (no other publication details are provided), p.9; 'L'Académie des beaux-arts alerte le gouvernement', *Le Figaro Magazine*, 28 March 1986, pp.126–8.
13. Quoted in 'Création des clubs "Zénith" au service de Jack Lang', *Le Quotidien de Paris*, 6 February 1986.
14. Reproduced in *Le Monde*, 30 January 1986, p.21, and in R. Desneux, *Jack Lang: la culture en mouvement*, Paris, 1990, p.246.
15. G. Hocquenghem, *Lettre ouverte à ceux qui sont passés du col Mao au Rotary*, Paris, 1986.
16. '"Poursuivre le mouvement"', *Le Matin*, 24 February 1986, p.2. A further version of the petition, from *Le Monde*, 2–3 March 1986, p.5, is reproduced in Desneux, *Jack Lang*, p.245.

17. 'Toubon crie haro sur Jack Lang', *Libération*, 1–2 March 1986; 'Haro droitiste sur Chéreau et Lang', *Le Matin*, 3 March 1986 (which attributes the 'megalomaniac' reference to Chirac).
18. 'Clinquant? Non, brillant', *Le Monde*, 11 March 1986; '"J'aime Jack Lang"', *La Croix*, 11 March 1986.
19. M. Hunter, *Les Jours les plus Lang*, Paris, 1990, p.245. An article in *Le Monde*, 25 March 1986, pointed out that Léotard's ranking was not in fact unprecedented: Malraux had been ranked first in the various governments of Pompidou and Couve de Murville between 1962 and 1969.
20. *Libération*, 21 March 1986; fuller details of de Villiers's political biography appeared in (among other sources) *Libération*, 1 April 1986, pp.6–8, *L'Evénement du Jeudi*, 3–9 April 1986, pp.18–19, and *Le Figaro*, 29 March 1986. De Villiers had resigned from the Alliance pour une nouvelle culture in March 1984. In June 1987, he left the Léotard Ministry to take up a seat in Parliament representing La Vendée and André Santini (UDF) was subsequently appointed Ministre délégué à la communication.
21. *Paris Match*, 9 May 1986, p.49.
22. M. Hunter, *Les Jours*, pp.246–7.
23. 'Zénith ou la guerre des étoiles contre la droite', *L'Unité*, no.645 (24 April 1986), p.25.
24. 'Côté culture, Balladur a des idées pour Léotard', *Libération*, 30 May 1986; and 'M. Dominique Wallon, directeur du développement culturel, donne sa démission', *Le Monde*, 25–6 May 1986, p.9.
25. For Léotard on the notion of cultural environment and the conventions, see his book *Culture: les chemins du printemps*, Paris, 1988, pp.90–2, and pp.120–2; also R. Wangermée and B. Gournay, *Programme européen d'évaluation: la politique culturelle de la France*, Paris, 1988, pp.74–6 and p.229.
26. 'Conférence de presse du mercredi 25 juin 1986' (Léotard and de Villiers), Ministry press dossier no.DP267.
27. Hunter, *Les Jours*, recounts that he did, however, at de Villiers's suggestion, set out to abolish another symbol of the Lang era, the Fête de la musique, but was persuaded by Ministry staff of the folly of doing so, pp.253–4.
28. All quotations are from de Villiers's speech at the 25 June press conference, press dossier no.DP267, unnumbered pages.
29. Lang quoted in '"Allons z'idées": Jack Lang en Mouvement', *Le Monde*, 22 April 1986, p.8. See also interview with Yves Mourousi on RMC, 10 April 1986, 7.00 p.m. (transcript available in DEP).

30. For Léotard's defence of his policies, see his interview '"Etre un bon gestionnaire de l'ingérable"', *Le Monde*, 12 December 1986, pp.1 and 26. See also Hunter, *Les Jours*, pp.263–6.
31. Quoted in Hunter, *Les Jours*, p.262.
32. 'Une Interview de Jack Lang (PS)', *La Croix*, 31 December 1986, p.13.
33. *Le Matin*, 1 July 1987, p.4.

– 9 –

Popularising the Past: *Lang et Léotard,*
même combat?

'Lang II', as the press soon dubbed him, presented the transformation he had recently undergone as the result of a new political maturity, which he also signalled by a more sober though still fashionable look and a marginally less lyrical idiom. 'Assez de discours', he declaimed at the 1988 Cannes Festival, 'on nous attend aux actes.'[1] The new image was also entirely in keeping with the sharper, more business-like style of the government as a whole. Both, however, were taken as indicating the absence of any 'grand design', though to an extent this was inevitable for a government returning to power. Lang himself was busily developing his profile as conventional politician rather than *homme de culture* – minister since 1981, MP since 1986, Mayor of Blois from the municipals of 1989 and regional councillor from March 1992. He also made it plain that he was returning to the rue de Valois in order to complete the task begun in 1981, which he insisted had been diverted during the Léotard years, those 'années d'antan' during which the Ministry had 'gone to sleep'.[2] Naturally, consolidating past achievements lacked the glamour and novelty of a project for civilisation.

The new Lang ministry mostly had a familiar look, with old faces like Renard, Dupavillon and Colin returning to his cabinet and some of the original directors still in post. It did, however, benefit from the Léotard interlude by keeping the Communication portfolio Lang had always wanted. In the reshuffle which followed the legislative elections of June, he also obtained responsibility for the bicentenary of the Revolution in 1989 and for the entirety of the *grands projets*. Yet his new powers were not as extensive as they appeared. Breaking with practice under Lecat and Léotard, Communication acquired a delegate minister, Catherine Tasca, who pointedly asserted her independence by occupying Fillioud's premises in the rue Saint-Dominique. The *grands projets* too became the responsibility of a newly created

Secretariat of State attached to the Ministry in June under Emile-Jean Biasini, formerly president of the Louvre project. His relations with Lang prior to 1986 had not always been 'idyllic' according to Jean Gattégno, but in any case, as Secretary of State, he dealt directly with the President and, in Pierre Bérégovoy's government of April 1992, was placed under the Prime Minister.[3] As for the bicentenary, day-to-day responsibility lay with an interministerial 'mission', also answerable to the Prime Minister. Lastly, in the first Rocard government, Thierry de Beaucé became Secrétaire d'Etat aux relations culturelles extérieures et à la francophonie within the Foreign Ministry, a step which, for Pascal Ory, was probably unprecedented in proclaiming the autonomy of foreign cultural relations.[4] In June, Francophonie itself was separated off and placed in the care of a delegate minister, the popular historian Alain Decaux, also under Foreign Affairs. Jeunesse et sports came under Education, with its own Secretary of State, Roger Bambuck.

Once again, then, for most of Lang's second term, culture was still far from a unified administrative sphere, though a move in this direction was fleetingly made in April 1992 when in Bérégovoy's government Lang at last achieved his dream of a 'Ministry of Intelligence' combining Culture, Communication (Tasca was replaced by Jean-Noël Jeanneney) and Education – a Ministry of State to boot, as Malraux's had been. But although Lang heavily underscored the historic nature of the twinning, conjuring up the spirit of Jean Zay and expressing the wish that Education and Culture never again be torn asunder, it was widely interpreted more as a presidential reward for his loyal service and good showing in the recent regionals, or as a consolation for not being appointed Prime Minister himself, than as a step towards a truly global policy. Either way, less than a year later the 1993 legislatives swept the Socialists from office and under his successor Jacques Toubon, the two portfolios again became free-standing.

One confused battleground on which Lang was anxious to distinguish himself from Léotard was the budget. After the furore caused by the *collectif budgétaire*, Léotard was criticised for further cuts in 1987 and 1988. In his defence, he rightly argued that these were entirely caused by the *grands projets*, some of which had been completed (Orsay and the IMA) and others modified or spread over a longer period. Expenditure on the *grands projets* was in fact calculated separately in both years. This had a dual advantage in that his remaining budget now actually registered an increase in 1988 of some 8 per cent, while Lang's historic rises pre–1986 looked less magnificent without the President's ever more costly projects. Léotard also aggregated in his calculations the estimated 800 to 850 million francs diverted from the Treasury by various taxation measures he introduced as part of his theological commitment to liberal forms of aid rather than subsidy. In this way, he could demonstrate that it was really he who had reached the 1 per cent, though in truth the savings on the *grands projets* still amounted to a cut since, as Mesnard points out, they might easily have been redirected into new regional projects but were not.[5] After Lang's return, culture was again listed as a priority, alongside education and research. His habitual lobbying over the summer paid off when his department was given a 12.5 per cent rise in the 1989 budget, reaching 9.9 billion francs or 0.86 per cent of state spending. This was considerable in an austerity budget which allowed only a 4 per cent rise overall, but it was not enormous. Subsequent increases were also eroded by vicissitudes like the Gulf War which forced the government to make cuts. It was not therefore until the 1993 budget that, over a decade late, 1 per cent (13.8 billion francs) was finally achieved, despite a 'no' vote by the RPR and UDF. But even this last, desperate symbol as new elections drew near was short-lived, as the figures had to be revised downwards in February 1993 for economic reasons.[6]

Another area in which Lang made some attempt to pick up where he had left off was *action culturelle*, though the establishments of that name, the EACs, were neither the main focus nor the main beneficiaries here, any more than in the pre–1986 period. After the damaging cut Léotard had had to make in 1986, neither the small increase he subsequently secured for *action culturelle* nor Lang's more generous 10 per cent rise in 1989 could offset a serious financial crisis in both the EACs and the subsidised theatre, for which underfunding by both Left and Right was often blamed. In 1990–1, this crisis helped bring about the transformation of all sixty-two EACs into what became known as 'Scènes nationales'. The measure continued Lang's pre–1986 reform by further limiting the extent to which the director is answerable to local representation (though association status was still not formally abolished) and by focusing the EACs even more on creation and the performing arts, away from the founding principles of *animation* and *polyvalence*.

At the same time, some effort was made to restore *action culturelle* as embodied in the DDC's work with new publics and practices, which Léotard had cut back. Significantly, though, Lang did not choose to reverse the structural transformation of the DDC but eventually set up a new unit, the Délégation aux développements et aux formations under Hélène Mathieu in February 1990, more flexible but according to Colin weaker than Wallon's full directorate.[7] The

Minister also took a particular interest in extending cultural action among the young in the troubled suburbs, particularly the 400 districts (*quartiers*) singled out as priority areas by the Ministre de la ville, Michel Delebarre. At the other end of the age spectrum, a neglected 'new public' was targeted by the Ministry-sponsored Mouvement de la flamboyance which encouraged cultural activity among the retired. Yet another, still less homogeneous, was the object of the Les Arts au soleil programme in summer 1990, which provided over 3,000 arts events for holiday-makers in France's coastal resorts. But as such measures suggest, the overarching and most publicised form of *action culturelle*, even more than in the 1981–6 period, was the one-off festivity, despite the somewhat stilted air of institutionalised fun such occasions had acquired: La Fureur de lire in 1989, Photofolie and La Fête du jardin in 1992, and so on.

Lang also continued to push the *tout-culturel* conception of creation, again extending a number of previous actions in this vein. The decoration of Chevalier or Commandeur des Arts et des Lettres was meted out to ever more incongruous figures, from Sylvester Stallone and Warren Beatty to a shepherd from Blois who imitated animal noises.[8] Lang was also more alert than ever to trends in youth culture. In May 1989, he appointed a young *chargé de mission* specifically for rock, Bruno Lion, dubbed by the British press the 'Minister for Rock 'n' Roll'. From world music he moved on to the craze, notably in France's disadvantaged suburbs, for rap and hip-hop, styles emanating from young urban African-Americans. Justifying this option, he would often describe these forms as 'un phénomène de civilisation' which at their best drew unconsciously on the commedia dell'arte. Amongst his initiatives for the *quartiers* was 'Hip-hop dixit!' in 1991 which involved mounting rap and graffiti exhibitions in a number of museums. The following year, he sponsored another graffiti exhibition at a particularly sensitive moment, shortly after sculptures at the Louvre metro station had been defaced. The exhibition even included a metro carriage covered in precisely the kind of graffiti the RATP was spending some 90 million francs a year erasing.[9]

Ultimately, however, even such archetypally Langian provocations did little to demarcate him from Léotard, whose policies he continued in a number of ways. This of course was largely inevitable since Léotard had often continued his, even enacting promises the Socialists had not kept. Youth culture was in fact a telling instance. In his 1981 campaign, Mitterrand had highlighted the urgency of cutting the luxury-goods VAT rate of 33.3 per cent imposed on records and cassettes to 18.6 per cent. But despite dogged attempts at each budgetary exercise, Lang had failed to persuade the Treasury to forego the substantial sum the tax brought in. In December 1987, Léotard did, though not without delay and difficulty. Even more galling for Lang, the implementation of the reduction from 1 January 1988 was followed by a 30 per cent rise in record sales in just one year, after a 40 per cent drop over the previous six years.[10] Léotard like Lang also saw the benefits of linking culture and the economy and promoted the cultural industries accordingly. He extended his predecessor's measures for individual and corporate sponsorship, passing a law in July 1987 which formalised and improved on the tax incentives the budget laws of 1982 and 1985 had introduced to encourage it. A Conseil supérieur du mécénat culturel set up in early February 1987 was also instrumental in developing a matching grants scheme (*cofinancements*), already considered a possible way forward by Renard the previous year.[11] In turn, Lang II did not undo these measures but modified them. By 1989, even the Avignon Festival was getting 15 per cent of its income from sponsorship.

The promised law on *enseignements artistiques* also had to wait for Léotard before being implemented. Chirac made it a priority in his first declaration of policy to the Assembly and in due course a bill was tabled jointly by the Education and Culture Ministries which became law on 6 January 1988. Its thrust was to reinforce and extend the obligation to provide at least one weekly hour each for music and art education, on a par with other subjects, to all years from the age of six to sixteen. This could also include other arts disciplines and there was provision for professional artists to be involved in these classes. In *lycées*, various new optional or compulsory programmes of study were to be available. Even so, the law did not innovate so much as modify and, although a few saw it as the most important cultural legislation of the Fifth Republic,[12] many felt it did not go far enough. By 1993, most also agreed, including Chirac, that it had not been properly applied. For Mesnard and others, its main weakness was that it was essentially only a blueprint law, not a *loi-programme* like Malraux's heritage legislation, which meant that the estimated two billion francs its implementation would require over the next ten years were not committed. 'La Bastille de l'Education nationale reste à renverser', wrote one disappointed observer.[13]

When Lang returned, he extended the kind of measures taken before 1986 until the joining of Education and Culture gave him his biggest opportunity yet for coordinated action. He then took a number of interministerial initiatives and in early March 1993 presented an extensive new package of measures backed by what was heralded as a 73 per cent budget increase for activities in educational establishments, though only days before the legislative elections swept him out of office. The following November, under Toubon, the package was thrown out and a new interministerial agreement reached on the need to apply the Léotard law fully.[14] Arguably, however, the problem cannot be solved by legislation or ministerial engineering but requires a more fundamental shift in attitudes from teachers, parents and local authorities. As the Wangermée report pointed out, bringing this about will be no easy task since it will necessarily involve either a shift in the accepted hierarchy of school subjects or a lengthening of the school day or year.[15]

The element of continuity in Lang's and Léotard's policies was most in evidence in the area of the national heritage. For the Right in 1986, *patrimoine* was Lang's Achilles heel and the anti-government press often delighted in drawing up lists of crumbling cathedrals and other monuments he was supposed to have neglected. In reality, after two years of prioritising the heritage, the budget Léotard allotted it was no greater than Lang's had been during the previous two years.[16] Where Léotard was more successful, however, was in passing a third major *loi-programme* (5 January 1988) on the heritage, called for in vain ever since the first two drafted under Malraux. Léotard's act authorised over five billion francs of capital expenditure (*autorisations de programme*) on historic monuments, parks and sites for the coming five years.[17] But Lang was not to be so easily outdone. In his first major policy statement at the Château de Chambord on 6 September 1988, he too announced that *patrimoine* was to be a priority, set to receive a 14.5 per cent increase when his overall budget for 1989 was going up by only 12.5 per cent. Funding for restoration work and general improvement was to top one billion for the first time.[18] Much of his post–1988 widening of the field of culture also took a patrimonial form, from protecting the bar at Le Fouquet's and the Piscine Molitor in Paris to launching an 'Inventaire du patrimoine culinaire'.

This new focus can be read in several ways. Clearly, on one level, he was systematically filling in the gaps left by his earlier policies while at the same time carving out a niche which remained all his own when so much of his ostensibly wide domain had been conceded to others. Secondly, it had become clear by the late 1980s that monuments, stately homes and museums were increasingly in demand, ideal demonstrations of the view that culture pays economically. Hence the new buzzword 'cultural tourism', already made much of by de Villiers, in which France's historic past played the major role. A third reason was that, although many of those who visited such monuments were foreign, their growing popularity among the French too breathed new life into the heritage's role as a lingua franca, bringing the nation together in a shared past. The policy can therefore be seen as integral to the 1988 presidential theme of *rassemblement* and consensus. This was equally true of another form of government homage to the past, the bicentenary of 1789.

After the cancellation of Expo 89, there had been fears that the bicentenary celebrations would end up a damp squib, especially as it seemed that little was being prepared. Léotard had set up a Mission du bicentenaire to prepare the celebrations in September 1986. But since then, another change of government, the deaths of the Mission's first two presidents, uncertainty over funding and other factors had delayed the finalising of the plans until October 1988. Beyond the practical details of sponsoring some 8,000 events in France and abroad which confronted the Mission, now chaired by the historian Jean-Noël Jeanneney, one of the government's preoccupations was to use the celebration as the Popular Front had the 150th anniversary: as an affirmation of the unity, prosperity and international stature France had achieved under Mitterrand. As a result, the emphasis was not on the conflictual but the consensual: the declaration of human rights, the birth of democracy and the Republic. Mitterrand also agreed to schedule the Paris conference of the G7, the seven richest countries of the world, for 14 and 15 July, deftly drawing world attention to France's diplomatic standing in the present as well as to its epoch-making past, though by combining popular festivities with the arrival of top politicians, he greatly complicated security arrangements and other practicalities, to say nothing of the symbolism of the bicentenary itself.

Some indeed, on both Right and Left, did not recognise their Revolution in this grand state occasion but felt it had somehow been confiscated. This was in part due to the massive security presence the summit demanded, including the closing off of central Paris to the *tiers-état* of motorists so that the powerful could cavort in peace. But it was also to do with the commercialisation and trivialisation of the human drama, 'une Révolution cadavérisée, momifiée, un Bicentenaire du toc et du truc à plume', as Gilles Perrault put it.[19] This approach was typified in the 'Oh Tuileries' theme park, where the souvenir stands sold Revolutionary underpants, or kitsch guillotines with the caption 'Ne perdez pas votre tête'. Some also felt it to be at work in the parade down the Champs Elysées organised for the late evening of 14 July by the French-American advertising wizzard and image-maker, Jean-Paul Goude, working closely with Jeanneney and Dupavillon.

For its critics, the choice of Goude was shocking; for others, as an illustrator and maker of advertising clips and pop videos he was the archetype of the 1980s *créateur*. His brief was to mark not just the storming of the Bastille but the universal message of both *La Marseillaise* and the Fête de la Fédération held on 14 July 1790, when representatives of all the departments of France had come to Paris and sworn to defend freedom. The message of the parade, then, was to be at once national and multicultural, for the French Revolution, it was declared, did not belong to any one community. Drawing principally on the idioms he knew best – pop, fashion, advertising – Goude translated this requirement into the global vocabulary of contemporary mass culture. His procession, conceived with world-wide TV transmission in mind, combined the self-conscious posing of the fashion parade with the flip, unfathomable iconography of the pop video, 'un ballet gracieux et gratuit', said *Le Monde* quoting Mona Ozouf.[20] What it conveyed above all, through its knowing parodies of national, regional and foreign stereotypes, was an ironic distance, the sense that while each community has something distinct in its cultural identity, each has become sufficiently detached from it by the global eye of television to be able to fuse with others in a sophisticated planetary cocktail. The tableau entitled *Les Valseuses*, for example, consisted of fourteen 'dancers' resembling catwalk models, all clad in the same extravagant designer hats and in dresses two and a half metres high. These concealed electric motors which rotated the dancers in time to a score by Michel Hardy comprising 'des bribes de toutes les musiques du monde sur un rythme funk'. Indeed, 'the real revolution', Goude claimed, was world music.[21]

As early as December 1981, Lang had declared that the Expo would be the culmination of the government's cultural policies and that only in 1989 could the true contribution of the Mitterrand septennium be judged.[22] Accordingly, the Goude spectacle, along with the grand opening of three *grands projets* the same day, the opera-house, the Pyramid and the Arch which now housed the Fondation des droits de l'homme, became 'la vitrine créative et surprenante de la France des années 90',[23] symbol of the Socialists' single-minded pursuit of modernity and a national multiculture. Of course, the idea that the bicentenary was a measure of what national culture had become under Mitterrand was double-edged, as Perrault's scathing comment showed. But the one million people who turned out to see the parade and the several million who watched it on TV seemed to drown out the critics, making opposition truants like Chirac, Giscard and Léotard, who stayed away, look like killjoys, and casting an aura of triumph over the entire Socialist era.

To an extent, this consensus extended to the *grands projets* too. As the 1980s drew to a close, the epic struggles of the pre–1986 period mostly fizzled out as one inauguration followed another and each new structure became quickly absorbed into the landscape, even those like the Pyramid once thought of as Trojan horses of aesthetic barbarism.[24] Under Léotard, Balladur remained obdurate for a while about vacating the Louvre. But with the Socialists back in power, it was agreed that the Louvre offices would be vacated by 14 July 1989, allowing the second phase, the conversion of the Richelieu wing, to begin in 1989. In August, six months after the opening of the Pyramid, Lang gave a press conference in which he pronounced the first phase a success. Opening hours and facilities had improved. Over three million visitors had passed through the Pyramid of whom 80 per cent had entered the museum itself, a 44 per cent increase over the same period (April to August) in 1988. Indeed, the only negative aspect was the time spent queuing to get in.[25] So by 1989, the Mitterrand monoliths were in the main a source of polemics only at budget time when the imbalance between Paris and the provinces was routinely deplored by the opposition and the PCF. There were, however, two notable exceptions, in both of which it was democratisation which continued to arouse passions.

The first was the Opéra-Bastille. The mission of the new opera-house was to be popular not by altering the sociological composition of the audience but simply by accommodating more people, which meant reducing operating costs and offering more seats, lower prices and more productions and performances. As the project took shape in the pre–1986 period, it became clearer how this was to be done, though not at what cost. Garnier would be given over mainly to dance, the Bastille mainly to opera. The new structure would have two auditoria which together could find room for 960,000 spectators a year as opposed to Garnier's 366,000. One would have 2,700 seats while the other, smaller and with a flexible layout (the *salle modulable*), would be put to more experimental uses including the staging of new work, one of the aims being to encourage creation. It would also have a number of peripheral stages identical to the main one to allow several productions to rehearse and prepare sets at the same time, and the spatial and technical facilities to allow sets to be stored and transported quickly between them. Scenery and costumes would be made within the building in purpose-built workshops (*ateliers*). These arrangements would allow a degree of *alternance* comparable to Covent Garden's, with a projected annual output of around twenty-five different productions, as against Garnier's ten, and 250 to 300 performances a year in the main auditorium alone, allowing prices to be halved.

Cost, however, remained the bugbear. After the 1986 elections, some in the new administration were concerned about the waste involved in running the Bastille and Garnier concurrently, estimated at half of the Ministry's entire Music and Dance budget. They also felt that the scenery workshops and *salle modulable* were a luxury. This led to a damaging stop-start approach from government and a trial of strength between Léotard on the one hand and Chirac and his Finance ministers on the other, from which Léotard emerged the somewhat dog-eared winner in August 1986, having saved the opera-house itself but sacrificed both the *salle modulable* and the scenery workshops. In the following months, however, he managed to restore both with only minor alterations, bringing the situation back more or less to that originally envisaged under the Socialists.[26]

Finally, a production programme for the first three seasons was announced on 31 March 1988, drawn up by a prestigious team Léotard had appointed the previous July headed by Daniel Barenboim as musical and artistic director, who from time to time would be working with Chéreau, Boulez and others, giving the new facility a dominantly modernist quality. The productions announced included *Don Giovanni*, Zimmermann's *Die Soldaten*, a strong emphasis on Wagner and Mozart, and a new work to be commissioned from Boulez.[27] However, troubled times lay ahead. Firstly, the programme did not earn universal approval. Particularly surprising was the small number of annual performances envisaged: 72 for the 1990–1 season and 120 for the following one, no higher than Garnier's average and a long way from the original 250.[28] Secondly, the director general Pierre Vozlinksy soon resigned over a disagreement about his contract and proved hard to replace. Barenboim in the meantime, only days before the presidentials, negotiated a financially attractive five-year contract which also gave him considerable powers. With the change of government in May, these three factors were to cause the rapid dislocation of the Barenboim team.

The first sign of trouble came on 31 August when Lang announced the appointment of Pierre Bergé, PDG of Yves Saint-Laurent and founder of *Globe*, as president of the Association des Théâtres de l'Opéra de Paris (ATOP), over the head of Léotard's appointee Raymond Soubie.[29] The recruitment of an active Mitterrandist from outside the opera world was resented and taken as a criticism of both the programme and Soubie, who resigned the following November. Bergé certainly was not happy with the programme or with Barenboim's insistence on retaining all artistic decision-making. Michel Schneider, the new Director of Music and Dance at the Ministry after Lang's return, was also opposed to the Barenboim contract. *Le Monde*'s Jacques Lonchampt, for a long time a vigorous defender of the new opera-house, then entered the lists after Soubie's departure, pointing up the failure to replace Vozlinsky and identifying the cause as Barenboim himself who, claimed Lonchampt, refused to relinquish power over programming to a new director general. Lonchampt also considered his high salary likely to have a knock-on effect on others in the establishment. A further problem he identified was the disappointing number of performances planned even for the third season, which would, together with the inflationary salaries, mean intolerably high costs and defeat the object, for which the taxpayer had been asked to pay such a high price.

But the most complex question raised by Lonchampt was about the meaning of 'popular' opera. Like Mitterrand and Bergé, he partly took it to mean more performances for more people at a more reasonable price. But he also seemed to see it as a certain kind of repertoire, without which the increased numbers could not be achieved: 'Pas un seul opéra vraiment populaire, en dehors de *Carmen*, aucun Verdi avant la troisième année, [...] aucune ouverture sur un répertoire un peu original. Ah! le bel opéra "nouveau".…'[30] In a later clarification, Lonchampt conceded that *Don Giovanni* may well be a popular opera and that works like *Die Soldaten* doubtless also had their place. But they alone could not increase the public. What was also needed were good productions, not necessarily by star names, of *Faust, Manon, Tosca*, 'et autres chefs d'œuvre "populaires", assurant par ailleurs des rentrées substantielles… Un Opéra populaire, ce n'est pas un Opéra au rabais, mais un organisme à des coûts économiques supportables et d'une forte rentabilité culturelle pour l'ensemble de la nation.'[31] This was also Bergé's view: 'Populaire avec tous les guillemets que vous voulez, mais tout de même cet opéra doit être destiné au public le plus vaste. A cet égard, peut-être faudrait-il penser à un "italien", à un Verdi au moins dans une programmation actuellement plus difficile.'[32]

Patrice Chéreau, stung by the criticisms voiced by both men, ardently took issue with this view of the popular. As well as challenging the criticism of Barenboim personally, he argued that it was dishonest to berate the cost and number of performances when nobody yet knew what the new facility was actually capable of, though he made it clear that the figure of 750,000 spectators a year being bandied about by Bergé and Lonchampt was in his view demagogic, especially as opera productions were available elsewhere in Paris: 'Est-ce qu'être populaire, cela veut dire répéter moins longtemps les spectacles? [...] En d'autres termes, est-ce qu'être populaire veut dire tirer la qualité des productions vers le bas?'[33] What the Lonchampt-Chéreau altercation brought out was a potential conflict between democratisation and creation: for what kind of artistic fare should actually be on offer in an establishment dedicated to widening public participation? The problem with Lonchampt's and Bergé's view was that it could lead to the tedious reviving of only the safest, least 'difficult' works. Chéreau, on the other hand, by querying the new opera-house's ability to attract vast audiences, was close to questioning the whole basis on which it had been so expensively created. Significantly, his article defined the 'chance historique' offered by the Bastille not as the chance to democratise but as 'la création d'un théâtre lyrique de haut niveau à Paris, c'est-à-dire d'un opéra de niveau international et fondé sur les critères de travail les plus professionnels et les plus rigoureux'. In this respect, his position was that of the other 1960s theatre directors who had moved away from cultural action. The government's position meanwhile was simply to avoid the theoretical debate altogether by assuming the existence of a sociologically unspecific demand for opera and therefore addressing only the mechanics of democratisation, not the more complex question of 'cultural needs' examined by Bourdieu and summarised by Michel Schneider: 'Les "masses" [...] ne rêvent pas d'opéra, pour une raison très simple [...]: elles n'en ont aucune envie. Et elles n'en ont aucune envie parce qu'on ne leur en a pas donné l'envie.'[34] In this perspective, the debate needed to be cast in terms not of repertoire, seat-prices or number of performances, but of mediation, of creating demand at the same time as improving supply.

The material outcome of the affair was predictable. Bergé, disputing Barenboim's contract on a technicality, attempted to persuade him to accept a new salary, new working conditions and reduced powers. Barenboim apparently would not compromise on his powers and Bergé accordingly declared the post of artistic director vacant. Boulez and Chéreau promptly resigned, the latter attacking Lang openly despite their friendship since Nancy. A petition of other big names was also organised which made it clear that, if Barenboim went, their own agreements to work with the Bastille were also in jeopardy.[35] Here then, for the first time since 1981, was a group of major international artists in revolt against the Socialist government, while the opposition, quick to side with the Barenboim-Chéreau camp, was able to make maximum capital from the affair. Worse still, the Bastille found itself six months before opening with no programme. In the event, a new team was put together, under the relatively unknown Korean director, Myung Whun Chung, in time for the official inauguration on 13 July 1989 and its real opening, with *Les Troyens* by Berlioz, on 17 March 1990, only two months later than scheduled. But the myth of a natural bond between the arts and the Left had irreparably shattered on the issue of creation versus democratisation. Nor was the Bastille even then able to function uncontroversially as a number of its fundamental problems remained, mercilessly summarised by the Ville de Paris's cultural spokesperson Françoise de Panafieu during the debate on Lang's last budget in November 1992: a series of resignations and strikes due to unaltered trade-union restrictions, continued uncertainty about the artistic purpose and financing of the *salle modulable*, and the fact that the number of performances was still lower than Garnier's used to be and that as many as 1,000 seats were on sale at the top price of 560 francs. 'Une "mauvaise réponse à une question qui ne se posait pas"', concluded Panafieu.[36]

A similar rift with a different cultural community was revealed in the polemics surrounding the last of the major presidential projects, the Bibliothèque de France (BdF). Although public reading had been a priority in 1981, by 1988 a number of problems remained regarding library provision, not least the BN where shortage of space and resources meant insufficient storage facilities, overcrowding, and delays in retrieval, computerisation and the microfilming of works being destroyed by natural acidification. Léotard therefore commissioned a report, which proposed a radical departure, even decentralisation. He also appointed the well known historian Emmanuel Le Roy Ladurie as *administrateur général*, who more modestly proposed a 'BN-bis' instead. But after his re-election, Mitterrand made it quite clear in an interview on 14 July 1988 that there would be no such half-measures. His inclination was to build one of the biggest and most modern libraries in the world. 'J'en ai l'ambition', he crisply asserted, 'et je le ferai.' A month later in a letter to Prime Minister Rocard, he spoke of 'une très grande bibliothèque d'un type entièrement nouveau' which would 'couvrir tous les champs de la connaissance, être à la disposition de tous, utiliser les technologies les plus modernes de transmission de données, pouvoir être consultée à distance et entrer en relations avec d'autres bibliothèques européennes'. But in his first-hand account of the project, Jean Gattégno, who left the DLL in 1989 to take charge of planning the content of the library under the overall administrator Dominique Jamet, contends that, due to pressure from Le Roy Ladurie and others, this grand ambition was steadily diluted and the library brought back to being a BN-bis.[37]

To flesh out Mitterrand's idea, a report was commissioned whose main recommendations were officially adopted in April 1989. The new library would be situated near the Pont de Tolbiac in the east of Paris, on a site provided free of charge by Chirac within a larger district earmarked for redevelopment. The former BN's collections would be divided between the two sites, all work published after 1 January 1945 going to Tolbiac. New communications technologies would allow networking with university libraries and the main municipal libraries, all pooling their resources with the aid of a nation-wide computerised catalogue. To meet Mitterrand's requirement concerning democratisation, the new establishment would include, alongside vastly improved facilities for professional researchers, an impressive public library with open access to books and substantial facilities for consultation of a wide range of audiovisual and computerised materials. An *établissement public* (the EPBF) would be created to see the project through to completion by 1995, the end of Mitterrand's second septennium. Selected architects would be invited to take part in an international competition, the best four being submitted to the President who would as usual make the final choice.[38]

Substantial objections to this plan did not arise until the summer, when academics and intellectuals on Left as well as Right suddenly seemed to notice the 1945 division, or 'caesura' as it became known. Some rejected it for practical reasons, the inconvenience of shuttling between the two sites and so on. Others objected to its intellectual arbitrariness, described by *Le Nouvel Observateur*'s Jacques Julliard as 'un véritable péché contre l'esprit'. But such complaints were often only symptoms of a more fundamental unease about the whole nature of the project. Since only three to four million volumes were to be transferred to a giant twenty-first-century building open to the general public and apparently offering all sorts of other hands-on facilities, would not scholarship and the printed word be marginalised, desecrated, sequestered in what one contributor to *Le Débat* called 'cette Babel du livre imprimé, microfilmé, microfiché, informatisé, vidéotisé, cassettisé'?[39] In an article entitled 'Alexandrie ou Disneyland?', Fumaroli joined in the criticism of the caesura but was clearly more bothered by what he described as 'la coexistence, sur le site Tolbiac, d'un super-Beaubourg, voué à attirer le grand public par tous les gadgets de la société de consommation et de spectacle, et de deux bibliothèques de recherche, vouées, elles, à la réflexion et au recueillement savant'.[40] However, on 21 August, at the height of the controversy and five days after Mitterrand had selected the young French architect Dominique Perrault to build the new library, Lang suddenly revealed that the President was willing to abandon the caesura and transfer all eleven or twelve million of the BN's printed holdings to Tolbiac. Clearly, appeasement was assumed to be the best way of silencing the critics, though this proved not to be so. For Gattégno, the alteration transformed the whole project and was a first victory for the Le Roy Ladurie camp, who could now legitimately see it as primarily a matter of moving the BN rather than of creating an entirely new library (p.214).

Dissent now switched inexorably to the building's design. This consisted of a huge open square under which were two levels, with a rectangular garden in the centre twenty-one metres below the square. On the upper level was the library for the general public with shelving for 500,000 volumes, extensive seating, the audiovisual department and general facilities like bookshops and restaurants. Also available for consultation here would be digitally reproduced patrimonial material. Below this was the 'garden level' or 'cloister', exclusively for researchers who alone would have access to the original collections of the BN. At each of the four corners of the square would stand a 20-storey glass tower shaped like an open book containing office space and half the stack area (see Figure 6). This design was partly criticised because it had been originally drawn up to house only the three to four million post–1945 volumes, not the eleven or twelve million now envisaged. But what most vexed its critics were the glass towers which, they argued, sacrificed functionality to monumentality, threatening to roast France's written treasures whenever the sun came out. The high-tech nature of the library, and particularly Jamet's ambitious audiovisual plans at this stage, also continued to cause grave doubts. But a third source of animosity, which Gattégno in fact believes was fundamental to the entire debate, remained the public library on the upper level. His team's interpretation of Mitterrand's democratising ambition was that they should avoid creating two separate libraries in one. Instead, the BdF was envisaged as forming a graduated whole which, argues Gattégno, could have led the reader step by step into the nation's heritage, 'une bibliothèque conçue comme un parcours continu, une familiarisation ou une initiation progressive à la lecture savante' (p.73).

In 1990 and 1991, a public campaign by academics and library specialists against the BdF began with a piece in the *TLS* by Harvard historian Patrice Higonnet, which attacked the political ambition underpinning the choice of architecture and called for it to be stopped: 'It will be a monument to the evisceration of French socialism', wrote Higonnet, 'as it inscribes in steel and glass the institutional triumph and moral bankruptcy of French social democracy, a "high-tech" substitute for reflective humanism.' A few months later, Fumaroli again deprecated a conception of democratisation which failed to distinguish adequately between a national library, a public library and a tourist attraction. But to complicate matters even further, the project around this time also came under fire from its own artillery. For the President's new cultural adviser, Laure Adler, criticised it for not democratising enough, complaining that the plan to introduce a user's card turned the library into 'une forteresse culturelle qui avait tendance à dissuader les gens d'y venir'.[41] Mitterrand therefore sent Lang and

Figure 6. The Bibliothèque nationale de France, January 1995 (architect: D. Perrault). Photo: Jim Dolamore.

Biasini a clarification in which he identified two 'equally interesting but quite distinct' publics: the 'élite intellectuelle' of researchers who have every right to expect peace and quiet on the lower level, and the general public who must equally 'se sentir chez lui' in this institution it has paid for.[42] For Gattégno, Mitterrand's letter was a second concession to academic pressure, clearly disavowing the democratic conception of a single library drawn up by the EPBF.

A third then came about as a result of an open letter sent to the President in August 1991 by a former head of the BN, Georges Le Rider, signed by around a hundred users who once more called for the design to be revised, though Gattégno again insists its real target was the attempt to widen access. By December, its signatories had reached 700. In October, Chirac went to see Mitterrand to express his support for the petition. Soon afterwards, Biasini announced that the President was asking the Conseil supérieur des bibliothèques under André Miquel, himself a former administrator general of the BN, to express a view. The Council duly put together a panel of experts which reported the following January. With some caution given that its brief was not to challenge either the design or the conception, the report called for storage of books in the towers to be stopped, for less use of highly vulnerable retrieval technology, for steps to be taken to ensure that the garden could be built on if necessary, and for the building to be made more compact (pp.92–4).

The government's response was lukewarm. Mitterrand agreed to remove two storeys from the towers and not to store the most precious books there. He also agreed to a clarification of the relationship between the BdF and the BN and to wider consultation. To this end, a commission of specialists was set up, again under Miquel, which would make proposals not to the EPBF but directly to the ministers responsible. The DAGEC's Jean-Luc Silicani was also given the task of investigating how the library could reach its goals as economically as possible. These proposals seemed to satisfy nobody. Le Rider and others were disappointed at their modesty; Gattégno saw them as a further disavowal which limited his own autonomy and bypassed Jamet. He immediately resigned as he was expected to, a scapegoat to avert the more embarrassing removal of his superior and appease the Le Rider faction as the 1993 elections approached. He interprets his departure as yet a further move away from Mitterrand's original democratising aim, back towards a BN-bis.[43]

What, then, is the significance of the apparently inexhaustible antipathy to the BdF? As with all the *grands projets*, it was partly the result of the *fait du prince* since, with the library's conception and design circumscribed by presidential diktat, it became extremely difficult to take any real account of the views of the academic community. This, together with the fact that the plans were insufficiently publicised in Gattégno's view, no doubt accounts for the suspicion and resentment the project aroused in the intellectual community. Gattégno also points out a variety of other causes, including the refusal of the library's intellectual opponents to recognise the credentials of Jamet's team and the tactical advantage they were afforded by the prospect of a change of government in 1993 (pp.240–2).

But there was arguably a deeper, cultural dimension to the polemics, to do with the centrality of the written word and the literary heritage to France's whole sense of national identity. As Jacques Julliard put it, 'une bibliothèque, ce "lieu de mémoire" par excellence, est un des éléments constitutifs de la conscience nationale au sens de Renan, c'est-à-dire un consensus fondé sur une histoire'.[44] The problem for the Bibliothèque de France as for the new British Library was how to adapt this 'lieu de mémoire' to the electronic age and to a late twentieth-century interpretation of cultural democracy in a mass society, both of which appeared to threaten it. The idea of democratising the BN in fact posed a dual problem. First, it led to fears of a Beaubourg syndrome, for as Fumaroli's allusion to Disneyland suggests, the new library seemed to some to involve transplanting the BN's tranquil classicism in a post-modernist madhouse, designed to attract crowds of milling tourists or casual users and kitted out with what even Jamet described as 'des espaces ludiques et culturels'.[45] Second, and perhaps more disturbing, it involved powerful new technologies capable of demythifying books and even dematerialising the library altogether as a building and a cultural totem. The deepest problem for the BdF project may therefore be that it provides one of the first major arenas in which French cultural tradition has to wrestle with the twenty-first century.

By the 1993 elections, the BdF was classed alongside the Opéra-Bastille as a future disaster zone with uncertain aims and horrendous operating costs. What both show is the continuing controversies and problems caused by a programme of *grands projets* combining presidential will and huge quantities of public money. Both also demonstrate that democratising the heritage can still be a live polemical issue in the 1990s. Finally, both indicate that despite official blandishments and a certain rallying prior to the 1986 elections, diplomatic relations between the PS government and many in the cultural and intellectual community, on both Left and Right, remained obstinately problematic. This was equally apparent in the other main area of cultural debate in the post–1988 period: television.

Notes

1. 'Urgences et priorités', *Le Monde*, 24 May 1988. The title 'Lang II' was modelled on the label 'Mitterrand II' given the President after his second election victory.
2. 'Les Six Sous de Lang', *Le Nouvel Observateur*, 19–25 August 1988, p.23.
3. J. Gattégno, *La Bibliothèque de France à mi-parcours: de la TGB à la BN bis?*, Paris, 1992, p.206. On the problems caused by this bicephalous relationship between Culture and the Grands Travaux state secretariat, see also pp.205–8; and S. Collard, 'Mission impossible: les chantiers du Président', *French Cultural Studies*, vol.3, no.8, June 1992, pp.118–19.
4. 'Une Etape', *Le Monde*, 10 June 1988, p.2.
5. F. Léotard, *Culture: les chemins du printemps*, Paris, 1988, pp.65–6; and A.-H. Mesnard, *Droit et politique de la culture*, Paris, 1990, p.137.
6. For a brief resumé of the 1989 budget, see *Lettre d'Information*, 31 October 1988, p.2; for the 1993 budget, see ibid., 12 November 1992, pp.4–5. *Le Monde*, 1 March 1993, p.11, estimated the revised February figure as either 0.93 or 0.98 per cent.
7. Colin believes that if Lang had stayed in office in 1986 he would not simply have reduced the DDC as Léotard did but abolished it altogether, because its cross-disciplinary nature was not accepted by the other directorates and no longer coincided with ministerial thinking (personal interview, 7 April 1992).
8. The decorating of the shepherd was pointed out to me by Robert Abirached (personal interview, 8 April 1992).
9. 'Jack the Lad', *Independent* (Saturday magazine supplement), 27 June 1992.
10. M. Hunter, *Les Jours les plus Lang*, Paris, 1990, pp.266–7.
11. J. Renard, *L'Elan culturel: la France en mouvement*, Paris, 1987, p.220. *Cofinancements* involve the state's undertaking to match franc for franc the income a company gains from sponsorship.
12. For example Alain Casabona, general secretary of the Comité national pour l'éducation artistique, reported in 'Culture: après le bluff socialiste, l'élan libéral', *Le Figaro Magazine*, 26 March 1988.
13. A.-H. Mesnard, *Droit*, pp.140–1; and R. Wangermée and B. Gournay, *Programme européen d'évaluation: la politique culturelle de la France*, Paris, 1988, pp.222–5. The quotation is from A. Schnapper, 'Une Bastille à renverser', *Commentaire*, no.48, winter 1989–90, p.720.

14. On the 73 per cent increase, see *Journal Officiel*, 2ᵉ séance du 7 novembre 1992, p.5,008. At the same sitting, Lang also summarised his new *enseignements artistiques* proposals for 1993, p.5,020; see also Ministry press dossier entitled 'Présentation du plan en faveur de l'éducation artistique à l'école', 1 March 1993. Toubon's November 1993 proposals are reported in *Le Monde*, 21–2 November 1993, p.9.

15. Wangermée and Gournay, *La Politique culturelle*, pp.223–5.

16. Ministry figures published in 1991 suggest that Lang's average annual budget for heritage between 1981 and 1986, excluding the *grands projets*, was actually higher than Léotard's at 1991 prices, 1,702 million francs as against 1,466 million, Ministry of Culture, 'La Politique culturelle 1981–1991': 'Patrimoine', 1991, p.18.

17. See Mesnard, *Droit*, p.140; and Léotard, *Culture*, pp.184–5.

18. His speech is reproduced in a supplement to *Lettre d'Information*, 19 September 1988, and was widely reported in the press.

19. 'La manifestation et le concert de la Bastille à Paris', *Le Monde*, 11 July 1989, p.12.

20. 'Un Ballet gracieux et gratuit', 16–17 July 1989, p.6.

21. First quotation (Hardy), Ministry of Culture, '"La Marseillaise", Jean-Paul Goude', press dossier no.DP400, p.12; Goude is quoted in 'Un Ballet gracieux et gratuit', *Le Monde*, 16–17 July 1989, p.6.

22. *Grand Jury*, RTL, 27 December 1981.

23. Charles Gassot, producer of the Goude event, quoted in press dossier no.DP400, p.35.

24. The Cité des sciences at La Villette was opened in March 1986, Orsay in December the same year, the IMA in December 1987, and the new premises for the TEP, now called the Théâtre de la colline, in January 1988.

25. Lang's speech at a press conference reviewing the Pyramid's first six months, 19 September 1989, press dossier no.DP419.

26. See Léotard's announcements in his interview with *Le Monde*, 28 May 1987, pp.1 and 17; see also M. de Saint Pulgent, *Le Syndrome de l'opéra*, Paris, 1991, pp.273–7, for a fuller account of this episode.

27. 'L'Opéra entre espoirs et pesanteurs', *Le Monde*, 2 April 1988, pp.1 and 18; and M. de Saint Pulgent, *Le Syndrome*, pp.290–1.

28. In the debates which ensued, the figure quoted for the 1991–2 season varied from 120 to 160.

29. The ATOP replaced the Association de préfiguration de l'Opéra-Bastille and grouped together the Bastille, Garnier and the Salle Favart.

30. 'Daniel Barenboim, oui ou non?', *Le Monde*, 9 November 1988,

pp.1 and 14 (quotation p.14).

31. 'La Bastille des artistes', *Le Monde*, 24 January 1989, pp.1 and 13 (quotation p.13).

32. 'Un Bon Génie pour la Bastille', *Le Monde*, 2 September 1988, p.17.

33. 'Une Réponse de Patrice Chéreau sur la situation de l'art lyrique à Paris', *Le Monde*, 11 November 1988, p.24.

34. *La Comédie de la culture*, Paris, 1993, p.137.

35. Catherine Tasca, delegate minister for Communication under Lang, was also rumoured to have sided with Boulez and Chéreau, both of whom she had previously worked with: see for example Lonchampt, *Le Monde*, 24 January 1989, p.1. Boulez resigned from the governing body of the ATOP but remained vice-president of the Bastille's *établissement public*.

36. *Journal Officiel*, 2ᵉ séance du 7 novembre 1992, p.5,012.

37. Mitterrand's letter to Rocard is reprinted in 'La "Grande Bibliothèque" avance', *Lettre d'Information*, 29 August 1988. The following analysis is indebted to information provided both in M. Gattégno's book, *La Bibliothèque de France*, and in the two interviews he granted me, 29 March 1991 and 7 April 1992, as well as subsequent correspondence, though a variety of other sources are used to provide as objective an account as possible. The analysis of the period up to spring 1991 also draws on my own article, 'The *Bibliothèque de France*. Last of the *grands projets*', *Modern and Contemporary France*, no.46, July 1991, pp.35–46; the same issue contains a transcript of parts of my 1991 interview with M. Gattégno, pp.73–6. Future references to his book will appear in brackets in the text.

38. P. Cahart and M. Melot, *Propositions pour une grande bibliothèque*, Paris, 1989. For a more detailed summary of the report, see Looseley, 'The *Bibliothèque de France*', pp.37–8. For Lang's press conference on 12 April 1989 announcing the first major decisions based on the report, see 'Un Grand Chantier: la Bibliothèque de France', in Ministry of Culture, 'Le Livre et la lecture', 24 May 1989, press dossier no.DP388.

39. Julliard, 'Monsieur le Président', *Le Nouvel Observateur*, 22–8 June 1989, p.31; M. Lever, *Le Débat*, no.55, May–August 1989, p.166.

40. Fumaroli, 'Bibliothèque de France: Alexandrie ou Disneyland?', *Le Figaro*, 21 July 1989.

41. Higonnet, 'A French Folly', *TLS*, 11–17 May 1990; Fumaroli, 'Bibliothèque de France: la charrue avant les bœufs', *Le Figaro*, 30 August 1990; Adler, *Passages*, November 1990, p.47.

42. '"Une Bibliothèque d'un genre entièrement nouveau"', *Le*

Monde, 2 March 1991, p.14.

43. In July 1993, J. Toubon announced that the BN and BdF would be brought together in one administrative structure from 1 January 1994, the Bibliothèque nationale de France.

44. Julliard, 'Monsieur le Président', p.31.

45. 'La Réponse de Dominique Jamet: les critiques ont tort', *Connaissance des Arts*, October [?], 1990, p.117.

– 10 –

Culture and the Audiovisual

From the moment Lang took a stand on Deauville, film and television became a major source of debate under the Socialists. Controversy, however, intensified from the mid–1980s as a deepening crisis in cinema, the arrival of new channels and new technologies like cable and satellite, and political decisions both before and after March 1986 all transformed the audiovisual landscape and made it the cultural issue of the decade. But as with the debates I looked at in Chapter 9, the opposing sides in these conflicts came to be less easily identifiable as the Left and Right.[1]

Due to the high costs and risks involved, film production in France is financed from a variety of sources, the greatest share coming from private producers and distributors, both French and foreign. It is also a classic case of a cultural industry operating in a market economy but needing public intervention to survive. Under Lang, the basic system of state aid to cinema set up in the 1940s and 1950s, chiefly in the form of the Compte de soutien à l'industrie cinématographique managed by the CNC, remained in operation but was steadily modified. In addition to Ministry subsidy (383 million francs in 1991) and income from TV companies (to which I shall return), the Compte is still supplied mainly by a tax levied on cinema tickets, amounting to approximately 11 per cent of the ticket price. This was estimated in the budget statement for 1991 as likely to yield some 435 million francs. The bulk of the Compte goes to producers of existing full-length films (*longs métrages*) who are willing to reinvest it in a further production. This aid is described as 'automatic' in that it is available to all French producers planning to reinvest and is calculated on the basis of the ticket sales of a previous film, irrespective of any judgment of quality. Although this inevitably favours those already successful, it has been a powerful instrument for maintaining the level of French film production at a time when that of other European countries has fallen off. A further proportion of the Compte is distributed as selective aid to production, by means of the *avance sur recettes*, which rewards aesthetic quality and innovation rather than previous commercial success. A theoretically reimbursable, interest-free loan is provided on the basis of a favourable pronouncement by a specialist commission on a scenario which would be unlikely to elicit the necessary financing from private sources. Thirdly, the Compte de soutien aids *diffusion* by providing subsidy to cinemas, again automatic in the case of cinemas generally and selective for *art et essai* venues.

Despite this well established system, the French film industry during the 1980s became caught in a downward spiral, as cinema admissions plummeted in the teeth of competition from television and new audiovisual technologies. In 1960, cinemas were attracting around 400 million spectators. Falling dramatically in the ensuing years then stabilising during the 1970s at 170 to 180 million, attendances began to fall again from the mid–1980s: 163 million in 1986, 117.4 million in 1991. Cinema receipts accordingly went down 19 per cent in real terms between 1982 and 1986.[2] Reflecting and aggravating the problem was the steady closure of cinemas in smaller towns and rural areas, halving the number of seats available between 1964 and 1986, so that by 1981 almost half the French population lived in communes which had no cinema. A further result of the admissions slump was the drop in investment by distributors, who in 1980 accounted for some 30 per cent of the finance available to French or majority-French film production, in 1986 18 per cent, and in 1989 only 2 per cent, and this at a time when production costs were soaring. Lastly, the American domination of the French domestic market was increasing all the time, driving the French share down from 49.5 per cent of tickets sold in 1981, to 44.3 per cent in 1985 and as low as 30 per cent in 1991.[3]

The Socialist government reacted to this crisis during the first quinquennium by increasing overall aid to the film and audiovisual industries sevenfold, the Ministry's contribution to the Compte de soutien rising from zero in 1981 to 113 million francs in 1986.[4] The assistance given through the *avance sur recettes* was also extended and improved in various ways. In addition, a new fund, *l'aide au développement des projets*, was devised to help in the very early stages of drawing up a first scenario, and a special form of direct aid was established which allowed the Minister personally to fund prestigious projects, often by foreign directors. This was used to assist work by Wajda, Jancso and Chahine and would also have been used for Scorsese's *Last Temptation of Christ*, had opposition from religious groups not made Lang back down.

For *diffusion*, aid was provided to selected projects for building or modernising cinemas in deprived areas via the Agence pour le développement régional du cinéma, which also assists in the immediate showing of new films in remote rural areas by covering the cost of copying. The government was also concerned to protect independent cinemas and at the same time ensure that quality work, such as the films backed by the *avance sur recettes*, was distributed as widely as possibly up and down the country. Both aims involved tackling the fact that distribution in France was monopolised by a handful of major companies, notably Gaumont-Pathé and various other groupings of cinemas into programming networks. This concentration, the PS argued, meant that in practice what the average cinema-goer was allowed to see in ordinary cinemas (as opposed to film clubs or *art et essai* establishments) was largely determined by the commercial considerations of a relatively small group of distributors. The audiovisual law of July 1982 therefore stipulated that all such groupings had to have the prior consent of the CNC and were forbidden where two or more nation-wide companies were involved. This forced the Gaumont-Pathé group to split and led to the appointment of a cinema ombudsman to arbitrate in all disputes regarding market domination and unfair competition.

But government intervention of these kinds was not enough, for to compensate for the dwindling revenue from distributors and for rising production costs, it was important to look for new sources of finance. One was the IFCIC, specially designed to aid the film industry by securing loans to producers, distributors and firms engaged in the technical aspects of the industry. Another involved further encouragement of private patronage. A law passed in July 1985 created a system of tax incentives by the setting up of Sociétés de financement des industries cinématographiques et audiovisuelles (SOFICA), which enabled investments in film production by both private individuals and companies to be made tax-deductible as long as the work concerned was in French and made in an EC country. Only two years on, in 1987, SOFICA investments accounted for 10.5 per cent of the total finances available for French or majority-French films, while IFCIC-assisted investments accounted for 6.5 per cent. In 1992, the SOFICAs brought in almost 180 million francs involving 58 films.[5] However, as the number and type of broadcasting media grew, the chief imperative, if the French film industry was to find new sources of finance and be shielded from 'l'anarchie du marché' and further decline, was to rationalise its relationship with television. And it was here that the Ministry's limited influence over the audiovisual sector was most problematic.

The Socialists' entire approach to the sector was in fact vitiated by contradiction. Before 1981, cultural and media policies had been considered indissoluble and, in the run-up to the presidentials, the PS's suspicion of the broadcasting media had led to a determination to impose cultural criteria upon them in three ways: by separating production from distribution in order to ensure creative quality in programme-making; by decentralising channels and programme production to make them serve local people and local creativity; and by insisting that television repay its debts to the more traditional cultural forms on which it lived parasitically. But after 10 May, attitudes imperceptibly changed. Although Bredin's report on cinema and Moinot's on broadcasting were designed to mesh, the decision to separate Culture and Communication meant that implementing these three interventionist principles largely became the preserve of the Culture Ministry alone, while measures freeing broadcasting from government control, initiated to an extent by the Communication Ministry but increasingly by a President acting independently of everybody, often pulled in a different direction.[6]

The prompt legalising of private local radio stations (*radios libres*) in November 1981, for example, seemed a positive step towards decentralisation and cultural diversity in that the stations were to be run by local community associations. In practice, it launched a multitude of stations many of which, especially once the President unilaterally allowed them to take advertising in 1984, expanded to become national commercial stations mainly given over to English and American pop. The following year, the historic bill of 29 July theoretically ended the state's tutelage of broadcasting by setting up an independent regulatory body acting as a buffer between the two, the Haute Autorité de la communication audiovisuelle. Here too, decentralisation was written into the law but made little headway between 1981 and 1986 because cable, the technology most likely to place television in local hands, was slow to develop. Instead, three private, Hertzian, national channels were launched, also presidentially initiated: the subscription channel Canal Plus in 1984, La Cinq and TV6 in 1986.

This is not to say that none of the three cultural aims was acted upon. As well as setting television to work in drawing attention to high-cultural forms like the visual arts and theatre, Lang took a number of important steps to protect cultural standards and favour audiovisual creation during the 1981–6 period, though not all were unequivocally successful. Unwilling to demote the cinema auditorium as the authentic environment for film, or to allow the free play of market forces, the Ministry saw television as the best way of injecting new cash into the film industry. Even excluding the 400-odd films screened annually by Canal Plus since 1986, the number of films on

TV increased from 500 in 1981 to 901 in 1989. This dependence, it was felt, needed to be recognised financially. TV companies already contributed to the Compte de soutien by paying both fifteen centimes per spectator and a lump sum of around 120,000 francs every time a film was broadcast, the equivalent of the tax on tickets that would have been levied if the film had been shown in a cinema to 70,000 spectators. But since this notional figure was lower than the average numbers actually attracted by a film screened in a cinema, and considerably lower than those watching it on TV, the Ministry no longer considered such payment adequate, replacing it in the 1986 budget with a 1.5 per cent tax on a channel's income.[7] Further measures since 1982 have also progressively obliged TV companies to devote a percentage of their turnover to co-producing films or buying broadcasting rights on new films (3 per cent since 1991).

Yet films alone could not satisfy the surge in demand for programmes generated by the new channels and technologies. If French television were not to be swamped by the inexhaustible supply of soaps and made-for-TV films issuing from America, many times cheaper than French products because they had already recouped their investment on their vast domestic market, it had to step up production of its own TV programmes. So once the Ninth Plan had opted to prioritise the cultural and audiovisual industries, a Compte de soutien à l'industrie des programmes was launched in 1984, designed to aid the making of 'creative' programmes – fiction, cartoons, documentaries and so on – and, like the Cinema fund, fed by a tax on TV channels' income. This was initially levied on the new networks alone but the Finance bill for 1986 extended it to the income of all TV channels, whether from advertising, subscription or licence fee. The bill also combined this Compte with the Cinema's to form the Compte de soutien financier de l'industrie cinématographique et de l'industrie des programmes audiovisuels. Today, the joint fund receives 5.5 per cent (922 million francs in 1990) of the total income of TV companies, 43 per cent of it going to its Cinema section and 57 per cent to its Audiovisual section. Since July 1993, the video industry too has been paying in 2 per cent of its turnover.[8]

Television was called on to help film creation in other ways too. For some time, the charters (*cahiers des charges*) which lay down the conditions under which TV channels are allowed to operate had regulated the number of films a channel could show per year and the times of the day and week at which they could show them, so that cinemas would not have to compete with TV when they were likely to attract their optimum audiences, such as Friday evening and all day

Saturday. But Lang wanted tougher restrictions still. The idea of a 'chronology' for showing new films was first introduced in the 1982 audiovisual law at his behest. What he initially had in mind was the new danger video cassettes represented to the more 'natural' exploitation of the film in cinemas. A *décret d'application* of the 1982 law duly stipulated that a new film could only appear on video twelve months after general release.[9] This was only one in a series of restrictions designed to ward off the video peril, including a swinging 33 per cent VAT rate and a tax imposed on VCR sales, to say nothing of the bizarre obligation for all imported VCRs to pass through the customs office in Poitiers. Then, as the private TV channels were launched from 1984, Lang attempted to include them in the chronology too, his preferred sequence being cinemas, video, Canal Plus, then the remaining channels.

But although his proposals were greeted enthusiastically by the cinema profession, they backfired in a number of ways. The video restrictions proved damaging to both the burgeoning French video trade, thereby contradicting Lang's cultural industries policy, and arguably to the cinema industry as well. Hunter points out that in America video in 1986 accounted for 36 per cent of the resources coming into the film industry yet had not damaged ticket sales in cinemas, while CNC figures showed only 7 per cent in France in the mid–1980s. Figures also indicated that while sales of VCRs were rising yearly in Britain and West Germany, they fell by 25 per cent in France after the Poitiers decision caused the import process to grind almost to a halt.[10] The video industry attempted to free itself from the twelve-month clause by taking the case to the European Court of Justice in 1984 but the Court ruled in the government's favour.

The creation of Canal Plus, the pay channel given over largely to feature films and sport, also represented a threat to Lang's cinema policy; hence his wishing to see it placed third in his chronology, with a time lapse of eighteen months. The channel's chairman André Rousselet, close to the President, had other ideas. He demanded only six months, to the dismay of the Minister and the film industry, trading this off against an undertaking to invest 25 per cent of the channel's profits in new films and to show a majority of French works. Fillioud and Mitterrand sided with Rousselet. Eventually a compromise was reached of eleven months provisionally (damaging the video industry further) and later twelve.[11] But Lang was in line for worse disappointments yet, this time over his efforts to have stiff new quotas accepted which would force new private channels, to which he was in any case opposed, to show a high proportion of French films. Although quotas of 60 per cent European and 50 per cent French films were imposed on Canal Plus, when La Cinq was being set up in 1985 its *cahier des charges* stipulated that only a quarter of its film output had to be national, though this would rise to 50 per cent after five years, bringing it into line with the public channels. To make matters worse, the consortium which was to run the channel included Silvio Berlusconi, known by some in the French film world as the 'gravedigger of Italian cinema' whose existing three channels dispensed a diet of American imports and game-shows. Lang's entreaties were ignored and he was rumoured to be contemplating resignation. His decision not to and the prudent silence he maintained on the matter for quite a long time drew the opprobrium of a cinema industry generally won over by his previous support. Bertrand Tavernier returned his 'Arts at Lettres' medal in disgust, later describing La Cinq's creation as 'une manœuvre criminelle'.[12]

After the March 1986 election, Léotard's new broadcasting bill was rushed through Parliament by autumn 1986. He had said that broadcasting was an ideal realm in which to put the regime's liberalism into practice and the law which bore his name came with an appropriate discourse of disengaging the state and shifting the weight from public to private.[13] Yet here too, apart from privatising TF1, the new government declined to dismantle the Socialists' earlier achievements, for the simple reason that in the main they were already liberal. What it did do was reattribute La Cinq and TV6 and replace the Haute Autorité, accused of being too easily manipulated by the state, with a similar body with increased powers and membership, the Commission nationale de la communication et des libertés (CNCL). Léotard also announced that the licence fee would be reduced by 17 per cent as a result of the loss of one public channel, the tax on VCRs lifted, and advertising on Antenne 2 reduced.

His audiovisual bill was poorly drafted and much criticised, with no fewer than 1,637 amendments put down when it passed through the Senate. The privatising of TF1 was particularly unpopular: Mitterrand expressed 'extreme reservations' about it, the PS's Culture spokesperson Jean-Jack Queyranne likened it to selling off the Comédie Française to Coca-Cola, and 100,000 people signed a petition against it. In spring 1987, the franchise was attributed not to Hachette as expected but to a consortium headed by the construction magnate Francis Bouygues, close to the RPR, and including Robert Maxwell. The music channel TV6 was sold to CLT and La Lyonnaise des Eaux and became the generalist M6, while La Cinq went to a group formed by Silvio Berlusconi and Robert Hersant. The CNCL immediately proved controversial since the majority of its thirteen members were close to the RPR and it opted to replace all the heads of channels. One controversy then followed another, culminating in a carefully aimed dart from the President in an interview in September 1987 when he expressed the view that the CNCL 'n'a rien fait jusqu'ici qui puisse inspirer le respect'.[14] The *paysage audiovisuel français*, or PAF as it became known, had swiftly turned into a minefield.

The most intractable problem for the CNCL was one which the Socialists had created and Léotard aggravated: rampant competition between public and private channels. The new Minister coined the somewhat obscure phrase 'le mieux-disant culturel' to indicate the high cultural standards which would be expected of those bidding for the private channels. In his book written at the end of his term of office, he also maintains that all the measures introduced to apply the law were in fact aimed at protecting and encouraging French audiovisual creation. An eventual total output of one thousand hours of creative new work per year had been insisted upon from TF1, M6 and La Cinq together. The cultural obligations Lang had had trouble obtaining were also pushed through in all three cases, via both their individual *cahiers des charges* and a number of *décrets d'application* of the audiovisual law issued in January 1987, which imposed a fixed quota of 50 per cent French and 60 per cent European films and 'audiovisual works'.[15]

But Léotard's account is only half the story, for in reality these obligations were often not met or enforced, and by late 1987 there was precious little evidence that deregulation was helping French creation or warding off Americanisation. On the contrary, many felt that the intense competition between channels, both public and private, for the finite advertising revenue on which they now depended had led only to 'la dictature de l'audimat'. Total spending on advertising in the various media rose by 65 per cent, while television's share of that spending went from almost 27 per cent to a projected 35 per cent between 1987 and 1991.[16] The consequence was a lowest common denominator policy involving very little cultural or educational programming at prime-time and a considerable quantity of game or variety shows. There was also a significant increase in the number of films shown, mostly American, and of cheap US series. And although the creation record of the two channels remaining in the public sector was better than that of the commercial ones, they were now minoritised within the PAF, losing audiences, and receiving insufficient funds from the licence fee alone to enact their public-service mission, and could therefore only compete with the private sector by imitating it. Not surprisingly, a BVA survey in September 1987 showed that 51 per cent of viewers felt that the quality of French television had deteriorated; those involved professionally were also unanimous in their discontent. To make matters worse, competition was leading to an inflationary spiral in the price of films, sports events and even salaries as the star names of one channel were snapped up by another. 'C'est toute la construction libérale de M. Léotard qui se lézarde', concluded *Le Monde*.[17]

As the presidentials approached, Mitterrand made the audiovisual one of the main themes of his campaign. Like the PCF, some in the PS leaned towards renationalising TF1, but the official line was simply to restore its mission as a public service. In the event, with television as with other areas of cultural policy, Rocard's government opted for continuity more than change, to the extent that the real originality of its position was actually the absence of upheaval. It did not immediately replace the heads of channels, and the new audiovisual bill it drew up retained the general structure of the 1986 legislation, contenting itself instead with reform.[18] Dated 27 January 1989, the law replaced the CNCL by the third regulatory body in seven years, the Conseil supérieur de l'audiovisuel (CSA). With its membership again reduced to nine, it had greater powers than both its predecessors, particularly concerning the imposition of penalties on private channels which did not respect their cultural obligations. To tackle the crisis in the public sector caused by private-sector competition, Lang announced an increase in the licence fee and an injection of cash. But just as vital was a strategy to eliminate competition between the two public channels themselves. The new government therefore opted to appoint a joint head of Antenne 2 and FR3.[19] The move was not popular in some quarters, including the PS, but it was the government itself which ended up dissatisfied as the CSA, anxious to assert its independence as its two predecessors had failed to do, chose a figure identified with the opposition as joint president, Philippe Guilhaume. He, however, eventually resigned under government pressure and was replaced by Hervé Bourges, head of TF1 until its privatisation and the Elysée's original preference for the post.

Like the Chirac government, the Socialists also pursued the culture and broadcasting issue at European level. EC ministers of culture had begun regular meetings in 1984 and the ruling on the video time-lapse by the European Court of Justice in 1985 had effectively widened the Court's sphere of activity to include the cultural domain. Since then, there had been a steady move towards harmonising member countries' legislation, particularly after the signing of the Single Europe Act, for example through the notion of a common system of aid to audiovisual and film production. A further means was the attempt, earnestly advocated by European cinema professionals, to establish a 60 per cent quota of European productions on all TV channels in member countries via a proposed EC directive called 'Télévision sans frontières'. Supported initially by the French government, the move misfired when Mitterrand was forced to back down under pressure from America which was extremely hostile to what it saw as a 'fortress Europe' policy.[20] The directive did not therefore impose obligatory quotas but merely adopted them in principle and whenever possible, leaving it to national legislation to regulate if it so wished.

This the French government duly did. Catherine Tasca introduced decrees in January 1990 which imposed new obligations on TV channels, including the requirement mentioned earlier to invest 3 per cent of turnover in new productions, and another to devote 15 per cent to commissioning home-produced programmes. She also plugged the loopholes which had allowed private channels to dodge Léotard's prescriptions. Although, as Léotard says, private channels had been required to invest more in French creation, the money had in practice often gone on cheaper types of programmes which were scheduled at non-peak hours rather than at prime-time. Tasca's new decrees therefore insisted that the majority of the French and European productions required by the quotas be scheduled between 6.00 p.m. and 11.00 p.m., and from 2.00 p.m. to 6.00 p.m. on Wednesdays. In 1991 and 1992, however, these restrictions were made more flexible in response to fears that their uniform application would threaten the existence of the smaller channels. The 50 per cent quota of French work was also reduced to 40 per cent.[21] Subsequently, in 1993, debate about such 'protectionism' became international again as the GATT negotiations brought further conflict with the US over France's insistence on treating culture as an exception where free trade is concerned. Lang's successor Jacques Toubon and Prime Minister Balladur now took up the torch of his resistance to American market domination in the closing stages of the seven-year-long 'Uruguay round', which finally had to be concluded without an agreement on the audiovisual issue being reached.

One further European initiative pursued by both Lang and Léotard was the Franco-German cultural channel in the public sector, known as La SEPT and later ARTE, which was initiated only a month before the Socialists' 1986 electoral defeat. For some time, it was only available via cable and then at restricted times on FR3, causing the SEPT team some frustration at the government's failure to find it a Hertzian frequency. But in April 1992, the ideal opportunity for its wider dissemination, and at the same time for an adjustment of the balance between private and public sectors, arose when financial problems being experienced by La Cinq, unresolved by a takeover in

1991 by Hachette, led to its demise. Shortly afterwards, the then Secretary of State for Communication, Jean-Noël Jeanneney, announced that part of its network would be attributed to La SEPT, somewhat to the consternation of two opposing camps: those who felt that there was no place for an 'elitist' cultural channel on prime-time TV, and those who feared that it would provide a convenient pretext for generalist channels to offload their cultural obligations.

This element of continuity in audiovisual policy running from the first Socialist quinquennium through cohabitation into the post–1988 period meant that Right and Left jointly came under attack over the continuing cultural fallout of the Socialists' original reforms. Again, America was at the heart of the debate, for much of the failure of certain channels to meet their obligations was due to the inability of European production capacity to meet the huge increase in television hours the new channels brought, to which the only short-term remedy was to import even more. With some irony in fact, shortly after Lang had begun to soften his position on America, parts of the cultural community, once sharply divided over Deauville and Mexico, began to come round to his earlier way of thinking. The roots of their discontent lay in the cinema's pre–1986 opposition to La Cinq. The privatising of TF1 and the failure of the CNCL to curb the commercialisation of French broadcasting then inflamed it, particularly as the Léotard reforms coincided with a further crisis in the cinema industry as 1987 saw another 15–20 per cent drop in attendances. Gradually, opposition began to take a more organised form. On 9 December 1985, a mass meeting of artists was held at la Mutualité to protest at the creation of La Cinq. A year later, the Communist mayor of Aubervilliers Jack Ralite, member of the Mauroy government in 1981 and a respected cultural militant, launched an appeal which led to the setting up of the Etats généraux de la culture. The organisation's first meeting was held in February 1987 and collected 247 signatures for the appeal. The second, in June, drew 1,500 people; the third, in November, 6,000. One of its objectives was to campaign against 'la grande marmelade contemporaine, souvent aplatie devant l'Amérique et son marché' that was French television, which had become merely a pretext for advertising.[22] At the second meeting, a 'draft audiovisual charter' was drawn up which claimed that the 'right of citizens to communication' had been hijacked by privatisation and called for a public-service mission which was not limited to the public sector alone.

After the Socialists' return to power, the movement remained active for a time, particularly over the government's climb-down on the Télévision sans frontières directive. On 21 May 1989, the Etats généraux and the Comité d'action pour l'Europe du cinéma et de la télévision organised a protest rally involving actors, producers and other artists in Strasbourg where the directive was due to be debated at the European Parliament.

In October 1988, hundreds of artists also took part in the 'Opération Garance' to draw attention to the 200,000 people of all persuasions who had signed the movement's petition for an end to advertising breaks in fiction programmes on television, described by Ralite as a mutilation. The Etats généraux did not, however, believe that advertising should be removed from public television altogether, though others did, detecting a contradiction in the idea of a public service being reliant on advertising and sponsorship for almost 70 per cent of its income. Those who took this view at first drew hope from the return of a Socialist government and a campaign was launched by Max Gallo, Pierre Bourdieu and others, soon joined by a large number of artists and intellectuals including Costa-Gavras, Lévy and Derrida.[23] Their proposal was that the private channels be given a free rein to develop whatever kind of programming they wished according to free-market principles, and that the public channels be financed via both the licence fee and a tax levied on the other channels' advertising revenue. In the event, however, despite some signs of wavering from Lang and a certain amount of pressure from the PS, the status quo was preserved.

Such criticisms of French broadcasting were part of a more general unease about the direction of cultural policy in the late 1980s. During cohabitation, for example, the Etats généraux did not limit its campaigns to audiovisual matters but saw the disorder of the PAF and the domination of television by money as symptomatic of a crisis of creation involving all the arts. As well as the audiovisual charter, the meeting in June 1987 drew up a bill of cultural rights which bluntly stated that 'for years' France had been abandoning its creative life to 'l'affairisme': 'Trop souvent l'encouragement nécessaire à la création contemporaine, signe extérieur et intérieur de richesse d'une nation, passe après l'exigence de rentabilité que les industries culturelles publiques et privées poursuivent à travers l'insatiable marchandisation de la culture. Dans le même temps, l'effort de l'Etat pour préserver et développer la culture originale s'étiole et s'abandonne aux mêmes règles.'[24] Ralite particularly underscored the dangers of state disengagement through sponsorship and matching grants, which meant that for the first time in French history it was private enterprise which determined what should and should not be encouraged. He lambasted the colonisation of culture by the financial interests of the big banks, multinationals and advertisers which were moving in on the cultural field dreaming of rich pickings. He criticised the SOFICAs whose financial assistance was made conditional on inadmissibly high interest rates; the Agence pour la gestion des entreprises culturelles which introduced the language of marketing and private enterprise into the arts; and the 'démeublement du pays' brought about by that 51st state of America, Eurodisneyland. With economic values thus overruling cultural ones, it was the very diversity and substance of the national imagination which was being eroded by the market economy.[25]

Naturally, the immediate object of his wrath was the right wing in power at the time. But most of his comments actually applied to measures introduced by a government of the Left of which he had once been a member, from La Cinq to Eurodisneyland (yet another initiative pursued with equal energy by the Fabius and Chirac governments). Fundamental to his position in fact was a theological certainty that culture and the economy were very definitely not the same battle as Lang had insisted they were, and he was voicing that certainty in the name of the original principles of May 1981: creation, pluralism, decentralisation, the defence of cultural identities. Of course, Ralite himself might be accused of speaking for a PCF weakened by its former ally and now on the defensive. But the numbers attracted to his movement could not be so easily dismissed. And although after 1989 it seemed to slip from the public eye, the doubts it had crystallised were by then being taken up by others, again from a variety of political standpoints. Indeed, from all the debates about specific issues around 1989–90 – the bicentenary, the Opéra-Bastille, the Bibliothèque de France and the audiovisual – it was growing clearer that the support of the cultural and intellectual community which the PS government had largely won back by 1986 was again breaking up. This was only confirmed by the more theoretical debate which emerged at much the same time about cultural policy as a whole.

Notes

1. It is not within the scope of this book to make a full examination of Mitterrand's audiovisual policies in their own right. I shall therefore concentrate on the relations between audiovisual and cultural policies, particularly concerning cinema and television.
2. Ministry of Culture, 'La Politique culturelle 1981–1991': 'Cinéma', p.1; and R. Wangermée and B. Gournay, *Programme européen d'évaluation: la politique culturelle de la France*, Paris, 1988, pp.201–3.

3. Ministry, 'La Politique culturelle 1981–1991': 'Cinéma', p.4; and *Cinéma*, Etat et Culture series, Paris, 1992, p.154.
4. Ministry of Culture, 'La Politique culturelle 1981–1985: bilan de la législature': 'Cinéma', p.8.
5. The 1987 figures are from R. Caron, *L'Etat et la culture*, Paris, 1989, p.59; the 1992 figure from Ministry of Culture, *Lettre d'Information*, 11 March 1993, Cinema supplement, p.1.
6. On presidentialism in audiovisual policy, see M. Harrison, 'The President, cultural projects and the mass media', unpublished paper read to the Maison Française, Oxford, 28–9 June 1991, especially pp.18–20.
7. Ministry, 'La Politique culturelle 1981–1991': 'Cinéma', p.1; and 'La Politique culturelle 1981–1985': 'Cinéma', pp.8–9. The tax is known as a *prélèvement* where public channels are concerned.
8. Ministry sources: 'La Politique culturelle 1981–1991': 'Cinéma', p.3; *Cinéma*, Etat et Culture series, Paris, 1992, p.199; and *Lettre d'Information*, 11 March 1993, Cinema supplement, p.1.
9. On the whole video-cinema issue, see Hunter, *Les Jours les plus Lang*, Paris, 1990, pp.158–62 and pp.205–8, to which I am indebted here.
10. Ibid., pp.207–8.
11. Ibid., pp.184–90. The 25 per cent was later brought down to 20.
12. Tavernier is quoted in J. Ralite, *La Culture française se porte bien pourvu qu'on la sauve*, Paris, 1987, p.16.
13. F. Léotard, *Culture: les chemins du printemps*, Paris, 1988, p.60.
14. 'Exclusif: Le Président parle des médias', *Le Point*, 21 September 1987, pp.26–7 (quotation p.27).
15. F. Léotard, *Culture*, pp.60–2. *Décrets d'application*, nos 87–1 and 87–2 (15 January 1987), 87–36 (26 January 1987), 87–43 (30 January 1987). The quota of European productions was 70 per cent for TF1.
16. Figures quoted in P. Bourdieu *et al*, 'Pour une télévision publique sans publicité', *Le Monde*, 29–30 April 1990, pp.1 and 9 (quotation p.9); and in A. Pedley, 'The Media', in M. Cook (ed.), *French Culture since 1945*, London and New York, 1993, p.167.
17. 'Le Krach du "mieux-disant culturel"', *Le Monde*, 21 October 1987.
18. S. Bachmann, 'Les Réformes de l'audiovisuel depuis 1974: "l'éternel retour"', *Quaderni*, no.10, spring 1990, pp.42 and 47.
19. Ibid., pp.42–6.
20. On the TV sans frontières issue, see Hunter, *Les Jours*, pp.290–7.
21. Tasca's decrees: nos 90–66 and 90–67 (17 January 1990). The first

of these was subsequently modified by further decrees in 1991 and 1992. See also M.-E. Alouf, 'Quotas de Tasca', *Politis*, 3–10 January 1991, p.13. On the 1991–2 measures, see *Le Monde*, 18 December 1991, p.16.

22. Ralite, *La Culture française*, p.15.
23. P. Bourdieu *et al*, *Le Monde*: 'Que vive la télévision publique', 19 October 1988, p.2; 'Tombeau pour une ambition', 11 May 1989; and 'Pour une télévision publique sans publicité', 29–30 April 1990, pp.1 and 9.
24. Ralite, *La Culture française*, p.63.
25. Ibid., pp.48–56.

– 11 –

A l'heure des bilans: The Ministry in Question

After the bicentenary, a mentality of commemoration seemed to set in at the Ministry: Mozart, Rimbaud, Columbus, the cinema centenary planned for 1995. The same spirit was extended to the Ministry's own past, with a major colloquium in December 1989 marking its thirtieth anniversary and the setting up in March 1993 of a Comité d'histoire du Ministère de la culture chaired by the recently retired Augustin Girard. Two years before, for the tenth anniversary of Mitterrand's election, the Culture department had commissioned a series of television films about its policies, also producing a box-set of twelve glossy brochures and a richly illustrated 'chronicle of a cultural decade' running to almost 400 pages.[1] As one might expect, the tone of these documents was irrepressibly upbeat, highlighting the generosity of the doubled budget and the two central ambitions which had instigated it: supporting creation as a way of being worthy of France's heritage; and bringing culture out of its 'elitist fortresses' into society. By these means, it was argued, the Ministry had changed perceptions of culture: 'A une vision étriquée, trop souvent tournée vers le passé, s'est substituée celle d'une culture vivante, multiple, en prise sur le présent.' And with the torch now being taken up by artists, local authorities, businesses and the public, culture had become a political and economic force to be reckoned with.[2]

The Ministry, however, was not alone in reviewing its accomplishments by this time. As we saw, Lang's policies during the first quinquennium were widely acclaimed by the public and the cultural community and such discordance as there was largely emanated from the opposition benches or the anti-government press. But his absence from office after March 1986 had the effect of breaking a spell, unleashing the series of critiques I alluded to in the Introduction. This will to take stock was intensified by a Ministry survey published in 1990 entitled *Les Pratiques culturelles des Français*, whose findings cast serious doubt on the efficacy of state voluntarism. Then there were the numerous journalistic assessments around the time of the Malraux and Mitterrand anniversaries, in particular a series run by *Commentaire* in 1989 and 1990 which asked artists, administrators and others, including Lang and some of his staff, to look back over the Ministry's first thirty years.[3]

The result of all this retrospection was that by the turn of the decade cultural policy was the subject of a modest but significant debate, one which again largely transcended party-political divergences in so far as the policies of Lang and Léotard were often not treated as distinct. Indeed, most of the debate was not about specific policies at all but about issues the Lang and Léotard years had jointly raised and which ultimately spanned the complete history of state intervention since 1959. At its core were the essays by Finkielkraut and Fumaroli, the Ministry survey, and two further articles by one of the survey's authors, Olivier Donnat, each successive text engaging in a somewhat tetchy dialogue with one of the others. Rigaud and Schneider also joined in from time to time by situating their own arguments in relation to Finkielkraut's or Fumaroli's. For all five, the heart of the matter was the nature of contemporary culture and, within that broad parameter, the legitimacy of state intervention, in particular the future of democratisation.

One of the most commonly felt concerns among surveyors of cultural policy in the 1980s and early 1990s was that it had become so fascinated by image, enterprise and spectacle that it had lost sight of its social mission. As Jacques Bertin put it in 1991: 'les années Lang resteront comme les années Kleenex, les années de la superficialité, du brio, du sonore. On ne changera plus le monde avec la culture, allez! Mais on repeindra nos façades dans de gaies et consensuelles couleurs.'[4] This transformation was, for example, visible in the way the EACs had been redirected towards high-gloss professional creation in the performing arts, away from *action culturelle*. Indeed, according to Bertin in an earlier article, the very term *action culturelle*, redolent of Copeau, Vilar and May 1968, had become thoroughly unfashionable in the Ministry, replaced by the slick glossary of marketing and *le look*. If the term is used at all today, he argued, it is merely as a sales pitch for a town or region. Nobody is to blame for this. It is just that the Left's assumption of power defused the revolt which had always driven it, turning yesterday's agitators into today's administrators.[5]

This lament was echoed at greater length in 1992 by Jean Caune, a writer with first-hand experience of the transformation of *action culturelle*, as a one-time actor, director and cultural administrator at the

MC in Chambéry. In his book *La Culture en action de Vilar à Lang: le sens perdu*, *action culturelle* is defined as particularly concerned with mediation, with reducing the gap between art and the people and thereby establishing what he calls 'social communication'.[6] Tracing how this concern grew up out of the pre-war *éducation populaire* movement, he dissects its shifts of meaning and gradual attrition between 1960 and 1986. In his view, the major turning-point came in the late 1970s when it fell victim to a crisis of legitimacy with the rise of the cultural industries and the new prominence given to an insufficiently theorised notion of creation. Here, Caune takes Girard's *Futuribles* article about the effects of those industries as an important signal since it demonstrated that official discourse was shifting towards a more pragmatic emphasis on simply satisfying existing demand, with no regard for problems of mediation or reception (pp.266–70). Thus, the EACs, instead of fulfilling their real civic function, have simply become a useful market for the creations of other institutions like CDNs. The kind of thinking Girard exemplified held sway at the rue de Valois throughout the 1980s, Caune maintains, in the form of the culture-economy argument and the infatuation with the new toys of communications technology which, the government deceived itself into thinking, held the key to the problems of social segregation (pp.332–3).

Other commentators, like Alain Finkielkraut, concentrated not on the withering of *action culturelle* but on what had replaced it. *La Défaite de la pensée* is not about cultural policy specifically but is a theoretical critique of the *tout-culturel*, based on a history of the two senses ascribed to the word culture: on the one hand, '[les] grandes créations de l'esprit'; on the other, the broader anthropological meaning which places great art on a par with more banal forms of creativity, habit or ritual.[7] Finkielkraut's thesis is that these two senses are grounded in an historical antithesis between the Enlightenment belief in the universal, emancipatory nature of traditional humanist culture, and notions of nationhood, ethnicity and particularism which, from Herder's idea of a national *Volksgeist* to the philosophies of post-war decolonisation influenced by Marx and Lévi-Strauss, are expressions of a determinism which mysteriously binds individuals to their community and distinguishes them irremediably from those similarly bound to different communities.

In the final part of his book, he introduces a third, very recent position, which he describes as 'post-modern'. To an extent, this is a development of the anthropological meaning in that, in both, everything is cultural and all cultures have equal legitimacy. But ultimately post-modernism goes beyond the earlier duality. It impugns

Enlightenment universalism for imposing on all a single, canonical, Eurocentric conception of culture. But it also distinguishes itself from the decolonialist philosophy in that it does not dethrone Western high culture but rather promotes other forms of artefact to the same nobility, particularly those associated with the consumer society such as advertising, fashion and the entertainment business, so that in the end there is nothing ultimately to choose between Shakespeare and a pair of boots (pp.151–3). The result is a pick 'n' mix form of cultural consumption akin to zapping, a hotch-potch in which the greatest artistic achievements of humanity, the popular cultures of non-Western societies, and mass-produced leisure products all become indistinguishable. This ideology has become a dominant discourse in the 1980s, Finkielkraut believes, for anyone who insists on discriminating between Beethoven and Bob Marley is accused of elitism, or worse still of sharing the racist's horror of *métissage*. But, he contends, the term elitism here has been turned inside out. Whereas Malraux shared the Enlightenment belief in the need to democratise a high culture reserved for an elite, elitism today is taken to mean refusing to recognise that whatever people do in their spare time is culture, irrespective of its aesthetic or intellectual worth.

This consumerist logic, he goes on, is accepted uncomplainingly by the majority of reconstructed intellectuals because, mistaking zapping for existential liberty, they see the market as an antidote to the kind of collectivism which leads to totalitarianism. Consumption, hedonism and youth therefore become values for all age-groups and walks of life: politics, the media, even morality and religion. Finkielkraut cites as instances Bob Geldof's Live Aid concert of 1985 and the mass rallies held by the Pope in his travels: both show a willingness to use the hedonistic spectacle as a means of appealing to the young, even though to do so is to make a bargain with the devil since spectacle by its nature disintellectualises, emptying heads and corrupting meaning. For Finkielkraut, the only effective rampart against this is education, in its most rigorous and republican sense, founded on the Enlightenment conviction that 'il n'y pas d'autonomie sans pensée, et pas de pensée sans travail sur soi-même' (p.169). He fears, however, that the element of bookishness this implies, of solitary reflection and intellectual rigour, is in fact being excised from the education system, as establishments make use of mass-cultural forms like television, cartoons, computer games and rock music as teaching materials, debasing culture in their haste to meet the young on their own narrow ground rather than teach them to grapple with universal aesthetic values. The same is true of cultural policy too, where rock music particularly has been adopted as a paradigm. The 'chaleur fusionnelle' created by rock's loud, insistent rhythms negates language and reason, dissolving the individual consciousness in a collective frenzy. This model has been applied by the government to all forms of cultural practice. Hence an annual book festival is christened 'La Fureur de lire', a name preposterously inappropriate to the contemplative and solitary act of reading but which perfectly demonstrates the idea of culture as an instant, fun experience: non-intellectual, non-verbal, spontaneous.[8]

Finkielkraut's book is an incisive indictment of the relativism behind the *tout-culturel* philosophy, but it is not without its weaknesses. There is something visceral in his disapproval of modern consumer culture, his tendency to identify all mass-cultural forms with brutishness and 'la non-pensée' (p.157). While his view of pop music, for example, has particular validity today when the synthesised monotony of techno-pop dominates, it is a reductive view which takes no account of those in Francophone or Anglophone countries (Ferré and Brel, the novelist and singer-songwriter Yves Simon, Leonard Cohen or Bob Dylan) who have used popular or even rock idioms not to produce the mind-numbing dance music Finkielkraut assumes to be the norm but as a late twentieth-century lingua franca whose boundaries are there to be explored. Michel Schneider likewise objects to Finkielkraut's indiscriminate generalisations and is himself quite happy to accept that 'le baroque de Jimi Hendrix' may well be more beautiful than that of Lully.[9] On the whole, however, Schneider's reading of *La Défaite de la pensée* is a sympathetic one, seeking to demonstrate that Finkielkraut's defence of a stable artistic hierarchy is more than just a young fogey's nostalgia for a lost cultural imperialism. For Schneider, universal moral and aesthetic values do exist – freedom and sexual equality, harmony and form (p.69) – though this does not mean they are deposited only in the West or the bourgeoisie. He also shares Finkielkraut's view that 'instruction', not festivity and fun, is the only means of achieving genuine equality of access, defining culture as quite simply 'la fréquentation lettrée de l'art' (p.149).

But what Schneider most usefully adds to the debate is the connection he makes between the Ministry's *tout-culturel* policies and its equally obstinate promotion of the avant-garde. In Schneider's view, the Ministry is not entirely to blame for today's aesthetic relativism, for its confusion on the matter has been aggravated by the crisis in contemporary art referred to earlier, which has cut itself off from the public and broken away from form, beauty and even meaning, to the point where reality is presented more or less untransposed. The result is that policy-makers have become persuaded that in art anything goes (pp.122–3). The Ministry could never have promoted 'tag' (graffiti), for example, if it had not been for this aesthetic uncertainty, though Lang still has to take some of the blame because by falling in with it, he made it worse. Schneider therefore opposes the whole principle of a state-driven creation policy.

Fumaroli's *L'Etat culturel*, described as the most violent, brilliant and sectarian attack on "'la culture Lang'" since *La Défaite de le pensée*, displays much of Finkielkraut's distaste for contemporary consumer culture.[10] But whereas the earlier text looks back briefly to Malraux to find the Enlightenment values its author admires, Fumaroli dismisses Fifth-Republic cultural policy entirely. What he means by 'l'état culturel' is the direct interference of the French state, on a scale unprecedented in the Western world, in mass leisure and the arts, the word 'culture' being used to fudge the distinction between the two. This interference allows the state to use culture to celebrate its own generosity so that, in the absence of the institutional checks and balances considered indispensable in other countries, culture has become just another name for propaganda and a new state religion. Little wonder, then, that the government's increasing munificence is in inverse proportion to contemporary artistic achievements. Today, in place of new Mozarts and Rimbauds, France has only 'événements', 'espaces' and statistics on cultural consumption (pp.20–1).

It is this conviction which prompts Fumaroli to rehabilitate the Third Republic's liberalism.[11] The big mistake in 1959 in fact was to depart from pre-war practice and separate the arts from education both structurally and philosophically. For it was Malraux's mistrust of learning and even books, his belief that an untutored public could relate spontaneously to the visual and the powerfully iconographic, that unintentionally paved the way for the domination of an 'audiovisual aesthetic' (p.188) based on passivity and spectacle (pp.124–5). May '68, which Fumaroli interprets as the work of a young generation demanding more Americanised leisure experiences and gadgets, brought confirmation of the awesome error Malraux had made. A new *soixante-huitard* Left soon came to power, ostensibly anti-American but in reality concerned only to develop French equivalents of the types of transatlantic kitsch and fashionable avant-gardism the Nancy Festival had already shipped over. The real means of resisting American influence would of course have been to cultivate in French schools the one thing the USA can never possess: France's cultural past. Instead, the state education system has found itself competing with an official counterculture administered by a government department sited somewhere between Greenwich Village and Disneyland and possessed of a 'semantic bulimia' (p.169) which turns the word culture into 'un énorme conglomérat composé de "cultures" dont chacune est à égalité avec toutes les autres' (p.171). Today's culture has thus been broken up into a thousand consumer demands, which the Ministry attempts to satisfy by resorting to statistical surveys and market research.

This definition of the *tout-culturel* doctrine does not add a great deal to Finkielkraut's. Fumaroli is more original when outlining its effects on traditional democratisation, which much of his book is concerned with. One of his favourite convictions is that the perennial concern with access to high culture has amounted to a kind of colonialist violence or state terrorism which attempts to force upon ordinary people artistic forms they previously had no 'natural' aptitude for, and to suppress those authentically popular forms which they do appreciate but which have been denounced as worthless or bourgeois by a coterie of Parisian intellectuals. For Fumaroli, true culture cannot be imposed from without in this way and democratisation would have been positively harmful if it had ever succeeded. Its failure, though, has led not to its abandonment but merely its commercialisation. With culture now just another mode of consumption, audiovisual technologies and the techniques of mass tourism are used to market the heritage, the patrimonial artefacts themselves becoming secondary to the gadgetry which disseminates them or the building which houses them. The Pompidou Centre and the Louvre Pyramid are cases in point but, as we glimpsed in the previous chapter, Fumaroli reserves his greatest opprobrium for the Bibliothèque de France, where France's literary inheritance will, he persists in believing, find itself in a vast cultural supermarket, Alexandria lost in Disneyland.[12]

Fumaroli is at his best on the psychology of this kind of cultural tourism, portraying the modern cultural institution as an upmarket Las Vegas in which the visitor is reduced to a window-shopper or idle onlooker ('badaud'), a remote-controlled zombie vacantly following the direction signs through the collections and compliantly donning the walkman supplied, rather than being allowed to engage with a work personally and in private. Paris, once the capital of 'l'Europe de l'esprit' (p.291), is thus transformed into one giant theme park. For Fumaroli as for Finkielkraut, the only way out of this tourist nightmare is the austere discipline of study. It is a deception to let people believe they can appreciate art effortlessly, in crowds or with the help of *animateurs* and audiovisual aids. It requires perseverance, concentration, a long apprenticeship, and ultimately 'un véritable abandon, la grâce' (p.221). Yet a society so captivated by modernity and the flux of the present needs to confront its past in this way and only a liberal education, detached from the temporal and the material, can equip it to do so. Cultural policy in the Fifth Republic demonstrates what happens when this need is ignored: the ruin of state education and 'l'humiliation de ses maîtres' (p.251).

L'Etat culturel caused an immediate stir in the media and in intellectual circles as it was meant to.[13] It is an elegant performance: stimulating, provocative, necessary. It suffers none the less from polemical excess, not least in its tendency to attribute too much blame to the Ministry and Lang personally for the commercialisation of French culture, rather than seeing it as part of a wider socio-economic transformation taking place in Western societies, most of which have no comparable ministry. The most common criticism levelled at the book was that of elitism, though this is unfair to an extent. He is certainly opposed to the ethic of democratisation and the rhetoric of that opposition is surely exaggerated. Yet he cannot strictly be accused, as he occasionally was, of believing in the born genius,[14] for the notion of reaching the heights through time and effort informs his entire position, the role of state education being to give everyone an equal opportunity to join a 'nobility of the mind' by acquiring an informed understanding of high culture. None the less, he does resign himself a little too easily to the idea that many are called but few chosen. A humanities education should be available to all, he seems to suggest, but not all will want to avail themselves of it or will come through it successfully. But the problem is what will become of those who do not? Or of those for whom it is already too late because they are, for whatever reason, today's educational misfits? Are they to be unwelcome in theatres, opera-houses and great libraries on grounds of incompetence or on the assumption that they do not have what Fumaroli mysteriously calls a 'spontaneous' interest?

His own position on these questions seems crystal clear from his comments on the Bibliothèque de France. Once again, Mitterrand's democratising ambition is described as an act of violence on the 'real' users of the BN, compelling them to 'se fondre dans la foule indistincte des badauds', a public he depicts as 'interchangeable, qui avale tout machinalement' and which has already deterred those who 'spontaneously' used to frequent other high-cultural institutions such as the Comédie Française or museums (pp.206–7). Yet those among the untutored who do not aspire to using such cultural institutions are no worse off, to Fumaroli's mind, as they have their own natural tastes – Maurice Chevalier or Charles Aznavour, Boulevard theatre or provincial opera, in a word the 'goût moyen et populaire qui convenait vraiment au plus grand nombre' (p.78). Here, Fumaroli differs from Finkielkraut in that he does not appear to believe that the 'low-cultural' practices of the many are necessarily worthless or that the appeal of high culture is universal, but that, as long as all have initially had the choice of taking the high road, the current social distribution of high and low is quite acceptable as it stands, and that people should be left to find their own level, untroubled by meddlesome attempts at cultural engineering. Ultimately, it would seem, his liberal indictment of state intervention is a paean to the status quo.

It is also of course a plea for the humanities and the eternal values of scholarship in an age of instant consumption, and as such may have considerable appeal to those in school and university systems where the short-term demands of a market ideology are increasingly dominant. None the less, writing from the vantage-point of a scholar with a sense of being 'humiliated' by the downgrading of the traditional educator, Fumaroli seems impervious to the possibility that, beneath the publicity-conscious, mercantile doings of an upstart ministry, there might be more serious ambitions than mere propagandising. The Ministry's own position in this debate was not in fact well served by Langian lyricism, but others were able to mount a more credible defence. Much of the weaponry for this had in fact already been mustered before Fumaroli's book, in *Les Pratiques culturelles des Français*, which analysed the findings of a survey carried out in December 1988 and January 1989 and compared them with those of earlier exercises in 1973 and 1981. What links Fumaroli to Finkielkraut, Schneider, Caune and Bertin, despite their obvious differences, is that all five look backwards, wanting to restore an approach to culture – via education in the first three instances, via *action culturelle* in the last two – which has been lost. The authors of *Pratiques culturelles* on the other hand look resolutely to the future, calling for the revision of cultural policies conceived in some cases years ago and quite out of touch with contemporary realities.

The main finding of the study is that, due to progress in educational level, spare time available, technology, and so on, the previous fifteen years have seen a shift in the 'centre of gravity' of cultural practices away from the written word and other traditional forms. With the regular falling off of the average number of books read, particularly among 15–24-year-olds, the trend is clearly towards a culture of sound and vision. Ninety-five per cent of households own at least one TV set and the advent of new channels, video and remote control has pushed up the number of viewing hours by 25 per cent to twenty a week, affecting all categories of population. This makes TV-watching the mass-leisure form par excellence since the differences in frequency and duration of viewing based on variables such as age and profession have progressively weakened. The other comparable change concerns listening to music, where again the development of domestic audiovisual facilities (CDs, personal stereos, FM radio stations, etc.) accounts for a massification of listening to music of all kinds, frequent listening having more than doubled since 1973. This surge in supply means that new mass products have now become accepted as 'cultural' and therefore that far fewer French people today can be classed as deprived of 'cultural' practices of some kind. It has also brought about a 'culture d'appartement' since the individual no longer has to go out to find cultural activity.

However, the authors do not share the early PS view that society has thereby been atomised and domesticised, for the survey also shows that French people actually go out more in the evening, giving rise to a more convivial form of activity, 'la culture de sorties'. In fact, these two forms of culture are not mutually exclusive in so far as those who enjoy the latter also enjoy the former. Yet although *la culture de sorties* does include high-cultural venues like theatres and art galleries, it is not these pursuits which have benefited most from the increase in outings but restaurants, discos and rock or jazz concerts, though the results do show that the elite which has always enjoyed high culture – graduates, *cadres*, the *professions intellectuelles supérieures* and Parisians – is still the largest sector to do so and that it is equally they who indulge most in outings. None the less, if some of the findings merely update those of Bourdieu in the 1960s, most seem to corroborate Girard's 1978 premise that cultural practice is being democratised by dynamic technological and economic forces rather than by state cultural action. For example, from a certain standpoint at least, the personal stereo may be said to widen access to music more effectively than all the subsidised orchestras and concert-halls put together. Nor can it be argued that the music thus democratised is entirely commercial pop as the recent Pavarotti phenomenon demonstrates in both France and Britain, though objections concerning the crucial differences between live and recorded performance carry more weight.

The authors of *Pratiques culturelles* see the pragmatic recognition of such contemporary realities as essential to a redefinition of cultural policy. Donnat himself aimed to further the point in two articles of his own, published in *Esprit* in 1988 and 1991, the latter singled out for criticism by Fumaroli in the debates which followed the appearance of *L'Etat culturel*.[15] Both articles provide one of the most cogent arguments in favour of such a redefinition and at the same time an insight, devoid of the usual self-congratulation, into Ministry doctrine under Lang. Like the introduction to *Pratiques culturelles* which Donnat co-wrote with Girard, the articles are partly replies to those like Finkielkraut whom he sees as guilty of 'la nouvelle déification de l'art et le repli frileux sur les valeurs du passé' (1991, p.71). The second article is also a reply to specific criticisms by Finkielkraut and others of the survey itself, accused of adopting a quantitative approach which condoned the reduction of culture to consumption.[16] Donnat sees their position as a hopelessly rearguard, *beaux-arts* one, adopted because they have a professional interest in maintaining the supremacy of the written word or of mediation. Accordingly, they diabolise TV and the cultural industries as alienating and manipulative and refuse to take account of the changes which in the last decades have transformed the conditions under which works of art are produced and disseminated.

In 1959, writes Donnat, Malraux's patrimonial view of culture as a body of great universal works, remote from economic and social realities, was widely shared, by initiated and uninitiated alike. The Ministry's purpose, therefore, was unequivocal: to enrich this heritage and democratise it. But over the last twenty-five years, the Malraucian conception of culture has been steadily drained of meaning. The idea of a universally agreed canon was challenged in 1968, while the rise of leisure technologies has revolutionised the reproduction of images and sounds and introduced industrial and commercial interests into the hermetic world of artistic production, making it impossible to distinguish culture from leisure as confidently as Malraux had done. The conventional model of an author writing a book, then handing it over to a publisher, used to allow a reassuring line to be drawn between the work of art and the marketable product. But this has now become obsolete as market demands impinge on the actual conception of a work and as technology often makes it difficult to distinguish who exactly its real creator is (1988, p.97). As a result, the relationship between creation and *diffusion* has been revolutionised.

In Donnat's model, Lang becomes the first minister to assume this new complexity. His ministry pragmatically acknowledged the existence of the mass-cultural industries alongside the high-cultural subsidised sector and saw that the role of a cultural policy must be to manage the relationship between the two rather than allow their further polarisation. This required the adoption of four sets of measures, all familiar today as Lang's trademarks: the recognition of cultural forms considered minor or commercial; the attempts to teach the subsidised sector some elementary rules of management and marketing; the recognition of the cultural dimension of economic crisis and technological change; and, particularly important in Donnat's perspective, the regulation of commercial mass culture to ensure that aesthetic criteria are protected. Within these new policies, Malraux's democratisation had little place, despite the Socialists' constant evocation of it while in opposition. Reality, he argues, 'obligeait à des révisions, déchirantes pour certains' (1988, pp.98–9). Instead, Lang and later Léotard brought the aesthetic closer to both the economic and the ludic. Little wonder, then, that he was criticised for contributing to the confusion of aesthetic values, for his *tout-culturel* philosophy seemingly legitimised a fun route to 'culture' which required no patient apprenticeship or intellectual effort and which also bypassed the usual forms of adult mediation and control.

What is most convincing in Donnat's analysis is that, while not being blind to the problems raised by Finkielkraut and Fumaroli, he has a more complex grasp of them. As a surveyor of cultural practices, he is aware of the impossibility of drawing a once-and-for-all line between culture and entertainment. He is also capable of seeing a positive side to the impact of the marketplace and new technologies which at times brings him close to the recent work of Paul Yonnet or Gilles Lipovetsky, who likewise reject the French intellectual's traditional antipathy towards the media and mass culture.[17] But he is equally conscious of the problems this position entails. He understands the worries about the demise of the written word caused by 'cultural machines'. And, while he casts doubt on the notion that this demise automatically heralds the 'defeat of thought', he does acknowledge the passing of the 'homme cultivé' in favour of new media heroes, and the need to consider whether the audiovisual is by nature an inferior form of intellectual or aesthetic experience.

He recognises too that at present research into the cultural industries and their effects, particularly TV, is lacking, as is an adequate vocabulary for conducting debate since the terms culture and democratisation are so debased by promiscuous usage that they are no longer precision instruments. Classical democratisation and the cultural industries also carry with them quite different sets of values, he notes, the one a political project to construct a more civilised society, the other driven by a purely commercial imperative. Indeed, this is perfectly apparent when he himself calls for democratisation to be replaced by a more focused, segmented approach:

cesser de rester en termes idéologiques pour passer à une approche plus professionnelle, et un peu comme le font les gens qui vendent des chemises et des lunettes, à savoir à quel type de population je m'adresse, comment faire pour que les gens qui devraient être intéressés par mon produit y viennent, et comment faire pour essayer d'accroître le marché en atteignant certains types de population. (Personal interview, 8 April 1992)

Such terminology is unlikely to reassure those like Ralite, Finkielkraut or Fumaroli who detest this intrusion of marketing values into what is perhaps the one domain where disinterestedness is still supposed to be a virtue. And whilst it may be true, as Donnat believes, that democratising high culture is no longer the central issue for cultural policy today, because high culture is no longer dominant and ordinary people no longer feel deprived of it, the truth of the matter is that such pragmatism simply has nothing to say either to those for whom the value of high culture remains immutable, or to those who see equality of access to it as the guiding ambition of any cultural policy worthy of the name. For them, Donnat's brave new high-tech world is just another guise for the same old undiscriminating consumerism. This is a dialogue of the deaf and, as Donnat acknowledges, likely to remain so in the foreseeable future.

Occasionally, however, contributors to the debate tried to find a third way between these extremes. In *Libre Culture* (1990), Jacques Rigaud, formerly Duhamel's *directeur de cabinet* and author of *La Culture pour vivre* which had spelt out the philosophy of *développement culturel* in the mid–1970s, begins by analysing the paradox of contemporary culture, nicely epitomised as 'une étrange victoire'.[18] On the surface, the apostolic dreams of the pioneers and early militants have come true, with culture now a major factor in national and local politics and signs everywhere of abundant cultural life. Yet like Bertin and Caune, Rigaud is well aware of the loss of energy and the progressive institutionalisation of the great democratising mission, and of the ambivalence of its achievements in a society dominated by unemployment, urban violence, persistent illiteracy and a consumption-driven economy which has locked the masses into passive, commercial forms of leisure. So in Rigaud's eyes, the need for a national debate about the place of culture in society is as urgent today as ever and he laments the poverty of current reflections on the subject. Finkielkraut's and Fumaroli's arguments in particular are dismissed; what is needed today is not academic nostalgia but a down-to-earth, all-embracing reassessment, without which the problems of individual sectors cannot be properly addressed. Rigaud in fact lays into Fumaroli with much the same animus as Fumaroli does those 'technocrats of culture' like Rigaud who have supplanted the traditional pedagogue.

This does not, however, make Rigaud an unconditional Langian since much of his book is an account of the Left government's vices as well as its virtues. In particular, he has important reservations about the excesses of the *tout-culturel*, which he claims was adopted only because it appeared to distinguish the Socialist position from Malraux's and at the same time allowed the real problems of cultural inequalities to be eluded. Rigaud also doubts whether rock, BD and so on constitute the authentic culture of contemporary youth. Indeed, he feels there is a very real risk of their confining many young people to mass-cultural forms for the rest of their lives. And yet he is not willing to dismiss youth culture completely as a degraded sub-culture, for he is able to see that it largely transcends class-based, national and ethnic divisions. He can also detect signs of hope in the surging 'social demand' for cultural tourism and mass-leisure activities generally among the young. Here, he tacitly subverts Ralite's and Fumaroli's use of Disneyland as a metaphor for the bankruptcy of commercialised leisure by discerning in the craze for theme-parks and audiovisual gadgetry (La Villette, the Futuroscope at Poitiers) an index, admittedly tenuous, of an unarticulated longing for more cultural, more demanding forms of leisure. True, this longing is easily diverted into mass consumption and turned into the glazed gawping of Fumaroli's *badaud*. But he believes that it could be coaxed out quite easily if the cultural content of such activities were enhanced (pp.354–60).

Rigaud therefore sidesteps any charge of aesthetic relativism by cleaving to a hierarchy in which culture is always superior to leisure and mass entertainment. But he equally rejects the classical conception which restricts the term cultural to those practices consecrated by the qualified few. What he proposes instead is a middle way, aligning himself with the several generations of *animateurs* and unrepentant partisans of *développement culturel* for whom 'la pratique culturelle ne doit jamais être passive. S'ils [these partisans] refusent de la subordonner à la possession d'on ne sait quel passeport intellectuel ou d'un diplôme, ils admettent qu'elle implique un effort d'attention, de connaissance, de réflexion, et, à la limite, une certaine ascèse' (p.409). Artistic reception is not a matter of spontaneous revelation à la Malraux but an active, difficult process which needs to be worked at. He fully accepts, therefore, that from any cultural event which has attracted crowds, many will come away untransformed. But he is also convinced that an indeterminate number will undergo 'un choc, ou, en tout cas, le frémissement initial' (p.410). This belief in the power of art to change people's lives effectively refutes Fumaroli's prescription that the *badaud* be kept away from high-cultural institutions. But what Rigaud is chiefly expounding is the importance of the mediator, those missionaries like himself who have in their different ways dedicated themselves to true democratisation. For Rigaud, this is not just a moral and social crusade as it was in 1945 but a practical necessity. What those nostalgic for high culture fail to grasp is that it will only survive in the modern world if it becomes a majority resource and thereby succeeds in influencing the great choices society now faces (p.426). Furthermore, the fact that large numbers of people now frequent cultural institutions should not disguise the problems which remain. In an age of audiovisual sensations and massive cultural tourism in which our ability to be aesthetically discerning has been deadened by constant exposure to the screen, the task of today's mediator is more important than ever: it is to teach people to see (p.427).

Rigaud's book is therefore a call for the restoration of democratisation through *animation*. He is not as unbending as Finkielkraut about what is and is not cultural, and he is the antithesis of Fumaroli who will not countenance mediation coming from outside the education system. By challenging this view, Rigaud in fact provides a way out of the dilemma left by Fumaroli regarding those who are already the failures of the education system. But opposing Fumaroli and Finkielkraut does not place him in the Donnat and Girard camp either. It is true that he shares their more pragmatic sense of the complexity of culture today and of the impossibility of avoiding 'l'image et l'argent'. But he believes in a conception of democratisation which Donnat sees as obsolete and he is more circumspect than Girard about the ability of new technologies to bring it about without corrupting the relationship between art and its recipient. Even so, he does help us understand the recent cultural debate as taking place not simply between intellectuals and pragmatists but between two types of professional mediator: those from the education system and those who work in the cultural field. In this respect, one may see both parties as engaging in a certain amount of special pleading.

The common denominator in all the texts I have examined is the perceived need for a complete reappraisal of the role of the state. None of the major contributors calls for its total withdrawal from the field of culture but all want change, even if there is no real consensus as to what form it should take. One fairly extreme position is Fumaroli's, who looks back fondly to the Popular Front's union of Leisure and Beaux-Arts with Education but nevertheless recommends that the swollen ministry of today renounce *le tout-culturel* and concern itself simply with the *patrimoine*, though he would still like to see this coordinated with policies for education and public-service broadcasting. What he definitely does not wish to see is precisely what the Right in March 1993 had in mind for 'l'après-Lang': a return to Malraux and democratisation.[19] Schneider too is radical in suggesting that the state cede its responsibilities for creation to the local authorities, private institutions and individuals, and in his belief that reducing taxation is preferable to direct subsidy. The tasks which do legitimately fall to the state are 'enseigner [in which he subsumes democratisation], conserver et réglementer' (p.150), but he would rather they were distributed among the Ministries of Education, Environment and Industry (pp.147–55).

Donnat's position is quite different. One of the questions he identifies for cultural policy today is how the Ministry's two objectives, supply and demand, creation and *diffusion*, can be articulated now that creation has come so much closer to a market ideology which can lead straight to standardisation (1991, p.78). Perhaps the primary role for the Ministry should therefore be not democratisation but protection of the quality and diversity of creation, making it above all a ministry for artists. He also ponders how the Ministry's enlargement of its sphere via the *tout-culturel* is to be reconciled with the need to maintain priorities; and how to harmonise 'le rapport cultivé et le rapport "spectaculaire" à l'art', when the latter, even where the traditional high arts are concerned, turns artists into media stars and works of art into mass products, with the attendant risk of high culture being marginalised (1991, pp.78–9, quotation p.79).

Others, however, are keener to see the recent – and in their view excessive – stress on creation counterbalanced by a reinstatement of the state's sociocultural mission. What is needed, in Caune's words, is 'la jonction entre une action de rayonnement national et une action de proximité; entre une pratique de fréquentation des œuvres et des pratiques d'expression artistique; entre la production artistique et une intervention sur les domaines de la vie quotidienne et du loisir, bref entre l'art et son insertion sociale' (p.359). Abirached similarly believes that the MCs could only have undertaken successful cultural action if they had been able to work with the dense network of MJCs, which came under a different department. Given the simmering social unrest in France's city suburbs, such action is just as vital today and he would therefore like to see Culture's responsibilities widened to include Jeunesse so that, without abandoning its concern with creation, it could also involve itself in *éducation populaire* and amateur practices.[20]

Rigaud again adopts a somewhat more complex position. As a result of continuous ministerial action over the last thirty years, much has been achieved, but the Ministry has increasingly fallen victim to its own success. The richer the cultural life it has helped generate, the more it has complicated its own mission, as the universe it administers has become denser, more self-willed, less susceptible of centralised control. Other structures and initiatives have evolved to challenge its supremacy: the local authorities, corporate sponsorship, cultural associations, harmonised European legislation such as Télévision sans frontières; while its own cultural institutions, vastly increased over the years, are reaching maturity and also engaging in an Oedipal struggle for autonomy. The budget is another complicating factor. Since the 1 per cent has yet to be achieved (at Rigaud's time of writing), the Minister's room for manoeuvre is steadily shrinking, as the capital expenditure and on-costs of the *grands projets*, as well as the vast array of earmarked subsidies, grow. Nor can a generous Culture budget be relied on for very much longer since the Single Europe Act will mean that national taxation arrangements will have to be revised and some taxes reduced (pp.347–8). And with the state already wrestling with a social security deficit and other constraints, there is no guarantee that culture will remain a priority.[21]

For all these reasons, Rigaud sees the traditional model of direct state management of culture as outdated and calls for it to be redefined in more modest and doubtless less gratifying terms: correcting the market where necessary, assisting the now highly active local authorities, encouraging institutions to stand on their own feet, discreetly helping creation and *diffusion*. Such a conception could no longer be embodied in the title Ministry of Culture but would be better conveyed by the original designation of Cultural Affairs. At the same time, though, he does argue for a government-wide 'global political project' (p.377) in which all ministries recognise the cultural dimension their activities have assumed (pp.376–9). This would of course address the pressing need for an arts initiation in schools and for an integrated approach to mass culture, broadcasting and the cultural industries, ensuring that cultural criteria are heeded in decision-making in these areas.

As I have tried to show throughout this study, successive governments since 1958 have generally declined to grasp this nettle and have ended up with the worst of both worlds, the Ministry having little real influence over connected administrations and yet still finding itself accused periodically of over-centralising cultural life. Reducing its remit has not been seriously entertained in recent years, even in 1986. Conversely, it has not been joined with Youth and Sport since Bourdan in 1947, while Bérégovoy's radical decision to couple it with Education came too late, though there are those like Jacques Renard who do not in any case believe that a huge 'Ministry of Intelligence' combining Education, Communication and Culture could ever be as effective as Culture has been alone.[22] Under Toubon in 1993, both Education and Communication became self-standing again, Culture itself being twinned with Francophonie (see Figure 7). Interesting though this initiative was, what it seemed to suggest was not a redefinition of the cultural so much as a return to a more classical,

Gaullist conception concerned with the 'defence' of the French language and France's international *rayonnement*, both prominent themes at an RPR colloquium in January 1993 and in Toubon's first statements as Minister, where he asserted the need to return to Malraucian democratisation. Of course, it remains to be seen precisely what this stance will amount to in the post-Mitterrand era. But for the time being, it does not suggest a dramatic new approach to the major issues of cultural policy which have been intermittently but persistently debated since 1936.

Notes

1. Ministry of Culture, 'La Politique culturelle 1981–1991', 1991; and *Vous avez dit culture? Chronique d'une décennie culturelle 1981–1991*, Paris, 1992.
2. Ministry, 'La Politique culturelle 1981–1991': '1981–1991: bilan d'une politique culturelle', pp.3–4.
3. Ministère de la culture et de la communication, *Nouvelle Enquête sur les pratiques culturelles des Français*, Paris, 1990, accompanied by O. Donnat and D. Cogneau, *Les Pratiques culturelles des Français 1973–1989*, Paris, 1990; 'La Politique culturelle en France', *Commentaire*, 4 issues, nos 48–51, winter 1989/90–autumn 1990.
4. 'Dieu que la culture est joyeuse!', *Politis*, no.121, 3–10 January 1991, p.7.
5. J. Bertin, 'A la recherche de la culture perdue', *Politis*, 9 June 1988, pp.39–41 (quotation p.41).
6. Grenoble, 1992, pp.21–4. Subsequent page references for this and other texts frequently alluded to in this chapter will henceforth appear in the text.
7. *La Défaite de la pensée*, Folio/Essais, Paris, 1987, p.11.
8. Finkielkraut interviewed on BBC2's 'The Late Show', 12 October 1992.
9. *La Comédie de la culture*, Paris, 1993, p.69.
10. *L'Etat culturel: essai sur une religion moderne*, Paris, 1991. The description of the book is from 'M. Fumaroli lance une bombe contre J. Lang', *L'Evénement du Jeudi*, 22–8 August 1991, p.96.
11. See Chapter 1.
12. Fumaroli, 'Bibliothèque de France: Alexandrie ou Disneyland?', *Le Figaro*, 21 July 1989.
13. Two of the chief forums for debate were *Esprit*, no.175, October 1991 (J. Roman), pp.149–57, followed by no.179, February 1992 (Fumaroli), pp.150–4; and 'L'Etat culturel: mythe ou réalité?',

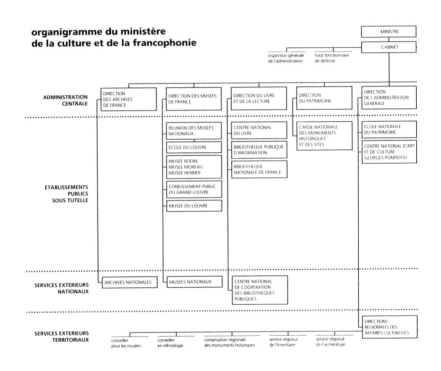

Figure 7. The Structure of the Toubon Ministry, April 1994. Source: Ministère de la culture et de la francophonie.

A l'heure des bilans

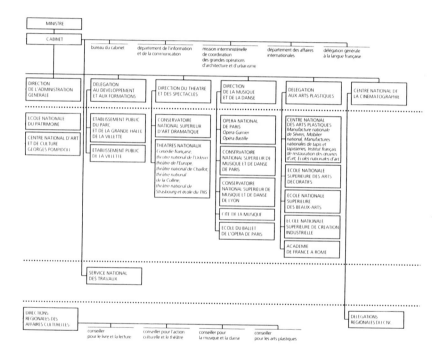

special issue of *Le Débat*, no.70, May–August 1992, pp.3–83.

14. 'M. Fumaroli lance une bombe', p.96.

15. Donnat, 'Politique culturelle et débat sur la culture', *Esprit*, November 1988, pp.90–101; and 'Démocratisation culturelle: la fin d'un mythe', *Esprit*, March–April 1991, pp.65–79. In future references in the text to these articles, they will be distinguished by their respective dates. My analysis of Donnat's position is also based on my interview with him, 8 April 1992. Fumaroli's reference to Donnat appears in *Esprit*, no.179 (Note 13 above), pp.152–3.

16. See for example the interview Finkielkraut gave *L'Evénement du Jeudi*, 'Finkielkraut persiste et signe: c'est la défaite de la culture!', 19–25 April 1990.

17. Yonnet, *Jeux, modes et masses: la société française et le moderne 1945–85*, Paris, 1985; Lipovetsky, *L'Ère du vide: Essai sur l'individualisme contemporain*, Paris, 1983.

18. *Libre Culture*, Paris, 1990, p.17.

19. Fumaroli, 'Pour une rupture', *Le Monde*, 25 March 1993, p.2; and *L'Etat culturel*, p.253.

20. Abirached, *Le Théâtre et le prince 1981–1991*, Paris, 1992, p.198 and personal interview, 8 April 1992.

21. Rigaud, *Libre Culture*, pp.96–104 and pp.333–54. The recent GATT trade talks also corroborated Rigaud's argument that a national cultural policy will be increasingly difficult to conduct in isolation.

22. Personal interview with J. Renard, 30 September 1993.

Conclusion

The story of the first ever left-wing Ministry of Culture in France, of the gestation and implementation of its policies, its confrontation with a set of cultural and economic conditions which transformed it, and the intellectual reticence and cultural debates it stimulated, is a tale of earnest idealism, political pragmatism and mixed achievement. How finally should its importance be judged? As I pointed out at the beginning, this is not an easy question to answer so soon after the events, so I shall limit myself to a few observations which flow from the preceding chapters and which may open up further lines of enquiry.

In April 1992, *Le Figaro* said of Lang that he had made a profound mark on the Mitterrand decade, by giving it a style.[1] This he certainly did for the Ministry itself, turning it into a more approachable, more lively and relevant institution and successfully establishing culture as a political priority for the 1990s. Today, despite Rigaud's worries about financial prospects, the future of the department looks assured, employing as it does over 12,000 people in 1993 as against the 377 originally transferred from Education in 1959. Of course, this upgrading was not entirely Lang's doing, since a change of both status and style was inevitable given France's rapid cultural and economic evolution since the 1950s. But he did facilitate and to an extent orchestrate it.

This he partly achieved simply by the doubling of the Culture budget, which he personally fought for though would probably not have obtained without the backing of a president equally determined to bring culture out of the shadows. Although the spectacular leap of 1982 was somewhat eroded during the last years of the first quinquennium and the 1 per cent was much slower coming than planned, to have spoken up for the arts and allowed them to take budgetary precedence at a time of world recession is the Socialists' greatest achievement in the cultural field, not only because it brought relief after years of penury but also because it set an example to private investors and, to a far greater extent, local authorities. The latter had of course begun to step up their involvement well before 1981. But by 1990, communes with a population of more than 10,000 had practically doubled their spending on culture since 1978, and cultural provision has become a vital factor in local and regional planning – vital both to wealth creation and to a town's chances of attracting investment. 'Tous les maires des grandes villes, toutes tendances partisanes confondues, *"font du Lang"* aujourd'hui', commented *Le Figaro*.[2] Furthermore, regional cultural facilities have vastly increased since 1981, with the new FRACs, FRAMs, BCPs, museums, *grands projets de province*, and so on.

Lang also gave the Ministry a style by virtue of his own unique talent for staging events and seeking notoriety, at times even turning himself into a walking cultural statement through his celebrated 'look'. His appointment to the number two position in Bérégovoy's government, and the occasional talk of his being *premier-ministrable* or even *présidentiable*, although far-fetched for the moment, is testimony to the change he brought about in the political stature of an unpromising department, and indeed in his own position as a rank outsider within the party.

None of this, however, alters the fact that, beneath the veneer of official self-congratulation, the Socialists' major achievements in the cultural sphere have an inescapable ambivalence. By intensifying and personalising ministerial action in the way he did, Lang in effect took state intervention to a point where its paradoxes became more apparent. This is true, for example, of the doubled budget itself, which despite its generosity was not always a panacea nor even a blessing. Neither the directorates nor their beneficiaries found so unprecedented a windfall easy to manage after the lean years and this, coupled with the Socialists' refusal to designate priorities, led to funds being distributed with too much largesse or too little thought to the 4,000 subsidised associations alluded to by Léotard. Another problem was the tendency for costs to rise simply because more money was available. This process was particularly identifiable in the decentralised theatre where the generous increase in funds in the early years did not often result in a corresponding increase in the number of creations undertaken, only in higher operating costs, greater use of film stars and bigger production budgets, some of which came close to those normally expected of a film.[3]

Furthermore, as Rigaud and others have pointed out, much of the budget increase has been or soon will be absorbed by the capital expenditure on the *grands projets* and then by the cost of running them on top of the existing high-spending institutions like the Pompidou Centre (see Figure 8(a)). A report by René Rizzardo on cultural decentralisation published in 1991 showed that there was some resentment of this at local level and called for the money due to be saved by the completion of the Parisian projects to be invested in equally prestigious institutions for the regions. At the Assembly discussion of the Socialists' doomed budget for 1993, Françoise de Panafieu estimated that the total costs of the Paris projects would be almost three billion that year as against a paltry 140 million francs for the regional ones.[4] But even though it is said that this imbalance is slowly being rectified, the *grands projets* will remain a costly commitment (around 29 billion francs so far).

The Mitterrand years have also demonstrated that, no matter how generously funded, a cultural policy cannot move mountains and may sometimes throw up new ones: the infamous '*effets pervers*' which critics delight in identifying and which are probably endemic to any voluntarist policy. In specific sectors, Lang's measures have often been greeted positively – book policy, the law on the *droits de l'interprète*, aid to cinema – but have still not been able to ward off disaster. In the book sector for example, despite the *prix unique*, the number of small bookshops is still diminishing, as are book sales, the rate of regular reading among the young, and library use. Aid to rock and *chanson* has not prevented a continuing drop in the sales of French records or in the number of record-dealers.[5] But the classic instance is cinema. It is often pointed out that the tradition of state support for French film, steadily strengthened since 1981 to the extent that the USA saw it as a major obstacle to free trade in the 1993 GATT talks, has allowed France alone among European countries to maintain a respectable production rate of some 140 films annually (156 in 1991), and Lang is commonly hailed as the saviour of the industry. Yet state action has been helpless to stem the haemorrhage of audiences or the slump in demand for French films. Mark Hunter, one of Lang's most vocal critics here, goes further. In his view, the Minister's over-protective reflexes actually proved detrimental to the industry: by forcing the big distributors and TV channels to programme French films, often *films d'auteur* which did not attract big audiences; by shielding French film-makers from competing for a wider public; and by delaying the emergence of a French video industry. The result, he contends, is a 'nationalised' film industry sycophantic towards those in power and indifferent to public demand.[6] A similar hothouse effect has been a cause for concern in both the subsidised theatre and the art market as I pointed out in Chapter 5, as well as in contemporary experimental music of the kind produced by L'IRCAM.

The most obvious *effets pervers* for culture, however, were not Lang's doing so much as his fellow ministers'. In the area of broadcasting, for instance, privatisation had dire consequences for his campaign against American audiovisual domination, and his 1981 ambition to create 'la meilleure télévision du monde' is today no more than a sad irony.

Indeed, the Socialists' failure to harmonise Culture and Communication and prevent the commercialisation of television as they promised is one of their two most serious flaws, privatisation being mischievously described at a conference in 1993 as the most important thing they ever did in the cultural field.[7] The other flaw, also a broken promise, is of course the continuing inadequacy of creative-arts teaching in the state education system, despite the Léotard law of 1988. For all Lang's talk of a festive culture and of 'irrigating' communities, a cultural policy which fails to have a significant say in the cultural content of television and education has little chance of making a really decisive impact on national life.

One last *effet pervers* of a kind has once again to do with style. For one may wonder whether Lang's efforts to publicise his action and heighten its appeal, successful though they were, did not create too many opportunities for politics to get in the way of policy. How far opting for maximum visibility actually made a difference to the reception of the measures themselves is hard to gauge, but there is reason to doubt whether, in this day and age, aid to rock, fashion or comic strips would have been interpreted as quite such a threat to civilisation if it had not been accompanied by so much hype. Even a close associate of Lang like Robert Abirached feels that the concern with image – 'ce rideau de perles chatoyant' – diverted attention from the serious back-room work being undertaken by particular directorates like his own, and he suggests that Fumaroli's hostility in particular may have had more to do with Lang than with his policies.[8] Certainly, what is striking from the silence of the intellectuals onwards is the personal element in much of the criticism of the Lang administration, exemplified with extraordinary acuity by the contributor to *Le Quotidien de Paris* in 1988 who spoke of 'l'espèce de sécrétion abrutissante que, pareille à une glu, son emmiellée parole répand sur les choses' and fantasised about tipping a jar of bilberries over his immaculate shirt.[9] A mistake made by many here was to identify the Ministry with the Minister when the former, as Abirached's and Schneider's books reveal and my own conversations with ex-administrators confirm, was far from homogeneous. But I would suggest that it was as much an error to reduce the Minister himself to one dimension when he too was, as I have tried to show here and elsewhere,[10] a complex figure combining media flair and political astuteness with the sincere, sometimes naive, and remarkably energetic dedication to disseminating culture which he has shown

Conclusion

LES CHIFFRES CLES
DU BUDGET 1995

	LFI1994	PLF1995	%95/LFI 1994
Part du budget de la culture dans le budget général de l'Etat	0,93%	0,91%	
Evolution du budget culture (DO + AP) en MF	12269	12754	4,0%
Evolution du budget de la culture (DO + CP) en MF	13506	13441	-0,5%
Budget culture en DO + AP hors GT	11016	11413	3,6%
Part des grands travaux dans le budget culture			
- dans le total des AP	25,4%	22,9%	
- dans le total des CP	48,2%	42,3%	
- en DO + CP	19,70%	17,40%	
Crédits consacrés aux enseignements artistiques dans le budget culture	1053	1065	1%
Loi de programme patrimoine en MF (référence 1994 : PLF)	1505	1538	2,2%
Francophonie (hors jeux de la Francophonie en 1994)	103,9	123,97	19,3%
dont budget culture	47,6	56,67	19,1%
dont budget affaires étrangères	56,3	67,3	19,5%
Opéra de Paris			
fonctionnement	540	581,5	7,7%
équipement	30	85	183,3%
Cité de la musique			
Fonctionnement	46,3	113,6	145,4%
BNF			
Fonctionnement	359	549	52,9%
Equipement AP	646	550	-14,9%
Equipement CP	1700	1423	-16,3%
CNAC-GP			
Fonctionnement	330	350	6,1%
Equipement	95	134	41,1%
Grands projets en région	0	50	

Figure 8(a). The Projected Ministry of Culture Budget for 1995. Source: Ministère de la culture et de la francophonie.

Distribution by sector of projected 1995 budget (DO + AP: indicates Ministry's capacity to undertake new operations)

Patrimoine écrit:	15%
Patrimoine monumental:	15%
Patrimoine muséographique et plastique:	21%
Spectacles:	27%
Développement culturel:	9%
Cinéma, audiovisuel:	3%
Administration générale:	8%
Recherche:	2%

Abbreviations

AP	Autorisations de programme (funds earmarked for long-term capital expenditure)
BNF	Bibliothèque nationale de France
CNAC-GP	Pompidou Centre
CP	Crédits de paiement (funds covering the annual expenditure needed for an AP)
DO	Dépenses ordinaires (funds covering operating and intervention costs)
GT	Grands travaux
LFI:	Loi de Finances initiale (a Finance bill already discussed, amended and passed by Parliament)
MF	Millions de francs
PLF	Projet de loi de Finances (a Finance bill not yet passed)

Figure 8(b). The Projected Ministry of Culture Budget for 1995. Source: Ministère de la culture et de la francophonie.

throughout his adult life.

But what of the place of the Mitterrand years in the history of cultural policy? Certainly, they have brought change, sometimes in unexpected ways. Cultural-policy debate has, for example, been largely depoliticised, as the Left swiftly adopted more market-oriented strategies and the Right, whose cultural policies under de Gaulle had been Left-inspired anyway, realised the importance culture had assumed at local and national levels and from 1983 moved in on the act. Since 1986, the process has carried on largely unabated, despite Lang's shadow-boxing during Léotard's period of office. That year, Jacques Toubon too was bullish about Socialist cultural policy, and even at the RPR colloquium in January 1993, strong reservations were still being expressed about it. Yet the colloquium's call for a return to a more sober policy of Malraucian democratisation really only amounted to a promise of continuity with a more distant Left; and Lang too by this time was making a point of invoking Malraux more frequently.[11] During the *passation des pouvoirs* the following March, Toubon significantly promised, much as Léotard had done, to 'faire sans défaire' and, despite his fairly rapid removal of some of the senior civil servants who had worked with Lang, and his announcement that the Mitterrandian Pierre Bergé's contract with the Opéra de Paris would not be renewed in 1995, his early statements and actions contained little to suggest that he intended to tackle policy very differently (see Figures 7 and 8(a) and (b)).[12] Indeed, the Balladur government's firm stand on protecting French audiovisual interests against further American domination during the GATT negotiations indicated a distinct commonality of purpose with Lang on the issue. Even in Toubon's colourfully enigmatic definition, shortly before the 1993 elections, of a cultural policy as 'mort aux cons', the 'cons' in question were taken to be not the PS but those on his own side who believed that Lang's departure would mean a fresh start and a reduced ministry.[13] At any event, appointed only two years before the 1995 presidentials, Toubon did not have time on his side any more than Léotard had.

The talk of a 'return to Malraux' is an indication of another transformation brought to completion under Lang: the demotion of *action culturelle*. As we saw in Chapters 3 and 4, the depoliticisation of culture after 1981 was not in fact a new phenomenon but had already begun during the 1970s, not only among former Leftist intellectuals but also among those in the theatre who had abandoned democratisation and *animation*. For a time, the PS itself was more hesitant on the matter for, although it had already shifted from the SNAC's *gauchiste* stress on grass-roots *animation*, it was still nominally harking back, in some confusion, to both Vilar and May 1968. But with the help of the intellectuals' defection after 1981 and the worsening economic situation, the new government was not slow to sense which way the wind was blowing and switched to the much more pragmatic discourse of the *tout-culturel*. Lang's chief innovation, therefore, alongside the budget increase, was to begin facing up to a development the state could neither control nor ignore without penalty: the rise of a civilisation of mass leisure in which culture was fast becoming a commodity, a prospect still shocking to the pre–1981 Left. It therefore fell to him to help the PS complete its metamorphosis into a modern party of government by accepting that its unbending disapproval of commercialism in the arts was no longer appropriate and that, as Donnat rightly observed, high and low cultures, public and private sectors, state voluntarism and market forces could be and had to be 'departitioned'.[14] Contrary to all expectations, then, it was a government of the Left, grimly ideological at the outset and backward-looking in many respects, which began to inflect cultural policy in a more forward-looking direction.

Nevertheless, the extent of the change needs to be qualified. Firstly, the focus on the *tout-culturel* and the cultural industries was not a brand new ministerial option but had its roots partly in the Sixth Plan and partly in what had come after it. As I argued in Chapter 3, the Sixth Plan's stress on creativity and difference had very soon had its day, swallowed up by the recession and Giscard's new economic liberalism. Somewhat ironically, given pre–1981 assaults on *le giscardisme culturel* by Lang and others, the Socialist ministry then combined these two approaches in the culture-economy formula. It still encouraged creativity and difference but redirected them, away from their post–1968 associations with regional autonomy and workers' emancipation towards a more 1980s concern with industrial and marketable forms of professional creation, while amateur practice and democratisation were largely taken care of by populism, festivity and fun.

Secondly, for all the feverish attention it received, the *tout-culturel* did not dominate policy as much as it was assumed to, for the pattern of distribution of the cultural budget actually changed little under Lang. Schneider reports that spending in his Music and Dance directorate on popular forms was only a tiny fraction of that on Boulez's IRCAM. Neither Gattégno nor Abirached had any sense of their respective high-cultural disciplines being marginalised by the new line, except on the level of ministerial discourse in Abirached's case.[15] Spending on the DDC's activities was deemed by the Council of Europe report to be inadequate. In hard budgetary terms, then, the Lang years actually focused less on new areas of intervention than on an admittedly enlarged but essentially Malraucian policy, initially prioritising creation, then after May 1988 *patrimoine*. Even democratisation was catered for after a fashion by such lavish initiatives as the Grand Louvre, the Opéra-Bastille and the Bibliothèque de France, though the *grands projets* as a whole, with their *fait du prince* and their *effet de vitrine*, were more suggestive of the Gaullist obsession with national grandeur than of a really brass-tacks concern with cultural inequalities at ground level. Indeed, a further continuity with the de Gaulle era is this perennial preoccupation, despite all the talk of diversity and eclecticism, with fostering a national culture, visible in a host of other ways: the insistence on maintaining the state's role as harmoniser when the decentralisation laws were being implemented, the promotion of French mass culture in opposition to American, the stress on collective fun, and the idea of a national multiculture enshrined in the Goude procession.

All these elements of continuity help us arrive at a somewhat sharper definition of the place of the Lang administration in the Ministry's history. Rather than challenging the fundamental tenets of cultural policy progressively defined since 1959, the Socialists, for all their millenarian oratory, soon contented themselves with reasserting them and to an extent redrafting them. National culture, creation, *patrimoine*, democratisation, presidential projects, cultural development, cultural industries, all were, to a greater or lesser extent, familiar options before 1981 which the Socialists variously took up, took further, funded better, or stripped of elitism as appropriate. All things considered, this is barely surprising. Firstly, continuity is always more likely than change since, as Rigaud points out, when a minister departs, the administration and the President usually remain.[16] But in this case, it was also the outcome of the Lang ministry's reluctance to choose between the orientations suggested by its diverse historical influences, preferring instead to pursue them all simultaneously. Given that its exchequer was not bottomless, this simply meant that priorities emerged automatically rather than by design. It is little wonder that those which did were the traditional ones, particularly given the participation in policy-making of a president who saw himself as the heir of the Popular Front and whose intellectual roots were therefore closer to Malraux's than to Lang's. This continuity also goes some way to explaining why the Socialists did not fundamentally redefine the Ministry itself.

What becomes clearer when one looks further back, beyond Malraux to the whole span of policy since 1936, is the complex position of the Popular Front in the narrative. Clearly, the Front set great store by the democratisation of high culture and this became its principal legacy where Laurent, Malraux and even Mitterrand were concerned. But the Zay ministry also left behind a blueprint for a more inclusive, global conception of culture which harmonised the high-cultural with the educational and the sociocultural, viewing art as deeply embedded in society. Since then, the ghost of this global conception has periodically stalked the corridors of power and aspects of the blueprint have been variously plundered, though it has never been re-used in its entirety. The Bourdan ministry briefly combined Beaux-Arts with Youth and Sport but separated it from Education. Malraux's department too broke away from Education but kept apart from Jeunesse et Sports and Education populaire, its autonomy symbolising a detached conception of art indifferent to the wider issues of education and leisure. Certainly, Malraux was concerned about ending the cultural dispossession of the masses. But he interpreted this task somewhat narrowly and experience soon showed that little would be achieved as long as schools, television and the network of grass-roots sociocultural organisations like the MJCs were not called upon to contribute to it.

By the mid–1970s, however, the ghost had manifested itself again, both to those who were drafting the Sixth Plan's cultural objectives and to a reconstructed Socialist Party now striding towards power. For a time, then, there seemed a real chance that the ideal of globality and harmonisation – whether by a superministry or by interministerial structures akin to the FIC – would become a reality. In practice, however, although that ideal produced some successful interministerial initiatives after 1981 and the occasional structural innovation such as the ephemeral Temps Libre ministry or the belated joining of Education and Culture, both of which were vestiges of 1936, it also suffered a number of setbacks, in particular Culture's difficult relations with Communication and Education, the disappearance of the FIC, and the resentment and later demotion of the DDC. What is more, another, crucial agency of policy-making emerged in the form of the President himself who, where both the *grands projets* and broadcasting were concerned, often went his own way. These factors, coupled with the shift away from the all-encompassing ideology of *action culturelle* and a resulting tendency, identified by Rigaud, to conduct policy on a sector-by-sector basis,[17] set the boundaries of what the PS's original global policy could achieve.

So it is that the central problem for cultural policy today is, to a large extent, still that which Zay and Lagrange attempted to address sixty years ago, though of course mass communications, mass leisure and mass unemployment make it infinitely more acute. What we have seen throughout this study is that, by its very nature, a cultural policy is about more than simply supporting art for art's sake. Rightly or wrongly, a 'policy' is also a concerted plan of action embodying a state view of the place and purpose, even perhaps the usefulness, of the arts and culture in the national community. The problem, then, for today's policy-makers is how to adapt traditional arts and heritage measures to the altered circumstances and requirements of contemporary society: to leisure practices transformed by new technologies, or to the wider social and economic needs being addressed by policies for the towns and cities, the young and various minorities, the environment, education and the media; how, also, to encourage artistic creation by professional artists while at the same time improving opportunities for all to find fulfilment in both the appreciation of high culture and in their own creativity, particularly those who are the victims of social and economic change. These are all questions which will have to be addressed if the principle of state involvement is to retain any legitimacy at the end of the millennium.

'Certes', said Donnat and Girard in their preface to *Nouvelle Enquête sur les pratiques culturelles des Français*, 'une politique culturelle n'a pas pour seul objectif de coller à la vie mouvante de la société; elle défend avant tout la création, elle conserve la mémoire. Mais elle ne saurait longtemps être décalée par rapport aux modes de vie sans perdre une partie de son ancrage dans la réalité contemporaine.'[18]

But moving with the times, adjusting policy to contemporary realities, is more problematic than it sounds. For although the question of whether the state should intervene does not for the moment seem to be the main focus of debate, the question of how and how far definitely is. And here, as Chapter 11 demonstrated, there appears to be no real consensus, either about what the 'cultural' in cultural policy means or about what kind of structure is appropriate to conduct such a policy, though there does seem to be a measure of agreement that a global strategy for the arts, broadcasting, leisure and education is as vital as ever. There is also little convergence of opinion about the weight to be given to creation, *patrimoine* or community arts respectively, other than a widespread feeling that foregrounding creation, i.e. 'supply', has gone too far and must now be balanced by a greater stress on encouraging 'demand'; particularly as a further question, about whether the state can support creation without interfering with it or institutionalising it, also remains unresolved.

Nor is there any firm answer to yet another issue which has reverberated through the history of policy since 1936 and which was raised particularly acutely under Lang. Is it the state's job, as Laurent and Malraux believed, to be prescriptive about national taste, to act as our aesthetic guardian and steer us towards an edifying culture supposed to do us good – 'imposer au public ce qu'il désire profondément', as Vilar once put it? Or is its task simply to go with the flow, to act as 'the nation's impresario' by providing improved access to whatever kind of entertainment today's 'customers' demand?[19] Interventionism or *clientélisme*? And finally, this dilemma points to what is possibly the most intractable problem of all for future policy, touched on by Jacques Toubon in a speech to the Senate in December 1993: the contradiction between a state policy still dedicated to promoting a shared national culture – 'des moments partagés d'identité collective' – and one espousing a communications revolution which is steadily isolating individuals within their private domestic space, unpicking the very fabric of community life.[20]

These are the principal questions the Mitterrand years leave us with. If the Socialists' own answers to them were ambivalent at times, not always strikingly original, and gave rise to no very dramatic changes in the ministerial structures for state intervention, they did serve to raise awareness and advance understanding of them. By attempting to rethink the dominant discourse of democratisation in terms of a reactivated discourse of globality, limited though that attempt may have been, they at least put up waymarks to assist others in the more fundamental remapping of cultural policy which cannot be eluded on the threshold of a new millennium. However one may judge the Mitterrand regime's motives and methods, or the reactions of its sternest critics, its chief virtue is not only to have supported the arts and culture in hard times but to have placed on the public agenda questions about them which are unlikely to go away.

Notes

1. 'Jack Lang, ou la politique de la mise en scène', *Le Figaro*, 3 April 1992.
2. Statistic taken from *Développement Culturel*, no.97, January 1993, p.1. The *Figaro* quotation is from 'J. Lang, ou la politique de la mise en scène'.
3. See, for example, R. Wangermée and B. Gournay, *Programme européen d'évaluation: la politique culturelle de la France*, Paris, 1988. p.155; and J.-P. Colin, 'La Culture et son administration', *Commentaire*, no.50, summer 1990, p.345. R. Abirached analyses the financial position of contemporary theatre in more detail in his chapter 'L'Argent', in *Le Théâtre et le prince 1981–1991*, Paris, 1992.
4. R. Rizzardo, *La Décentralisation culturelle: rapport au Ministre de la culture et de la communication*, Paris, 1991, pp.27 and 107; Panafieu,

Conclusion

Journal Officiel, 2ᵉ séance du 7 novembre 1992, p.5,011.

5. For a brief description of books and other problem sectors, see J.-P. Rioux, 'L'Impératif culturel', *L'Histoire*, no.143, April 1991, pp.54–60. A study of cultural industries in Europe dated May 1989 indicates that the number of record-dealers had been divided by ten in the previous ten years, X. Dupin and F. Rouet, *Mesures des pouvoirs publics à l'égard des industries culturelles en Europe 1988–1989*, rapport intermédiaire, DEP, May 1989, p.44.

6. 'Un Américain juge la politique de Lang', *Reader's Digest Selection* (French edition), 1 December 1991; and Hunter, *Les Jours les plus Lang*, Paris, 1990, *passim*.

7. Pierre Sorlin, intervention from the floor at the Society for French Studies conference, University of Warwick, 30 March 1993.

8. *Le Théâtre et le prince*, pp.194–5; and personal interview, 8 April 1992.

9. 'La Langue de Lang', *Le Quotidien de Paris*, 7 July 1988.

10. D.L.Looseley, 'Jack Lang and the politics of festival', *French Cultural Studies*, vol.1, no.1, February 1990, pp.5–19.

11. E.g. his 'Hommage à André Malraux', speech unveiling two sculptures in tribute to Malraux, 14 September 1992.

12. Those recently departed include Evelyne Pisier (DLL), Christian Dupavillon (Patrimoine), Thierry Leroy (Music and Dance) and François Barré (DAP). On these changes, see 'Culture: les professionnels de la Rue de Valois', *Le Monde*, 31 December 1993, p.9.

13. *Le Quotidien de Paris*, 1 February 1993, p.17. Toubon later defined 'les cons' as 'les gens qui ont des préjugés, qui sont fermés', *Libération*, 15 April 1993, p.37.

14. 'Politique culturelle et débat sur la culture', *Esprit*, November 1988, pp.98–9.

15. Schneider, *La Comédie de la culture*, Paris, 1993, p.77; Gattégno, personal interview, 7 April 1992; Abirached, personal interview, 8 April 1992.

16. *Libre Culture*, Paris, 1990, pp.93–4.

17. See Rigaud's preface to Caune, *La Culture en action de Vilar à Lang: le sens perdu*, Grenoble, 1992, p.15.

18. Paris, 1990, p.11.

19. 'The Late Show', BBC2, 12 October 1992; the quotation from Vilar is from *De la Tradition théâtrale*, Paris, 1963, p.43.

20. Extracts from Toubon's speech are reproduced in 'Vers une rénovation de la politique culturelle', *Lettre d'Information*, 30 December 1993, pp.2–4 (quotation p.3).

Bibliography

I have listed here only the works cited in this study, as space does not allow an exhaustive inventory either of the works consulted or of the vast literature on French cultural policy generally, though most of the key texts do appear below. In addition to these, I would refer the reader particularly to A. Girard (with the collaboration of G. Gentil), *Développement culturel: expériences et politiques*, édition révisée, Paris: Dalloz, 1982; and J.-P. Rioux (ed.), *L'Histoire culturelle de la France contemporaine: bilans et perspectives*, 4 vols, Paris: Ministry of Culture/ IHTP, 1987, which contains, among other invaluable material, S. Rab, 'Histoire des politiques culturelles', vol.2, pp.87–127, and M. Blouin, 'Histoire des institutions d'Etat', vol.2, pp.128–63. I have also used the end-of-chapter notes to direct the reader to further appropriate sources. I am happy to offer any extra assistance I can to those who do not find here the information they are looking for.

Where the press is concerned, I have only listed articles of some substance, omitting here the shorter or more ephemeral pieces I have had occasion to cite in the end-of-chapter notes. The unpublished Ministry documents I have referred to are available for consultation at the Centre de documentation of the Ministry's Département des études et de la prospective (DEP), 2 rue Jean-Lantier, 75001 Paris.

Works are listed in alphabetical order unless otherwise stated.

BOOKS AND CHAPTERS

Abirached, R., *Le Théâtre et le prince 1981–1991*, Paris: Plon, 1992
Bécane, J.-C., *L'Expérience des Maisons de la culture, Notes et Etudes Documentaires*, no.4,052, Paris: Documentation Française, 1974
Bodin, L., and Touchard, J., *Front populaire 1936*, Paris: Armand Colin, 1961
Bonnier, H., *Lettre recommandée aux fossoyeurs de la culture*, Monaco: Editions du Rocher, 1992
Bourdieu, P., and Darbel, A., *L'Amour de l'art: les musées d'art européen et leur public*, 2ᵉ édition revue et augmentée, Collection Le Sens Commun, Les Editions de Minuit, 1969

Bibliography

Busson, A., *Le Théâtre en France: contexte socio-économique et choix esthétiques*, *Notes et Etudes Documentaires*, no.4,805, Paris: Documentation Française, 1986

Cabanne, P., *Le Pouvoir culturel sous la V* *République*, Paris: Olivier Orban, 1981

Cacérès, B., *Histoire de l'éducation populaire*, Paris: Seuil, 1964

Cahiers de l'IHTP, *Politiques et pratiques culturelles dans la France de Vichy*, no.8, June 1988

Caron, R., *L'Etat et la culture*, Paris: Economica, 1989

Caune, J., *La Culture en action. De Vilar à Lang: le sens perdu*, Grenoble: Presses Universitaires de Grenoble, 1992

Chaslin, F., *Les Paris de François Mitterrand: histoire des grands projets architecturaux*, Folio Actuel, Paris: Gallimard, 1985

Clément, C., *Rêver chacun pour l'autre: sur la politique culturelle*, Paris: Fayard, 1982

Colin, J.-P., *La Beauté du manchot: culture et différence*, Paris: Publisud, 1986

Desneux, R., *Jack Lang: la culture en mouvement*, Paris: Editions Favre, 1990

Emmanuel, P., *Pour une politique de la culture*, Paris, Seuil, 1971

Faure, C., *Le Projet culturel de Vichy*, Lyon: Editions du CNRS/Presses Universitaires de Lyon, 1989

Favier, P., and Martin-Roland, M., *La Décennie Mitterrand*, Paris: Seuil, 2 vols: 1, 'La Rupture', 1990; 2, 'Les Epreuves', 1991

Fédération Léo Lagrange, *1936, Léo Lagrange*, Paris: Editions Temps Libres, 1980

Finkielkraut, A., *La Défaite de la pensée*, Folio/Essais, Paris: Gallimard, 1987

Forbes, J., 'Cultural policy: the soul of man under Socialism', in S. Mazey and M. Newman (eds), *Mitterrand's France*, London: Croom Helm, 1987, pp.131–65

Foucart, B., Loste, S., and Schnapper, A., *Paris mystifié: la grande illusion du Grand Louvre*, Paris, Julliard, 1985

Foulon, C.-L., 'André Malraux, Ministre d'Etat et le Ministère des affaires culturelles (1959–1969)', in Institut Charles de Gaulle, *De Gaulle et Malraux*, proceedings of colloquium held 13–15 November 1986, Collection Espoir, Paris: Plon, 1987, pp.221–40 (also contains other papers on Malraux the Minister by Anthonioz, de la Gorce, Takemoto)

Fumaroli, M., *L'Etat culturel: essai sur une religion moderne*, Paris: Fallois, 1991

Gattégno, J., *La Bibliothèque de France à mi-parcours: de la TGB à la BN bis?*, Paris: Editions du Cercle de la Librairie, 1992

Gaudibert, P., *Action culturelle: intégration et/ou subversion*, 3ᵉ édition revue et augmentée, Collection Synthèses Contemporaines, Tournai: Castermann, 1977

Gontard, D., *La Décentralisation théâtrale en France 1895–1952*, Paris: Société d'Edition d'Enseignement Supérieur, 1973

Hocquenghem, G., *Lettre ouverte à ceux qui sont passés du col Mao au Rotary*,

Bibliography

Collection Lettre Ouverte, Paris: Albin Michel, 1986

Hunter, M., *Les Jours les plus Lang*, Paris: Editions Odile Jacob, 1990

Jackson, J., *The Popular Front in France: Defending Democracy, 1934–38*, Cambridge: CUP, 1988

Jeancolas, J.-P., 'The setting-up of a "method of production" in the French cinema 1946–50', in B. Rigby and N. Hewitt (eds), *France and the Mass Media*, Warwick Studies in the European Humanities, Basingstoke: Macmillan, 1991, pp.59–67

Jeanson, F., *L'Action culturelle dans la cité*, Paris: Seuil, 1973

Kelly, M., 'Humanism and national unity: the ideological reconstruction of France', in N. Hewitt (ed.), *The Culture of Reconstruction: European Literature, Thought and Film, 1945–50*, Basingstoke: Macmillan, 1989, pp.103–19

Kergoat, J., *La France du Front populaire*, Paris: Editions de la Découverte, 1986

Lacouture, J., *André Malraux, une vie dans le siècle*, Collections Points, Paris: Seuil, 1973

Lang, J., *L'Etat et le théâtre*, Paris: Librairie Générale de Droit et de Jurisprudence, 1968

Lang, J., and Bredin, J.-D. (notes by A. Vitez), *Eclats*, Paris: Simoën, 1978

Langlois, C., *Pour une véritable culture*, no publication details, 1985

Laurent, J., *La République et les beaux-arts*, Paris: Julliard, 1955

——, *Arts et pouvoirs en France de 1793 à 1981: histoire d'une démission artistique*, 3ᵉ édition revue, corrigée et augmentée d'une annexe, Travaux 34, Saint-Etienne: Centre Interdisciplinaire d'Etudes et de Recherches sur l'Expression Contemporaine, Université de Saint-Etienne, 1983

Léotard, F., *Culture: les chemins du printemps*, Paris: Albin Michel, 1988

Looseley, D.L., 'Paris versus the provinces: cultural decentralization since 1945', in M. Cook (ed.), *French Culture since 1945*, London and New York: Longman, 1993, pp.217–40

Mesnard, A.-H., *L'Action culturelle des pouvoirs publics*, Paris: Librairie Générale de Droit et de Jurisprudence, 1969

—— *Droit et politique de la culture*, Paris: PUF, 1990

Mitterrand, F., *Ici et maintenant*, Paris: Fayard, 1980

Mollard, C., *La Passion de l'art*, Paris: Editions de La Différence, 1986

Mossuz, J., *André Malraux et le gaullisme*, Cahiers de la FNSP, Paris: Armand Colin, 1970

Nouvel Observateur, Le, En France aujourd'hui: idées, arts, spectacle, Paris: CLE International, 1987

Ory, P., *L'Aventure culturelle française 1945–1989*, Paris: Flammarion, 1989

Ory, P., and Sirinelli, J.-F., *Les Intellectuels en France, de l'Affaire Dreyfus à nos jours*, Paris: Armand Colin, 1986

Petit-Castelli, C., *La Culture à la une, ou l'action culturelle dans les mairies socialistes*, Paris: Club Socialiste du Livre, 1981

Pinto, D., 'The Left, the intellectuals and culture', in G. Ross, S. Hoffmann and S. Malzacher, *The Mitterrand Experiment: Continuity and Change in*

Modern France, Oxford: Polity Press, 1987

Plunkett, P. de, *La Culture en veston rose*, Collection Place publique, Paris: Table Ronde, 1982

Poujol, G., 'La Création du Ministère des affaires culturelles', in R. Abirached (ed.), *La Décentralisation théâtrale*, 2 vols, vol.2, 'Les Années Malraux 1959– 68', Cahier no.6, Paris: Actes Sud-Papiers, 1993, pp.25–37

Ralite, J. (Etats généraux de la culture), *La Culture française se porte bien pourvu qu'on la sauve*, Paris: Messidor/Editions sociales, 1987

Reader, K., *Intellectuals and the Left in France since 1968*, Basingstoke: Macmillan, 1987

Rigby, B., *Popular Culture in Modern France: A Study of Cultural Discourse*, London and New York: Routledge, 1991

Rioux, J.-P., *The Fourth Republic, 1944–1958* (translated by G. Rogers), Cambridge History of Modern France, no.7, Cambridge: CUP, 1987

Ritaine, E., *Les Stratèges de la culture*, Paris: Presses de la FNSP, 1983

Ruby, M., *La Vie et l'œuvre de Jean Zay*, Paris, no publisher or date (printed 1969)

Saint Pulgent, M. de, *Le Syndrome de l'opéra*, Collection Accords, Paris: Laffont, 1991

Schneider, M., *La Comédie de la culture*, Paris: Seuil, 1993

Shennan, A., *Rethinking France: Plans for Renewal 1940–1946*, Oxford: Clarendon Press, 1989

Starkey, H., 'Bande dessinée: the state of the ninth art in 1986', in J. Howorth and G. Ross, *Contemporary France: A Review of Interdisciplinary Studies*, 3 vols, vol.1, London: Frances Pinter, 1987, pp.168–91

Various, *Le Complexe de Léonard ou la société de création*, Paris: Editions du Nouvel Observateur/Lattès, [1984]

Vilar, J., *De la Tradition théâtrale*, Paris: Gallimard, 1963

Wachtel, D., *Cultural Policy and Socialist France*, Contributions to Political Science, no.177, New York: Greenwood Press, 1987

Zay, J., *Souvenirs et solitude*, Paris: Julliard, 1945

ARTICLES IN JOURNALS, CONFERENCE PAPERS

Bachmann, S., 'Les Réformes de l'audiovisuel depuis 1974: "l'éternel retour"', *Quaderni*, no.10, spring 1990, pp.29–48

Biasini, E.-J., 'Les Grands Travaux: l'héritage de demain', *Après-Demain*, no.322, March 1990, p.8

Chaban-Delmas, J., 'Jalons vers une nouvelle société', *Revue des Deux Mondes*, January 1971, pp.6–16.

Collard, S., 'Mission impossible: les chantiers du Président', *French Cultural Studies*, vol.3, no.8, June 1992, pp.97–132

Donnat, O., 'Politique culturelle et débat sur la culture', *Esprit*, November 1988, pp.90–101

——, 'Démocratisation culturelle: la fin d'un mythe', *Esprit*, March–April 1991, pp.65–79

Fumaroli, M., 'De Malraux à Lang: l'excroissance des Affaires culturelles', *Commentaire*, no.18, summer 1982, pp.247–59; and 'L'Excroissance culturelle (suite): sur les autoroutes de la création', *Commentaire*, no.30, summer 1985, pp.658–63

——, 'Les Anciens et les modernes', *Esprit*, no.179, February 1992, pp.150–4

Girard, A., 'Industries culturelles', *Futuribles*, no.17, September–October 1978, pp.597–605

Harrison, M., 'The President, cultural projects and the mass media', unpublished paper read to the Maison Française, Oxford, 28–9 June 1991

Holleaux, A., 'Il y a deux ans mourait André Malraux: Le Ministre des affaires culturelles', *Revue des Deux Mondes*, November 1978, pp.354–5.

Laurent, J., 'Lettre ouverte au Ministre de la culture', *Acteurs*, no.1, January 1982, pp.68–72

Looseley, D.L., 'Jack Lang and the politics of festival', *French Cultural Studies*, vol.1, no.1, February 1990, pp.5–19

——, 'The World Theatre Festival, Nancy, 1963–88: a critique and a retrospective', *New Theatre Quarterly*, vol.6, no.22, May 1990, pp.141–53

——, 'The *Bibliothèque de France*. Last of the *grands projets*', and 'La Bibliothèque de France: interview de M. Jean Gattégno, délégué scientifique', *Modern and Contemporary France*, no.46, July 1991, pp.35–46 and pp.73–6

Ory, P., 'Front populaire et création artistique', *Bulletin de la Société d'Histoire Moderne*, vol.8, 1974, pp.5–21

——, 'La Politique culturelle du premier gouvernement Blum', *Nouvelle Revue Socialiste*, no.10–11, 1975, pp.75–93

——, 'La Politique du ministère Jack Lang: un premier bilan', *French Review*, vol.58, no.1, October 1984, pp.77–83

Peyrefitte, A., 'Il y a un an mourait Malraux: le Ministre', *Revue des Deux Mondes*, November 1977, pp.335–8

Poujol, G., 'The creation of a Ministry of Culture in France' (translated by M. Kelly), *French Cultural Studies*, vol.2, no.6, 1991, pp.251–60

Riggins, S.H., and Pham, K., 'Democratizing the arts: France in an era of austerity', *Queen's Quarterly*, vol.93, no.1, spring 1986, pp.149–61

Rioux, J.-P., 'L'Impératif culturel', *L'Histoire*, dossier 'Les Années Mitterrand', no.143, April 1991, pp.54–60

——, 'L'Evolution des interventions de l'Etat dans le domaine des affaires culturelles', *Administration*, no.151, 15 April 1991, pp.10–12

Roman, J., 'L'Etat culturel', *Esprit*, no.175, October 1991, pp.149–57

Saez, G., 'Politique culturelle: suivez le guide!', *Pour*, no.101, May–June 1985, pp.36–45

——, 'Emergence et institutionnalisation des cultures régionales et minoritaires comme objets de politique publique', unpublished paper read to colloquium on 'L'Etat devant les cultures régionales et communautaires', Association française de science politique and the Institut d'études politiques d'Aix-en-Provence, 23–5 January 1986, 16pp.

——, 'La Politique de développement culturel de 1981 à 1986', unpublished paper read to the Séminaire du Centre de Recherches Administratives, FNSP, 31 January 1987, 15pp.

——, 'De l'autonomie des politiques culturelles territoriales', in *Les Papiers du GRESE*, no.6, autumn 1989, Presses Universitaires du Mirail, pp.5–16

Saez, G., and Saez, J.-P., 'Peuple et Culture et le renouveau de l'Education populaire à la Libération', unpublished paper read to the Colloque du CRHIPA on 'Education populaire et Formation permanente en France et en Italie', Grenoble, 6–7 October 1989

Vaisse, P., 'Dix Ans de grands travaux', *Contemporary French Civilization*, vol.15, no.2, summer/fall 1991, pp.310–28

Various, *Communications*, special issue 'La Politique culturelle', no.14, 1969

——, 'Quelle "Très Grande Bibliothèque"?', *Le Débat*, no.55, May–August 1989, pp.136–67

——, *Commentaire*, 'La Politique culturelle en France', no.48, winter 1989–90, pp.699–720; no.49, spring 1990, pp.105–28; no.50, summer 1990, pp.343–54; M. Fumaroli, 'La Culture et les loisirs', no.51, autumn 1990, pp.425–35

——, 'L'Etat culturel: mythe ou réalité?', *Le Débat*, no.70, May–August 1992, pp.3–83

——, *Cahiers Français*, 'Culture et société', no.260, March–April 1993

SELECTED PRESS ARTICLES

Académie des beaux-arts, 'L'Académie des beaux-arts alerte le gouvernement', *Le Figaro Magazine*, 28 March 1986, pp.126–8

Algalarrondo, H., 'Les Six Sous de Lang', *Le Nouvel Observateur*, 19–25 August 1988, p.23

Baudrillard, J., 'La Gauche divine', *Le Monde*, 2 parts: 1, 'La Fin des passions historiques', 21 September 1983, pp.1 and 10; 2, 'Social: la grande illusion', 22 September 1983, p.8

Beaux-Arts (text by J. Girard and G. Boyer), special issue *La Pyramide du Louvre*, no date, unnumbered pages

Bertin, J., 'A la recherche de la culture perdue', *Politis*, 9 June 1988, pp.39–41

Billard, P., 'Jack Lang: la grande parade', *Le Point*, 10 June 1985, pp.127–34

Boggio, P., 'Le Silence des intellectuels de gauche', *Le Monde*, 2 parts: 1, 'Victoire à contretemps', 27 July 1983, pp.1 and 6; 2, 'Les Chemins de traverse', 28 July 1983, p.6

Bourdieu, P., *et al*, 3 articles in *Le Monde*: 'Que vive la télévision publique',

19 October 1988, p.2; 'Tombeau pour une ambition', 11 May 1989; and 'Pour une télévision publique sans publicité', 29–30 April 1990, pp.1 and 9

Bredin, J.-D., 'Les Intellectuels et le pouvoir socialiste', *Le Monde*, 22 December 1981, pp.1 and 22

Chéreau, P., 'Une Réponse de Patrice Chéreau sur la situation de l'art lyrique à Paris. Un opéra à la Bastille, oui ou non?', *Le Monde*, 11 November 1988, p.24

Connaissance des Arts, special issue *Grands Travaux* (English edition), 1989

Enthoven, J.-P., 'Jack Lang comme si vous y étiez', *Le Nouvel Observateur*, 25 November 1983

Fumaroli, M., 'Bibliothèque de France: Alexandrie ou Disneyland?', *Le Figaro*, 21 July 1989

——, 'Bibliothèque de France: la charrue avant les bœufs', *Le Figaro*, 30 August 1990

——, 'Pour une rupture', *Le Monde*, 25 March 1993, p.2

Gallo, M., 'Les Intellectuels, la politique et la modernité', *Le Monde*, 26 July 1983, p.7

Garcin, J., 'Marc Fumaroli lance une bombe contre Jack Lang', *L'Evénement du Jeudi*, 22–8 August 1991, pp.96–7

Girard, J., and Martin, C., 'L'Art et l'état', *Beaux-Arts*, 3 parts: 1, 'Les FRAC en question', no.104, September 1992, pp.63–9; 2, 'La Commande publique', no.105, October 1992, pp.65–72; 3 (discussion, no author), 'Les Politiques de l'art', no.106, November 1992, pp.97–103

Gravelaine, F. de, *et al*, 'Art et industrie', *L'Unité*, no.622, pp.22–8

Hauter, F., 'Jack Lang, ou la politique de la mise en scène', *Le Figaro*, 3 April 1992

Higonnet, P., 'A French Folly', *TLS*, 11–17 May 1990

Hocquenghem, G., 'Les Culturocrates', *Libération*, series of 4 articles, 21–4 July 1981, pp.20–1, p.24, pp.20–2 and pp.24–5 respectively

——, 'La Culture par la joie', *Libération*, 18 November 1981

Hunter, M., 'Un Américain juge la politique de Lang', *Reader's Digest Selection* (French edition), 1 December 1991

Julliard, J., 'Monsieur le Président', *Le Nouvel Observateur*, 22–8 June 1989, p.31

Konopnicki, G., 'A des années-lumière', *Le Monde*, 7 August 1982, p.2

L——, F., 'Le Bilan Malraux', *Le Nouvel Adam*, no.9, April 1967, p.32

Lacouture, J., 'Dix ans de règne sur la culture', *Le Monde*, 4 parts: 1, 'L'Espoir', 5 July 1969, pp.1 and 15; 2, 'Le Musée imaginaire', 6–7 July 1969; 3, 'Les Conquérants', 8 July 1969, p.9; 4, 'Un Organisme bâtard', 9 July 1969, p.15

Landevennec, Y., 'Faut-il brûler Jack Lang?', *Royaliste*, 16–29 September 1982, pp.6–7

Landowski, M., 'Un Grand Ministère de la culture', *Le Monde*, 26–7 April

Bibliography

1981, pp.1 and 12

Lonchampt, J., 'Daniel Barenboim, oui ou non?', *Le Monde*, 9 November 1988, pp.1 and 14

——, 'La Bastille des artistes', *Le Monde*, 24 January 1989, pp.1 and 13

Mignon, S., 'Culture: suivez Jack Lang!', *Le Point*, 5 April 1982, p.121

Mitterrand, F., 'La Démocratisation voie de la vraie réforme architecturale', *Architecture*, no.22, April 1981, p.43

Plunkett, P. de, 'Le Système Lang', *Le Figaro Magazine*, 25 January 1986, pp.15–23

Politis, special issue 'Les Années Lang', no.121, 3–10 January 1991

Rey, A., 'L'Opéra entre espoirs et pesanteurs', *Le Monde*, 2 April 1988, pp.1 and 18

Rollat, A., 'La Bataille de la culture entre la gauche et la droite: les nouveaux chouans', *Le Monde*, 3 November 1983, p.8

Simon, Y., 'Les Temps changent', *Le Monde*, 18 June 1981, p.17

Slama, A.-G., *et al*, 'Faut-il un ministère de la Culture?', *Le Figaro*, 21 May 1984, p.2

Spire, A., *et al*, '"Poursuivre le mouvement"', *Le Matin*, 24 February 1986, pp.2–3

Various, 'François Mitterrand vu par...', *Le Matin*, numéro hors série, no date [April 1981]

——, 'Culture: les choix des quatre grands', *Le Matin*, 3 parts: 1, 21 April 1981, pp.30–1; 2, 22 April 1981, pp.28–9; 3, 23 April 1981, pp.26–7

——, 'Sept Ans de culture', *Les Nouvelles Littéraires*, 23 April 1981, pp.30–43

Warnod, J., 'Les FRAC: une bonne idée trop souvent détournée', *Le Figaro*, 12 March 1986, p.34

PUBLISHED INTERVIEWS (the first name cited is that of the interviewee)

Baumel, J., 'Quelle action culturelle demain?', *Le Figaro*, 1–2 March 1986

Buren, D., 'La Modernité souffle où elle veut', *Le Figaro*, 21 January 1986

Duhamel, J., 'L'Avenir des Maisons de la culture', *Le Monde*, 4 May 1972, p.17

Finkielkraut, A., 'Finkielkraut persiste et signe: c'est la défaite de la culture!', *L'Evénement du Jeudi*, 19–25 April 1990

Guy, M., 'Michel Guy au *Quotidien*', *Le Quotidien de Paris*, 25 July 1985, pp.12–13

Jamet, D., 'La Réponse de Dominique Jamet: les critiques ont tort', *Connaissance des Arts*, October [?] 1990, p.117

Lang, J., 'Dialogue entre Jack Lang et Jean-Denis Bredin', *Le Monde*, 2 parts: 1, 28 February 1978, pp.1–2; 2, 1 March 1978, p.2

——, 'Jack Lang: "La Vraie Finalité d'un ministère, c'est de dépérir et de disparaître"', *Le Quotidien de Paris*, 1 June 1981, pp.16–17

——, 'Jack Lang: "Rien n'est prioritaire puisque tout l'est"', *Les Nouvelles Littéraires*, 4–11 June 1981, p.16

——, 'Les Deux Urgences du Ministre de la culture', *France-Soir*, 12 June 1981

——, 'Un Entretien avec le Ministre de la culture', *Le Matin*, 18 June 1981, p.7

——, 'L'Interview de *Playboy*: Jack Lang', *Playboy* (édition française), September 1981, pp.21–103 *passim*

——, 'Un Entretien avec M. Jack Lang', *Le Monde*, 5 September 1981, pp.1 and 8

——, 'Il faut une riposte au niveau européen', *Journal du Dimanche*, 6 September 1981

——, 'Jack Lang: "Je ne suis pas un ayatollah!"', *L'Express*, 10 September 1982, pp.8–11

——, 'Jack Lang: "Je ne suis pas anti-américain"', *Les Nouvelles Littéraires*, 28 October 1982, pp.10–12

——, '"C'est le choix des personnes qui guide d'abord nos actions" nous déclare le Ministre de la culture', *Le Monde*, 19 July 1983, pp.1 and 15

——, 'Jack Lang parle à *Paris Match*', *Paris Match*, 3 February 1984, pp.24–7

——, 'La Création industrielle sera le pétrole de l'an 2000', *Le Matin*, 11 October 1985

——, 'Zénith ou la guerre des étoiles contre la droite', *L'Unité*, no.645 [24 April 1986], pp.24–5

——, 'Une Interview de Jack Lang (PS)', *La Croix*, 31 December 1986, p.13

Léotard, F., '"Etre un bon gestionnaire de l'ingérable"', *Le Monde*, 12 December 1986, pp.1 and 26

——, 'L'Opéra, de Garnier à la Bastille', *Le Monde*, 28 May 1987, pp.1 and 17

Mauroy, P., 'Ce qu'ils nous veulent', *Les Nouvelles Littéraires*, 4–11 June 1981, pp.14–15

Mitterrand, F., 'Un Entretien avec M. François Mitterrand', *Le Monde*, 2 May 1974, p.2

——, 'François Mitterrand: "Le Premier des patrimoines, c'est l'homme"', *Les Nouvelles Littéraires*, 7–14 May 1981, pp.27–30

——, 'François Mitterrand: "Parce que je suis amoureux de Paris..."', *Le Nouvel Observateur*, 14 December 1984, pp.66–86

——, 'Exclusif: Le Président parle des médias', *Le Point*, 21 September 1987, pp.26–7

Peyret, J., 'Le Ministère de la culture deviendrait-il le ministère de la pub?', *Stratégies*, 2 December 1984, pp.54–8

Pompidou, G., 'Le Président de la République définit ses conceptions dans les domaines de l'art et de l'architecture', *Le Monde*, 17 October 1972, pp.1, 12 and 13; reprinted as 'Déclarations de M. Georges Pompidou Président

Bibliography

de la République sur l'art et l'architecture', Actualités-Documents, Comité interministériel pour l'information, no. 94, November 1972

MINISTERIAL STATEMENTS, SPEECHES, PRESS RELEASES

Lang, J., 'Discours de Jack Lang' (July 1981–March 1985), 5 vols, Ministry of Culture, unpublished Ministry transcripts of his major speeches excluding the following
——, Presentation of *prix unique* bill to Senate, *Journal Officiel*, séance du 29 juillet 1981, pp.1,205–7
——, 'Discours prononcé par M. Jack Lang, Ministre de la culture, à l'Assemblée nationale le mardi 17 novembre 1981, lors de la Session Budgétaire', unpublished Ministry transcript (also *Journal Officiel*, séance du 17 novembre 1981)
——, 'Intervention de M. Jack Lang, Ministre de la culture' (Mexico City), 27 July 1982, *Après-Demain*, no.250, January 1983, pp.4–7 (also unpublished Ministry transcript)
——, Press conference of 3 October 1983, 'Les Orientations nouvelles de la politique des industries de la culture', dossier d'information no.118
——, Speech presenting the Plan Son, 23 October 1984, unpublished Ministry transcript
——, Speech to a colloquium at the Ecole des hautes études commerciales, 29 November 1984, unpublished Ministry transcript
——, 'Discours de Jack Lang', Chambord, 6 September 1988, supplement to *Lettre d'Information*, no.245, 19 September 1988
——, Ministry of Culture, 'Le Livre et la lecture', press conference, 24 May 1989, Ministry press dossier no.DP388
——, 'Eléments du discours de Jack Lang' (on the first six months of the Pyramide du Louvre), 19 September 1989, press dossier no.DP419
——, 'Hommage à André Malraux 1901–1976: allocution de M. Jack Lang, au Palais-Royal, passage des Fontaines', 14 September 1992, unpublished Ministry transcript
Léotard, F., and de Villiers, P., 'Conférence de presse du mercredi 25 juin 1986: discours de François Léotard et Philippe de Villiers', Ministry press dossier no.DP267
Malraux, A., Speech inaugurating MC of Bourges, 18 April 1964 (extract) in 'Malraux: paroles et écrits politiques 1947–1972 inédits', *Espoir. Revue de l'Institut Charles de Gaulle*, no.2, 1973, pp.58–9
——, Speech inaugurating MC of Amiens, 19 March 1966, reproduced in Ministry of Culture, 'Trentième Anniversaire du Ministère de la culture' (see **Other Official Documents** below); and in R. Abirached (ed.), *La Décentralisation théâtrale*, 2 vols, vol.2, 'Les Années Malraux 1959–68', Cahier no.6, Paris: Actes Sud-Papiers, 1993, pp.223–30
——, Speech to National Assembly, 27 October 1966, *Journal Officiel* of this

day, 2ᵉ séance; partly reproduced in ATAC Informations no.3, December 1966, p.3

———, Speech to National Assembly, 13 November 1968, *Journal Officiel*, 2ᵉ séance du 13 novembre 1968, pp.4,351–5; partly reproduced in 'Les Maisons de la culture posent un problème', *Le Monde*, 15 November 1968, p.7, accompanied by 'Affaires culturelles: les crédits représentent 0.427% des dépenses de l'Etat', pp.6–7

Ministry of Culture, '"La Marseillaise", Jean-Paul Goude', press dossier no.DP400

Toubon, J., Speech to Senate, 6 December 1993, extracts reproduced as 'Vers une rénovation de la politique culturelle', *Lettre d'Information*, no.358, 30 December 1993, pp.2–4

OTHER OFFICIAL DOCUMENTS (Ministry publications, reports, etc.)

Ministry of Culture (and Communication) Publications

Cinéma, Etat et Culture series, Paris: Documentation Française, 1992

Développement Culturel (DEP, in chronological order):
'Prospective et développement culturel', no.13, May–June 1972, pp.2–3
'Le Budget du Ministère chargé des affaires culturelles de 1960–1985', special issue, no.67, October 1986
'"Le 10 pour cent culturel"', no.97, January 1993
'Les Conventions de développement culturel: un milliard en dix ans', no.98, February 1993

'Dix Ans après une loi qui fait fureur!', supplement to a special Salon du Livre edition of the DLL's newsletter *Lettres*, March 1991

Dupin, X., and Rouet, F., (Council of Europe), *Mesures des pouvoirs publics à l'égard des industries culturelles en Europe 1988–1989*, rapport intermédiaire, DEP, May 1989

Lettre d'Information (Département de l'information et de la communication, in chronological order):
'Le Texte de la plate-forme commune de gouvernement UDF/RPR', no.191, 28 April 1986, pp.3–4
'Exposition: "grands projets culturels en France"', no.241, 4 July 1988
'La "Grande Bibliothèque" avance', no.244, 29 August 1988 (letter from Mitterrand to Rocard)
'Orientations budgétaires pour 1989', no.248, 31 October 1988, p.2
'Orientations budgétaires pour 1993', no.335, 12 November 1992, pp.4–5
Supplement 'Cinéma: bilan et nouvelles mesures', no.342, 11 March 1993

Le Livre, Etat et Culture series, Paris, Documentation Française, 1993

Ministère de l'éducation nationale et de la culture (Délégation au

Bibliography

développement et aux formations), *L'Art à l'école: enseignements et pratiques artistiques*, Paris: Hatier/L'Etudiant, no date [1993]

Ministère de l'éducation nationale et Ministère de la culture, 'Les Enseignements artistiques de 1981 à 1986. Ce qui a été fait, ce qui reste à faire', no date

Moulin, F., and Moulinier, P., *Les Conventions de développement culturel*, Ministry of Culture (DEP), May 1993

Musées, Etat et Culture series, Paris: Documentation Française, 1991

Nouvelle Enquête sur les pratiques culturelles des Français, Paris: Documentation Française, 1990, accompanied by O. Donnat and D. Cogneau, *Les Pratiques culturelles des Français 1973–1989*, Paris: La Découverte/Documentation Française, 1990

'Les Orientations de la politique culturelle de Jack Lang', dossier de presse réalisé pour le voyage du Ministre aux Etats-Unis, November 1990

Patrimoine, Etat et Culture series, Paris: Documentation Française, 1992

'La Politique culturelle 1981–1985: bilan de la législature' [1986?] (collection of booklets)

'La Politique culturelle 1981–1991', 1991 (collection of booklets)

Rigaud, J., 'La Politique culturelle: bilan de deux années d'action', internal Ministry document taken from the review *Défense nationale*, February 1973

'Trentième Anniversaire du Ministère de la culture. Journées d'étude sur la création du Ministère de la culture', 30 November–1 December 1989 (dossier, including *Eléments provisoires de chronologie sur les débuts du Ministère de la culture* and Bernard, A., see following section)

Vous avez dit culture? Chronique d'une décennie culturelle 1981–1991, Paris: Centre national de la photographie, 1992

Other

Belleville, P., *Pour la culture dans l'entreprise: rapport au Ministre de la culture*, Paris, Documentation Française, 1982

Bernard, A., *Le Ministère des affaires culturelles et la mission culturelle de la collectivité*, internal document dating from March 1968, Paris: Documentation Française, 1989

Cahart, P., and Melot, M., *Propositions pour une grande bibliothèque*, Paris: Documentation Française, 1989

Commissariat général du Plan, *Rapport de la Commission des affaires culturelles*, Paris: Documentation Française, 1971

Commissariat général du Plan (M. Guillaume), *L'Impératif culturel: rapport du groupe de travail long terme culture*, Paris: Documentation Française, 1982

Commissariat général du Plan d'équipement et de la productivité, *Rapport général de la Commission de l'équipement culturel et du patrimoine artistique*, Paris: Imprimerie Nationale, 1961.

Commission du Bilan (F. Bloch-Lainé), 'Politique culturelle et vie collective',

Bibliography

La France en mai 1981, 6 vols, Paris: Documentation Française, 1982, vol.1, pp.224–38; and 'La vie culturelle', vol.3, pp.295–317

Donnat, O., and Cogneau, D., see *Nouvelle Enquête*... under **Ministry of Culture (and Communication) Publications**

Giordan, H., *Démocratie culturelle et droit à la différence: rapport au Ministre de la culture*, Paris, Documentation Française, 1982

Ministère de l'économie et des finances, 'Projet de loi de finances: budget de la culture', *Les Notes Bleues*, no.43.

Puaux, P., *Les Etablissements culturels: rapport au Ministre de la culture*, Paris, Documentation Française, 1982

Querrien, M., *Pour une nouvelle politique du patrimoine: rapport au Ministre de la culture*, Paris: Documentation Française, 1982

Rizzardo, R., *La Décentralisation culturelle: rapport au Ministre de la culture et de la communication*, Paris: Documentation Française, 1991

Wangermée, R., and Gournay, B. (Council of Europe), *Programme européen d'évaluation: la politique culturelle de la France*, Paris: Documentation Française, 1988.

DOCUMENTS CONNECTED WITH POLITICAL PARTIES

Parti Socialiste

Anon., *Projet socialiste pour la France des années 80*, Paris: Club Socialiste du Livre, no date [1980]

FNESR, 'La Création dans la cité. Rencontre de Rennes, 24–5 octobre 1980, Rencontre d'Avignon, 21–3 juillet 1981', *Communes de France*, no.16; also typed report dated January 1981 of the October 1980 meeting, 'La création dans la cité'

Mitterrand, F., 'Action culturelle débat majeur de notre temps', *Nouvelle Revue Socialiste*, no. 4, 1974, pp.5–11 (extracts)

Parmantier, P., 'Feu le livre?', *Communes de France*, March 1981, pp.21–3

SNAC, 'Orientations générales d'une politique d'action culturelle' (introduction by D. Taddei), *Nouvelle Revue Socialiste*, no. 4, 1974, pp.12–31 (document dated June 1974)

———, 'Orientations générales d'une politique d'action culturelle', typed draft document dated July 1974

———, 'L'Action culturelle dans le combat politique', typed draft document dated January 1975

———, handwritten anonymous summary of the draft document and ensuing discussions in the various working parties at the Rencontres nationales, Ministry document (DEP) (no date)

Bibliography

Other

Various, *Un Projet culturel pour demain dans le cadre d'une véritable décentralisation*, actes du colloque de Lyon, 21 October 1985

'Texte de la plate-forme commune de gouvernement UDF/RPR' (culture and communication), *Lettre d'Information*, no.191, 28 April 1986, pp.3–4

TV AND RADIO PROGRAMMES (in chronological order)

Lang, J., 'Grand Jury RTL-Le Monde', RTL, 27 December 1981 (extracts in DEP)

Lang, J. and Garcin, J., 'Ouvert le dimanche', FR3, 12 September 1982, 3.00 p.m.(DEP transcript)

Lang, J. and Mourousi, Y., 'RMC Choc', RMC, 10 April 1986, 7.00 p.m.

'The Late Show', programme devoted to the Lang years, BBC2, 12 October 1992, 11.15 p.m.

Brief Chronology Since 1959

1959
8 January: Malraux Ministre d'Etat chargé des affaires culturelles
3 February: Decree lays down sectors to transfer to the new ministry
24 July: Further decree defines the Ministry's mission

1960
Cleaning of Parisian buildings begins

1961
24 June: Malraux inaugurates the first MC, Le Havre

1962
31 July: First 5-year *loi-programme* for the restoration of monuments
4 August: Law creates *secteurs sauvegardés*

1964
Structures set up for Inventaire général

1968
May–June: Malraux's conception of culture contested

1969
28 April: De Gaulle resigns, replaced from 19 June by Pompidou
21 June: Malraux replaced by E. Michelet, with same title

1970
27 September: Michelet replaced by A. Bettencourt, *par intérim*

1971
Commission des affaires culturelles for 6th Plan (1971–5) reports
7 January: Bettencourt replaced by J. Duhamel, Ministre des affaires culturelles

1973
5 April: M. Druon replaces Duhamel, with same title (until 1 March 1974)

1974
May–June: Giscard wins presidential elections; M. Guy Secrétaire d'Etat à la culture (8 June; A. Peyrefitte had stood in after Druon)
26–8 July: SNAC debates and Mitterrand's press conference at Avignon

1975
18–19 January: SNAC holds Rencontres nationales de la culture

1976
25 August: Guy replaced by F. Giroud, with same title

1977
29 March: Giroud replaced by M. d'Ornano, Ministre de la culture et de l'environnement (until 31 March 1978)

1978
3 April: D'Ornano replaced by J.-P. Lecat, Ministre de la culture et de la communication (until 4 March 1981)

1981
19 March: Mitterrand outlines his cultural policy at PS symposium
May:
10: Mitterrand beats Giscard in presidentials
21: Investiture and visit to Panthéon
23: J. Lang Minister of Culture in P. Mauroy's government
June: PS gains absolute majority in legislatives (14th and 21st); 2nd Mauroy government
10 August: Prix unique du livre law (in force from 1 January 1982)
September:
4–6: Lang turns down invitation to Deauville Festival
24: Mitterrand reveals big budget increases for Culture and outlines his programme of *grands projets*
17 November: Lang presents his doubled budget to the Assembly

1982
January: creation of DDC
8 March: Presidential communiqué on *grands projets*

10 May: Decree modifies the Ministry's mission laid down 24 July 1959
21 June: First Fête de la musique
July:
27: Lang's Mexico City speech
29: Broadcasting bill ends state monopoly
15–16 October: Decrees set up CNAP and DAP
November: 9th Plan report (1984–8), *L'Impératif culturel*

1983
11–13 February: Sorbonne colloquium on 'Culture and Development'
March:
6 and 13: Socialists lose a number of councils in the municipals
23–5: New austerity measures; Lang demoted to *ministre délégué*
July:
2–5: Cancellation of Expo '89
26: M. Gallo launches *Le Monde*'s 'silence des intellectuels' debate
3 October: Lang outlines new cultural-industries policy

1984
January: Beginning of campaign against Pei's Pyramid
17 July: Mauroy replaced as Prime Minister by Fabius
4 November: Canal Plus begins broadcasting
December: Lang's full ministerial status restored

1985
3 July: Law on *les droits des artistes-interprètes*
21 October: Lyon opposition colloquium, *Un Projet culturel pour demain*
December: Buren Columns begin to cause controversy

1986
Lang's budget reaches 0.95 per cent of state spending
20 February: La Cinq begins broadcasting
March:
1: TV6 begins broadcasting
16: Victory for RPR-UDF in legislatives; first 'cohabitation'
20: F. Léotard Minister of Culture and Communication
16 April: *Collectif budgétaire* for 1986 cuts Culture by 4 per cent
14 May: Léotard announces privatisation of TF1
25 June: Léotard's press conference on culture; DDC to be dismantled
30 September: Léotard's broadcasting law
18 December: Street protest at cultural and audiovisual policies

1987
Spring: Finkielkraut's *La Défaite de la pensée*
23 July: Law on *mécénat*

1988
5–6 January: Laws on heritage and creative-arts education
May:
8–9: Mitterrand re-elected; M. Rocard Prime Minister
12: Lang Minister of Culture and Communication
5 and 12 June: Legislatives: PS does not obtain an absolute majority; Lang Minister of Culture, Communication, the Bicentenary and Grands Travaux
14 July: Mitterrand announces plan for a new national library
6 September: Lang announces that *patrimoine* is now a priority

1989
January:
13–15: D. Barenboim sacked from the Opéra-Bastille
27: Lang's new broadcasting bill
February: Opening of Pyramide du Louvre
12 and 19 March: Municipals: PS does well
13–15 July: Highpoint of bicentenary celebrations: grand opening of Opéra-Bastille, Pyramide and Arche de la Défense; Goude's *Marseillaise* parade in evening of 14th

1990
Spring: *Nouvelle Enquête sur les pratiques culturelles des Français*
Summer: Rigaud's *Libre Culture*

1991
15 May: Rocard replaced by E. Cresson; Lang Minister of Culture, Communication and Grands Travaux
August: Fumaroli's *L'Etat culturel*

1992
April:
2: Cresson replaced by P. Bérégovoy; Lang Minister of Education and Culture (including Communication)
12: Eurodisneyland opens; La Cinq closes
7 November: Culture budget adopted in Assembly: at 13.8 billion francs, it will at last reach 1 per cent

1993

January: Schneider's *La Comédie de la culture*

February: Economic constraints take the Culture budget below 1 per cent again

21 and 28 March: Socialists ousted in legislatives. E. Balladur forms new government; J. Toubon Minister of Culture and Francophonie

December:

9: Lang loses his seat in Assembly

14–15: In the GATT talks, Europe and USA agree to differ in the heated debate over *l'exception culturelle*

Index

Abadie, François, 71
Abirached, Robert, 73, 106, 113, 168,
    170, 240
  Théâtre et le prince, Le, 3, 53, 112n39,
    227, 236
academicism (*académisme*), 12–13, 18, 38
Académie des beaux-arts, 12–13, 28, 163
action culturelle, 6, 37, 44, 46, 72, 242
  after May 1968, 49–51, 53–4
  Socialist conception of, 57–8
  under Lang, 72, 120, 150, 177–8, 213–
    14, 239–40
action internationale, 168–9
action socioculturelle, 6
  see also sociocultural, the
Ader, Jean, 120
Adler, Laure, 189
advertising, 51, 126
  in broadcasting, 200–4 *passim,* 207–8
Agence nationale pour la création en
    milieu rural, 117
Agence pour le développement régional
    du cinéma, 95, 198–9
aide au développement des projets, 198
Alliance pour une nouvelle culture, 161,
    166, 173n20
Allons z'idées, 169–71 *passim*
America, 86, 207, 209
American 'majors', 77
Americanisation and American
    competition, 26–8, 124, 198, 200–4
    passim
  Lang and, 76–9, 159–60, 207, 217, 236
  Socialists' position on, 57, 59, 83
Angrémy, Jean-Pierre, 142, 153n22
animateurs culturels, 23, 39, 42, 44, 218,
    225
  Socialists and, 59–61, 80
animation, 25, 41, 54–5, 105–7, 226
  post-1968 conceptions of, 44, 59–60,
    239

Année du patrimoine, 55
Antenne 2, 203, 205
Anthonioz, Bernard, 39, 73
Arc et Senans colloquium, 50–1
Arche de la Défense, 135–9 *passim,* 143,
    149, 167, 182
archives, 150
Archives du monde du travail de
    Roubaix, 137, 143
Arp, Jean, 38
Art et industrie exhibition, 131
Art et Lumière, 161
art schools, 114
Artaud, Antonin, 42
ARTE, 206–7
artothèques, 100
arts and heritage, 4–5, 11, 16, 157, 243
Arts au soleil, Les, 122, 178
arts plastiques, see plastic arts
Association des écrivains et artistes
    révolutionnaires (AEAR), 14
Association des élus pour la liberté de la
    culture, 161
Association des expulsés du 12ᵉ
    arrondissement, 150
Association des Maisons de la culture et
    des cercles culturels (AMC), 14
Association des Théâtres de l'Opéra de
    Paris (ATOP), 184
Association populaire des amis du musée
    (APAM), 14
Association pour la gestion des entreprises
    culturelles (AGEC), 107, 209
Association pour la promotion des radios
    rurales, 117
Association pour le développement de la
    lecture publique (ADLP), 16
Association pour le développement du
    mécénat industriel et commercial
    (ADMICAL), 130
Association pour le renouveau du Louvre,

148, 153n32
audiovisual (media, policy, technologies),
    34, 128–30 *passim*, 209, 218, 226
    excluded from GATT 1993, 206
    under Lang, 72, 77–9, 81, 162, 199–
        203, 205–8
    under Léotard, 167–8, 203–5, 207
    see also broadcasting, cinema, radio,
        television, video
Audon, Michèle, 153n22
autogestion, 56
avances sur recettes, 39, 197–9 *passim*
avant-garde, the
    Lang and, 59–60, 102, 104–5, 216–17
    Malraux and, 39, 42, 43, 45,
        pre-1958, 13, 18, 26
Avice, Edwige, 71, 90
Avignon, 58, 59, 62, 108
Avignon Festival, 25, 43, 56, 76, 94, 179
Aznavour, Charles, 219

Balladur, Edouard, 1, 167, 169, 183, 206,
    239
Bambuck, Roger, 176
Banlieues 89, 141
Barenboim, Daniel, 64, 184–6
Barrault, Jean-Louis, 39
    Renaud-Barrault company, 40
Barré, François, 146, 245n12
Barre, Raymond, 115
Barrès, Maurice, 19, 84
Bastille, La, 64, 85, 121, 142
Baudrillard, Jean, 85–6
Baumel, Jacques, 115, 162
Baumol, William, 109, 142
Bazin, Hervé, 78
BD (comic strips), 125–6, 215, 225
    see also Centre national de la BD
Beatty, Warren, 178
Beaubourg, *see* Pompidou Centre
Beaucé, Thierry de, 176
beaux-arts, 12–13, 56, 95, 113
    Beaux-Arts (department), 12–13, 15,
        20, 23–8 *passim*, 242
    and Malraux, 34, 38, 40
Beckett, Samuel, 42, 165
Beethoven, 215
    Ode to Joy, 64
Belfort, 58
Belleville, Pierre, 72, 117
Bérégovoy, Pierre, 167, 176, 228, 234
Bergé, Pierre, 126, 169, 184–6, 239
Bergman, Ingmar, 165
Berlusconi, Silvio, 203

Bernard, Antoine, 36–7
Bertin, Jacques, 213, 220, 222
Beurs, 118, 160
Biasini, Emile-Jean, 35, 41, 139, 142,
    176, 191
bibliobus, 16, 24,
Bibliothèque nationale (BN), 73, 162,
    187–92, 219
Bibliothèque (nationale) de France (BdF),
    143, 187–92, 196n43, 209, 218–20
Bibliothèques centrales de prêt (BCPs),
    24, 54, 94, 97, 114
bicentenary of the French Revolution,
    62, 137, 176, 181–2, 209
    see also Expo 89
Blech, René, 14
Bloch-Lainé, François, 65n9, 95, 96–7,
    99, 142, 153n22
Blum, Léon, 14, 18, 27, 86
Blum-Byrnes agreements, 27, 76
Bogianckino, Massimo, 142
Bonnier, Henry, 3
    *Lettre recommandée aux fossoyeurs de la
        culture*, 3
books and bookshops, 34, 51, 54
    under Lang, 72, 94, 96–9, 220, 235
    see also Monory, *prix conseillé, prix
        unique du livre*
Bordeneuve, Jacques, 24
Borotra, Jean, 20
Boulez, Pierre, 125, 184–6 *passim*,
    195n35, 240
Bourdan, Pierre, 24, 34, 228, 242
Bourdieu, Pierre, 43, 119, 186, 208, 221
Bourges, Hervé, 205
Bouygues, Francis, 203
Braque, Georges, 35, 38
Bread and Puppet, 42, 60
Brecht, Bertolt, 42
Bredin, Jean-Denis, 67n30, 72, 85, 200
Brel, Jacques, 216
Breton, André, 18
British Library, 192
broadcasting (media), 50, 58, 72, 199–
    203, 207, 228
    failings of policies since 1981, 235–6
    Mitterrand's interventions in, 200, 202,
        242
    see also audiovisual, radio, television,
        video
Brook, Peter, 165
budget for Culture, 228
    before 1981, 12, 49, 55, 58
    moves towards 1 per cent of state

Index

spending, 58, 61, 67n31, 228, 233
  from 1981, 77, 81, 90, 162, 176–7,
    193n6
  under Lang, 80–1, 92n19, 150, 233–4
  under Léotard, 167–8, 176–7
  under Malraux, 34–5, 42, 44, 49
  under Toubon, 237–8
Buren, Daniel, 102–4
  see also Colonnes Buren
Busson, Alain, 109–10
Byrnes, James, 27

Cabanne, Pierre, 18, 39, 148
Caillebotte, Gustave, 13, 104
Cain, Julien, 24
Canal Plus, 200–3 passim
Canard Enchaîné, Le, 141
Cancun summit conference, 77
capitalism, 56–7, 89
Carrefour supermarkets, 98
Cassou, Jean, 28
Castro, Fidel, 78
Castro, Roland, 141, 148
Caune, Jean, 213–14, 220, 222, 227
  La Culture en action de Vilar à Lang, 6,
    56, 213–14
Centre national d'art contemporain
  (CNAC), 39
Centre national de la BD et de l'image
  d'Angoulême, 126, 137, 143
Centre national de la cinématographie
  (CNC), 27–8, 34, 197–9 passim
Centre national de la photographie, 126
Centre national des arts plastiques
  (CNAP), 99–102 passim
Centre national des lettres (CNL), 54,
  66n13, 97, 126
Centre national supérieur de formation
  aux arts du cirque, 123
Centres d'action culturelle (CACs), see
  Etablissements d'action culturelle
Centres d'art, 100
Centres de développement culturel, 94
Centres de lecture publique, 16
Centres dramatiques nationaux (CDNs),
  25–6, 39, 40, 42, 44
  after Malraux, 49, 53–4, 76, 94, 105–
    10 passim
Centres Leclerc supermarkets, 98–9
Certeau, Michel de, 50, 87
  La Culture au pluriel, 87
Chaban-Delmas, Jacques, 50
Chagall, Marc, 38
Chaix, P., 144

Chancerel, Léon, 16, 21
chanson, 72, 124–5, 235
chartes culturelles, see cultural charters
Chaslin, F., 146, 148
Chemetov, Paul, 138
Chéreau, Patrice, 53–4, 86, 112n32, 165,
  184–6
Chevalier, Maurice, 219
Chevènement, Jean-Pierre, 118
Cheysson Claude, 86
Chirac, Jacques, 61, 173n17
  as Mayor of Paris, 60, 102, 136, 161,
    187, 191
  opposition to Expo 89/bicentenary,
    147–8, 182
  as Prime Minister, 99, 166–70 passim.
    179, 184, 205, 209
Christo, 112n25
Chung, Myung Whun, 186
ciné-clubs, 23
cinema, 26–8, 39, 197–203, 207, 210n11,
  235
Cinémathèque, 40
Cinq, La, 200, 203–4, 206–7, 209
Cité des sciences et de l'industrie, see
  Villette, La
Cité internationale de la musique, see
  Villette, La
Clavé, André, 16, 21
Clément, Catherine, 64, 85, 140
  Rêver chacun pour l'autre, 85
CLT, 203
Club Zénith, 163–4, 169
Clubs Léo Lagrange, 23
Cocteau, Jean, 38
Cogniat, Raymond, 18
cohabitation, 1,
Cohen, Leonard, 216
Colbert, 11
Colin, Jean-Pierre, 73, 116, 175, 177,
  193n7
  La Beauté du manchot, 116–19 passim,
    133n14
colloquium on 'Création et
  développement' (Sorbonne), 84, 88–
    90, 158–9, 160, 169
Colonnes Buren, 102–4, 162–3, 167,
  169
Comédie Française, 17, 18, 102, 112n32,
  203, 219
comic strips, see BD
Comité d'action pour l'Europe du
  cinéma, 208
Comité d'histoire du Ministère de la

culture, 212
Comité d'organisation de l'industrie
 cinématographique (COIC), 20, 27
Comité pour l'identité nationale, 77
comités d'entreprise, 24, 117
Comités régionaux des affaires culturelles,
 40
Commentaire, 213
Commissariat à l'éducation générale et au
 sport, 20
Commission de la création artistique, 39
Commission des affaires culturelles, 50–2
Commission nationale de la
 communication et des libertés
 (CNCL), 203–5, 207
Commission supérieure des monuments
 historiques, 102, 148
Communists (PCF, communism), 13–14,
 22, 33, 56, 58
 after 1981, 85–6, 183, 205, 209
community cultures, 57, 72, 118, 133n14
compact discs (CDs), 128–30, 221
Compte de soutien à l'industrie
 cinématographique, 197–8, 201
Compte de soutien à l'industrie des
 programmes (1984), 201
Compte de soutien financier de
 l'industrie cinématographique et de
 l'industrie des programmes audiovisuels
 (1986), 201
computers (all aspects), 128–31 *passim*,
 215
Conseil de développement culturel, 52
Conseil national des langues et cultures
 régionales, 117–18
Conseil supérieur de l'audiovisuel (CSA),
 205
Conseil supérieur des bibliothèques, 191
Conseil supérieur du mécénat culturel,
 179
conseillers artistiques régionaux (regional
 artistic advisors), 100
conservation, 4, 55, 80
Conservative Party (UK), 2
Conservatoire de musique de Lyon, 137
Conservatoire national de musique, 137
conservatoires, 40
Conservatoires nationaux de région, 94
contrats de Plan, 115–16
conventions de développement culturel
 (contracts policy), 115–16, 149, 168
Copeau, Jacques, 16, 22, 25, 213
copyright legislation (1957), *see droits des
 artistes-interprètes*

COREPHAE, 95, 115
Cornu, André, 23
Cortazar, Julio, 76
Costa-Gavras, 165, 208
Cotonou conference, Lang's speech at,
 78–9
Council of Europe evaluation of French
 cultural policy, 4, 104, 109, 120, 125,
 180, 240
'Coup de talent dans l'Hexagone', 128
creation (*création*), 5, 37–41, 53, 55, 62
 and creativity, 53, 57–62, 67n29, 122,
 157, 240
 and *diffusion*, 123, 222, 227–8
 grands projets and, 139–41
 under Lang, 80–3, 94–6, 106, 123,
 209, 240–1
 see also creation in the community,
 tout-culturel, le
'création artistique dans la cité' colloquia,
 59, 61, 95
creation in the community (*création dans la
 cité*), 95–110
 books, 96–9, 110
 principles, 95–6
 theatre, 105–10 *passim*
 see also plastic arts
créations collectives, 42–3, 45
creative-arts education in schools
 (*enseignements artistiques*), 15, 34, 52,
 61, 228, 242
 Socialists' position on, 57–8, 62, 119
 under Lang, 82, 119–20, 162, 179–80,
 236
 under Léotard, 168–9, 179
creativity, 44–5, 50–2, 243
 Socialists' approach to, 57–61, 67n29,
 89, 95, 169
 under Lang, 81–3, 119–22, 127–8, 240
Cuba, 78, 158
cultural associations, 14–16
cultural charters (*chartes culturelles*), 54–5
cultural democracy, 5, 44, 46, 52, 110,
 192
 Socialist policies for, 114–22, 157
 Socialist views on, 59, 60, 113, 128
cultural development (*développement
 culturel*), 50–2, 113, 120, 224–5, 241
cultural identities, 44, 50, 57, 117, 160,
 209
'cultural imperialism', 77, 160
cultural industries, 51, 54–6 *passim*, 65n4,
 159, 179, 241
 in recent cultural debates, 214, 222–4,

228
Socialists and, 56–8 *passim*, 88, 113,
    123–31
cultural needs, 40, 43
cultural policy, meaning of, 3–6, 242–4
cultural relations/action abroad, 24, 34,
    168
cultural revolution, 43–4, 56, 84
cultural studies, 4
cultural tourism, 180, 218–19, 225, 226
culture/the cultural
    and leisure, 5, 15, 37, 217–19, 222
    and the economy, 80–4, 86–90, 109,
        128–31, 139–40, 169
    criticism of, 209, 214
    under Léotard, 179
    and the workplace, 72, 117
culture cultivée, 4, 43, 50
    meaning and use of term 'culture', 3–5,
        24, 50–1, 214–18, 222–6
    under Lang, 81–4
    under Malraux, 34–7, 45
    under Popular Front, 14
    see also cultural policy, 'global'
        conception of culture, high culture,
        mass culture, national culture,
        popular culture
culture scientifique et technique, 115, 143

'Dallas', 77
dance, 137
Dasté, Jean, 16, 21, 25, 106
Dauge, Yves, 148
Deauville Festival, *see* Lang, Jack
Débat, Le, 188
Debray, Régis, 85
Debré, Michel, 34
Decaux, Alain, 176
decentralisation, 20, 24–6, 40–5, 53–5,
    62
    laws of 1982–3, 114, 241
    under Mitterrand-Lang, 82, 101, 106,
        113–16, 150, 162
décloisonnement (decompartmentalisation),
    17, 123–4, 146
Défense, La, 104, 135–6
    see also Arche de la Défense
Defferre, Gaston, 114–15
Delebarre, Michel, 178
Délégation à la création, aux métiers d'art
    et aux manufactures, 73, 99
Délégation aux arts plastiques (DAP), 73,
    99–104 *passim*, 126, 168
Délégation aux développements et aux

formations, 177
Délégation aux enseignements et aux
    formations, 168
Délégation nationale à l'action culturelle,
    60
Delbée, A., 112n32
Delors, Jacques, 81, 90
Delpire, Robert, 126
democratisation, 5, 87, 97
    during Third and Fourth Republics,
        12, 14–16, 18, 20–8 *passim*
    grands projets and, 141–3, 192, 241
    in recent cultural debates, 5, 215, 218–
        26
    in the 1970s, 50–6 *passim*, 105
    under Lang, 82–3, 94–5, 98–9, 109,
        123, 240
    under Malraux, 36–7, 40–5, 231
Département des études et de la
    prospective (DEP), 6n2,
Department of National Heritage (UK), 2
departmental archives, 114
Derrida, Jacques, 88,, 89–90, 208
Desneux, Richard, 3
Devaquet, Alain, 170
    Loi Devaquet, 170
développement culturel, *see* cultural
    development
difference, 44, 50, 82, 113–19, 122, 240
diffusion, 5, 41, 44, 51, 96–9, 198–9
    see also creation, democratisation
Direction de l'administration générale et
    de l'environnement culturel (DAGEC),
    168, 191
Direction de la jeunesse et des sports, 24
Direction de la musique et de la danse,
    240
Direction des bibliothèques, 24
Direction des mouvements de jeunesse et
    de l'éducation populaire, 24
Direction des musées de France, 28, 167
Direction du développement culturel
    (DDC), 73, 106, 113–20 *passim*,
    133n18, 143, 240
    and cultural industries, 122, 124, 125,
        129
    budget for, 120, 150, 167
    dismantled, 167–8, 177, 193n7, 242
Direction du livre, 54, 80
Direction du livre et de la lecture (DLL),
    97, 126
Direction du patrimoine, 55, 167
Direction du théâtre et des spectacles
    (DTS), 106, 113, 168

Direction générale des arts et des lettres (DGAL), 23–4, 28, 34
Direction générale des relations culturelles, 24
Directions régionales des affaires culturelles (DRACs), 40, 54, 100, 115, 120, 133n18
Disney, Walt, 79
Disneyland, 188, 192, 217–18, 225
Eurodisneyland, 209
Donnat, Olivier, 213, 221–4, 226, 227, 240, 243
dotation culturelle spéciale, 114
dotation générale de décentralisation, 114
Douffiagues, Jacques, 120
droit à la différence, 44, 114
droit d'auteur, 17
droits des artistes-interprètes (law), 96, 125, 235
Druon, Maurice, 50, 52, 81
Dubedout, Hubert, 58
Dubuffet, Jean, 44
Duhamel, Jacques, 49–51, 53, 224
Dujardin-Beaumetz, 29n6
Dullin, Charles, 16, 25
Dupavillon, Christian, 73, 121, 175, 245n12
Dylan, Bob, 64–5, 216
The Times They Are A-Changin', 65

Eco, Umberto, 89–90, 165
Ecole nationale de la photographie d'Arles, 126, 137
Ecole nationale des arts culinaires, 123
Ecole nationale des beaux-arts, 12
Ecole nationale supérieure de danse de Marseille, 137
écomusées, 55
Eiffel Tower, 137
Elysée palace, 95, 126
EMI, 124
Emmanuel, Pierre, 50, 52
éducation populaire, see popular education
education system, 51–2, 58, 215, 217, 226, 243
Enthoven, Jean-Paul, 159
entreprise culturelle, 108–9
Esprit, 20–3, 221
Essel, André, 98–9
Etablissements d'action culturelle (EACs)
    association status of, 107–8, 177
    CACs and MCs, 45, 55
    from 1981, 72, 94, 107–10, 113, 148, 161

from 1986, 168, 170, 177
    redirected towards creation, 105–10 *passim*, 213–14
    see also Maisons de la culture
établissements publics, legal status of, 138
Etats généraux de la culture, 207–9
ethnic cultures, *see* community cultures
European audiovisual quotas, *see* Télévision sans frontières
European Council of Culture Ministers, 159, 205
European Court of Justice, 99, 202, 205
Expo 89, 137, 140, 146–8, 158
Exposition universelle (1937), 17, 18
'extra-territorial' cultures, *see* community cultures

Fabius, Laurent, 81, 158, 160, 161, 209
Fainsilber, Adrien, 136–7, 145
fashion, 51, 126
Fédération nationale des élus socialistes et républicains (FNESR), 59, 61, 62
Ferré, Léo, 216
Ferry, Jules, 12, 41
Festival d'automne, 53
fête, 17–18, 20–1, 28, 120–2, 163, 178
Fête de la musique, 2, 121–2, 123, 160–1, 173n27
Fête de l'industrie et de la technologie, 131
Fête du cinema, 162
Fête du jardin, 178
Fifth Republic and cultural policy, 19, 33, 52–3, 217–20 *passim*
Figaro, Le, 163, 233
Figaro Magazine, Le, 158, 170
Fillioud, Georges, 71, 90, 202
fine arts, *see* beaux-arts
Finkielkraut, Alain, 3–4, 78, 85
    Défaite de la pensée, La, 3, 213, 214–16, 217–26 *passim*
Fleuret, Maurice, 76, 121–2, 124, 133n27
FNAC, la, 97–9
folk cultures (music, dance, folklore, etc.), 17, 19, 21, 124
folk museums (*écomusées*), 55
Fondation des droits de l'homme, 182
Fonds d'aide à la commande publique, 101
Fonds d'incitation à la création (FIACRE), 99–101, 126
Fonds d'intervention culturelle (FIC), 51–2, 119, 120, 123, 133n18, 242
Fonds de promotion des cultures d'outre-

Index

mer, 117
Fonds national d'art contemporain (*le FNAC*), 100–1
Fonds régionaux d'acquisition des musées (FRAMs), 100, 114
Fonds régionaux d'art contemporain (FRACs), 100–1, 104, 114
formation, la, 5
Foucault, Michel, 85–6
Fouquet's, Le, 180
Fourth Republic and cultural policy, 22–9
FR3, 205, 206
François Mitterrand vu par ..., 63–4
Francophonie, 78–9, 168, 176, 228–31
Frank, Bernard, 83
French Revolution, 11–12, 13, 62, 182
Front National, 165, 166
Front populaire, *see* Popular Front
Fumaroli, Marc, 83, 188–9, 192, 236
Etat culturel, L', 3, 24, 27, 213, 217–20, 221–6 *passim*
on Third Republic and Vichy, 19, 21, 31n25, 31n27, 217
fun, 2, 45, 122, 161, 169, 216, 223, 240–1
Fureur de lire, La, 122, 178, 216
Futuroscope (Poitiers), 225

Gai-Pied, 171
Gallo, Max, 84–5, 208
GATT negotiations, 79, 206, 231n21, 235, 239
Gattégno, Jean, 73–6, 97, 99, 176, 187, 240
Bibliothèque de France à mi-parcours, La, 3, 188–92 *passim*
gauchistes, 43, 56–7, 114, 143, 239
Gaulle, Charles de, 29, 33–6, 45, 63, 135, 241
Gaullism, 33, 41, 52, 55, 73, 228–31
and the Left, 44, 94, 116, 241
Gaullists (and RPR), 1, 61, 102, 115, 136
Gaumont-Pathé, 199
Geldof, Bob, 215
Gémier, Firmin, 12, 22, 25
Genet, Jean, *Les Paravents*, 39
Gide, André, 14
Gilman, Bernard, 73
Giordan, Henri, 72
Démocratie culturelle et droit à la différence, 117–18
Girard, Augustin, 50, 122, 212, 221, 243

article on cultural industries, 55–6, 214, 226
Giraud, Michel, 147
Giscard d'Estaing, Valéry, 50, 52, 61, 85, 161, 182
giscardisme culturel, 58, 64, 240
his cultural policy, 53–6, 58, 62, 95, 98, 111n13
'global' conception of culture, 5–6, 242–4
before May 1981, 19, 34, 51, 56, 61–4 *passim*
in recent cultural debates, 228–9
theory and practice from 1981, 82, 87, 122, 146, 157, 176
Globe, 163, 184
Glucksmann, André, 85–6
Goude, Jean-Paul, 181–2, 241
graffiti, 178, 216–17
Gramsci, Antonio, 57, 161
grands projets, 2–3, 241
before Mitterrand, 49, 53, 135–6, 151n1
under Léotard, 167–70 *passim*, 176
under Mitterrand-Lang (1981–6), 102, 131, 135–51, 161
and Socialist cultural policy, 139, 151
competitions for, 137–8, 152n7
costs, 148–50, 234–5
hostility to, 146–51, 183–7, 187–92, 218
motives behind, 139–46
presidential nature of, 137–9, 242
regional projects (*grands projets de province*), 137, 149
support for, 163–5
under Mitterrand-Lang (1988–93), 175–6, 182–7, 187–92
Secrétariat d'Etat aux grands travaux, 175–6
see also individual projects (Louvre, etc.)
grands travaux, see grands projets
Grenoble, 42, 48n26, 58, 62, 73, 108
Grotowski, Jerzy, 42
Guéhenno, Jean, 14, 24
Guilhaume, Philippe, 205
Guillaume, Marc, 87
L'Impératif culturel, 87, 88–9, 96, 113
Guimard, Paul, 140
Guy, Michel, 49, 53–6 *passim*, 60, 106, 115
as critic of Socialist policies, 148, 162

Index

Hachette, 54, 203, 207
Halles, Les, 53, 60, 135, 136, 139, 148
Hallier, Jean-Edern, 86
Hardy, Michel, 182
Haut Commissariat à la jeunesse et aux sports, 34
Haute Autorité de la communication audiovisuelle, 200
Hautecoeur, Louis, 20
Hendrix, Jimi, 216
Henry, André, 71
Herder, J.G. von, 214
heritage (*patrimoine*), 4, 12, 29n3, 226, 243
  grands projets and, 141, 192, 218
  Socialists' approach to, 62, 72
  under Giscard, 55, 58, 62
  under Lang, 73, 94–5, 102–4, 180, 194n16, 241
    his policies criticised, 162, 180
  under Léotard, 168–9, 180
  under Malraux, 37–8, 45
  wider definition of, 37–8, 95, 117
  see also conservation
Hersant, Robert, 203
'Heure de vérité, L'', 161
high culture (*haute culture*), 4, 243
  before Malraux, 14, 18, 21, 22, 241–2
  in recent cultural debates, 214–17, 218–20, 221–7 *passim*
  under Lang, 87, 94–6, 120
  see also creation in the community
  under Malraux, 36, 41, 43–4
Higonnet, Patrice, 189
hip-hop, 178
Hip-hop dixit!, 178
historic buildings and monuments, 4, 55
  under Lang, 81, 95, 101–4, 150
Hocquenghem, Guy, 84, 94, 96, 165
Holleaux, André,
Huidobro, Borja, 138
Hunter, Mark, 3, 121–2, 235

L'*Impératif culturel, see* Guillaume, Marc
industrial design (*création industrielle*), 126–7
information technology (IT), *see* computers
Institut de France, 12
Institut du monde arabe (IMA), 135–6, 138, 176, 194n24
Institut pour le financement du cinéma et des industries culturelles (IFCIC), 129–30, 199

intellectuals, 56, 63, 192, 209, 226
  role of, in developing cultural policy 13, 14
  silence of, 84–6, 89–90, 93n30, 240
interculturel l', 118
Internationale, L', 17, 85
Inventaire du patrimoine culinaire, 180
Inventaire général des monuments et des richesses artistiques de la France, 37–8
IRCAM, L', 125, 235, 240

jacobinism, 114, 116, 117
Jamet, Dominique, 165, 187, 191–2
Jaujard, Jacques, 23, 28, 34
Jaurès, Jean, 64, 86
jazz, 124–5
Jeanneney, Jean-Noël, 176, 181, 207
Jelloun, Tahar Ben, 78
Jeune France, 20–24
Joffrin, Laurent, 88
Jospin, Lionel, 64, 86
Journée portes ouvertes dans les monuments historiques, 95, 162
Journées du prêt-à-porter, 126
Julliard, Jacques, 188, 192
Juppé, Alain, 167, 169

Kahnweiler, Daniel-Henri, 104
Konopnicki, Guy, 79, 165
Kundera, Milan, 76

'La France a du talent' event, 127–8
Labour Party (UK), 2
Lacouture, Jean, 40, 45
Lagrange, Léo, 15–19, 20, 71, 242
Lamirand, Georges, 20
Landowski, Marcel, 40, 61, 71
  Landowski plan for music, 40, 45, 52, 94, 121
Lang, Jack, 1–2, 3, 6n3, 59–61, 236–9
  and Americanisation, 76–9,
  and Deauville Festival, 77–9, 84, 86, 159, 197, 207
  and *grands projets*, 138–9, 147, 175–6
  and Nancy Festival, 42–3, 59–61, 73, 120, 122, 217
  as *animateur*/organiser of events, 60, 63–4, 80, 88
  as director of Chaillot, 53–4, 60–1, 72, 80
  as Minister,
    1981–6, 79–80, 90, 120–2, 161, 222–3
    1988–93, 175–6

overall assessment of, 233–9
budget speech November 1981, 80–4,
  88, 96, 123
criticism of, 86, 158–9, 162–3
first weeks in office, 71–6
image and popularity of, 3, 71–2, 158–
  61, 163–5, 236
Mexico City speech, 78–9, 82, 86,
  159, 207
out of office 1986–8, 166–71 *passim*
see also Ministry of Culture (place of
  Mitterrand-Lang years)
Langlois, Christian, 163, 165
  Pour une véritable culture, 163
Langlois, Henri, 40
latinité, 79
Laurent, Jeanne, 12, 29n5, 53–4, 243
  and Lang-Mitterrand, 76, 94, 105–6,
    142
  and Malraux, 28–9, 33, 38, 40–1, 44,
    47n16
  and Popular Front, 241–2
  creates CDNs, 24–6
  République et les beaux-arts, La, 12, 28–9
Lavaudant, G., 112n32
Le Corbusier, 18, 35, 38, 148
Le Rider, Georges, 191
Le Roy Ladurie, Emmanuel, 187–8
Lecat, Jean-Philippe, 49, 54, 55, 71, 113,
  166
leisure, 15, 34, 35, 37
  the leisure industry, 89, 128, 217–19,
    222, 240, 242–3
Léotard, François, 1, 166–71 *passim*,
  173n19, 173n27, 176–83 *passim*, 239
Leroy, Thierry, 168, 245n12
Lévi-Strauss, Claude, 214
Lévy, Bernard-Henri, 78, 85, 91n15, 165,
  208
Lévy, Professor Maurice, 146
liberalism
  Third Republic's, 12, 217
  from Giscard to Léotard, 53–6, 96,
    163, 166–9 *passim*, 203–5 *passim*
Libération, 84, 88, 90, 162, 166
libraries (public reading), 34, 50, 54, 62,
  114
  under Lang, 72, 80–1, 82, 96–7, 114,
    150, 235
  his policies criticised, 162
Lille, 58, 62, 76, 163
Lion, Bruno, 178
Lipovetsky, Gilles, 223
literature, 4, 62

Live Aid, 160, 215
Living Theater, 42
Llorca, D., 112n32
local authorities, 24–5, 39, 41, 42, 44–5,
  114
  growing involvement in cultural
    provision, 49–50, 54–5, 116, 233–4
  Socialists and, 58–9, 90, 101, 141
  see also municipal elections
Loi d'aide temporaire à l'industrie
  cinématographique, 27–8
Loi Lang, *see prix unique du livre*
Loi Malraux, 37
loi-programme for restoration of historic
  monuments, 37
Loir-et-Cher, 162
Lonchampt, Jacques, 184–5
Loren, Sophia, 88
Louis XIV, 11
Louvre, the, 12, 16, 28, 37, 126, 183
  Grand Louvre, 136–9 *passim*, 142–3,
    148, 149, 167
  Pyramide du, 112n25, 138, 141–3,
    148, 182–3
  Fumaroli on, 218
Lully, J.-B., 216
Lyon conference on cultural
  decentralisation, 115, 117
Lyonnaise des Eaux, La, 203

M6, 203–4
Maisons de la culture (MCs), 14, 21, 105,
  227
  after Malraux, 49, 53–5 *passim*
  Amiens, 41, 42, 46n9, 48n26
  Bourges, 46n9, 48n26
  Grenoble, 42, 48n26, 73, 143
  Le Havre, 41, 48n26
  Nanterre, 112n32, 165
  under Lang, 72, 107–9
  under Malraux, 40–5, 48n26, 135
  see also Etablissements d'action
    culturelle
Maisons des jeunes et de la culture
  (MJC), 23, 53, 227, 242
Maisons Jeune France, 21
Malraux, André
  and Lang, 73, 94–5, 113, 125, 241
    respective conceptions of culture,
      81–4 *passim*, 88, 116, 127, 146
  and Popular Front, 14, 19, 33, 41
  and Vichy, 19
  as Minister, 29, 33–7, 45, 173n19, 243
  his policies, 37–45, 105

rethought by successors, 49–53, 55
in recent cultural debates, 215, 217, 222, 225–6
RPR's 'return' to, 226, 231, 239
manifeste pour la République, 63
Manufactures nationales, 38
Marchais, Georges, 61
Marley, Bob, 215
Marseillaise, La, 17, 64, 182
Martin-Barbaz, J.-L., 112n32
Marx, Karl, 214
Marxism, 22, 43, 85, 108
Socialist cultural policy and, 56, 62–3, 71
mass culture, 228
and the bicentenary, 182
critiques of, 215–16, 217–19
during Third and Fourth Republics, 13, 16–17, 22, 26
Malraux and, 36, 45, 215
Socialists' view of, 57–9, 77–9
under Lang, 123–7, 241
see also popular culture
mass media, 243
hostility to, 22, 36, 58, 62, 83
rise of, 35, 45, 51
Masson, André, 38
matching grants (*cofinancements*), 179, 193n11, 208
Mathieu, Hélène, 177
Matin, Le, 63, 83, 165
Matra, 54
Mauroy, Pierre, 23
as Mayor of Lille, 58, 163
as Prime Minister, 71, 76, 80, 121, 158, 207
Maurras, Charles, 19, 77, 159
Maxi-Rock, Mini-Bruit, 124
Maxwell, Robert, 203
May 1968, 2, 60, 64, 213, 217
and culture, 39–40, 43–5
legacy of, 50, 57, 81, 85, 116, 240
Mécénat, see patronage and sponsorship
Mesnard, André-Hubert, 100, 101, 176, 179
métissage culturel, 78, 118, 146, 160, 163, 215
MGM, 77
Ministère de la jeunesse, des arts et des lettres, 24
see also Bourdan, Pierre,
Ministry of Communication, 49, 71, 90
relations with Culture, 228, 236
under Lang, 72–3, 82, 131, 166,

175, 199–203
under Léotard, 203–5
Ministry of Culture (generic title), 1–2, 102, 228
antecedents, 21–6 *passim*
creation of, 33–5
critiques of Lang ministry, 84, 162–3, 222
critiques of Léotard and Lang jointly, 207–9, 213, 223
critiques of role of state, 19, 163, 217–18, 226–8
effets pervers of voluntarist policies, 235–9
mission statements, 37, 82–3, 92n24
nature and remit of, 2, 5, 226–31, 233
under Lang 1981–6, 72–3, 80, 90, 113, 115, 122
under Lang 1988–93, 175–6
under Léotard, 168–9
under Malraux, 33–7
place of Mitterrand-Lang years in history of, 1–2, 19, 239–44
Ministry of Education
during Fourth Republic, 23–4, 29, 242
during Third Republic, 12, 15, 20,
relations with Culture, 34, 37, 40, 51, 61, 228, 242
from 1981, 71, 82, 119–20
from 1988, 176, 179–80, 242
Ministry of Finance, 28, 34, 126, 129
new building (Bercy) for, 136, 138, 149, 167
Ministry of Free Time, 71, 90, 242
Ministry of Information, 24, 33, 40
minority cultures, *see* community cultures
Miquel, André, 191
Miró, Joan, 38, 40
Mission du bicentenaire, 181
Mission du développement culturel, 52, 113
Mission économie culturelle et communication, 129
Mission pour la création industrielle (Mission for industrial design), 127
Mitterrand, Danièle, 126
Mitterrand, François, 60, 64–5, 76, 85, 102
and Malraux, 241
and Popular Front and Vichy, 19, 241
conception of culture and society, 62–3
culture in his 1981 campaign, 61–4
development of a cultural policy, 56–8

Index

UNESCO symposium speech, 62–3, 80–2, 88, 136
see also grands projets, Ministry of Culture (place of Mitterrand-Lang years)
Mnouchkine, Ariane, 165
mobile libraries, see bibliobus
Mœbius, 128
Moinot, Pierre, 41, 72, 200
Mollard, Claude, 73, 99, 101, 104, 168
Mona Lisa, 38
Monde, Le, 23, 77, 84–6, 90, 121, 161, 182, 184, 205
Monory, René, 54, 76, 97
freeing of book prices, 54, 76, 80, 97–9
Montagne Sainte Geneviève, new facilities for, 137
Montbéliard, 58
Moravia, Alberto, 165
Morel, J.-P., 144
Morin, Edgar, 44, 50
Motion Picture Export Association, 77
Moulin, Jean, 35, 64
Moulin, Raymonde, 101
Moulinier, Pierre, 133n18
Mounier, Emmanuel, 20–2
Mouvement de la flamboyance, 178
MPO, 129
Mugler, Thierry, 162
multiculturalism, 117–18, 169, 182
municipal elections
    1983, 90, 108, 147–8, 161
    1989, 175
Musée de l'affiche, 126
Musée des arts décoratifs (Louvre), 126
Musée des arts et traditions populaires, 17
Musée d'Orsay, 135–6, 139, 141, 176, 194n24
Musée national d'art moderne (MNAM), 28, 39, 43
museums, 50, 55, 104–5, 114
    under Lang, 76, 81, 82, 95
music, 4, 45, 52, 220–1
    before 1958, 12, 13, 19, 21,
    Socialist policy for, 62, 124, 137, 235
    under Malraux 41
    see also Fête de la musique, Landowski plan for music
music schools, 114
musical baccalauréat, 40

Nancy World Theatre Festival, see Lang, Jack
Napoléon, 12,

national culture, 11–12, 13–14, 18, 26, 44
    bicentenary and, 182
    grands projets and, 139–46
    under Mitterrand-Lang, 76–7, 116–19, 241
National Music Day (UK), 2
national revolution, 19–20
neo-liberalism, see liberalism
new practices and publics, 113, 116, 120, 177–8
new technologies, 87, 128, 197, 226, 243
    growing importance before 1981, 45, 50, 55
    Lang's policies for, 77, 128–31 passim, 214
New Wave, 27
'non-public', the, 44
'North-South' relations, 77–8
Nouvel, Jean, 138
Nouvel Observateur, Le, 76, 139–41 passim, 188

Occupation, the, 19–22
OCTET, 129–30
Odéon-Théâtre de France, 38, 39–40, 43
'one per cent for art' mechanism, 28, 38–9, 101
opera, 4, 125
Opéra-Bastille, 137–42 passim, 148–50, 182, 183–7, 194n29, 209
    under Léotard, 167–8, 183–4, 194n28
Opéra de Paris (Palais Garnier), 18, 38, 55, 142, 150, 183–4
Opération Garance, 208
Orchestre de Paris, 64
'Orientations générales d'une politique d'action culturelle', 56–8, 66n16
Ornano, Michel d', 71,
Ory, Pascal, 16–18, 20–1, 73, 122, 125, 176
Oscars de la mode, 162
Ott, Carlos, 138
Ozouf, Mona, 182

Palais de la Découverte, 143
Palais Royal, 102–4
Panafieu, Françoise de, 187, 235
Panthéon, Le, 64, 76, 80, 121
Paris city council (Ville de Paris), 60, 136, 147, 161, 167
Parisianism, 19, 25, 54, 109
Parti socialiste unifié (PSU), 73
Pasqua, Charles, 170–1

Index

patrimoine, le, see heritage
patronage and sponsorship (*mécénat*), 11, 54
  under Lang and Léotard, 82, 90, 130, 179, 199, 208
Pauwels, Louis, 170
Pavarotti, L., 221
PCF (Parti communiste français), *see* Communists
Pei, Ieoh Ming, 138, 142–3
performing arts, 107–10 *passim*, 213
'permanent correspondents', 40
Perrault, Dominique, 188, 190
Perrault, Gilles, 181–2
personal stereo (walkman), 160, 218, 221
Pesce, Rodolphe, 97
Pétain, Philippe, 19, 20, 86, 92n15
Petit-Castelli, Claude, 59
Peuple et Culture, 23, 73
Peyrefitte, Alain, 33
Peyret, Juliette, 127
Philip, André, 23
Photofolie, 178
Picasso, Kiki, 166
Pinto, Diana, 85
Piscine Molitor, 180
Pisier, Evelyne, 245n12
Pivot, Bernard, 3, 7n5
Plan, five-year, 23
  Fourth, 37, 41, 42, 47n11, 143
  intérimaire 1982–3, 82
  Ninth, 87, 89, 117, 129, 201
  Seventh and Eighth, 53
  Sixth, 50–2, 56–7, 59, 242
  legacy of after 1981 victory, 82, 101, 113, 240
Plan Recherche Image, 130
Plan Son, 130
plans-reliefs, 163, 167
Planchon, Roger, 53–4
plastic arts (*arts plastiques*), 4, 18, 28, 38–9
  under Lang, 72, 99–105, 110, 235
  acquisitions, 81, 100–1, 104–5
  commissions, 99, 101–5
  see also 'one per cent for art' mechanism
Playboy, 77–8, 81
Plunkett, Patrice de, 158–9, 162
  La Culture en veston rose, 158–9
pluralism, 50, 82, 113–20, 122, 143, 209
Poland, military coup in, 86
Pompidou, Georges, 33–4, 45, 49, 52, 53, 137
Pompidou Centre (Beaubourg), 49, 53,

73, 135, 143
  cost of, 150, 234
  Fumaroli on, 218
pop music, *see* popular music
Pope, the, 162, 215
popular culture, 13–17, 21, 22–6, 76
  see also mass culture
popular education, 13, 15, 23–4, 97, 214, 227
Popular Education (department), 23–4, 34, 242
Popular Front, 2, 13–19, 20–8 *passim*
  and cultural policy of Fifth Republic, 34, 41, 226, 241–3
  and *grands projets*, 142, 143
  and meaning of culture, 14–15
  continuity with Vichy and Resistance, 19–21
  Socialist government and, 71, 76, 82–3, 96, 120–1
popular music, 57, 123–5, 200, 215–16, 225, 235
Pratiques culturelles des Français, Les, 212–13, 220–1, 243
Prévert, Jacques, 18
private galleries, 104
prix conseillé, 54, 97–8
prix/grand prix de Rome, 12, 137
prix unique du livre (Loi Lang), 76, 97–9, 111n13, 131, 235
Projet socialiste des années 80, Le, 58–9, 61
PR, 1, 166, 171
PS, *see* Socialist Party, French
Pyramide du Louvre, *see* Louvre

quartiers, 115, 178
quotas (audiovisual), 27, 77, 202–6 *passim*, 210n15
Quotidien de Paris, Le, 138, 165, 236
Queyranne, Jean-Jack, 203

radio, 13, 15–17 *passim*, 24, 26, 61, 221
  under Mitterrand, 77, 200
  see also audiovisual, broadcasting
Ralite, Jack, 207–9, 224, 225
Ramadier government, 24
rap, 178
Rebérioux, Madeleine, 136
record dealers, 235, 245n5
recorded music, 13, 17, 26, 51, 235
  Lang's policies for, 123–5, 128–30 *passim*
  VAT on records, 125, 178–9
regional councils, 114, 116

Index

regional cultures, 19, 55, 57,
  under Lang, 72
regional languages, 13, 19, 117–19
regional opera houses, 40, 107
regional orchestras, 40, 95, 107
Renard, Jacques, 90, 109, 127, 129, 175,
  179, 228
Rencontres de Fontevraud, 161
Rencontres internationales sur les libertés
  et les droits de l'homme, 160
Rencontres nationales de la culture, 56,
  67n29
Resistance, the, 21–2
Rétoré, Guy, 137
Rideau gris de Marseille, 16
Rigaud, Jacques, 3, 34, 130, 136, 139,
  242
Culture pour vivre, La, 224
Libre Culture, 3, 213, 224–8, 231n21,
  233–4, 241
Ritaine, Elisabeth, 18
Rivette, Jacques, 40
Rizzardo, René, 234–5
Rocard, Michel, 171, 187, 205
rock music, see popular music
role of the state in culture, see Ministry of
  Culture
Rolland, Romain, 17
Quatorze Juillet, Le, 17
Rousselet, André, 202
Royaliste, 78
RPR, 147, 162, 162, 165–6, 177, 203
  colloquium on culture January 1993,
  231, 239
Ruée vers l'art, La, 122, 162
rural culture, 13, 117

Sagan, Françoise, 63
Saint-Laurent, Yves, 126, 169, 184
Salles, Georges, 28
Sallois, Jacques, 73, 83, 121
Santini, André, 173n20
Savary, Alain, 119
Savary, Jérôme, 106, 112n32
Scènes nationales, 177
Schaeffer, Pierre, 20
Schneider, Michel, 3, 184, 186
  Comédie de la culture, La, 3, 213, 216–
  17, 220, 236, 240
Schoelcher, Victor, 64
Scorsese, Martin, Last Temptation of Christ,
  198
sculpture, 99, 101, 102–4
Secrétariat d'Etat aux arts et lettres, 24–5

Secrétariat d'Etat aux beaux-arts, 23
Secrétariat d'Etat aux relations culturelles
  extérieures et à la francophonie, 176
Secrétariat général à la jeunesse, 20
Secrétariat national à l'action culturelle
  (SNAC), 56–60, 121, 127, 239
secretary of state for Tourism, 71
secteurs sauvegardés, 37–8
Séguéla, Jacques, 63, 169
Senghor, Léopold Sédar, 78
SEPT, La, 206–7
Service de la création artistique, 39, 73
Service de la musique, 40
Service des expositions, 38
Sevran, Pascal, 72
SFIO, 2, 23, 56, 76
Silicani, Jean-Luc, 191
Simon, Yves, 64, 216
socialism, 57, 60, 62, 63, 64, 121
Socialist Party, French (PS), 1–3, 85–6,
  147, 171, 240, 242
  and broadcasting, 61–2, 199, 205, 208
  development of a cultural policy, 56–
  64, 114
Société pour la protection des paysages et
  de l'esthétique de la France, 102, 148
Sociétés de financement des industries
  cinématographiques et audiovisuelles
  (SOFICA), 199, 208–9
sociocultural, the, 6, 227, 242
  before 1958, 15, 18, 23
  since 1968, 44, 53, 56
  Socialists' approach to, 56, 59
  under Malraux, 37, 41
Sollers, Philippe, 85, 165
Sorbonne, the, 43, 88, 90
SOS Racisme, 118, 160
Soubie, Raymond, 184
Sous-Secrétariat d'Etat à l'organisation
  des loisirs et des sports, 15
Soustelle, Jacques, 14–15, 33
sponsorship, see patronage and
  sponsorship
Spreckelsen, Johann-Otto von, 138
Stallone, Sylvester, 178
Starck, Philippe, 126, 131
Strehler, Giorgio, 165
Styron, William, 165
Surintendance des bâtiments du Roi, 11
SYNDEAC, 106, 108, 170

Taddei, Dominique, 56, 67n29
tag, see graffiti
Tapie, Bernard, 158, 169

Tasca, Catherine, 112n32, 175, 195n35, 206
Tavernier, Bertrand, 203
télé-clubs, 23
television, 39, 41, 61, 215, 242
    charters for (*cahiers des charges*), 201–2
    hostility to, 36, 61, 62, 222
    Léotard's policies for, 167–8, 203–5
    private channels, 200–8 *passim*
    rise of, 26, 35–6, 220
    Socialist policies for, 62, 77, 199–203, 205–8
    Tasca decrees, 206, 210n21
    see also audiovisual, cinema, broadcasting, individual channels (TF1, etc.)
Télévision sans frontières, 206, 207–8, 227–8
TF1, 167–8, 203–5, 207, 210n15
theatre, 4, 16, 41, 105
    as public service, 22, 94
    Fonds d'aide au théâtre privé, 105
    in the provinces, 13, 16, 24–6
    independent companies, 105–6, 170
    public sector defined, 105
    street, 60
    under Lang and Léotard, 82, 94, 105–10 *passim*, 170, 177, 235
    under Malraux, 39–40, 105
    Union des théâtres indépendants de France, 16
Théâtre de l'est parisien (TEP), 137, 194n24
Théâtre national de Chaillot, 53–4
    see also Lang, Jack
Théâtre national populaire (TNP), 12, 53
    see also Vilar, Jean,
Third Republic, 12–19 *passim*, 101, 119
    see also Popular Front
tiers-mondisme, 76, 79, 86
Toubon, Jacques, 1, 147, 165, 167, 169, 173n17
    and Ministry of Culture, 176, 228–31, 244
    as Minister, 180, 196n43, 206, 239
Tourlière, Michel, 168
tout-culturel, le, 122–31, 143, 160, 169, 178, 240
    circus, 123
    commercial and industrial structures associated with, 128–31
    cookery, 123
    criticism and debate on, 162, 169, 214–18, 223, 224–7

industrial design (*création industrielle*), 126–7
    meaning of, 127–8
    operetta, 123
    photography, 126
    puppet theatre, 123
    'talent', 127–8
    see also advertising, BD, fashion, popular music, variety
Treaty of Rome, 99
Trigano, Gilbert, 147
Troupes permanentes de décentralisation, 40, 42
Tschumi, Bernard, 138, 144
TV6, 200, 203

UDF, 147, 162, 165–6, 177
unemployment, 86, 170, 242
Union des Maisons de la culture (UMC), 108
Uriage (Ecole des cadres), 20–24
USA, *see* America

Vaisse, Pierre, 139, 143, 148, 150
variety, 124–5
Venus de Milo, 38
Vichy, 19–21, 26–7, 77
video, 51, 220
    under Lang, 77, 128–30, 201–2, 235
Vilar, Jean, 16, 21, 76, 142, 213, 240
    and Avignon Festival, 25, 43
    and TNP, 25–6, 31n35, 39
    public-service ideal of, 22, 53, 94, 106, 244
Villette, La, 135–7, 225
    Cité des sciences et de l'industrie, 135, 143–6, 149, 194n24
    Cité internationale de la musique, 136–8 *passim*, 146, 149, 167
    Géode, La, 145, 149
    Grande Halle, La, 149
    Parc de, 136–9 *passim*, 144–6
Villeurbanne, 44–5, 53–4
Villiers, Philippe de, 166–9, 173n20, 173n27, 180
Vincent, J.-P., 112n32
visual arts, *see* plastic arts
Vitez, Antoine, 60, 80, 108, 159
Vozlinksy, Pierre, 184

Wallon, Dominique, 73, 106, 113, 115, 167
Wangermée, Robert, 104–5, 180
    see also Council of Europe

Warner Brothers, 77
Western, the, 57, 79
Wiesel, Elie, 64, 165
Willerval, Jean, 136
Wonder, Stevie, 124, 133n27
workers' self-management (*autogestion*),
  56
working-class culture, 13, 57
world music, 160, 178, 182

Yonnet, Paul, 223
youth, 15, 19, 20–1, 76, 159–61, 169–70

Youth and Sport department (Jeunesse
  et sports), 15, 20, 23–4,   61,
  227–8, 242
  under Mitterrand, 71, 90, 176
youth culture, 45, 50, 123–6, 160–1,
  178–9, 225

Zay, Jean, 15–19, 24, 26, 30n13, 176,
  242
Zénith, Le(s), 124–5, 143–4, 146
  originally planned for Porte de
  Bagnolet, 137, 149